CLEMENT ATTLEE

CLEMENT ATTLEE

THE INEVITABLE PRIME MINISTER

MICHAEL JAGO

\B^b\

First published in Great Britain in 2014 by
Biteback Publishing Ltd
Westminster Tower
3 Albert Embankment
London SE1 7SP

ISBN 978-1-84954-683-6

10 9 8 7 6 5 4 3 2 1

A CIP catalogue record for this book is available from the British Library.

Set in Baskerville by Soapbox

Printed and bound in Great Britain by
CPI Group (UK) Ltd, Croydon CR0 4YY

ACKNOWLEDGEMENTS

I am greatly indebted to a large number of people who have contributed in innumerable ways to the completion of this book.

Above all, members of the Attlee family have been generous with their time and helpful in correcting errors of emphasis and fact. Pre-eminent among these has been Anne, Dowager Countess Attlee (daughter-in-law), the keeper of the archive and the flame. Her comprehensive collection of photographs, memorabilia and memories provided many happy hours in her 'Clement' room. I am also indebted to the 3rd Earl Attlee (grandson) for his hospitality and willingness, amid House of Lords business, to spend time with me. Additional help was provided by Air Vice-Marshal Donald Attlee (nephew), Tom Roundell Greene (great-grandson), Jo Roundell Greene and Jenny Lochen (granddaughters), and Charles Attlee (great-nephew), who helped me set the family wheels in motion.

The book has been read, either in its entirety or in part, by Dr Patricia Owens (University of Sussex), Dr Robin Darwall-Smith (University College, Oxford), Michael Parsons (University of Pau), Dr Daniel Lomas (University of Salford), Olivia Harris (Middle Temple), Chris and Frances Pye, Bryan Engler, Robin Martin, by Anne, Lady Attlee, and by long-suffering members of my family. Their help and suggestions have been immeasurable. Dr Darwall-Smith, archivist of 'Univ', additionally opened the University College archives for inspection. Naturally, any errors of fact or omission are mine alone.

Research was also greatly aided by Simon Fowler, formerly of the Public Records Office; Helen Langley, Rebecca Wall, Dr Anne Mouron, and the staff of the Special Collections Reading Room at the Bodleian Library; Julian Reid and Harriet Fisher, archivists at Corpus Christi College, Oxford; the Librarian and staff of Churchill College, Cambridge; Edmund King, late of Wadham College, Oxford; Sam Mallinson of Brasenose College, Oxford and Jon Roycroft of the University of Oxford; the Librarian of the Oxford Union; by Bill and Jean Whaley, who provide a home for authors visiting Oxford, and by Toby Parker, archivist at Haileybury College.

Additionally, in various ways, the following have provided invaluable input and support: Edward Cootes, Professor Jonathan and Sarah Dancy, Iain Harris and Juliet Jamieson, James and Dr Elizabeth Jago, Claire Jamieson, Major Dr Seth Johnston (US Army), Richard Savage, Jerry and Jane Scott, Robin and Amanda Shield and Mark Vandevelde of the *Financial Times*. Much of the book was written in France, where I must thank Benoît Pelletier and Chantal Pourget for maintaining order in my house and affording the same respect for calm that they would have afforded Marcel Proust.

For help in locating photographs I must especially thank Will Carleton of Press Photo History. For help and permissions I am grateful to Anne, Countess Attlee; Michael Rhodes representing the Ernest Fawbert Collection; Charlie Masson-Smith, Chief Press Officer of Wandsworth Council; Colin Panter of Press Association Images; Mark Blumire of Alpha Press; Simon Flavin of the *Daily Mirror*; John Balean and Mark Dowd of Top Foto; Laura Wagg of PA Images; and Darryl Lundy of The Peerage.

As ever, I am in the debt of my agent, Andrew Lownie, and of Mick Smith and Olivia Beattie of Biteback Publishing who have provided encouragement and a remarkable degree of tolerance as deadline after deadline slipped by.

Somehow, in the midst of a heavy lecture schedule, my wife Carol has found time to read each chapter; her comments and suggestions have added felicity of expression and a transatlantic perspective to my efforts.

Finally, I must offer belated thanks to the late Edric William Hoyer Millar CBE and the late Thomas Simons Attlee for stimulating the interest of the author, then a twelve-year-old boy, in the 1945–51 Labour government. It is to the memory of those two outstanding gentlemen that I dedicate this book.

CONTENTS

INTRODUCTION

Taking tea at the House of Lords – Indian tea and digestive biscuits – with the 3rd Earl Attlee, I look across the table at a remarkable incarnation. Stouter than his wiry grandfather, as follically challenged on the crown of his head, sporting a trim military moustache, given to smiling definitively at the end of a sentence, John Attlee has not only the appearance but also the mannerisms of his grandfather. I expect him to pull out a well-chewed pipe and fill it with Golden Bar tobacco at any moment.

Unlike Clement, he was not a career politician, but, like his grandfather, had many years outside politics before he entered the House of Lords on the premature death of his father, Clement's only son, in 1991. 'It was vital experience,' he recalls. 'One thing led to another and each step prepared me for the next. Too many politicians and civil servants have never set foot outside the safety of the system, never had to run their own business.' I smile, for by the time Clement Attlee stood for Parliament in 1922 he too had a wealth of different experiences. And every step that he took from then until 1945 seemed planned to prepare him for the next. There was an inevitability about his path to 10 Downing Street.

'How would he have fitted into today's House of Lords?' I ask. 'Like a glove,' my host replies. And how about today's Labour Party? That's a different matter. Clement, whose later years were devoted to world government and a quest for world peace, might not have treated Iraq in quite the way that Tony Blair did. 'Harold Wilson kept us out of Vietnam,' says Lord Attlee. 'Why did we go to war in Iraq? Clement and Blair would not have seen eye to eye on that war.'

John Attlee answers questions in the same way, albeit more loqua-
ciously, as the famously taciturn Clement. He considers his answer, fits it
into historical context and gives a succinct reply. I asked what memories
he had of his grandfather, thinking that perhaps he deliberately imitated
his manner. 'Very few,' he replied. 'We were living in Belgium when I
was a boy. I would be picked up at Heathrow by Laker[1] and taken to
lunch in the Temple. Then Laker would drive me to Victoria for the
train to prep school.' Born in 1956, the present Earl Attlee knew only
the last years of Clem's life.

For an hour and a half we talk about John's life in politics, how he
spent a while as a crossbencher before joining the Conservative Party,
how he might easily have followed his grandfather into Labour's ranks
if he had been asked. ('Tony Blair has enormous charm and I'm sure
he would have persuaded me if he'd wanted to.') How he rose to be a
government whip in the Lords and what the job entailed. Again, there
was a directness in the telling of the story that was reminiscent of his
grandfather.

At one point the images fused and I asked him why the government
had not pressed its plans for reform of the House of Lords, how they had
missed that opportunity. A pardonable confusion followed and I had
to explain that I meant the 1949 proposals. For a moment I must have
believed that I was talking to the 1st Earl.

The Houses of Parliament are majestic and it is easy to imagine oneself
in another century. This augments my sense of being transported back
to the thrilling days of 1945, when the first majority Labour government came to power, of being a witness to the remarkable years of the
Clement Attlee administration. A devoted parliamentarian, he spent
thirty-three years in the House of Commons, twenty of them as leader
of the Labour Party. When he stepped down in 1955 and was awarded
an earldom he became a regular attender at the House of Lords, dutifully taking the train and Underground each day to St James's Park. As
much as any Prime Minister, Clement Attlee had an undying faith in
Britain's parliamentary system.

British peers tend to be men and women of a certain age and I imagine that I am seeing not the lords of today but Christopher Addison,
Pethick-Lawrence, 'Wedgie' Stansgate, Jowitt, the peers of the 1945–51

Labour government. That my host is a Conservative blurs the image not at all. For Clement Attlee, socialist to his fingertips, was far from being a radical. At times he must have envied Ernie Bevin, Herbert Morrison and Aneurin Bevan their humble origins. No less must he have envied their more charismatic styles. Bevin, a larger-than-life figure, doggedly English and unashamed to refer to Nuits Saint Georges as 'Newts', was by far the most visible of the Cabinet. Morrison, 'the Cockney sparrow', had a shrewd ability to appeal to the common man's concerns, while Bevan's cheeky brilliance appealed to a broad-based constituency. Attlee, by contrast, never quite shed his middle-class Victorian upbringing. Gladstonian Liberal principles learned in sober, secure Putney never quite vanished from his make-up. For all his reforming zeal and his pride in his government's achievements in India and the shift from Empire to Commonwealth, Clement Attlee was a Britain-first patriot in the tradition of Joseph Chamberlain and Leo Amery.

Two long periods of Labour administrations have intervened since 1951, when Clement Attlee's government fell from power, and those administrations were very different from their post-war predecessor. By 1964, when Harold Wilson became Prime Minister, Clement Attlee was already a man of the past, a pre-war relic in the 'white heat of technological revolution'. And, as his grandson points out, he would have hardly have been at ease with the micromanaging central control of Tony Blair and Gordon Brown. He might very easily have taken the same path as Roy Jenkins, Shirley Williams and David Owen in 1981. Shadows of three more former Labour Party peers flit across the neo-Gothic fabric of the House of Lords.

Two hours have slipped by while I juggled past and present. As I step out into a dark November evening, I imagine the fog swirling about Parliament Square and a news vendor calling out, 'India partitioned. Read all about it.'

John's grandfather Clement Attlee is the man most applauded (or blamed) for the partitioning of India, Britain's 'Jewel in the Crown'. As Prime Minister of the first majority Labour government from 1945 to 1950, the slight, angular figure ('Little Clem' or 'the little man', as Ernest Bevin fondly referred to him) led a government that transformed Britain after the Second World War. The achievements of that administration, of which the granting of independence to India is perhaps the most famous example, have become legendary. The landslide election of 1945 is perceived as the yardstick against which subsequent elections are judged; Clement Attlee, who became the 1st Earl Attlee in 1955, as commanding general of that remarkable victory, has become a cult figure.

Few of his colleagues would have predicted such elevation when he became deputy leader of the Labour Party after nine years as a Member of Parliament. Even when he succeeded to the leadership in 1935 it was widely assumed that he was a stop-gap leader, soon to be replaced by the better-known Herbert Morrison or Stafford Cripps. Indeed, even as he prepared to 'kiss hands' with the King after the election victory of 1945, several of his colleagues were conspiring to replace him with Morrison as leader and, therefore, as Prime Minister. His rise was attributed to good fortune rather than ability. He remained something of an enigma to the electorate; as time went on, the legend grew up that he was somehow an 'accidental' Prime Minister, a caretaker who inexplicably remained *in situ* and led the Labour Party for twenty years.

Neither of the two widely different images of Clement Attlee – as an infallible socialist icon to be venerated, or as a fortunate interloper – is wholly accurate. His style of leadership was distinctive, though occasionally flawed; his rise to power was neither accidental nor surprising. He was an ambitious man with a clear mission; he differed from his predecessor Winston Churchill in that he governed not as a charismatic champion on a charger but as chairman of a Cabinet. But the suppression of individual persona indicated no lack of ambition or purpose.

On occasion, that modest man became the legatee of the unfortunate appointments he made. Even in the departure from India in 1946–47 – perhaps especially in that episode – Attlee found that the going was appallingly slow, principally because the wrong man occupied a key position. It was a pattern that repeated itself throughout his six years as Premier.

Yet by the time the Conservatives returned to office in 1951, far-reaching, radical reform had been achieved at a breathtaking pace. The legacy of Attlee's government formalised the shape of the post-war consensus that survived until the Margaret Thatcher era nearly forty years later. For those reforms Attlee cannot take sole credit, but his ability to consume official business at stunning speed, his skill and diplomacy in keeping in harness a disparate, vocal group of able men, his relentless drive to bring projects to conclusion without compromise of principle – all these qualities combined to create a redoubtable leader. As Bevin famously commented in 1950, 'Clem never put forward a constructive idea in his life, but no one else could have kept us all together.'[2]

Without doubt the elevation of Attlee to cult status contains an element of nostalgia. The triumph of politics since Attlee's heyday brings with it a wistful contemplation of a Prime Minister motivated by the highest principles: patriotism, loyalty, decency in the internecine Labour Party, meticulous honesty in his dealings with politicians of all parties. Even his removal from office can be attributed to an altruistic motive: he insisted that an early election be held before King George VI set off on a tour of the Commonwealth, as he was adamant that the monarch's tour should not be vitiated by concerns about the state of his government in Britain. In this light Attlee becomes less a cult figure than a symbol of political decency that may have vanished for good. As to his rise to power, it was achieved entirely on merit, aided, it is true, by the tergiversations of Ramsay MacDonald's government, by the electorate's dim view of the Tory Party of the 1930s, by the absence from the House of Commons of his Labour Party rivals at critical moments.

Closer scrutiny reveals a committed patriot who returned from service in the First World War and, most wisely, retained his military rank, becoming affectionately known in his East End constituency as 'the Major'; a Member of Parliament who earned the deepest respect of his parliamentary colleagues between 1931 and 1935; a dedicated and competent Deputy Prime Minister in the coalition government during the war of 1939–45. Just as he had won the loyalty of the Parliamentary Labour Party, he earned his spurs in the wider Labour movement despite his lack of proletarian origin. By the end of the Second World War he had won the respect of the electorate, having been the voice of the government when Churchill was absent – as he frequently was.

At every critical point in his rise to power, Clement Attlee was simply the right man in the right place at the right time. Napoleon, it is true, would have approved of him, for he had that virtue that Bonaparte valued most in a general – he was lucky. It was greatly more than luck, however, that thrust power upon him. As Frank Field has astutely observed,[3] his later writings after he stepped down as Labour leader illustrate most clearly the ethical values that he brought to the exercise of politics and power. He led by example and was never ashamed to do so.

His tenure of power, sandwiched between two periods when Winston Churchill occupied Downing Street, inevitably results in comparisons between the two very different men who handled the business of being Prime Minister in widely different ways. General Sir Ian Jacob remembered that to Churchill 'what mattered most ... was not so much that he was Prime Minister and Minister of Defence as that he was Minister of Defence and Prime Minister ... He saw himself first as the man running the war, and second as the Prime Minister.'[4] While Attlee for a brief period occupied both those offices on first attaining power, it is definitively not as a head of a government department that we think of him. In the pre-war Labour government his most visible ministerial role was as Postmaster General. When Sir Stafford Cripps plotted to unseat the Prime Minister in 1947, his proposal that Attlee should become Chancellor of the Exchequer was absurd.

It was as Prime Minister that he excelled; by skilful and patient management that he governed. Bevin was correct in his assessments of himself and his colleagues, identifying Attlee's ability to sum up the majority view of his Cabinet with succinct accuracy, and concluding that no other of his colleagues could have done the job.

In no sense was Clement Attlee an 'accidental' Prime Minister. As one traces his path from Haileybury to Oxford to the Inns of Court and his first visit to the East End of London, as we fit together his family's commitment to social service, his wartime record, his passionate view of the obligations (and the limitations) of a socialist government and his contributions to that goal, his rise becomes not accidental but inevitable.

ENDNOTES

1   Alfred Laker, his grandfather's manservant from 1964 until Clement's death in 1967.
2   Leslie Hunter, *The Road to Brighton Pier*, p. 26.
3   Frank Field (ed.), *Attlee's Great Contemporaries*. 2009, London: Continuum Books.
4   *The Observer*, 'Churchill By His Contemporaries', p. 70.

CHAPTER 1

A VICTORIAN UPBRINGING, 1883–1904

Clement Richard Attlee was born on 3 January 1883 into a large Victorian family in a large Victorian house, 'Westcott', in Portinscale Road in the village of Putney, six miles from central London, a haven of peace and respectability. For twelve years a child had been born at regular intervals of two years to his parents, Henry and Ellen Attlee. Clement was the seventh child, the fourth boy; late in the following year another boy was born and the family of eight children was complete. It was a close-knit family, conformist, God-fearing, modestly prosperous, socially secure with no ambition to rise further. The family attended church at least twice every Sunday; each morning, family and live-in servants gathered for morning prayers at 7.30. Ninety minutes later Henry Attlee took the train to his place of work, the solicitors Druces and Attlee. Each evening he drank one glass of claret with dinner before withdrawing to his study to prepare his work for the following day.[1]

Family tradition has it that the Attlees originated at Great Lee Wood, north-west of the village of Effingham. There are traces of a moat in Lee Wood which enclosed the manor of Effingham-La-Leigh, mentioned in local records as early as AD 675. The Domesday Book lists the manor as held by the manor of Wotton, owned by Oswold de la Leigh; in 1320 it passed into the estate of Effingham Place Court and thence to the Crown. Henry VIII often rode the dozen miles from Hampton Court to hunt there. In 1550 Edward VI granted the manor to Lord William Howard, in whose family it remained until the eighteenth century. In the 1920s Effingham Golf Club was built on the land of the original manor.

Lee House (or 'Leigh House'), part of the landholding of Effingham Place Court, was not only the home of the family but also the origin of their name – 'At the lee' becoming 'Attlee' and accounting for the curious double 't'.[2] They were long-established as tenant farmers in Effingham and by the early eighteenth century they had moved the short distance to Dorking, establishing a milling business at Rose Hill and living in Westcott, a village to the south-west of the town. Not only did Henry Attlee rename his first two homes in Putney 'Westcott' as a memento of the family's source of affluence, Clement used the name for the house he later built near Great Missenden, and his sister Mary for her house in South Africa.

By the late eighteenth century the mill was prosperous. Richard Attlee, father of seven sons, accommodated two in the milling business, set two up as brewers and provided an allowance for Henry, Clement's father, to be articled at the age of sixteen to Druces, a firm of solicitors in the City of London. Henry became senior partner, adding his name to create 'Druces and Attlee', a firm that exists today under the umbrella of Druces LLP, a thriving commercial law firm, still based in the City. Henry's career flourished and he rose to be president of the Law Society.

After twelve years with Druces, Henry was sufficiently established to marry Ellen Bravery Watson, 23-year-old daughter of Thomas Watson, secretary of the Art Union of London. Established in 1837 'to aid in extending the love of the Arts of Design within the United Kingdom, and to give encouragement to artists beyond that afforded by the patronage of individuals', the Art Union was a successful and enterprising society. By 1865 there were over 15,000 subscribers and in 1867 *Curiosities of London* recorded that it had, 'unquestionably, fostered a taste for art'.[3]

Ellen, the oldest of six children, managed the Watsons' house on Wandsworth Common and brought up her younger siblings after her mother died. At the time of the 1871 census Henry and Ellen and one live-in servant were established at their first house, their first 'Westcott', in Keswick Road, Putney. They were a devoted couple, despite superficial differences. Ellen was a staunch Conservative, while Henry was a Liberal who made no secret of his 'radical' Gladstonian principles. Ellen, treating political differences as matters never to be aired in public, carefully stifled discussion of politics in her home.

Both were traditional Protestant Christians, philanthropists with a strong sense of duty and public service. Henry's politics aside, they were a typical middle-class Victorian couple and, as their family grew, a prosperous professional family. By the time of the April 1881 census, Henry and Ellen, six children and three servants lived at 'Westcott' in Portinscale Road, literally around the corner from their first house. From here, for thirty-seven years until he died in 1908, Henry would walk to the station, attired in his top hat and frock coat, sometimes accompanied part of the way by Clement, and take the 9.00 train to his office. The family never owned a carriage; if rain or snow prevented walking he would take a hansom cab.

Ellen ran the house, applying discipline and structure but without tyranny. She instilled in all her children the idea of the family as the most important element of life, an organism that supplied all its members' needs. Modern notions of 'unique identity' were unknown. As Attlee recalls, 'We were not encouraged to have a good conceit of ourselves.'[4] The ambition of the older boys was to become like their father, while the younger boys wanted to become their elder brothers.[5]

Physically, Clement was the baby. Slight of stature, he lacked the physique of his elder brothers – and of his younger brother Laurence, twenty-two months his junior, who soon overtook him in height. It was a source of amusement that, unlike other families where a younger brother wore the hand-me-down clothes of elder brothers, Clem would inherit clothes as Laurence grew out of them. His slight figure concealed a wiry toughness, but was a source of concern to Ellen, who kept him at home in his early years, unlike his older brothers, who went to school in Putney.

Until he was nine, Clement lived among women: his mother, his sisters who were schooled at home, their governesses, and his four unmarried aunts, two miles away in Wandsworth. Ellen took charge of his education, supplemented in time by a French governess who instilled a good French accent. This, Clement recalled in his autobiography, 'with other nonsense was speedily knocked out of me when I went to school'.[6]

When his brothers were at home there were endless games but, alone for long periods, Clement combed the shelves of his father's library, reading indiscriminately. He acquired an early love for poetry, venerated Alfred Tennyson, and memorised lengthy passages. His brother Laurence recalled that his memory and ability to absorb everything he read was his most impressive skill.

Among Clement's early memories were Queen Victoria's Golden Jubilee of 1887, when the family decorated the house with bunting,[7] and the annual Oxford and Cambridge Boat Race. It is a half-mile walk from Portinscale Road to Putney Bridge, the start of the Boat Race course, and Clement recalls that 'Any visitor to our house was at once asked, "Are you Oxford or Cambridge?" Our general view was that the Universities existed solely for the purpose of this race.' The Cambridge crew used to stay in the house next door to the Attlees and Clement 'always hoped that one day the crews would meet in the street, when, if they followed our example, there would be a fight'.[8]

Every summer Ellen and the children spent a month by the sea, where Henry joined them for two weeks. Clement's earliest memory of summer holidays was of Lowestoft when he was two. In later years the family went to Seaton in Devon, which became an idyll for him. When he visited Normandy after D-Day, he wrote to his elder brother Tom that it was very like Devon.[9] In 1945, when he attended the first meeting of the United Nations in San Francisco, he bestowed the highest praise on the California countryside, writing that it too reminded him of Devon.[10] In 1896, at a cost of £2,000, Henry bought Comarques, a red-brick house with 200 acres of land and several cottages in the village of Thorpe-le-Soken, close to the Essex coast.[11] From then on, Easter and summer holidays were spent there.

Although sparse in the finished account of his life, Attlee punctiliously recorded events in obsessive detail. These notes constitute a remarkable collection of his memories. Remarkable, that is, in what he chose to record, rather than as a coherent version of childhood and adolescence. He wrote, wistfully and nostalgically, then halted and made a list of something or other. Lists punctuate the record. Lists of boys at Haileybury and what they had achieved since. Lists of speeches that he made in the House of Commons, showing the length of each speech and the number of columns taken up in *Hansard*. For no apparent reason, he once made a list of the boys who had been contemporaries at Northaw Preparatory School.[12]

It is as though Attlee were trying to discover where he had found direction, writing an objective but uncertain biography of a different person, striving to grasp the secret of that person's success. The practical and pragmatic politician looks back at the callow youth and barely recognises him. He is objective about that person, as if he existed in another era, on the other side of some great divide. Then, when he became too wistful, recording in detail family outings, details of school or conversations with fellow officers, he would put an end to the memories and demonstrate his need for facts by constructing another list.

Perhaps most remarkable is the catalogue of summer holidays gone by, presented in painstaking detail. Where the family went, what they did, where they stayed, whom they met, how the brothers would amuse themselves, playing cricket or bicycle polo – all are meticulously recorded as if the events were recent, so fresh are they in the writer's mind. While the memories are eclectic, almost random, a framework of Attlee's early life emerges. There was the structured home life – weekday routine, Sunday worship, family visits and summer holidays – that lasted for as long as he lived at home; on these are superimposed clearly defined moments when his life changed, definitive points at which he made a decision that altered his conduct, his philosophy and, ultimately, his entire life.

That 'other person', the pre-socialist Attlee, did exist in another era: the Victorian age. Whereas Queen Victoria's Golden Jubilee, which occurred when he was four, was 'his' Jubilee, her Diamond Jubilee in 1897 was 'Laurence's'. He writes of Victorian London as a civilisation vanished forever. Curiously romantic about the city in the 1890s, he recalls the smell of horse manure in the streets when transportation was horse-drawn, the Stygian gloom of the Underground where thin shafts of light penetrated the smoke-filled tunnels, the hansom cabs of the affluent, 'the gondolas of London'. This is more than a paean to a lost innocence; the descriptions form the background to his later renunciation of the comfort of those years. He could be nostalgic for the nineteenth century while being totally objective about what was morally amiss. There was a fundamental distinction between public amenities and private living conditions. Later, as Alderman and the first Labour Mayor of Stepney, he was relentless in enforcing improvements. He was equivocal about change but singleminded in his determination to reform.

Clement was nine and a half years old when he followed Tom to preparatory school at Northaw Place, near Potters Bar. He was shy, tending to blush easily. He also had a fierce temper which Ellen taught him to restrain; this he inherited from his father, who strove to suppress any outburst. The image that Clement later developed of a placid politician, calm and ostensibly unflappable, owes more to self-control than to any natural equanimity. In his papers from his time as Deputy Prime Minister and Prime Minister one stumbles on examples of his rage, expressed in blunt responses scrawled on documents, subsequently toned down to more diplomatic language for distribution. In 1892, Henry thought Clement should learn to cope with his shyness and tendency to rage. Boarding school, that great leveller and stiffener of upper lips, was the solution.

The headmaster at Northaw, the Reverend F. J. Hall, was a long-standing friend of Henry's, a mathematician who had taught at Haileybury and persuaded him to join the Board of Governors of Haileybury College. Hall is remembered in *Haileybury College, Past and Present* as a master 'whose own skill in cricket and football was always at the service of the School, who has sent us many good players of his training since he left'.

That sentence merely touches the surface of Hall's greatest love. He and his assistant master, the Reverend F. Poland, were passionate cricket lovers. Cricket was the dominant priority at Northaw; religious knowledge, the only subject deemed worthy of intellectual enquiry, came a poor second. Clement later described the school's function: 'As a nursery for producing gentlemanly professional cricketers,' he wrote, 'the school could hardly have been bettered.'[13] While he was never an outstanding cricketer ('a good field, nothing of a bowler and a most uncertain bat'),[14] he did distinguish himself in religious knowledge, winning the Bishop's prize.[15]

Despite his lack of success on the field, he remained throughout his life an avid follower of the game, an ardent reader of *Wisden*,[16] able to recite batting and bowling averages of leading cricketers. Labour Members of Parliament, when conversation was desultory, would draw him out by referring to the progress of a county match, a technique that would make the taciturn leader positively garrulous. When he flew to Washington for meetings with President Truman in 1945, he took *Wisden* to read on the plane.[17] When, in Luddite-like fury, he objected to having a ticker tape at 10 Downing Street, he was persuaded of its value when his press officer Francis Williams pointed out that it would bring him up-to-date scores of cricket matches. For ever thereafter he referred to it as 'my cricket machine'.

Clement's memories of Northaw, while objective and realistic about its eccentric teaching methods, are entirely pleasurable. Although he doubted the value of the teaching – with reason, as his sketchy knowledge of Latin and Greek was to impede his academic progress at public school – fifty years later he had only fond recollections of forty youngsters gambolling about the school grounds.

Among Clement's contemporaries were two future ministers. One future colleague was William Jowitt, four years younger than Clem, who was put in his care when he came to the school. Jowitt was elected to Parliament as a Liberal in 1922. He later joined the Labour Party and served as Lord Chancellor throughout the two post-war governments. Another future Labour minister was Hilton Young, head boy when Clem entered the school. On one occasion, Young, observing him at tea, staring disconsolately at his meagre ration of bread and butter, promptly fetched his own jar of jam and let Clement help himself, a remarkable breach of stratified school etiquette. Young was later Minister of Health in Ramsay MacDonald's government and was created Baron Kennet in July 1935; Attlee recalled that when he was in the government, he was able to do Kennet some slight service. The latter, remembering the incident, wrote to him, 'It seems that if you cast your jam upon the water, it will, like bread, come back to you after many days.'[18]

Aged thirteen, having received the scantest of education at his preparatory school and spectacularly ill equipped academically, Clement went to nearby Haileybury to sit the entrance examination in the spring term of 1896. He passed and followed in the footsteps of his three older brothers.

Haileybury is a handsome school. Approached by a long drive, the school buildings are grouped around the main quadrangle. The arrangement of buildings is not only aesthetically pleasing, it is also practical; the different 'houses' are less physical buildings than administrative units. In many public schools, houses are scattered over a large area, while at Haileybury, boys from different houses shared the same living space. Four boys from different houses often shared a study; all boys, except those in one remote house, ate all their meals together. This was important to Clement, who felt that he had a wider acquaintance than boys at other public schools.

Few contemporaries would have picked out the young Attlee as a future Prime Minister. He spent four years in the middle of his class, never identified as a candidate for a scholarship to Oxford or Cambridge. Sports counted for much, and it was generally from the ranks of athletes that the college's prefects were chosen. Here, too, Clement was of only average ability. He stepped in occasionally as a second-rank player in the house rugby team but never with regularity. He was outstripped by Laurence, who arrived a year later and became a fixture in the Lawrence House cricket and rugby teams. A talented cricketer, he displayed the one skill that Clem would dearly have loved to possess.

The headmaster, Canon Edward Lyttleton, was, in Clement's view, 'a great man in his way … a hopeless headmaster'. To junior boys he was a remote figure; when they reached the sixth form they came more into contact with him. Clem, therefore, would not have known him well until his last year. They did, however, have close contact in March 1900, when Ladysmith was relieved by British forces in the Second Boer War.

The war had erupted in October 1899 and by the end of the month the Boers had encircled General White and 8,000 men at Ladysmith. The siege lasted for four months. When the siege was lifted, the Haileybury boys, amid the national rejoicing, expected Lyttleton to grant a half-holiday, normal procedure on such an occasion. Lyttleton, an anti-imperialist with pro-Boer sympathies, refused to do so. The majority of boys decided to cut school and stage a march through Hertford in defiance of the headmaster, who, predictably, regarded this as a flagrant breach of discipline. He reached a curious decision. The prefects were too senior to be beaten and the juniors too young, so the boys of the upper school 'expiated the sins of the rest'.[19] That evening Lyttleton caned seventy-two boys of the upper school, including Clement. Fortunately, Clement recorded, 'the Canon was tiring when he got to me'. This was just as well, as 'he had a lovely wrist'.

Clement had more contact with his housemaster Frederick Headley, a natural scientist. Eight years after Clem left Haileybury, Headley published his anti-socialist diatribe, *Darwinism and Modern Socialism*. The principal theme of the book is a defence of capitalism, specifically of the ingenuity of capitalists large and small, concluding that socialism would never take root in Britain. Capitalism, particularly monopolies or trusts, is not without its faults, Headley admitted. On the other hand, socialism would inevitably have a 'crushing, deadening influence' and would 'introduce unjust and impossible economics'. It would, Headley maintained, 'destroy the main motives for enterprise and put an end to the struggle for existence, the action of which maintains the health and vigour of human communities'.[20]

It is a beautiful irony that the man most responsible *in loco parentis* for Clement's moral education in his teens should be convinced that there was no future for socialism in Britain. It is equally ironic that Clement, an instinctive, unquestioning Conservative during those years, would certainly have agreed with him.

In one sphere of school life he did ask questions, however. He had been brought up in a family where religion was an essential part of the fabric. His mother held daily readings of the Bible in which all the children still at home participated. On Sunday evenings in Putney he allowed his mind to drift during evening service, setting himself puzzles to solve while the service ground on. At Northaw he was taught by two Protestant ministers and, now at Haileybury, the ineluctable Christian education led to his confirmation into the Protestant Church. Although he had begun to reject the 'mumbo jumbo' of religion, he kept his doubts to himself. It would have wounded his mother deeply if he had refused to be confirmed; the tactful course of action was to let the system absorb him as every Protestant public school absorbed its charges. He believed in Christian values, but not in the ceremony of it all. It could do no harm to proceed. To resist would cause damage.

Throughout his life he was at ease with men of the cloth and he never quarrelled with Tom, a thoughtful, committed Christian.[21] Once Clem adopted socialism, he saw its aims as substantially the same as those of Christianity – indeed, of most religions. In the climate of the late Victorian age, however, it was politic to mask his doubts with apparent conformity.

In September 1900, at the beginning of his last year at Haileybury, Clem was elected to the College Literary Society, joining the intellectual leaders of the school. He also belonged to the Shakespeare Society and the Antiquarian Society. Although never a leading actor, he performed in several school productions of Shakespeare during his last three years.

The Literary Society met on Monday evenings to debate typical issues of the day: free trade, whether the female sex encroached on men's rights, whether old school customs were dying out and should be revived – the standard fare of school debating societies. Clement was a platform speaker on two occasions, in each of which his Conservatism was given full rein.

On the first motion Clement opposed the motion 'that museums and picture galleries should be open on Sundays'. The record of the debate in *The Haileyburian*, the college magazine, reported the thread of his argument. What class, Attlee asked, would benefit from the opening of museums and galleries? Certainly not the poorer class, as they could not appreciate them. He thought that it would be giving the upper class another excuse for not going to church. It was introducing the thin end of the wedge.[22]

When Clement recalls that he was a Conservative in his early years, he understates the extent of that position. He must have blushed, as a socialist convert, to recall the vapid arrogance of his teenage views.

Three weeks later he opposed the motion 'that Members of Parliament should receive pay'. On this occasion he was on the winning side.[23] In this debate too his position was solidly reactionary; there is no political similarity between Clement Attlee at the age of eighteen and the young man of a mere seven years later after a spell in the East End of London.

Clem was also active in the Antiquarian Society, of which his friend Charles ('Char') Bailey was secretary. He was elected at the beginning of his last year and gave papers on Colchester and Saxon London, highlighting the strategic value of each.[24] His principal academic interest was in history and it was to read that subject that he applied to Oxford University that year.

Haileybury had a strong military tradition and Clement joined the Officer's Training Corps, known at the time as the 'Haileybury College Rifle Volunteer Corps'. In this activity he won various awards and rose to be a sergeant. In the spring term of 1901 he was part of the team that won the Army Cup, awarded for drill. In the summer of 1901, the end of his last term at Haileybury, he went to military camp at Aldershot and was judged the most outstanding cadet. He enjoyed the military discipline, an essentially physical pursuit in which athletic skill counted for less than on the rugby field.[25]

His four years at Haileybury were overall enjoyable, although he later recalled 'considerable periods of black misery'.[26] He records that the winter term of 1899 was his worst; Char Bailey moved into another study and Clement felt friendless. He made friends at first through Tom, but in the stratified world of a public school it was difficult to mix with boys two years his senior. Equally, Laurence, almost two years his junior, was as remote as Tom within the system. Clem suffered his fair share of bullying at the hands of 'an uncouth and brutal youth called Archer Clive'[27] and he did not mix easily. The ethic of the public school was quite alien to the ethic of family that he had absorbed in Putney.

Accounts of Clement's life traditionally treat Tom as his closest sibling, largely through the voluminous correspondence between the two. It is scarcely surprising that those letters have survived as Tom, a splendid eccentric, threw nothing away. His home at Perranarworthal housed fifty years of copies of *The Times*, piled high in his study and in a small annexe built for the purpose of storing his 'things'.[28] In fact, the two youngest brothers were also close and met for lunch almost weekly during the war, when Laurence was working in Whitehall.[29]

By the time Clem left Haileybury he had established himself as a reasonably solid and worthy individual. While no great athlete, he had played a few good rugby matches for his house. His academic performance was adequate but less impressive than that of two of his friends, Char Bailey and George Day, both of whom went up to University College, Oxford ('Univ') with him in October 1901.

School and home intersected little but he remained close to his family and the summer holidays spent at Comarques were integral elements of his life. Henry had changed little as his children grew up. In 1901 he maintained the same household in Portinscale Road as he had for a decade, with four live-in servants. Robert, now aged twenty-nine, still lived at home, as did Mary, Tom, Clem and Laurence. Dorothy had married Wilfrid Fletcher, a chartered accountant, and was living in Wiltshire. Henry, now turning sixty, was more likely to join his children for a game of billiards than a vigorous game of cricket, but he remained a benign and influential presence in their lives.

He also remained a Liberal, committed to Home Rule for Ireland. He had many friends and connections in the Liberal Party, one of whom was John Morley, another Liberal in the Gladstone tradition. A politician and writer, Morley served as Chief Secretary for Ireland and Secretary of State for India. He also published a biography of Oliver Cromwell in 1900 and a three-volume life of Gladstone in 1903. Morley lived nearby, between Putney and Wimbledon, and, consciously or not, had an influence on Clem, who read his biography of Cromwell more than once. During the Simon Commission's visit to India, Clem wrote to Tom, reminding him of passages in the book and referring affectionately to 'JM'.[30]

It is speculative but tempting to imagine that the young Clement saw Oliver Cromwell as a model for his own life. Certainly the first sentences of Morley's *Cromwell* could have flowed from Clement's mouth: 'I was by birth a gentleman, living neither in any considerable height, nor yet in obscurity.' There are other similarities in their early years: one of ten children, Cromwell too grew up surrounded by females; he was educated by a Protestant minister who believed the Pope to be the Antichrist; he was a good student but, wrote Morley, 'there is no reason to suppose that [he] was ever the stuff of which the studious are made'. It was assumed in the family that Clement would follow his father and oldest brother Rob into the legal profession. Cromwell too had been destined for the law, a period at Lincoln's Inn being 'the fashion for young gentlemen of the time'.

Cromwell's ethical stance would certainly have appealed to Clem. His view of the role of the established Church, particularly the Catholic Church, was congruent with Clem's respect for Christian values, as distinct from what he considered the peripheral flummery of ritual. Cromwell's brutally logical approach to the primacy of Parliament, tempered by respect for the existing social order, would have struck a chord with Clem's selective conservatism. As to his military ability, Clem considered Cromwell simply the greatest strategist in Britain's history.[31] Whether or not Clement, seventeen years old when Morley's book was published, cherished a secret desire to emulate the Lord Protector, the book's subject impressed him deeply. Once Clement experienced the almost spiritual conversion to socialism, the parallels between his and Cromwell's ethical motivation are striking.

Clem's progression to Oxford was a natural step, another necessary stage in his journey to becoming a lawyer like Henry and Robert. There is no sense of excitement in his autobiography, no modest awe at the reputation of Oxford or of the intellectual community he was about to join. Preparatory school, public school, the University – one followed the other without causing undue excitement. In autobiographical notes he described himself as 'very much a prig' and 'apt to turn to pharisaism'.[32] Sadly, that description seems to have fitted him well at that stage of his life.

Some of this was echoed in his final report from his housemaster, who commended him on his ability to think about things and form opinions, but commented that 'his chief fault is that he is very self-opinionated, so much so that he gives very scant consideration to the views of other people'. For a young man about to enter a community where the majority of his contemporaries would be self-opinionated, this was a worrying character trait.

In the Michaelmas (autumn) term of 1901, Clement went up to Oxford to read Modern History. His analysis of himself at the age of eighteen is starkly objective. A typical product of his era and class, he was, he wrote, 'mentally very young. Better read than most especially in poetry and history.' He knew nothing of science, little of government and political institutions 'except from the imperialist angle'. His knowledge of social conditions was derived entirely from home not school. He was decidedly fed up with public school religion. The whole trend of his mind was 'definitely romantic and imaginative'.[33]

His three elder brothers had also chosen Oxford. Robert was an undergraduate at Oriel, Bernard at Merton. Tom was already in his final year at Corpus Christi, and Clement, as a freshman, found his brother's knowledge of Oxford ways helpful as he settled in. Char Bailey and George Day from Haileybury had also been admitted to Univ to read Modern History. Both remained friends with Clement throughout their time at Oxford, Bailey remaining in touch for much longer. The college friendship most important to Clem, however, was the immediate bond he formed with a young man who had returned from Australia and been to school at Repton before Oxford.

Hugh Linton was the second son of Sydney Linton, the first Bishop
of Riverina, a new diocese in New South Wales. Born in 1882 into a
family with a long Oxford tradition, Hugh was the grandson of two
deans of Christ Church and was, himself, destined for a career in the
Anglican Church. His father Sydney was an undergraduate at Wadham
College from 1860 to 1863 and twice played for the University against
Cambridge at Lords. A missionary of remarkable energy and zeal, he
was appointed Anglican bishop in a diocese embracing a third of New
South Wales in 1885. An indefatigable worker, he devoted himself to his
mission, literally working himself into an early grave in 1894.

The young Hugh revered the memory of his father and, from the age
of eleven, when his father died, nourished a desire to return to Australia
and continue his work. His early years had been spent on the edge of
the outback in the western part of the state and he certainly shared with
Clement his memories of the huge sprawling diocese. Whether or not
Clem was attracted by the ideals of missionary work, the thrill and the
purpose of it remained vividly alive for Linton. After going down from
Oxford, he was ordained, serving in the Southwark diocese for four
years before returning to Australia to continue his father's work in 1910.

Linton was one among many sons of churchmen at Univ in Clement's
time. Of his contemporaries, Arthur Preston from Charterhouse,
reading Modern History, became Bishop Suffragan of Woolwich
and Archdeacon of Lewisham; Adam Fox from Winchester College,
reading 'Greats',[34] became a Canon of Westminster Abbey. A further
half-dozen of Clement's contemporaries, younger sons of well-to-do
families, became ordained ministers. The Church was a common choice
of career for younger sons but, even so, there was an unusual number
of future churchmen among the undergraduate body at Univ between
1901 and 1904.

The friendship between Clement and Linton remained central to
both their lives in Oxford. In the tradition of the era, each acquired a
nickname. Linton was 'Loony', while Clement rejoiced under the cogno-
men of 'Monkey'. Toward the end of the Michaelmas term in their
final year, in December 1903, they gave a joint coming-of-age birthday
dinner. Taking a mid-point between their twenty-first birthdays, they
offered their guests a spectacular seven-course meal: Sole Mornay,

Chicken Vol-au-Vents with Oysters, Welsh Leg of Lamb, Golden Plover, Chicory Salad, Pastry with Sabayon Sauce, finishing with Mushrooms a la Gorgona.[35]

This was a departure from Clement's normal life. He was not an extravagant undergraduate. Nor did he wear a hairshirt, for he had an adequate allowance of £200 from his father. After a year 'living out', when he shared lodgings adjacent to Univ with Bailey and Day, he moved into college. He lived decently but not excessively. His rooms overlooking the High Street were among the more expensive in college at five guineas a term (the most expensive cost six guineas) and his expenditure on other items – coal, candles, dinners and buttery bill – was about the average among his peers. In the matter of personal hygiene he appears to have been more punctilious than his contemporaries; his bill for the laundress was above average.[36] During the 1930s, Attlee, ever watchful of his pennies, calculated that his time at Oxford had cost £637 for the three years. Meticulous accounting itemised expenditure of nearly twenty pounds on clothes in his first year, an extravagance that was not repeated. Unlike most undergraduates, he carefully balanced his books, emerging with a surplus of £43.[37]

By the late 1890s Univ had developed a reputation for being 'a particularly friendly college; we all seemed to know each other, regardless of background, wealth (or lack of it), and academic or athletic ability'.[38] Clement was captivated by Oxford, and by Univ, the oldest college. It was, above all, a friendly college with a mix of athletes and intellectuals and – important after Haileybury – 'a lack of cliques'.[39] 'We do not seem to have produced scholars of distinction just then, or lawyers,' one old member reminisced, 'but prided ourselves on attracting men of general ability and varied interests which I still think is the best aim of a College.'[40]

This *esprit de corps*, the unwritten code of being a 'Univ man', involved taking more than a passing interest in sports, especially rowing, and participating in the various activities that collectively represented 'college life'. This embraced a balance between *mens sana* and *corpore sano*. Mornings were devoted to academic work, afternoons to physical activity, Sundays to God. Clement fitted easily into this routine, not least because it was a fair replica of his life in Putney.

The wages of deviation were potentially serious. Lewis Farnell, a Fellow during Clem's time, wrote of the public school influence that it demanded uniformity and was intolerant of aberration from the norm. Eccentric behaviour varied from harmless chaff to 'something much graver'.[41] Fred Bickerton, head porter at Univ, recorded with apparent unconcern the fate of one undergraduate who refused to be a 'Univ man'. One night, when Bickerton was on duty in the lodge, the under-graduate rushed in, naked, tarred and feathered, 'like a chicken in a nightmare. He was gibbering with terror, shaking and shivering all over, and in hysterics. His room had been upended, pictures and furniture thrown into the quadrangle.'[42]

Undergraduates were expected to make their friends principally among other members of their college and 'outside' friendships were regarded as undesirable. For Clement, however, there was an important influence on his undergraduate career in the person of his older brother. Through him, Clement became friendly with a group of young intel-lectuals at Corpus Christi College.

Tom Attlee and Edric Millar went up to Corpus Christi College in 1899. Millar was the more accomplished academically – he won an Exhibition (a minor scholarship) and took a First in both Honour Moderations and Greats. Active in the literary and intellectual life of the college, he was something of a mentor for Tom and, through him, for Clem.

Corpus Christi had two essay clubs, the Tenterden Essay Club and the Pelican, at which members read papers on principally literary topics. Millar belonged to both, reading papers on George Sand and Gustavus Adolphus to the Tenterden and on Matthew Arnold to the Pelican. He was subsequently elected president of both clubs.[43]

When Clem arrived in Oxford in 1901, therefore, Millar was an estab-lished figure at Corpus Christi and Tom decided that he should give his brother advice on how to deport himself in Univ. Millar, the oldest of eleven children, was quite accustomed to bossing six younger broth-ers about and he happily accepted Tom's suggestion.[44] Clem became friendly with Millar[45] and, on his advice, became 'someone in college' using the ladder of the University College literary clubs, the Martlets and the Churchwardens.

Members of the Martlets were a self-consciously intellectual group, brimming with undergraduate pretentiousness, but ultimately serious. Their minute book opens with the grandiose statement that: 'The Martlets Society dates from dim antiquity but after a temporary disappearance, it was constituted in its present form on May 8th 1897 when it was decided that the efforts of the society should in the main be devoted to literature … The society has no rules.'[46]

On 13 February 1903, shortly before Clem was elected a member, the members voted that 'this Society shall meet at 8.30 but this must not be taken to imply that the Society has any rules'.

Despite this tendency to frivolous anarchy, the papers at the Martlets were generally conventional. Among the favourite subjects were Wordsworth, Keats, Coleridge, Charles Lamb, Jonathan Swift and Tobias Smollett. Clem was far less conventional in his choice of subject for his first essay, delivering a well-received paper on William Blake, who enjoyed a reappraisal at the end of the nineteenth century. The record of Clem's essay is a brief summary but it quotes him as separating Blake's work into two classes, of which the second, in epic form, 'contains the prophetic and symbolical works which to the ordinary mind are unintelligible'.[47]

By the conventional standards of the time this was an ambitious departure. The cult of regarding Blake as a 'glorious luminary' had gathered momentum, but among the majority of contemporary critics Blake was still regarded as a mad visionary.

In general, however, the young Clement was conventional; one curious matter may indicate an ardent desire to conform. The minutes book of the Martlets and one other entry in University College archives refer to him as 'Mr R. Attlee'. Whether this is a simple error, as friends habitually addressed each other by surnames or nicknames, or whether Clem toyed with the idea of using his more common – and less Roman Catholic – second name 'Richard' is unknown.

The other Univ society that Clem joined was the Churchwardens, inevitably known in the slang of the time as the 'Chuggerwuggers'. This, according to A. D. 'Duncs' Gardner, first an undergraduate and later a Fellow of Univ, was 'for the lower, but not the lowest brows'. The members 'smoked long clay pipes, drank coffee, and enjoyed the

solemnly ribald reading of the works of Shakespeare'.[48] Clem joined
this convivial group and was elected Beadle (president) in 1904. His
close friend Linton was also a member and was Beadle in Michaelmas
term 1903.

Clem also belonged to the Oxford Union, the debating society any
aspiring politician or lawyer joined as a matter of course. Thirty years
later the Union debated daring and controversial motions, the most
famous being the motion 'that this house will in no circumstances fight
for king and country', which passed by 275 votes to 153 in 1933, but it
gained no such notoriety in Clement's time.

Not only was the famous 'king and country' motion decidedly
more adventurous than the motions proposed in the early 1900s, but
the Union itself, a famous breeding ground for politicians in the later
twentieth century, was tame and ill attended during Attlee's years. On
29 May 1902 a motion 'that a revolution in Russia is both probable
and desirable' was carried by twenty-eight votes to thirteen. On such a
momentous motion a mere forty-one members attended.[49]

Prominent among Union men at the time was William Temple of
Balliol, active in the university Liberal Club. Temple, a future Archbishop
of Canterbury, was president of the Union in the Hilary term of
1904. A year before, he had successfully opposed the motion 'that this
House would welcome the Disestablishment and Disendowment of the
Established Church'. Temple may have been a Liberal as an undergraduate, but he later moved further to the left, while remaining true to
conventional views about the relations of Church and state throughout
his life. It is tempting to wonder, if Clement's discovery of socialism had
occurred when he first arrived in Oxford, rather than five years later,
whether he and William Temple, Premier and Prelate of the future,
might have combined in the Union to affect the social consciences of
their contemporaries.

Clement adored the fabric of the Union, regularly working in its
comfortable library.[50] In common with Anthony Eden, Alec Douglas
Home, Harold Wilson and Hugh Gaitskell, however, he took no part
in Union debates,[51] even when George Day, his friend from Haileybury,
spoke against a motion condemning the government's Irish policy.
Naturally shy, he would have been uncomfortable doing so. Ironically,

in 1946, when the reforms of Attlee's first government were debated, 800 undergraduates attended. When Attlee himself spoke at the Union in 1952, coyly mentioning that it was his maiden speech, he received, according to the sitting president, the longest and loudest ovation that the debating hall had ever heard – despite the fact that the members carried the motion that he was opposing.

In that Edwardian era, a decade and a half before the Russian Revolution, issues of class in political debates were curiously absent. In the real world of the House of Commons, middle-class Liberals debated with middle-class Tories; class warfare and revolution were not on the political menu. So in Oxford, a conservative stronghold of public-school men, there was little trace of radical socialism.

Writing for *Isis*, the university magazine, soon after he had been elected leader of the Labour Party, he contrasted the large and active Oxford Labour Club of 1936 with the political climate in his day, commenting that the party 'has drawn support from those classes who were hardly represented in the Union of my time, but it also increasingly draws adherents from the comfortable classes who question not only the ethical but also the rational foundations of their comfort'. By the time he wrote that article, the left almost always carried the day in the Union.[52] A motion in the same year 'that this House prefers Chamberlain to Attlee' was roundly defeated.

Even if Clement had wanted to be part of a young socialist movement he would have been hard pressed. There simply was no fashionable left for him to join. Moreover, his interests were neither radical nor reformist. Politically, *faute de mieux*, he remained an unquestioning Conservative.[53]

The Attlee family, in the Victorian tradition, performed 'good works'. Clement, in common with his two oldest brothers Robert and Bernard and unlike the more free-thinking Tom, was a conformist. His idea of social work was paternalistic, certainly neither participatory nor based on religion. While Clem fully accepted Christian ethics, the illogical absolutes of religious doctrine frustrated him.[54] In his ideal world the enlightened prince would decree; the populace would obey; the established order would continue to thrive. Béziers would never have been sacked for the simple reason that Cathar doubt would not have existed. Conformity would have prevailed.

Bernard, previously a curate in south London, had recently been granted the vicarage in Wolvercote, within Merton's gift. During regular walks across Port Meadow with Tom to visit Bernard for Sunday tea, the brothers discussed social questions, for in this period Tom, future architect and social worker, was greatly more interested than Clem in the social system and reform.

If Clem imagined his future as an Oliver Cromwell or a Renaissance prince, that figure would have been of a fairly reactionary kind. He was simply 'not attracted' to the 'societies seeking support from undergraduates, especially in the religious field'.[55] Curiously, in the light of his later experience, 'he attended some meetings but remained uninterested' in the University Settlements – Oxford House, Toynbee Hall and the Oxford and Bermondsey Mission. He admits to having 'adopted a rather common pose of cynicism'.

Concerning the young Clement's sporting ability, one curious story has become accepted fact, frequently mentioned in accounts of his life. He was an accomplished billiards player who in his teenage years spent hours in the new billiards room that his father installed in Putney. It has become unchallenged truth that Clem, while he might have preferred to win a 'Blue'[56] for cricket, won a 'Half-Blue' for billiards. Whether or not this story originated from him, it is, sadly, a fabrication. Not only was billiards not recognised as a sport deserving of a 'Half-Blue', Clement's name does not appear on the roster of billiards players who represented Oxford against Cambridge between 1901 and 1904.[57] Even if Clement did translate this wish into imagined reality, this was the whitest of lies that would hardly impugn the integrity of perhaps the most fundamentally honest of Prime Ministers.

Which leaves us with the issue of academic work, which for many undergraduates was the least important aspect of Oxford life. Clem, reading Modern History, took as his special subject the Italian Renaissance. Again we encounter the shade of a romantic in the choice. Yet it was a choice tinged with *realpolitik*; the possession and ruthless exercise of power intrigued him. The age of the Renaissance produced princes in the mould of Machiavelli as well as a wealth of glory in the visual arts. Like Robert Adam, Attlee believed that 'all the arts flourish under great princes'.[58]

The quality of teaching did not impress him. He was never noted for patience, and it is easy to imagine how a dry, bloodless, academic approach to what he regarded as romantically stirring events would not have satisfied him. The teaching of most subjects in early-twentieth-century Oxford was highly academic and Modern History was only 'modern' in the sense that it was not ancient. Ancient History formed part of 'Greats', then considered the path to success in any professional walk of life. The methods of instruction in the Classics influenced the teaching in the Modern History school, whose syllabus ended at 1815. The interpretation of recondite sources cut a great deal more ice than a broadly based appraisal of the importance of a Renaissance ruler. It is easy to imagine Clement, fascinated by Leonardo's relations with Ludovico Sforza, chafing at the dispassionate analysis of fifteenth-century texts.

One tutor who taught Clem was Arthur Johnson of All Souls, known as 'The Johnner', who employed off-hand, if not eccentric, methods of instruction, often attired in hunting clothes after a good ride. Once, having reduced a Univ student to tears, Johnson put his arm around the man and said, 'Don't be a fool. I'm paid to talk to you like that.'[59]

Attlee was dismissive not only of Johnson, but of almost all the History dons he encountered. The exception was Ernest Barker, then a young don, who taught him in his last year. He was the only don, Clement later said, who 'made much impression on me'.[60]

Clem, like Tom and his friends from Haileybury, gained a second-class honours degree. His three years at Oxford were enjoyable; indeed, he later described them as the happiest days of his life. During the First World War he calmed himself while under shell fire by imagining himself taking a walk around Oxford. He had followed Millar's advice and become 'someone in college'; he had made close friendships, many of which – and one in particular – were to influence his later life.

With the nostalgia common to those who feel that they have unfinished business in the city of dreaming spires, Clement looked back later in life and wondered how his life would have evolved if he had won a first-class honours degree, stayed on at Oxford and become an academic Fellow of Univ. Such speculation is, in every sense, academic. A First was not and is not a guarantee of a fellowship, and he was not driven by a thirst for academic research. When he did teach, ten years later, at the London School of Economics, he taught, as he later governed, from the standpoint of practical knowledge and experience. He was vastly more effective at being Prime Minister than he would have been as a professor of History.

The picture that emerges of Clem at twenty-one years old is of a young man of laudable social conscience waiting to be woken up, looking, not too actively, for a receptacle for his non-specific vocation. By his own account he was a conservative, although he never belonged to any political club. Nor did he involve himself with religious groups, although it was common ground between him and Tom that they both accepted Christian ethics. By no stretch of imagination was he a socialist, principally because socialism was not spoken of in his set.[61]

Even if he had wanted to, there was no procedure for an individual to join the Labour Party. Two political parties dominated British politics, either of which would have been acceptable for a young man of his social background, neither of which appealed to him. Talk of social reform was as far as he and his contemporaries ventured. Clem intellectually endorsed the need for reform; as a budding barrister, he took his honours degree to the Inns of Court, exchanged the quadrangles of Oxford for the quadrangles of the Inner Temple, and prepared for conventional middle-class life as a lawyer.

Oxford retained its magical significance throughout Clem's life. When he was elected an Honorary Fellow of Univ in 1942 he was enormously flattered, writing to Tom that 'Univ have just made me an honorary Fellow which is rather pleasing.'[62] In his letter of acceptance to the college he was more formal, saying that 'No honour could be more gratifying to me than to become a Fellow of my old college.'[63]

There was, however, a problem. In Michaelmas term 1921 Clement's name had been removed from the books of the college and it would cost seven guineas to restore it. At matriculation in his first term, he had paid 'caution money', which stayed on the books as a credit and was used to keep his name on the college roll – a small subscription each year. By 1921 that credit had been used up, and he relinquished all the privileges offered to Old Members, such as the right to dine at High Table. The College Registrar, faced with the recognition that the college had elected an ineligible Honorary Fellow, wrote to Clement, by then Deputy Prime Minister, requesting a cheque for seven guineas.[64]

Once this small debt was cleared, Clement was installed as an Honorary Fellow and showed his appreciation by donating a superb silver-gilt standing wine cup to the college. Inscribed *Coll Magn Aul Universitatis D. D. C. R. Attlee, Hon. Causa Socius, In Usum Magistri et Sociorum*,[65] it is a copy of a James I original made in the reign of George III with a hallmark of 1807. Before it was delivered to the college, Attlee sent it to Queen Mary, who had a passion for fine silver. She was touched by the gesture and pronounced the cup most handsome.

Recognising his wartime service in the coalition, the university elected Attlee, by then Prime Minister, to receive an honorary Doctor of Law degree in March 1946. In his own view, however, the most signal honour came in December 1943 when a speech of his was set for translation into Latin as part of the Balliol entrance scholarship. This was recognition of a high order, placing him alongside Cicero in the firmament. With almost childish pride he wrote to Tom that 'I am told that this may be considered a high compliment'.[66]

Clement stayed in touch with the college and with its activities, particularly on the river. During the complex preparations for Encaenia[67] – arrangements for the delivery of his robes, transportation for his wife to the luncheon at All Souls, the organising of lunch for his chauffeur – Clement added a note in his own hand to the official letter confirming arrangements. 'I am so pleased', he wrote, 'to see our success in the Eights.' It seems that the secretary of the Univ Boat Club regularly notified the Prime Minister of Univ's performance in the Summer Eights, for in 1949 his private secretary P. P. Osmond wrote to the Boat Club secretary to thank him for sending a copy of the Eights' Week programme. 'Mr Attlee', he wrote, 'very much appreciated having this.'[68]

Univ is rightly proud of its only Old Member to become Prime Minister of Great Britain.[69] In the dining hall hangs a superb portrait of Clement, painted by Oswald Birley. Showing him in his robes as a Doctor of Civil Law, it perfectly captures the self-imposed restraint of the subject.

Although his loyalty remained firmly with the Dark Blues, he later developed an association with Cambridge University. In 1951, Harvey

Cole, president of the Cambridge University Labour Club, invited Attlee to be joint president of the club. Attlee at first refused, suggesting that they invite a Cambridge man. Cole replied that, since there were few Cambridge men among his ministers, the Prime Minister might agree to reshuffle his Cabinet. In the meantime, he should think of himself as an 'honorary Cambridge man'. Attlee, doubtless with a good-humoured chuckle, accepted the invitation.[70]

When Clement came down from Oxford, few, least of all Clem himself, would have predicted how his relations with the university would develop. Romantic and ambitious, possessed of a very respectable degree, yet, in his own words, 'too shy to speak', he was compelled to accept that he should start on the path carved out for him. 'This pleasant time came to an end,' he recalled, 'and I started work in London, reading in chambers with Sir Philip Gregory, one of the leading conveyancing counsels of that day.'[71]

ENDNOTES

1   General descriptions of the young Clement's life are from the first (unpublished) draft of Attlee's autobiographical notes in the archive at Churchill College, Cambridge, and from the greatly truncated published version, *As It Happened*.
2   Throughout Clement Attlee's life his name was frequently misspelt with only one 't'.
3   John Timbs, *Curiosities of London*. 1867, London: J. C. Hotten.
4   CAC: ATLE 1/7.
5   Kenneth Harris, *Attlee*, p. 7.
6   Clement Attlee, *As It Happened*, p. 6.
7   Ibid., p. 7.
8   Ibid., p. 7.
9   Letter to Tom Attlee, 15 August 1944.
10   Letter to Tom Attlee, 29 April 1945.
11   CAC: ATLE 1/7.
12   All these are preserved in the esoteric collection in Churchill College, ATLE/1 and ATLE/2.
13   *As It Happened*, p. 10.
14   Ibid., p. 10.
15   CAC: ATLE 1/7.
16   *Wisden*, 'The Cricketer's Almanac', is the longest-running sports annual in history, having been published annually since 1864.
17   Williams, *Nothing So Strange*, p. 232.
18   *As It Happened*, pp. 12–13.
19   *As It Happened*, p. 18.
20   Headley, *Darwinism and Modern Socialism*. 1909, London: Methuen.
21   A myth has grown that Clem and Tom quarrelled over Clem's signing up in 1914. This is false. They fundamentally disagreed, but each brother accepted that the other was following his conscience.
22   *The Haileyburian*, reporting on the debate of 18 February 1901.
23   *The Haileyburian*, reporting on the debate of 11 March 1901.
24   *The Haileyburian*, 8 March 1901.
25   In his early notes on his life, his time in the Haileybury Cadet Force receives more attention than almost any other subject – except summer holidays – until he describes his Oxford days.

26   CAC: ATLE 1/8.
27   CAC: ATLE 1/8.
28   As seen and marvelled at by the author when he first met Tom and Kathleen Attlee in 1960.
29   Conversation with Anne, Countess Attlee, October 2013.
30   Letter to Tom Attlee, 20 March 1929.
31   'The Churchill I Knew', *Churchill By His Contemporaries*, p. 14.
32   CAC: ATLE 1/8.
33   CAC: ATLE 1/8.
34   Oxford parlance for the course of *Literae Humaniores*, or 'Classics' in short. It is a four-year course that requires examinations in Greek and Latin language and literature in the second year and in ancient history and philosophy at the end of the fourth year.
35   Details of Clement's friendship with Hugh Linton are recorded in a note of Linton's death in the *Univ Record*. Details of the birthday meal are at University College Archives, UC:P32/X/1/5.
36   College 'battels' (accounts), University College, Oxford.
37   CAC: ATLE 1/8.
38   L. F. Rushbrook Williams, 'Recollections of a pre-1914 Oxford', *Univ Record* ('UCR') VII, 1, 22–29.
39   These and other comments by old members are cited by Robin Darwall-Smith, *A History of University College, Oxford*. 2008, Oxford: OUP, p. 433.
40   A. M. Moore, *Recollections of University College, 1896–1900,* pp. 31–32.
41   L. R. Farnell, 1934, *An Oxonian Looks Back*, pp. 141 and 143.
42   F. Bickerton, Fred of Oxford; Being the Memoirs of Fred Bickerton, Until Recently Head Porter of University College, Oxford (1953) pp. 34–35.
43   Minutes of the Tenterden and Pelican Essay Clubs, Corpus Christi College Archive E/7/1 and E/5/3.
44   Conversation, Edric Millar and the author, June 1960.
45   Clement also attended the Tenterden Club as a guest. Peggy Attlee, *With a Quiet Conscience*, p. 24.
46   Minutes of the University College Martlets Society, Bodleian: MS. Top. Oxon, d. 95/2 12.
47   Ibid.
48   A. D. Gardner, *Reminiscences*, typescript, University College Library.
49   Details of the officers and debates are from the records of the Union in the Oxford Union Library.
50   David Walter, *The Oxford Union: Playground of Power*, p. 20.
51   Christopher Hollis, *The Oxford Union*, pp. 145 and 231.
52   David Walter, *op. cit.*, p. 100.
53   *As It Happened*, p. 23.
54   Harris, *Attlee*, p. 564.
55   *As It Happened*, p. 23.
56   To win a 'Blue' at Oxford, an athlete has to play not only for the university but be part of the team that plays against Cambridge in the University Match.
57   According to records made available by the Director of Sport at Oxford University.
58   As the architect Robert Adam wrote in a letter to George III.
59   *UCR* vol. 5, no. 3 (1968), 160 and Carritt, *UCR*, vol. 3, no 3 (1958), 183–192. Cited by Darwall-Smith, p. 411.
60   *As It Happened*, p. 22.
61   *As It Happened*, pp. 22–3.
62   Letter to Tom Attlee, 29 March 1942.
63   University College Archive, UC:CO1/1/A/2/2.
64   University College Archive, UC:CO1/1/A/2/2.
65   'To the great hall of University College, Oxford C. R. Attlee, Honorary Fellow, gave this gift for the use of the Master and the Fellows.' University College Archive, UC:CO1/P3/1 fol. 32.
66   Letter to Tom Attlee, 1 January 1944.
67   The ceremony at which the university awards honorary degrees to distinguished men and women and commemorates its benefactors.
68   21 May 1949, Letter from P. P. Osmond, University College Archive, UC:CO4/C/1/1.
69   Old members of University College also include Bob Hawke, Prime Minister of Australia from 1983 to 1991, Festus Mogae, President of Botswana from 1998 to 2008, and Bill Clinton, President of the United States from 1993 to 2001.
70   CRA to Harvey Cole, 4 February 1951. Bodleian: MS. Attlee, dep. 118.
71   *As It Happened*, p. 25.

CHAPTER TWO

I AM A SOCIALIST TOO, 1904–1914

When Clement left Oxford in June 1904 he had taken the first steps towards a career as a barrister, 'eating his dinners' to acquire membership of the Inner Temple. He felt no strong calling to the Bar; it was a gentlemanly profession in which his father's eminence might help him. Moreover, there was nothing else that he particularly wanted to do. Possibly he envied Tom and Edric Millar who had chosen their careers – Tom as an architect, Miller at the Treasury. Perhaps he envied Bernard for having the calling that he did not. Certainly he envied Hugh Linton, who had a clear purpose thrust on him by his father's premature death. In Clement's case, his choice of career would please his father while at first appearing a perfectly acceptable option.

In the autumn of 1904 he began to apply himself to the Law in New Square, Lincoln's Inn. After Oxford, the environment was familiar, combining the portrait-laden dining hall, the rabbit warren of barristers' 'rooms' (for no lawyer was so vulgar as to call them 'offices') and spacious quadrangles. As is the nature of pupillage, it was demanding work, and Attlee later wrote that Gregory was a task-master.[1] It was a year of absorbing as much as possible of someone else's experience, while struggling to garner his own. Experience of precise drafting was a useful, if exacting, skill and, a year later, Clem passed the Bar examination.

Convinced that Clement could succeed at the Bar, Henry did all he could to further his career. This included buying him a share of a shoot organised by the secretary of the Law Society on the Sussex Downs.[2] To broaden his experience and understanding of a solicitor's function, he brought him to work in his office. Barristers and solicitors performed very different and rigidly separated tasks; the offer of work at Druces and Attlee was therefore unusual. Henry's firm was a depressing anachronism: gloomy, almost pre-Victorian in its working conditions. Typewriters were forbidden on the grounds that they diminished the quality of calligraphy; the telephone was used only to make appointments.[3] The filing of documents was an arcane process, understood only by Mr Powell, the clerk.[4] Clement sat at a small table in his father's office, taking notes during interviews with clients. This was not at all the profession that he had thought to have joined.

In time he diplomatically negotiated his release and recrossed the divide between solicitor and barrister to work as a pupil with Theobald Mathew, a well-known 'character' at the Inns of Court and long-standing friend of the Attlee family. The son of a High Court judge, Mathew deliberately contained his practice to allow time for writing literary and historical articles related to the law. His most famous work, *Forensic Fables*, is a delightful miscellany of legal humour, published in 1926. When Attlee was his pupil he was thirty-nine years old, had been a barrister for fifteen years, and was well established at 4 Paper Buildings, a thriving set of chambers.

Attlee, having been called to the Bar in March, enjoyed a year of hard work enlivened by the caustic, iconoclastic wit of Mathew. He worked with Lord Robert Cecil, third son of the Marquess of Salisbury and the King's Counsel of the chambers, and earned his first fee of ten guineas, drafting a bill for the Licensed Victuallers Association.[5] In the following year he worked with Cecil on the celebrated Norfolk peerage case, in which Lord Mowbray claimed the Earldom of Norfolk, a title created and bestowed on his ancestor in 1312, and, ultimately, won his case. On the basis of this success, Attlee was invited to review a book on peerage law which, he recalls, he did 'with all the assurance of youth'.

Another member of the chambers was Malcolm Macnaghten, who later became a King's Counsel in 1919 and a High Court judge in 1928. Macnaghten entered the House of Commons as Ulster Unionist MP for North Londonderry in the year that Attlee was elected to Parliament. During Clem's time with Mathew, an opportunity occurred which, with a different outcome, might have changed British political history. A vacancy came up for a conveyancer on the Ecclesiastical Commission

and Philip Gregory recommended Attlee for the job.[6] He was a promising candidate – until it became clear that he 'lacked some months of
standing at the Bar'. Had he been offered a permanent job, he might
never have left the comfortable profession of the law.

At first undeterred by lack of work, he travelled between the Assize
Courts of south-east England and handled just one brief at Maidstone
Quarter Sessions. A young barrister was presumed to have private means
to support him, as he could not expect to be offered lucrative briefs in
his early years. As he still enjoyed an annual allowance of £200 from
his father, Attlee felt no financial pressure while he lived at home and
persevered at the Bar. His pupillage completed, he joined the chambers
of Henry Dickens, son of the novelist, who had taken silk in 1892.

Dickens had achieved fame in 1902 through his spirited defence of Kitty
Byron, accused of stabbing to death her alcoholic and violent lover. Despite
his reputation, however, very little work trickled down to the juniors. Attlee
had time on his hands and he duplicated his Oxford life in agreeable fashion.[7] He spent an unhurried morning after breakfast at Portinscale Road,
sometimes walking into chambers, sometimes taking the steamer that had
started sailing from Putney to the Temple. Each Wednesday he met Tom,
Edric Millar and other Oxford friends for lunch in the Strand;[8] he joined
a literary society in Putney and attended meetings of a Hazlitt essay club.[9]
This untaxing existence might have persisted but for what turned out to be
a life-changing event one evening in October 1905.

Many leading public schools had founded boys' clubs in the poorer
parts of London and the Haileybury Guild had been founded in 1890
to do what could be done for the diocese of St Albans, particularly in
the district known as 'London over the border'. This euphemism, like
'London across the bridges' for south London, referred to those parts of
the city close to the docks, heavily overpopulated slums clustered by the
marshes beside the Thames. Ten miles separated Putney and Limehouse,
where the Guild had founded Haileybury House, but the districts were
culturally worlds apart. The East End of London, stretching from east
of Tower Bridge to the marshes of Beckton, was *terra incognita*.

Clement was working at Druces and Attlee when Laurence proposed
that they spend an evening at Haileybury House, ostensibly to see
how their donations to the Guild were being spent. Together they

walked from Billiter Square and took a train from Fenchurch Street to Limehouse. Emerging into a thick autumn fog shrouding the unwelcoming surroundings, the brothers walked to Haileybury House, where Cecil Nussey, an old Haileyburian and a founder of the settlement, greeted them. Nussey, while at Oxford, had become a disciple of the generation of social thinkers that influenced settlements in the third quarter of the nineteenth century, adopting the thinking of Thomas Green, Professor of Moral Philosophy from 1878 until his death in 1882.

Green's ethical socialism was based on the premise that human self-perfection could only be achieved through society, and that society therefore had the moral obligation to ensure the best conditions for everyone. This entailed for the individual not random and remote acts of charity, but the obligation on the more fortunate to share their fuller lives with the poor. Nearby Toynbee Hall, founded in 1884, put into action Canon Barnett's principle that 'little can be done *for* that is not done *with* the people'. Haileybury House under Nussey was a similar experiment that immersed Haileyburians as residents rather than as occasional visitors to the lives of the Cockney youth of Limehouse and Stepney.

Attlee was no stranger to the principles of social service. His mother and sisters were active in working with the underprivileged. Rob and Bernard had been involved with boys' clubs and the younger brothers had helped Bernard, a curate in Hoxton before going to Wolvercote, with his work in the East End.[10] While they willingly accepted their social obligations, their arm's-length experience of social work was very different from the commitment that Nussey made to the Haileybury Guild.

The Guild was founded as a religious organisation, with Old Haileyburians such as Edwyn Hoskyns, Rector of Stepney from 1886 to 1896, and Francis Gurdon, captain of cricket at Haileybury and Rector of Limehouse from 1894 to 1906, among its leading lights. By the turn of the century, however, recognising the deep suspicion of organised religion in the poorer districts, settlements adopted a non-sectarian approach, a reassuring facet for Attlee. As he and Laurence were shown over the premises, seeing the range of activities from drilling of the Cadet Battalion to draughts, bagatelle and boxing, he overcame his initial fear of his surroundings and listened with growing interest to Nussey's description of his mission.

By the time he left and headed home to Putney he had agreed to volunteer time to Haileybury House. At first he visited once a week; later, spending two or three evenings a week in Limehouse, he found himself increasingly drawn to the boys who at first had seemed to emanate from another world. In a much-quoted passage from *The Social Worker*, published in 1920, Attlee described his own conversion with poignant simplicity. He described the progress towards socialism of

a boy from a public school knowing little or nothing of social or industrial matters, who decides, perhaps at the invitation of a friend or from loyalty to his old school that runs a mission, or to the instinct of service that exists in everyone, to assist in running a boys' club.

Gradually, the boy overcomes shyness in this novel environment and finds himself 'with a new outlook and shedding old prejudices'. The boys, of a type that 'he always regarded as bounders, become human beings to him, and he appreciates their high spirits, and overlooks what he would formerly have called vulgarity'. After a year or two of acting as referee in their football matches, becoming involved with the boys' families, discussing the problems of their daily lives, all new to him,

the thoughtless schoolboy will have become interested in social problems in the concrete, and from this it is but a step to studying them in the abstract, and he soon sees how little his efforts can accomplish, and will perceive that the faults he sees are only the effects of greater causes.[11]

This frank step-by-step analysis of his growing involvement in the boys' lives led Attlee to the obvious but novel conclusion that settlements were 'artificial and transitory, as if a worker marries he has to move out'. It was vital to 'break up the huge collection of people of one class living as it were among the natives and create a more "natural" system'. Training should take place at the settlement but social workers should then move out and live in the district. Settlements must move with the times, he argued. They had rested on the idea that a few 'well-meaning cultured people could become neighbours to the poor at their discretion'. This bourgeois monopoly of good works was simply out of date.[12]

The 'thoughtless schoolboy' had found direction for his non-specific vocation. He found a means of giving, distinct from the religion he found tedious and irrelevant to daily life. He moved from envy of Hugh Linton's calling to solid respect for Cecil Nussey's dedication. In the autumn of 1907, when the manager of Haileybury House resigned, Nussey asked Attlee if he would be interested in taking the job, a residential position with a modest salary. With an alacrity that he could not have imagined on his first visit, he accepted.

Once he moved into Haileybury House he saw the boys more regularly and became more involved in their daily lives, often visiting their homes and talking with their parents. He became, in short, part of the life of the neighbourhood. Five months after he first visited Haileybury House, he took a commission in the 1st Cadet Battalion of the Queen's London Regiment, becoming a second lieutenant, the junior of three company officers.[13] In the summer of 1906 he accompanied twenty-seven of the boys to camp at Rottingdean. He enjoyed the experience and the company received a good report from the senior officer who remarked on their discipline and improved drill.

Thus opened a period of a decade and a half, interrupted by the First World War, in which Attlee, now a resident of the poorest district of London, initially lived a three-cornered life between Limehouse, the Temple and Putney. From his family, who imagined that his residence in Limehouse was temporary, he concealed his growing commitment. Not from fear that his father would impede or forbid him to make such a move, for Henry, in spite of his fixed habits, had a remarkably open mind. But for Clement, the journey to socialism was just beginning and he was content to wait and see in which direction it took him. On the one hand, he knew with growing intimacy and insight the challenges of life in Limehouse; on the other hand, he knew nothing of the theoretical background to ethical socialism. With the thoroughness that characterised his later life, he resolved to learn all he could about the movement that he had joined.

As his description of the schoolboy becoming a social worker made clear, the growing consciousness of the shameful facts of working-class London initiated a parallel growth in his political awareness. The closing decades of the nineteenth century had seen the foundation of the Fabian

Society and the Independent Labour Party, the theoretical and practical arms of the growing Labour movement. With typical pragmatism Attlee resolved to learn more about the theoretical base of socialism. However interesting his experiences, however diverting the anecdotes, unless he could see a way to alleviate the harsh conditions of life in Limehouse, he knew that they were merely studies in zoology.

Attlee's autobiography is terse and truncated concerning many phases of his life. His description of his life in the East End and the path to his becoming a socialist, by contrast, is filled with detail, a miscellany of events that brought into focus all the unquestioned values that he had previously accepted. From cardinal virtues to the smallest convention of good manners, everything was subjected to the East End test. One example will suffice. Attlee discovered that it was considered bad manners among his new neighbours to talk at meals. Without taking a view on the subject, he simply questioned the *dictum* of etiquette that a man spent the first half of dinner talking to the lady on his right and, after the fish course, turned and began speaking to the lady on his left. Why was this so rigidly observed? Why should Putney be invariably right and Limehouse invariably wrong in matters of etiquette?

The process of conversion, then, was logical and direct. Poverty was an evil to be eradicated. It was not, as he had been taught, a result of moral delinquency. Instead it was an inevitable result of prevailing social conditions. For things to improve, given that the ethics of the East End were not intrinsically invalid, then change was required in the social conditions rather than in the ethics of the poor. And, if change were needed, how could he go about achieving it?

Reverting to the habits of childhood, he began to read voraciously and was amazed by how much had been written on subjects of which he knew nothing. Of particular amusement to him was that he had attended at Haileybury a lecture on William Morris entitled 'Morris the Poet, Morris the Upholsterer, Morris the Socialist' and that Morris's pioneering work with the Democratic Federation, the predecessor of the Social Democratic Federation, had totally passed him by. For further enlightenment he turned to Tom, an admirer of Morris.

Tom, now training as an architect, was helping to run a boys' club in Hoxton, another depressed district north-west of Limehouse. He had a willing pupil in his brother, desperate to make up for lost time. Morris had maintained that art could only flourish in a society that returned from selfishness to fraternity, from the profit motive to British values of before the Industrial Revolution. Was this not, Tom asked, the goal of the Whitechapel Art Gallery, founded in 1901? Clement must have blushed to remember that he had argued in a Haileybury debate that the 'lower orders' would not appreciate art.

Successively he examined the ideals of different proponents of socialist thought. Sidney Webb of the Fabians he rejected as 'gas-and-water socialism', dependent on state institutions rather than human idealism; the Charity Organisation Society he saw as employing moral bribes in their charitable gifts; co-partnership he had dismissed as impractical after he and Tom had bought some ill-fitting, poorly made suits from a co-partnership tailor.[14] As he rejected, one by one, the theories of contemporary socialist thinkers, he became impatient that his work at the club was treating the symptom and not the disease. Only by street-corner agitation could the mass of the people be stirred to exert their power at the ballot box; only by working within the framework of the state could long-lasting radical reform be achieved.

Which brought him back to the Fabians. The process of edging closer to socialism and rejecting his inherited values took two years, and in October 1907 he was ready to take a significant step and join the movement. He and Tom went to Clement's Inn to join the Fabian Society. Edward Peace, the secretary, Attlee recalled, 'regarded us as if we were two beetles who had crept under the door, and when we said we wanted to join, he asked coldly, "Why?" We said humbly that we were socialists and persuaded him that we were genuine.'[15]

Once admitted, Clement found the proceedings lively but daunting, as his account of a meeting he and Tom attended at Essex Hall revealed. His first impression was that 'The platform seemed to be full of bearded men – Aylmer Maude, William Sanders, Sidney Webb and Bernard Shaw.' Clement turned to Tom and whispered, 'Have we got to grow a beard to join this show?' As he listened to H. G. Wells, Chiozza Money and Sidney Webb, he was transfixed. 'They all seemed pretty impressive to a neophyte.'[16]

Joining the Fabian Society was a step significant but not definitive, as the society embraced liberals as well as socialists. Superficially, he had much in common with the Fabian movement but found the society uncongenial, frivolously referring to Beatrice and Sidney Webb as 'The Beauty and the Beast'. He was 'repelled' by their rigidity and their distance from everyday life, finding them strong on facts but unrealistic and ineffective when it came to dealing with people.[17]

The Labour Party gained admission to the House of Commons in 1906 and Attlee attributes his conversion to socialism to the 1907 by-elections in Jarrow and Colne Valley that saw Pete Curran, the first Labour MP in the north-east, and the 26-year-old Victor Grayson elected, winning for the Labour movement seats previously held by Liberals.[18] In January 1908 he made the decision that linked his work at Haileybury House with a political purpose. One evening, a 'fiery little Welshman' named Tommy Williams, a member of the Crane Drivers' Union, called on Nussey to express his indignation at the iniquity of a decision of the Charity Organisation Society, the charitable group established to promote self-help rather than government intervention to assist the needy. Attlee listened attentively and, when Williams pronounced that he was a socialist, calmly stated, 'I am a socialist too.'

It was a defining moment. In a single bound Attlee vaulted from socially conscious conservatism, over the middle ground of benevolent liberalism – at a time when Campbell-Bannerman's Liberal government was hailed as the harbinger of reform – to a position that would have shocked him two years before. His father was a Liberal; he had grown up in a family with a tradition of social work. Without doubting their genuine commitment to reform, he questioned their efficacy. Remote benevolence would not solve the problems of the East End; if real reform required socialism, then he was a socialist.

In that declaration Attlee committed himself to action that extended beyond mere philanthropy. Williams invited Attlee to a meeting of the local branch of the Independent Labour Party, a group of about a dozen people who organised street-corner meetings three or four times a week. Attlee joined the ILP, joined the National Union of Clerks, attended at least one open-air meeting a week of the party and, without fanfare, found himself on the far side of a fundamental social divide.

Until that moment he had hesitated to admit that performance of good works would inevitably distance him from the backstop of life in Putney. His family shared a sense of social duty and thus his initial interest was not out of character. Yet he was as hazy about the nature of a socialist as a country parson who, observing Attlee at a meeting to which he had cycled on a hot day, observed, 'I suspect that man is a socialist. He wears a soft collar.'[19]

Initially, in the Victorian ethic of his time, he believed that poverty was a manifestation of moral turpitude, caused by lack of those values – thrift, sobriety, hard work – that the Victorian middle class held dear. Early in his visits to Haileybury House he was shocked to hear that an educated man admired Keir Hardie. He was later to have the opportunity to play back that surprise to an acquaintance. He records with suppressed glee an event in 1911 when he was staying with a local magnate. Asked by the magnate's daughter if he was a keen supporter of Lloyd George and the Liberals, he denied the charge. The daughter relaxed and concluded that he must be a Conservative. There was 'a distinct sensation' when he replied that he was a socialist.[20]

He began to understand how poverty and insecurity dogged families in Limehouse, where dockers and building workers might earn £1 a week and see perhaps half of that evaporate in rent payment. He saw women exploited, 'sweated' as seamstresses, earning as little as seven shillings and sixpence for a week's labour; he saw two women who worked at trouser-finishing paid a penny-farthing a pair, from which they bought their own thread; he learned from boys how, when they left school at fourteen, they would work twelve or more hours daily for a weekly wage packet of five shillings, only to be dismissed when they were old enough to demand an adult's wage. He began to understand the communal fear of the landlord, how families would consign their furniture to a neighbour's keeping and do a 'moonlight flit', the only alternative to eviction and distraint of their goods.

As he walked home one day, a small girl whom he knew attached herself to him and asked where he was going. 'Home to my tea,' said Attlee. 'I'm going home to see if there is any tea,' the girl replied.[21] That exchange lingered as a reminder that the next meal was less than assured for many of his new neighbours.

Discovery of such permanent uncertainty and insecurity was accompanied by a discovery of virtues that he had not imagined could coexist with poverty. He encountered fortitude and not shiftlessness in dealing with adversity; generosity, which undermined the middle-class virtue of thrift. He discovered that the boys, uninformed by Oxford standards, were quite capable of forming their own ideas on a wide range of subjects. One discussion in an attempt to define a gentleman particularly struck him. 'A gentleman', one boy ventured, 'is a bloke what's the same to everybody.'[22]

Most importantly, he discovered the self-respect that the boys possessed. Church-run settlements that offered coffee and buns to those who attended events were distrusted; Haileybury House charged a half-penny a week for membership and was oversubscribed while church events were ill attended. The boys had a visceral distrust of any organisation that offered something for nothing. By contrast, they trusted Attlee because 'He came to us as a shy little man. He became our friend because he had lived with us and got to know our problems and because he had no swank.'[23]

Discoveries about prevailing conditions of poverty and the revelation that it was within his power to effect change, not as an abstract concept for the masses – the Webbs' approach – but as an individual among individuals, had prompted his response to Tommy Williams. His avowal was a dramatic statement that marks a dramatic change of direction, but it must be construed alongside the young Attlee, comfortable in the company of fellow officers in the Cadet Battalion, professional men like him, Old Haileyburians, Conservatives with a conscience. Admitting that he was a socialist involved no reform of the structure of society, no abolition of the public schools. Attlee's core values remained essentially conservative, the nineteenth-century values absorbed by every public schoolboy: respect for the monarchy, patriotism, devotion to the British Empire and an obligation to those less privileged. While his social conscience had been awakened and he allied himself firmly with the growing Independent Labour Party, he remained essentially a liberal conservative.

In the first decade of the century, the Labour movement was struggling to find a political foothold. Individuals could not join the Labour Party directly but were required to belong to an affiliated organisation such as a trade union or the ILP. The party, which had grown out of the Labour Representation Committee in 1900, was very much the junior partner in the 'Lib–Lab' alliance of 1906. Its objective was to further 'working-class opinion being represented in the House of Commons'. This was far from revolutionary.

The gulf between the more radical Independent Labour Party and the Liberal Party, the necessary ally of the nascent Labour Party, was vast. Mutual suspicion undermined any collaboration and many working-class areas, including Stepney, had only minuscule groups of committed social-ists prepared to overstep more fashionable liberalism. This was realistic politics, as the Liberal Party had won 397 seats in the 1906 election against the Labour Party's twenty-nine. In the popular vote the Liberal landslide captured two and a half million votes, roughly ten times the support for Labour. Nonetheless, for the Labour movement it was an important elec-tion, laying the foundations of a parliamentary party.

In retrospect, the notion of Attlee, painfully shy and quite untrained in politics at street level, committing himself to social change through the instrument of a tiny group of activists seems akin to tilting at windmills. Soon elected branch secretary, he became the lead speaker for meetings held at street corners across the borough. As for overcoming shyness, anec-dotes in his autobiography reveal that he learned to swim by being thrown into the deep end. 'It is not easy to speak to an empty street in order to attract the passers-by,' he wrote, 'but I did a lot of it in those days.'[24]

During his first two years in Limehouse he continued to practise as a barrister despite the lack of work it offered, and had opportunities to travel. In September 1907 he sailed to North America. His sister Mary had travelled to Saskatchewan to help a cousin who was expecting her first child. With time on his hands, Attlee was deputed to escort her home. When he arrived in Montreal, finding that he had three days free, he visited Harvard and New York City, sailing up the Hudson River to Albany to meet Mary at Toronto.[25]

For ten months in 1908 his compartmentalised life continued as before. He had moved into different chambers, commuting from Haileybury House, and involved himself increasingly in the business of the ILP; at weekends he was involved in football matches and other excursions with his boys. When club activities permitted, he would cross town to Putney on Sunday. His weeks were full, but he remained essentially unemployed. The death of his father in November brought home to him both that he had lost an important bond to his family and, unsurprisingly, that he had no interest in the legal profession. That conclusion had been forming for some time but only after Henry's death could he publicly announce his changed philosophy. He had become immersed in Stepney affairs and lost interest in a profession bringing him little work. He decided to abandon law and to work for the Webbs on their propaganda in favour of the Poor Law Report.[26] Despite his disdain for the 'Webby' approach, the Poor Law was a massive obstacle to constructive reform.

In February 1909 the Royal Commission on the Poor Law submitted a majority report and a minority report, both ultimately dismissed by the Liberal government. The majority report, an unadventurous document, perpetuated the doctrine that poverty was a moral condition, recommending that the Poor Law remain in force. The minority report, the product of Beatrice and Sidney Webb, urged the abolition of Boards of Guardians and establishment of local authority organisations; in the breadth of its approach it has been hailed as the foundation stone of the Welfare State.

Ignored by the Liberal government, the Webbs founded what became the National Committee for the Prevention of Destitution and offered Attlee a job as meetings officer, responsible for organising meetings and finding speakers across the country. While the job itself was manifestly temporary, the commitment was permanent. The committee failed to achieve anything and, early in 1910, when Attlee was invited to become secretary at Toynbee Hall, he seized the opportunity. The move was not a success. Dispirited by the tired Liberalism of the settlement, Attlee lasted a short time before, probably by mutual agreement, he left the job at the end of the year. His interest lay more in his own 'manor', in Limehouse rather than Whitechapel – and, abidingly, in Haileybury House.

The move from Toynbee Hall deprived him of both job and accommodation. Henry Attlee had left £70,000 to his eight children and Clem's portion of the inheritance earned him £400 annually, enough to live on. Convinced that settlements were intrinsically artificial, he suggested to Tom that they move together into a council flat overlooking the Limehouse bend in the Thames. For 8/6 a week they occupied four rooms for a year until Tom married Kathleen Medley, a social worker and Labour councillor in Poplar. Yielding his place to Kathleen, Attlee moved back to Haileybury House.

Nearly seven years had elapsed since he came down from Oxford and Attlee was still without gainful employment. He supplemented his private income by occasional lecturing, including a course of weekly lectures on the trade union movement at Ruskin College, the independent college in Oxford, established in 1899 to provide 'educational opportunities for adults ... who need a second chance in education'.

In 1911 the Unemployment and Health Insurance Bill became law. Lloyd George accompanied the Bill with the innovative policy of hiring a number of 'explainers' who toured the country, explaining its content and purpose. Once again Attlee took on a job whose duration, he knew, would be short, but of whose purpose he approved. When it came to an end in December, Attlee returned to work for the Webbs at the NCPD.

In April 1912 that elusive job, both allowing him time to pursue his political activities and providing an income, materialised. Sidney Webb, an ardent promoter of the new London School of Economics, secured a large grant from a company in Bombay to establish a social science department. Webb proposed Attlee as a lecturer and tutor, citing his practical knowledge of social conditions. Attlee, for the first time, felt that his future was reasonably secure.[27] The pattern of his life became established: the LSE, Haileybury House and an increasing variety of social work, much of it uphill work in the teeth of Poor Law supporters. He recalls a parson who, in accepting the new system of school dinners, proposed that the children be served burnt porridge at inconvenient times and places.[28]

Suffusing his recollections of that period of his life is his pride at being part of a pioneer movement. He met most of the leaders of the Independent Labour Party – Keir Hardie, George Lansbury, Will Crooks, J. R. Clynes, Philip Snowden – the pantheon of architects of the Labour movement. He was becoming known beyond the borders of Limehouse and Stepney, speaking to public meetings across London at the rate of seventy or eighty meetings each year. He twice stood for election to the National Administrative Council of the ILP, but without success. He strove to 'regularise' his status and stood twice for the Stepney Borough Council and twice for the Limehouse Board of Guardians. He started a newspaper, the *Stepney Worker*, and put out three weekly issues, ceasing publication when a doctrinal issue arose between the ILP and their Marxist partners. His availability to support a host of causes gained him recognition among party leaders and, despite lack of tangible change to his formal status, he enhanced his local and national reputation.

One may speculate how his career might have developed in the second decade of the century if it had continued without interruption. Despite

lack of success in local council elections, he was widely respected in the
Labour movement and, ever pragmatic, was poised to enter politics as
a career. It was the next logical step. His socialism was no longer an
abstract theory but a personal conviction.

'Somewhere about this time', Attlee recalls, he made his first trip to
Italy with Tom, Mig (his sister Margaret), Edric and Winifred Millar.[29]
Otherwise, two and a half years passed during which Attlee followed
much the same course of life.[30] The days were spent lecturing and tutor-
ing at the LSE, evenings at the club and in political activities. There
would have been an election not later than 1915; Attlee would by then
have been very well positioned as a prospective Labour candidate. He
was never put to that test, as, on 4 August 1914, while he was on holiday
in Seaton with Tom and Kathleen, Britain declared war on Germany.

ENDNOTES

1   *As It Happened*, p. 25.
2   CAC: ATLE 1/8.
3   CAC: ATLE 1/8.
4   CAC: ATLE 1/9.
5   *As It Happened*, p. 25.
6   *As It Happened*, p. 26.
7   CAC: ATLE 1/9.
8   *As It Happened*, p. 27.
9   CAC: ATLE 1/8.
10   CAC: ATLE 1/9.
11   Clement Attlee, *The Social Worker*, pp. 211–12.
12   Ibid. The steps described are from pp. 213–21.
13   CAC: ATLE 1/9.
14   CAC: ATLE 1/9.
15   *As It Happened*, p. 31.
16   *As It Happened*, pp. 31–2.
17   CAC: ATLE 1/9.
18   CAC: ATLE 1/9.
19   *As It Happened*, p. 42.
20   *As It Happened*, p. 42.
21   *As It Happened*, p. 45.
22   *As It Happened*, pp. 32–3.
23   A former Haileybury House boy interviewed by Hannen Swaffer in 1945. *Daily Express*, 23 June 1945.
24   *As It Happened*, p. 51.
25   CAC: ATLE 1/18.
26   CAC: ATLE 1/8.
27   Another candidate for the job that Attlee was offered was Dr Hugh Dalton, later Attlee's Chancellor of
     the Exchequer.
28   CAC: ATLE 1/9.
29   CAC: ATLE 1/9. Winifred was Edric Millar's mother.
30   CAC: ATLE 1/9.

CHAPTER THREE

MAJOR ATTLEE, 1914–1921

The sequence of events that led to the declaration of war in 1914 ultimately yielded in importance to one action: the invasion of neutral Belgium. German strategy was based on the Schlieffen Plan, the outflanking of the French Army through Belgium rather than through the forests of the Ardennes. Until the Germans crossed onto Belgian soil, the ultimate cause of the war, the assassination of an Austrian Archduke in Serbia, was too remote to fan patriotic fires in Britain. The 'rape' of Belgium provided all the propaganda necessary to arouse British feeling against 'the Hun'.

Labour's initial policy, to prevent a capitalist war by international worker solidarity, was reasonable, if imprecise, as kings and emperors squared off after the murder of one of their own. Once the proximate cause for action by Britain was presented as a reprisal for the 'violation' of Belgium, with all the usual attendant atrocities, the party's position changed.

That change resulted in the resignation of Ramsay MacDonald, pacifist chairman of the Parliamentary Labour Party. Succeeded by Arthur Henderson, MacDonald paid the price for pacifism, suffering almost a decade of vilification. The British war propaganda machine was swift and fierce in discrediting dissenters. There was a rush to the Colours; Labour leaders supported the defence of Belgium. To have opposed the government's call for war credits of £100 million would have done possibly terminal damage to the emerging party. After all, the popular view proclaimed, the war would be over by Christmas.

In 1914, unlike his experience twenty-five years later, Attlee was uninvolved in the formulation of the party's policy. In Seaton, he and Tom discussed the war in terms more immediate to themselves. For Tom, the decision was simple. As a Christian he was unable to participate. At that stage, as enlistment was entirely voluntary, there was no legal stigma in his position; that would come later.

For Clement, thirty-one years old and single, the choice was equally simple. Britain's cause was just; the German aggressor must be stopped; he, who had trained at Haileybury and in Limehouse, had a duty to fight. He understood but could not subscribe to Tom's pacifism. As a socialist, he opposed war, but as an unmarried man, he felt it was immoral to stand by while others made the sacrifice.[1]

On 6 August he returned to London and attempted to join up, only to be turned down as the upper age limit was thirty. A further attempt to enlist in the ranks was blocked as he already held a volunteer commission in the Cadet battalion. Undeterred, he joined the Inns of Court regiment but, as he drilled recruits in the quadrangle of Lincoln's Inn, he seemed to be making no progress towards the 'real' army. Determined to 'do his bit', he asked a former student from the LSE to intercede with her brother-in-law, who commanded a battalion in Kitchener's new all-volunteer army.[2] In due course he was ordered to report to the 6th South Lancashire Regiment at Tidworth. Tom attempted to dissuade him; socialist colleagues in the East End argued violently with him, but Attlee was convinced of his duty and determined to serve, not merely drilling men in Lincoln's Inn but at the front.

At many points in Attlee's life it seems that, by unrelated accident, he had recently been engaged in activities that prepared him for the job in hand. This was the first of those occasions. A second lieutenant with six years of experience in the reserves, with administrative and organisational experience of a thoroughly practical nature, was a rare bird. He was promptly given temporary command of a company, commanding seven officers and two hundred and fifty men, 'mostly from Wigan, Warrington and Liverpool ... excellent material'.[3] When the adjutant, Captain Marsh, was posted to France in March 1915, Attlee was appointed to replace him and promoted to captain.[4] In a very short time he had found a position for which he was eminently qualified.

In April, Marsh returned to his post as adjutant and Attlee took over B Company permanently.[5] After training in Hampshire and Surrey, maps of France were issued to officers and the regiment seemed destined for the Western Front, where British and German forces were locked in a stalemate after the Second Battle of Ypres. When tropical kit was issued, however, Attlee surmised that they were destined for either Mesopotamia or Gallipoli. He was correct; embarking the *Ausonia* at Avonmouth, the regiment sailed via Alexandria to Gallipoli and joined British forces already at the Gully Ravine.

The Gallipoli campaign, the controversial brainchild of Aristide Briant and Winston Churchill, then First Lord of the Admiralty, was designed to open the Dardanelles for supplies to Russia, to bring Greece, Romania and Bulgaria into the war, and to relieve the stalemate in France. In Attlee's view, it was an innovative piece of strategy that ultimately failed because the Allied High Command, myopic in its concentration on the Western Front, failed to allot necessary forces in timely fashion.[6] During July the 29th Division, including the South Lancashires, joined what had become a battle from entrenched positions and prepared for a massive assault on Turkish positions.

Attlee's memories of the Gallipoli campaign highlight its static nature. Night watch duty he found particularly tedious:

> *It was very boring on night watch. The only way to keep awake was to get a good talk going with the sergeants. I remember a long discussion on industrial and craft unionism with my CSM of the NUR and a platoon sergeant of the NUVW. We agree very well.*[7]

The image of the company commander keeping himself and his non-commissioned officers awake by talking what his fellow officers would have considered seditious propaganda beside the Hellespont, 2,000 miles from England, constitutes one of the absurdities of war.

Conditions were appalling. Unburied corpses from both Turkish and Allied lines attracted swarms of flies; water was in short supply; dysentery was rife – as Attlee commented, 'a complaint for which our diet of bully beef, biscuit and tea without milk was not very suitable'. At the end of July, Attlee too contracted dysentery and was carried unconscious to the beach to be embarked on a hospital ship. Given the choice of going to England or Malta, he chose the latter, fearing that he would be posted out of the regiment if he returned to England. He was admitted to hospital at Hamrun, close to Valletta harbour.

Attlee was spared by his illness from participating in the Anzac assault between 6 and 8 August 1915. His division suffered enormous casualties and he wrote to Tom from the officers' convalescent centre in the Sicluna Palace that his company had caught the worst of the attack. Five officers had been killed and 'a dozen or so' wounded. His immediate concern was to avoid being sent back to England and to rejoin his regiment.[8]

He succeeded, and by late September was on his way back to Gallipoli. At Alexandria, knowing that Bernard had joined the Royal Navy as a chaplain and sailed to join the Gallipoli campaign, he asked if a Chaplain Attlee was among those present. To his delight, he learned that Bernard had arrived half an hour before, and the brothers had a chance to spend time together before both went to Gallipoli, Bernard to Helles, Clem to Suvla.

Rejoining his battalion in early October, Attlee found that the failure of the August assaults had drained all momentum from the campaign. As heavy rain and, later, snow made any operations difficult, his principal responsibility was to keep his men in shape. By regular exercise and 'fairly frequent issues of rum', he 'bullied' his company to stay alive while dysentery, frostbite and drowning decimated other companies.[9] It was only a matter of time before evacuation was ordered; on 28 December the Lancashires prepared to withdraw the five miles from the front line to the beaches. As the withdrawal began, Attlee looked around him, fixing images of the territory he was about to yield – 'the beauty of Samothrace standing up all white out of the sea', 'a very jolly terracotta statuette of a seated goddess about a foot high, very stately'[10] – images of civilisations on which the twentieth century had superimposed this carnage. They were brief moments as he worked with General Maude to save the battalion.

By the morning of 8 January 1916 the last Allied soldiers were evacuated. Attlee, in command of the rearguard, and Maude were the last to embark. The campaign had failed and Attlee had distinguished himself as a leader of men and an officer under fire. Many of his colleagues felt that he deserved a mention in dispatches.

In later years Attlee never wavered in his belief that Churchill had been right in urging the assault at Gallipoli, that its failure was not one of planning but of disastrously mismanaged execution – a case of too little and too late.[11] Contrafactual history, particularly of military events, is a dangerous subject, but Attlee, perhaps because of his later wartime association with Churchill, maintained that the campaign could have succeeded if it had been pursued with energy, pre-empting the Turkish concentration of force under Mustafa Kemal. As it was, it was a grisly bloodbath from which he and his regiment were fortunate to escape. It also caused Churchill's departure from the Admiralty.

Meanwhile, losses on the Western Front were mounting horrifically and in January 1916 the Military Service Act was passed, introducing conscription for single men aged between eighteen and forty-one. Tom, a married man of thirty-five, was not eligible until May, when the Act was extended to include married men. Thereafter, conscientious objectors were tried by courts martial and those who, like Tom, refused any form of service, for example as stretcher bearers, were imprisoned.

After refitting and training at Port Said, the South Lancashires sailed to Mesopotamia. Attlee recalls shipboard evenings of bridge with his superior officer, Colonel Vigne, a 'cheery old gunner colonel … one of the world's worst bridge players'. He rejoiced in the colonel's description of him to the CO: 'a charmin' feller, just going to play bridge with him, but a damned democratic, socialistic, tub-thumping rascal'.[12] An officers' mess during the Great War was hardly the most receptive audience for socialist doctrine.

Once again, Attlee's part in the campaign was to be short, to end in his being shipped out, after an injury that possibly saved his life. When the regiment attacked at El Hanna on 5 April he carried a red flag to guide artillery fire, but was hit from behind in 'friendly fire', punched into the air, and carried from the field. In subsequent attacks General Maude's division was badly mauled and, once more, Attlee was fortuitously absent.

From Basra he was shipped to hospital in Bombay, where he wrote to Tom, describing his condition:

> *Just a line to let you know that I hope in a few days to be sailing for England
> … I shall not be sorry to leave the East … bullet through the left thigh and …
> a considerable hole in my right buttock … but I still can't move [my legs] at all.*

Something wrong with the transmitting apparatus, I suppose. It's most absurd. I
send along a direct order to my leg to lift itself and it takes not the slightest notice
… By the way, it may interest the comrades to know I was hurt while carrying the
red flag to victory. I had a large artillery flag of that hue and was just planting it
on the parapet when strafed. I pointed out to the CO that I thought the colour was
a delicate compliment to my political persuasions.[13]

A medical report from Bombay of 30 April[14] describes his injuries
vividly. There were three distinct wounds: one to his left thigh, described
as 'severe – not permanent', one to his right buttock and one to his
groin, both described as 'slight – not permanent'. Collectively they were
enough to incapacitate him for six months and Lieutenant Heathcote
of the RAMC commented that he should be shipped to Britain for six
months of recuperation as 'a change of air is absolutely necessary for
his recovery'.[15]

On 2 May Attlee, barely able to walk, embarked at Bombay for
England. The summer was spent in slow convalescence. On 5 June he
was given a prognosis of six months before he would be fit for active duty.
By 17 July he could not 'walk any distance without becoming lame'. By
September he was described as 'fit for light duties'[16] and he was posted
to a 'not very lively' training battalion in Shropshire.

To his delight, by 11 October he had largely recovered; a medical
board determined that he was 'much improved', reporting that he
could 'ride a cycle for ten miles and march eight miles'.[17] Agitating to
rejoin the action in France, he was posted to a tank battalion under
the command of a South Lancashire colonel in Dorset; the appointment brought promotion to the rank of major and took him twice to the
Western Front. On the second occasion he was involved in preparations
for the Battle of Poelcapelle, a three-army assault launched in October
1917 during the second phase of the Passchendaele campaign. Back
in England, he was initially left in Dorset to form a tank battalion but
returned to the infantry when a new colonel took command.

The last year of the war began with Attlee at a training camp in
Barrow-in-Furness. With time on his hands, he renewed his correspondence with Tom, still imprisoned as a conscientious objector. His
thoughts ranged over his experiences, Tom's imprisonment, and the

future of socialism. He longed to 'pick up the threads of happenings and thoughts'.[18]

Stuck in the north of England, Attlee realised that he was a southerner;[19] he enjoyed Dorset, the county of Thomas Hardy and Tolpuddle, where he 'did pious respect to the memorial of the martyrs'. Meanwhile he was 'kicking his heels waiting to rejoin the fighting but stuck in this godforsaken hole'.[20] He was optimistic that Tom would soon be released as there had been motions for the release of conscientious objectors in both Houses, but 'they break down before the mass of British stupidity … strongly entrenched in the Cabinet'.

Throughout 1917 a series of revolutions had toppled the Russian Tsar and by October the Bolsheviks had overthrown the provisional government and taken control, leading to the Treaty of Brest-Litovsk and Russia's withdrawal from the war. Attlee, already a committed enemy of communism, was sceptical about the ability of the Bolsheviks to govern, writing to Tom, that he 'should like to have a long talk … and discuss all sorts of things'. The 'Russian debacle' he found 'rather appalling but quite explicable' as he imagined a country 'run by the Whitechapel branch of the SDP'.[21]

As to the future of socialism in Britain, he speculated how the war would affect community and private affairs. Deprived for four years of the chance to explore socialism with Tom, he longed to discuss the looming 'after the war'. Toying with guild socialism, he read Orage and Hobson's book which advocated trade-based guilds, rather than trade unions or governmental control, as the means of regulating industry. He concluded that he had 'never read a reasonably good case so badly put – the arguments puerile, mostly of the *non sequitur* type and the book infused throughout by petty malice'. The war, he felt, had given him 'slightly more catholicity' and dissipated the pre-war rigidity that made his and Tom's views unacceptable to the general public. His socialism had lost its middle-class veneer, and he wondered how Tom's values had evolved. 'I do not see how your principles can be applied in practice in the actual carrying on of the community,' he wrote. 'Doesn't this logically lead to anarchic individualism?'[22]

Tom expressed general approval of guild socialism, and Clement replied, accepting its potential but decrying its 'tendency to erect all such schemes into complete social systems'. He was struggling to find a basis for socialism. 'The Webbs', he wrote, 'with their local government bias tend to base everything on the locality and the local authority – the industrialists on industry and so on – the difficulty lies of course in the demarcation.'[23]

On differences between their positions regarding responsibility of the individual to fight to defend society, Clement was adamant that a debt to society was a valid debt, whatever the principles of the individual. Only if the state threatened to diminish the quality of life could the debt be avoided. The issue of war, moreover, was a red herring as sacrifices were made in peacetime too.

Of particular annoyance to him was a comment by Bishop Weldon in *The Times*, arguing that the German attack during Holy Week was one of the most tragic events of the war. Clem exploded at the 'absorption of the church in non-essentials'. As to personal responsibility, he continued:

> *My point is that I don't like the work but the community calls on me … and my particular objections to doing the work cannot weigh with me if the work has to be done … your antithesis between the state existing to make life better and fuller and asking you to take it is a false one. The true antithesis must be that the state asks you to make life less good and less full. Now despite the sacrifice of life in the war … life under German dominance would be less good and less full. If the Persians had not been defeated at Salamis would life have been fuller and better for the Greeks or if Attila had not been stopped at the Catalaunian Fields would life have been fuller and better for the province of Gaul? … your objection to taking life is fallacious in that it is at times necessary … I do not think that death is the worst evil or that taking life is the worst crime.*[24]

Attlee was feeling his way towards a clear definition of the individual's responsibility to the state and Tom was the ideal sounding board for his inchoate ideas, expressed in his letters with great honesty. His idealism of pre-war days had not only persisted but had been made more acute by his wartime experiences. While he saw that certain of his pre-war positions were too theoretical and doctrinaire ('Webby'), he was the more convinced of the individual's obligation to extend the benefits of a good society to all members. To ignore the opportunity and the obligation to do so was to suffer a defeat on the scale of Salamis or to have stood by while Attila rolled past Chalons-sur-Marne into France in AD 451. Totally objective about his military service, he glorified it not at all; he had merely followed his conscience with the same conviction as Tom had followed his. That conscience had led the brothers in opposite directions was not a matter for reproach but an inevitable fact; conscience entailed action. The question was already what action would be necessary after the war.

Indeed, conscience still pressed. Instead of waiting the war out in Barrow-in-Furness, Attlee lobbied to be sent back to the front. In April, General Ludendorff had launched an attack on Givenchy-lès-la-Bassée between Béthune and Lille, an assault repulsed at heavy cost by the 55th (West Lancashire) Division. In August he was posted to the 5th Territorial Battalion of the 55th and took part in their advance through Artois in the final stages of the war. His commanding officer, Lieutenant General Sir Hugh Jeudwine, commended him when he heard Attlee's troops singing as they advanced to the line, a rare occurrence.

Jeudwine instilled powerful regimental pride in his officers and Attlee recalled an occasion when he saw this at work. Commenting on how many officers had been promoted from the ranks by 1918, he wrote of a young subaltern, a former miner who had been asked during an officer's course for a tactical appreciation. 'Dost think Ah'm Douggy 'aig, lad?' the man replied. He was reported as being unfit to be an officer, and this infuriated Jeudwine, who asked for Attlee's opinion. Attlee commended the man as an excellent officer, a good disciplinarian, whom the men would follow anywhere. The general was delighted and gave the school commandant 'a raspberry' for suggesting that one of his officers was unworthy of his rank.[25]

For Attlee, the final offensive of 1918 once more saw him carried from the battlefield when falling timber struck him as he led an attack near Lille. He left his unit on 6 October, returning to England three weeks later, where he 'celebrated the Armistice in hospital … suffering from some painful boils, which seemed to get no better. A Canadian brought in some champagne to cheer us up.'[26] Despite a recurrence of dysentery,[27] he was determined to be home for Christmas. He filled in a pass, managed to get an unwitting surgeon to sign it, and left the hospital where his brother Rob was waiting outside in a taxi. So ended Major Attlee's wartime service.

Attlee's record of the war is sparse in the extreme. He devoted a mere ten pages of his autobiography to the war years; the fragments preserved in Churchill College are also uninformative, written principally to chart his war service for his children. Slightly more revealing is the record he wrote for himself, but even there he avoids any personal involvement in the action around him.[28] He remains objective, dispassionate, logical. His memory of the events is detailed; his chronology precise. Only in his relations with fellow officers and with the men under his command does the reader have a sense of his humanity. The 'Roll of South Lancs Regiment', listing officers by company and their fates – 'Wounded El Hanna', 'Killed Sari Bair' – is eloquent in its baldness.

He was horrified by the senselessness of the carnage. Belgium, the cause of Britain's entry into the war, was overrun; the Gallipoli campaign, which, properly supported, might have broken the deadlock, was grossly mishandled. Fellow officers in the 6th Battalion believed he would receive a decoration after the evacuation from Gallipoli; Attlee himself never mentions it. He describes himself as 'the only amateur company commander'; he writes of suffering from dysentery with the dispassion of someone experiencing a mild headache. A seam throughout the record is his responsibility – to his men whose lives depended on him and to his fellow officers. On the high command he is silent. It was not until March 1923 that he aired his feelings about the 'stupid' and 'class-based' army that he had served in for four years. Meanwhile the Lancashire roll survived: 'Killed Sunn I Yat', 'Died from wounds Mudros', 'Killed France 1918'.

Officially demobilised on 16 January 1919 and finally gazetted out on 16 February,[29] Attlee promptly set out for the East End to reconstruct his life on pre-war lines: a place to live, a job and local politics. In the first of these he was disappointed, as Haileybury House was closed, its staff having been lost, one by one, to the war. Fortunately, Toynbee Hall was able to offer temporary accommodation, which he accepted for its location alone. Employment was easier to arrange, as the LSE had expanded its Department of Social Science, and Professor Urwick was happy to take him back on the staff. With those two fundamentals arranged, he surveyed the political and social landscape.

It has become a cliché to say that the Great War changed Britain fundamentally. Much was altered by the war and much evolved of its own force during the war years; for Attlee, a committed socialist returning to the East End with a distinguished wartime record, the social and political changes combined to offer prospects radically different from the options open to him in 1914.

The most far-reaching change was a questioning of the old order. This was not a narrow political movement but a universal recognition that relations between the governing class and the masses were antiquated and based on indefensible assumptions. Over seven million men had served in the British Army and 750,000 had died. Until the Representation of the People Act in February 1918, some 40 per cent of adult males – and all women – were ineligible to vote. The passing of the act almost tripled the size of the electorate and granted the vote to most women over thirty. The previous year had seen the toppling of the Russian Tsar, followed by full-blooded revolution nine months later. The prospect of several million returning British soldiers with no right to vote prompted the government to rapid reform.

The Liberal Party had split in 1916, and Herbert Asquith, triumphant winner of the 1906 election, now led a group of Liberals opposed to the war while David Lloyd George headed a Conservative–Liberal coalition. In spite of Lloyd George's immense popularity as 'the man who won the war', there had been a Liberal migration to the Labour Party as the only credible party to oppose the coalition.

In Ireland, the Easter Rising of 1916 had led to the establishment of the first Irish Parliament in Dublin. The adherence of Irish voters to the Liberal Party that had championed Home Rule was thus dramatically eroded. The seventy-three Sinn Fein members elected to the new Parliament disdained to take their seats at Westminster.

All these trends were evident in the general election of November 1918, which returned Lloyd George and the coalition to power but saw the Labour Party win more of the popular vote than either Lloyd George's or Asquith's party. Despite winning only fifty-seven seats, the Labour leaders rightly identified a movement that would establish their party as the authentic voice of progress.

Within the Labour Party itself there had also been significant change. The heterogeneous nature of the party allowed differing views to coexist during the war. The overwhelming majority of members believed that

German nationalism should be checked, accepting the government's position that the only solution was through victory. On the left there had been calls for a negotiated peace, but once war was declared most branches of the party supported the national effort. The international aims of the party were at first unaffected, as contempt for the 'capitalist' nature of the war entailed support for German workers rather than jingoism. This support diminished as the war dragged on.

While the party generally co-operated with the government, they demanded a plain statement of war aims from Asquith. When a Cabinet reshuffle took place in May 1915, Arthur Henderson joined the Cabinet as president of the Board of Education in a broader national government. Almost immediately, the fissures in the party once more became evident over the issue of conscription.

The split in the Liberal Party posed another threat to Labour unity but, once more, support for government policy overcame visceral distrust of Lloyd George. The fall of Asquith was considered regrettable but the party was heavily in favour of joining the coalition in the interests of national unity, provided that Labour could retain some measure of independence. Demands for clarification of war aims intensified; concern that the end of the war should bring a just and lasting peace fanned criticism of the relentless fighting. By the end of 1917 the Labour Party was more vocal in its criticism of Lloyd George; Henderson resigned from the Cabinet; the party set out its *desiderata* clearly: a world 'safe for democracy', elimination of imperialism, and the foundation of the League of Nations.

After three years of war the Labour Party's position was widely welcomed and Lloyd George was forced to respond. Labour was gaining ground as a responsible national party, a development reflected in the general statement of policy, *Labour and the New Social Order*, drawn up in January 1918 and adopted at the party conference in June.

Starting from the principle that 'what has to be reconstructed after the war is not ... this or that piece of machinery; but, so far as Britain is concerned, society itself',[30] the paper condemned 'reckless profiteering and wage-slavery'. The Labour Party would 'do its utmost to see that it is buried with the millions whom it has done to death'.[31] After this ritualistic condemnation of capitalism, the paper assumed a more sober theme, speaking of a 'deliberately planned co-operation in production and distribution for the benefit of all who participate by hand or by brain'. It moved towards a responsible and rational statement of policy, 'whether in opposition or in due time called upon to form an Administration'.[32]

By the time the general election was held in December, the Labour Party had achieved a position unimaginable four years before. Thanks to tireless work by Henderson, smoothing out differences between the wings of his party, a system of local Labour parties was in place. The party's status was confirmed by its winning over 2 million votes, more than 20 per cent of the turnout – a result better than that achieved by either branch of the divided Liberal Party. Although this resulted in disproportionately low representation in the House of Commons, it established the party's credentials as never before.

Such was the situation when Attlee, demobilised in January 1919, 'went to Stepney to see how things were moving'.[33] The era of utopian dreaming was over; the party was impatient to gain power. Dismissive of its history of spotless idealism on the fringes of British politics, its leaders scented the real possibility of displacing the divided Liberal Party in the mainstream. Major Attlee, 35-year-old war veteran, college lecturer and practical social worker, could hardly have been more congruent with the revitalised party organisation. Every wartime development of the party added to his electability to political office; the enlarged franchise most affected boroughs such as Stepney and Limehouse. The timing of his return to the East End, moreover, was opportune, for local elections to the London County Council were to be held in March.

Standing as a candidate in the Limehouse division, Attlee was defeated by a narrow margin – a mere eighty votes – but he succeeded in establishing his local reputation. Having failed to keep out a coalition Liberal in the 1918 general election and conscious of the vulnerability of the Lloyd George coalition, the local party needed a strong candidate for the next battle; they selected Attlee. He had won the respect of two local political bosses who controlled very different groups within the party: Oscar Tobin,[34] a Romanian Jew, and Matt Aylward, an Irish trade unionist. Neither Jewish nor Catholic, Attlee, with the support of these two respected leaders, was a unifying figure in the Limehouse party.

To establish residency in his prospective constituency, he took a lease on Norway House, a large, dilapidated house in Limehouse with fine

features such as classical eighteenth-century Adam fireplaces. He made
extensive repairs and moved into a flat on the first floor, letting two other
flats in the house to members of the Labour Party and converting the
ground floor into a Labour club. Behind the house were stables, one of
which he let to a socialist coal merchant; the other, at a higher rent, to
a Tory butcher. To help run the house he hired Charlie Griffith, a local
ex-service lad. 'Griff' became his trusted and admiring factotum and a
lasting friend.

The following three years gave Attlee a rapid but thorough appren-
ticeship in local government. In April the elections for the Boards of
Guardians were held. Attlee did not stand but was co-opted to the
Limehouse board when Labour won twelve of the sixteen seats. From this
base he served as chairman of the children's home and the Limehouse
representative on the Metropolitan Asylums Board. Fortunately, a light
schedule of lectures and tutorials at the LSE allowed him ample time.

In November he managed the local Labour campaign for election to
the borough councils. Adopting the root-and-branch slogan of 'Sack
the Lot', a phrase used by Admiral John ('Jackie') Fisher in a letter to
The Times on government overmanning and overspending,[35] he had the
satisfaction of seeing Labour win forty-three of the sixty local seats,
including all fifteen in Limehouse.

Despite not having won an election, Attlee was now a highly visible
and respected figure in Stepney and Limehouse. As an organiser and a
hands-on social worker he had enhanced and broadened his pre-war
reputation. The strength and value of that reputation was rewarded
when the newly elected, inexperienced councillors appointed him mayor
of Stepney. At the age of thirty-six, the youngest mayor in Stepney's
history, he had been given a platform on which to build his reputation
across the constituency.

It is hard to imagine a more favourable vantage point from which to
fight a parliamentary election than that which Attlee occupied for the
year from November 1919. Suddenly, and quite unexpectedly, he was
elevated to an executive position that would give him valuable experience and wider visibility. From being a trusted and reliable operative he
became one of a group of Labour Party notables. George Lansbury, an
iconic figure in the movement, was mayor in neighbouring Poplar and

in 1920–21 Herbert Morrison became mayor of Hackney. The appointment was a rite of passage for an aspiring London politician.

Attlee undoubtedly had aspirations at this point, but he had been shrewd enough to maintain a low personal profile while being active in borough work. His sincerity as a socialist was established; his ability as an organiser was becoming recognised. When he was elected chairman of the group of fifteen London Labour mayors he demonstrated his most enduringly famous skill: the ability to determine the majority view amid dissent, and to implement it. Looking ahead to an election that needed to be held before December 1923, he could envisage himself entering Parliament at the age of forty with solid administrative and executive experience to his credit.

His year as mayor of Stepney was, to say the least, active. Using all the powers at his disposal, he set about reform with zeal to create what his daughter-in-law describes as 'a small welfare state within the borough'.[36] His first priority was housing – the lack of it and the physical condition of such housing as was available. Appointing surveyors to inspect buildings, he served some 40,000 notices to property owners to bring properties up to standard. Moreover, he ensured that, as far as possible, these were enforced. He set about reducing the shocking infant mortality rate, appointed sanitary inspectors and health officers. The cost to the borough was considerable and the local rates soared to over twenty shillings in the pound. As this cost fell upon landlords and local businesses, to the benefit of the less affluent tenants, he was unperturbed. While it was impossible to eradicate the evils of slum properties in a single year, the progress made was remarkable.

Of his achievements as mayor, Attlee was proudest of reducing Stepney's infant mortality rate to one of the lowest in London. When a vote of thanks was to be made to the chairman of the Public Health Committee, he suggested that this achievement be recognised. To his consternation, the proposer congratulated the borough on 'a great increase in the birth rate, mainly due, as we all know, to the personal efforts of the chairman'.[37]

Because the work of a borough involves several inter-related committees, he ensured that he sat on those that were central to progress, chairing the Valuation Committee; he was also the council representative on three Joint Industrial Councils, a member of the committees of three hospitals and of the governing boards of four schools.

In addition to these strictly local responsibilities, he was invited to act as chairman of the Association of London Labour Mayors, a group formed by Morrison as secretary of the London Labour Party. He called a national conference of mayors and civic leaders in Shoreditch to address the issue of rising unemployment. This *démarche* gained attention from the press and the twenty-eight London mayors were invited to the Mansion House, where the Lord Mayor, James Roll, 'was proposing some mild measures' to reduce unemployment in London. Breaking with protocol which dictated that the assembled company listen respectfully to the Lord Mayor and then go away, Attlee responded with 'a forcible appeal for more vigorous measures', which was echoed by the other Labour mayors, 'rather to the consternation of the City Fathers'.[38]

Realising that no constructive action could be expected from the Mansion House, Attlee and his colleagues resolved to stage a peaceful demonstration. A deputation of London mayors went to Downing Street for a meeting with Lloyd George. At several visible points along the Embankment and in Westminster stood assembled groups of unemployed men, awaiting the return of the mayors. The peaceful demonstration threatened to turn ugly when a number of activists called for bolder action. When the mayors emerged after an inconclusive meeting with the Prime Minister, Attlee foresaw a violent outcome, located his group from Stepney and led them home in military style. The image of the mayor, a Pied Piper leading a group of potentially violent men away from trouble, can only have contributed to his growing reputation as a committed but moderate leader.

There remained one dimension that Attlee needed to add to this political persona. As a young party, Labour had few prepared positions that it would implement if elected. The party effectively divided into the 'cloth cap' members from the trade unions and the 'intellectuals' who discussed doctrine – in Attlee's view, in a vacuum removed from realities of social work. He was distrustful of doctrinaire ('Webby') solutions and, while he would have shivered at being termed an intellectual, he recognised the need for practical answers to theoretical questions. He needed to make his impression on party thinking.

Towards the end of his tenure as mayor, he published *The Social Worker*, a statement of his own experience and his journey from complacent Victorian middle-class charity to social work that 'bothers to find out what the problems are before applying remedies'.[39] Once arrived in the latter position, he argued, the social worker acquires the perception that 'the root of the trouble is an entirely wrong system altogether, a mistaken aim, a faulty standard of values, and we shall form in our minds more or less clearly a picture of some different system, a society organised on a new basis altogether'.[40]

Foreshadowing his later career, he differentiated between what can be achieved at the local level and issues that require the intervention of central government. He stressed the limitations of imposed theory, as:

> *The social reformer must beware of trying to act as God and making man in his own image ... the failure of many well-intentioned schemes has been due to people giving to the poor what they thought would be good for them, without studying the psychology of those for whom they were going to cater.*[41]

He perceptively described the limitations of religious organisations, quoting the Bishop of Southwark, who confessed that 'we clergy, with our public schools and universities behind us, lack the imagination to see all it means for those who are suffering from social injustice ... we, as a whole, instinctively sympathise in our hearts with the employers.'[42] The settlement movement he characterised as well-intentioned, but remote from the problems it sought to solve. Addressing broad theoretical issues facing social reformers, *The Social Worker* is a concise work that proposes solutions, based not on abstract theory but, as the reader grasps from the first pages, on Attlee's own experience.[43]

In a single year Attlee added enormous substance to his stature in the Labour Party. It was a tiring year, however, and when Edric Millar suggested that they make a tour of northern Italy together, he jumped at the offer. It would be his first holiday since his trip to Italy with Edric in 1912 and, absent any signs of an impending election, he could afford the time. A few weeks before they left, Edric asked Attlee if he might invite his mother and younger sister to accompany them. Attlee, who had already met both mother and sister, readily agreed.

The four set off from Victoria Station toward the end of August on a five-week itinerary to Tuscany, Umbria and Lake Como. There would be no politics for five weeks, and Clement Attlee had no idea how the trip would alter his life.

ENDNOTES

1   CAC: ATLE 1/11.
2   *As It Happened*, p. 57; CAC: ATLE 1/11.
3   *As It Happened*, p. 57.
4   CAC: ATLE 1/11, War account, p. 5.
5   Ibid., War account, p. 6.
6   *The Observer*, 'The Churchill I Knew', in 'Churchill by His Contemporaries', p. 15.
7   CAC: ATLE 1/11, War account, p. 10.
8   Letter to Tom Attlee, 27 August 1915.
9   CAC: ATLE 1/11, War account, p. 15.
10   CAC: ATLE 1/11, War account, p. 15.
11   *As It Happened*, p. 60.
12   *As It Happened*, pp. 61–2.
13   Letter to Tom Attlee, 19 April 1916.
14   TNA: WO 339/10870.
15   TNA: WO 339/10870.
16   Ibid.
17   Ibid.
18   Letter to Tom Attlee, 20 March 1918.
19   CAC: ATLE 1/18.
20   Letter to Tom Attlee, 20 March 1918.
21   Ibid.
22   Ibid.
23   Letter to Tom Attlee, 2 April 1918.
24   Letter to Tom Attlee, 2 April 1918.
25   *As It Happened*, pp. 63–4.
26   Ibid., p. 65.
27   TNA: WO 339/10870.
28   Unpublished record in the possession of Anne, Countess Attlee.
29   Ibid.
30   Attlee, *Labour and the New Social Order*, p. 3.
31   Ibid., p. 4.
32   Ibid., loc. cit.
33   *As It Happened*, p. 66.
34   Attlee was equivocal about Tobin's morals, recording that he 'possessed great energy and considerable organising ability. He had unfortunately other qualities, a tendency to intrigue and a promiscuity in his marital relations which led to his changing the sphere of his political activities from time to time in the course of his political career.' Overcoming any ethical doubts he may have had, Attlee recognised the importance of a charismatic local boss in boosting his own political career. CAC: ATLE 1/11, Post War, p. 1.
35   *The Times*, 2 September 1919.
36   Anne, Countess Attlee, conversation with the author, November 2013.
37   *As It Happened*, pp. 71-72.
38   *As It Happened*, p. 73.
39   Attlee, *The Social Worker*, p. 9.
40   Ibid., p. 10.
41   Ibid., p. 141.
42   Ibid., p. 172.
43   The book was favourably reviewed but sold only 600–700 copies. Attlee estimated that he made about £25 from the entire venture – £850 in today's money. (CAC: ATLE 1/25).

CHAPTER FOUR

MEMBER OF PARLIAMENT, 1922–1931

The holiday in Italy was a much-needed respite. Not only had 1920 been an exhausting year; it was also the year in which he perforce took stock of his life and direction. In May his mother died of cancer; in the same year his sister Dorothy died, aged forty-three. The house in Putney was sold and the last ties with comfortable Victorian life were severed. Attlee, a 37-year-old bachelor, felt alone.

During his year as mayor of Stepney there had been occasions when he needed to be accompanied; being unmarried handicapped him. His sister Mig often went to Stepney to act as mayoress but, living in Putney and needing to spend time with their mother, she could not attend events as frequently as Attlee would have liked.[1]

Kenneth Harris records an interview with Attlee's friend Jack Lawder, when Lawder recalled asking Clement why he didn't marry. In response, 'Attlee looked into his Adam fireplace, puffed at his pipe and said nothing.'[2] Clearly he had considered the problem but, with little time available for 'stepping out', had found no solution. In his political life fortuitous timing had greatly aided his progress. Now, in his personal life too, Fate intervened. As the trip to Italy progressed, he spent more and more time alone with Millar's sister Violet and, by the time they reached Lake Como, he realised that he wanted their friendship to become a permanent attachment. His interest had grown gradually as they travelled through Umbria and Tuscany, taking a detour to Rimini. On the night train from Rimini to Milan, watching Violet asleep, upright in her seat, he realised the extent of his affection – and Violet recognised the symptoms.[3]

Before that trip to Italy, Attlee's love life is a mystery. He had proposed marriage once before,[4] but specifics remain obscure. Edric Millar, who never married, was astounded at how totally, passionately and enduringly his friend, whom he imagined to be an instinctive bachelor, had fallen in love with his sister. He was delighted to have been the matchmaker.[5]

The Millars lived comfortably in Hampstead, a close-knit family not unlike the Attlees. Violet and her twin sister Olive were the youngest of eleven children, fifteen years younger than Edric. Attlee was concerned not by the gap in their ages but by the gulf that separated Violet from his life in the East End. The families knew each other well, but, conscious that he was 'just a street-corner agitator', he gave Violet the opportunity to observe him orate before he proposed marriage.[6]

Her baptism into 'street-corner agitation' passed off well at a meeting on Hampstead Heath. Throughout their life together she understood Attlee's social conscience but never quite accepted that he was a socialist; she saw him as a man of essentially conservative values with a burning desire to improve the lot of the less fortunate. She had no doubts about compatibility when she accepted his proposal.

By October they were engaged; they married on 10 January 1922. In a neat symmetry, underscoring similarities of family background, Violet's brother Basil and Clement's brother Bernard officiated at the service, while Rob was Clement's best man. After a brief honeymoon in Dorset they returned to London.

Violet wisely decided not to live in Limehouse; her husband would never quite leave his work behind. Laurence had married Letitia ('Letty') Rotton and they were living in Woodford Green. They learned of a house available in Monkhams Avenue, an adjacent street which they thought suitable for Clement and Violet.[7] 'We lost no time,' Clement wrote, 'and secured it within three days.' Woodford was a short train ride from Liverpool Street and the East End; Violet had a home that did not also accommodate the local Labour club.

Attlee continued his involvement with Limehouse and Stepney politics, although, he admitted, 'with somewhat less intensity'. He continued to teach at the LSE and to work with the Independent Labour Party on a committee set up to define and modernise policy. Most importantly, as the party waited for a rupture between the Conservatives and the Lloyd George faction of Liberals, he tended his political patch in Limehouse.

That rupture was triggered in mid-September as Turkish forces led by

Mustafa Kemal, having retaken Izmir from Greece, advanced towards the demilitarised zone south of the Straits. Britain unilaterally threatened Turkey with war on the grounds that she had violated the Treaty of Sèvres, an action that infuriated the French, irritated Commonwealth members who had been included as parties to the British threat, and alarmed the British public with the prospect of another Dardanelles campaign. Lloyd George's brinkmanship prompted the Conservative party to discuss withdrawal of support from the government.

When, on 10 October, the Cabinet resolved to call an election, the alignment of parties was uncertain. Within the Conservative Party, a movement to dissolve the coalition and fight the election as a single party led to the Carlton Club meeting of 19 October at which Conservative Members voted decisively to renounce Lloyd George. The long-awaited election was to be fought between four parties – Conservative, Labour, Liberal and National Liberal – on 15 November.

Attlee, challenging Sir William Pearce, a Liberal who had held the seat since 1906, entered the campaign well prepared. His election address was a careful blend of radical slogans ('I stand for life against wealth' and 'No more war and no more secret diplomacy'), of condemnation of the coalition ('The Great Betrayal') and positive undertakings to improve the quality of life in Limehouse. There must be jobs for all, homes for all: 'What could be done for the war must be done for the peace.' Stressing his record of local commitment, he concluded simply, 'Help the man who has worked for you.'

He was confident of the result. Both Liberal parties suffered significant setbacks nationally, collectively winning 113 seats with 29 per cent of the popular vote. Unsurprisingly, the Conservative Party won an overall majority, but the results were significant for Labour. Major Attlee was one of 142 Labour Members of the new House; the Labour Party for the first time won more votes than the two Liberal parties combined – over 4 million votes, almost 30 per cent. His own majority of 1,899 was hardly overwhelming, but in unseating the Liberal candidate he joined a parliamentary party that had every reason for optimism.

A significant result of the election was the ascendancy of Labour Members with middle-class origins. Attlee, the first Oxford graduate to be elected a Labour MP, continued to use his army rank and was known around Limehouse as 'the Major'. The image of the Labour members as trade union men in cloth caps, merrily marching through the divisions singing 'The Red Flag', was no longer representative of the party. Socialism, absent revolution, was now acceptable, and respectable Major Attlee was the very image of reasoned socialism. When J. R. Clynes, who had led Labour into the election, was replaced by Ramsay MacDonald, Attlee fitted perfectly with the style of the team that MacDonald wanted to create. Once more, with impeccable timing, he found himself contemporary.

Roy Jenkins, describing MacDonald's election as Labour leader, maintains that the differences between Attlee and the new leader ultimately contributed to Attlee's rise. Contrasting MacDonald, a 'physically impressive Scotsman with his dithyrambic style and his biological similes', with Attlee, 'the precise and pragmatic Englishman, whose qualities showed so little above the surface', he treats the alliance as one that could only increase Attlee's stature.[8] Thus, when Attlee was chosen by MacDonald as one of his two Parliamentary Private Secretaries, he gained visibility; when MacDonald broke with the Labour Party and Attlee willingly toed the party line, his preparedness to go into the wilderness added more to his credit balance. His accession to the leadership in 1935 was substantially aided by his appointment as PPS to MacDonald in 1922. It is a persuasive argument that once more highlights how Attlee, who 'could act with circumspection and muffle his cunning with a diffident personality,'[9] enjoyed good luck to support his instinctive timing.

The first two years of Attlee's long career in the House of Commons were a period when the three leading parties strove to establish ownership of issues and redefine their policies in a changed world. Among Conservatives there was a new awareness of the possibility of a Labour government in the near future, which could only temper their approach to social issues. For the Liberals, with Asquith again in the ascendant, it was vitally important to re-establish their status as the natural opposition to the Tories. For the Labour Party, now fewer than a million votes away from power, perception was crucial. If it were to capture the middle-class electorate, sober statesmanship was as important as a radical social programme. This called for greater tact and party unity than ever before.

Attlee, after a competent but unremarkable maiden speech on 23 November 1922,[10] maintained a discreet profile in the House, as 'the competition from our Benches was intense and a Parliamentary Private Secretary is not expected to speak often'.[11] In that position, however, he kept himself well informed on the widely variant trends among his colleagues. Parliamentary work, together with his new role as a father, necessitated his giving up teaching at the LSE. His first daughter Janet was born on 25 February 1923 and Violet suffered a bad bout of post-natal depression. His presence was now much needed at home during a critical period in his career.

During 1923 he began to speak out on disarmament. In the House on 15 March he made a provocative speech, stating clearly the socialist position that there should be no armies and no wars. While Britain had an army, however, it should not be a stupid, class-based organisation, but should promote younger officers and be run economically and efficiently.[12] Ideology and practical politics were not always in step, as he discovered at the party conference in June, when he clashed with former party leader Arthur Henderson over disarmament. The Conservatives, observing signs of discord in the party, believed that a short and unsuccessful period in office might damage Labour terminally. Stanley Baldwin, who had succeeded Bonar Law as Prime Minister in May, unexpectedly called an election for 6 December, ostensibly on the issue of tariffs.

In his second election in two years, Attlee had as his opponent Miller Jones, a local manufacturer, 'a pleasant man [with] not much platform ability'.[13] At a joint meeting Jones opened his remarks by saying, 'I know nothing of politics or economics,'[14] a remark greeted with derision by his largely unemployed audience. Attlee increased his majority to 6,185 in the two-sided contest. The national result was inconclusive: the Tories remained the largest party with 258 seats, but vulnerable in any vote that united Labour (191 seats) and the Liberals (158 seats).

Baldwin, faced with the option of resigning or carrying on until a defeat in the House forced resignation, chose to carry on. When a defeat occurred on 21 January 1924, the Liberals having joined the Labour Opposition on an amendment to the Address, Baldwin promptly resigned and the King requested MacDonald to form a government.

Without a majority and constrained on all sides, Labour took office for the first time.

MacDonald described the first Labour government as 'an insane miracle'.[15] Attlee believed that he had not expected to take office and, as a result, 'the party programme, except on foreign affairs, was very much a minority document'.[16] The Labour Party in office resembled a coalition of minorities, riven as they were with differences on a host of issues. MacDonald set the scene for dispute when, in contravention of party principles, he put together his own Cabinet without reference to the National Executive. Equally fundamental was his taking office at all, as many within the party, including Ernest Bevin of the Transport and General Workers' Union (T&GWU), opposed forming a minority government. Attlee defended MacDonald on both issues, arguing that if Labour wished to be seen as a credible party, it must accept the responsibility of government.

Having served as MacDonald's PPS, Attlee was certain of a ministerial post and, ironically after his position on disarmament the previous year, he went to the War Office as Under-Secretary with particular responsibility for the Territorial Army. On his first day at the War Office, the Permanent Secretary introduced him to the Director of the Territorials – none other than General Jeudwine, formerly of the 55th Division, who had commended Attlee for his leadership in the closing months of the war. The former major was much amused to find himself the civilian 'master' of his wartime chief.

It was clear that no measures of radical reform could be implemented by a minority government. Nonetheless, Attlee and several of his colleagues feared that MacDonald was more interested in remaining in power than in honouring election pledges. These were disillusioning times for Attlee, who, despite gaining wide understanding of the functioning of an important department, was not privy to the workings of the Cabinet. He later described those months, saying, 'We had little to do in the House except vote and answer a few questions.'[17] It was scarcely the uplifting experience he must have hoped for in his first term as a minister.

He credited MacDonald with success in achieving a step forward with the Geneva Protocol, as the League of Nations had previously received too little attention. Important measures were passed with John Wheatley's housing policy and Philip Snowden's budget; otherwise, the glorious experiment of the first Labour government achieved little. Even its demise was unremarkable.

In September, Attlee returned from a holiday in Southwold as the government was embroiled in a manufactured crisis. *Workers Weekly*, a publication of the Communist Party of Great Britain, published a provocative article in the form of 'An Open Letter to the Fighting Forces'. The letter contained one sentence that was seized on by the government as seditious:

> *Soldiers, sailors, airmen, flesh of our flesh and bone of our bone, the Communist Party calls upon you to begin the task of not only organising passive resistance when war is declared, or when an industrial dispute involves you, but to definitely and categorically let it be known that, neither in the class war nor a military war, will you turn your guns on your fellow workers, but instead will line up with your fellow workers in an attack upon the exploiters and capitalists, and will use your arms on the side of your own class.*[18]

The editor, J. R. Campbell, was accused of sedition and incitement to mutiny, a charge withdrawn after protests from left-wing Labour backbenchers. In a debate in the Commons on 30 September, MacDonald denied having been consulted on the matter, an implausible position that led to a Tory demand for a Vote of Censure. When the Liberals joined the attack, demanding a committee of inquiry, MacDonald requested a dissolution of Parliament, and an election was called for 29 October. During the ensuing campaign, four days before the election, a letter purporting to originate from Grigory Zinoviev of the Comintern, addressed to the CPGB and calling for extension and development of Leninism in Britain, was published in the *Daily Mail*. The letter, subsequently demonstrated to be a forgery,[19] fanned fears of socialist revolution and, coming on the heels of the Campbell case, drove enough voters into the Tory camp to ensure the defeat of the government.

The effect – as well as the origin – of the Zinoviev letter has been exhaustively discussed, for it apparently caused slight damage to the Labour vote but far greater damage to the Liberals. The Conservatives gained 154 seats, largely at the expense of the Liberal Party, and emerged with an overall majority of 221 seats. The Labour Party, having captured over 5 million votes, was relatively undamaged, now armed with a convenient excuse for its loss of the election. The Zinoviev affair distracted attention from the election result as a verdict on Labour's performance in power and became a symbol of supposed 'dirty politics'. The short-term effect, therefore, was the return of the Conservatives, but the long-term effect of Labour's defeat was minimal; with the collapse of the Liberal Party, Labour's position was consolidated.

Despite having to trade the post of a junior minister for a seat on the Opposition's front bench, Attlee could be reasonably satisfied with his position in the autumn of 1924. His seat at Limehouse seemed secure, as he increased his vote to 11,713 and had a majority of 6,021 in a three-cornered fight. He had acquired valuable experience at the War Office in a position that was of great interest to him. Without close association with MacDonald, he bore no stigma for Labour's defeat. In two years he had established himself as a likely future Cabinet minister without giving out political markers to any faction. His single complaint was that 'three elections in successive years had been rather a strain on my finances'.[20]

On the larger issue of Labour's experience in its first government, Attlee had mixed views. He had come to doubt MacDonald's political dexterity, although his belief in the leader's ideals remained intact. He had mounting concerns about relations between a Labour government and the trade unions, believing that Bevin's support of union members' interests amounted to disloyalty when those interests clashed with a socialist government's policy. This ambivalent attitude to trade unions and their growing power continued to bother him throughout his career.

One advantage of being in opposition was the ability to spend more time at home. Violet had suffered a bad bout of depression after Janet's birth and been advised not to have more children. Despite this, Felicity had been born in the following year, fortunately without post-natal difficulties. Weekends were blissful escapes from politics, principally periods that he could spend alone with Vi. During the day, he would follow her command – digging the garden, mending furniture, French polishing, handling the 'grunt' work around the house. In the evenings he would read aloud to her. They were a remarkably self-contained couple, loving but not doting parents, happy to be alone as a family. Entertaining belonged to the week's official business; friendships outside the immediate family could be honoured by a weekday lunch at the Oxford and Cambridge Club. Once Attlee went home on Friday night, only the family had claims. The similarities with his early life in Putney became marked.

For two years he enjoyed a reasonably 'normal' life. It was a brief period of calm, with regular holidays by the seaside in Suffolk, Devon or the Isle of Wight, often spent with other members of the extended family – a way of life not to be enjoyed again for three decades. They continued to live at Woodford but, when Martin was born in 1927, made much-needed additions to the house.

During the first three years in Opposition, three principal activities occupied Attlee's working days. He was appointed a temporary chairman of committees, an undemanding post but one that offered great insight into parliamentary procedure, as he was required from time to time to chair committees whose membership was drawn from all parties. In 1925 he led for the Opposition on the Rating and Valuation Bill, a subject on which he was well informed after his experience as mayor of Stepney.

His third and most important area of activity was in the vexed issue of electricity supply. The government introduced a Bill, 'the purpose of which was to co-ordinate main-line transmission and generation and to make possible joint action by smaller authorities'.[21] In effect, this was a first step towards nationalisation and Attlee, appointed to the committee examining the Bill, consistently promoted its stated aims: to facilitate co-ordination between local authorities and resist involvement of private enterprise. He was chairman of the Electricity Committee of the Stepney Borough Council and when the Bill created the London and Home Counties Joint Electricity Authority, he was its vice-chairman. As a result, his understanding of the issue of co-ordination of supply was considerable and greatly respected in committee. Indeed, Attlee recalled, 'This was so marked that when we came to the report stage a Conservative objected to the undue deference shown to my views.'[22]

For Attlee, there was greatly more than the issue of nationalisation involved in the question of supply. It was possible in 1926 to offer economically a utility that had previously been a luxury. He believed that local authorities, in concert with a centralised supply system, would be in the interests of users large and small. The accusation that this amounted to municipal socialism cut no ice with him; compared with the potential abuses by private companies, this was a minor issue.

When the general strike was called on 3 May, Labour boroughs such as Stepney were faced with a conflict of interests. As owners of the means to supply electricity to users in the borough, the councils had contractual obligations to keep plants operating. As representatives of a working-class constituency, many of whom would be on strike themselves, they could scarcely employ 'blackleg' labour to break the strike and keep all the lights on. Attlee arranged an emergency meeting between the Electrical Committee and the Trades Union Congress (TUC) general council at which a compromise was reached. Electrical workers, all members of the Electrical Trades Union, would continue to supply light for the borough but would supply power only for hospitals. Because it was impossible to separate the means of supply of light and power, it was agreed that if any consumer was found to be using power in defiance of the agreement, then its light and power would be shut off.

The arrangement – an early example of Attlee's ability to find a compromise that mutually hostile groups could accept – ultimately depended on an 'honour system'. When Scammell and Nephew, lorry and van manufacturers in Spitalfields, defied the restrictions, all their electricity was shut off. The company, run by Colonel Alfred George Scammell, the great-nephew of the founder, had its own generating plant and could have operated independently of any electrical supply from the council. The company's decision to defy the council, therefore, was certainly taken for political motives, a conclusion supported by Scammell's subsequent action: the company issued writs for damages against Attlee and the Labour members of the Stepney Electricity Committee, alleging conspiracy and malice. When, after a long delay, the case came to court, the court found for Scammell, and Attlee was ordered to pay £300 in damages. While this was not an enormous sum, he envisaged the precedent encouraging other firms to follow suit, in which case 'I should have gone bankrupt and my political career would have been interrupted, if not terminated'.[23]

Attlee and his fellow Labour councillors decided to appeal, briefing Malcolm Macnaghten KC, Attlee's colleague from chambers twenty years before. Eighteen months after the general strike, the appeal was successful. Attlee, by then in India with the Simon Commission, wrote to Tom from Lucknow, thanking him for his congratulations on the outcome and adding, 'The result of the appeal was a great load off my mind.'[24] Two weeks later he confessed to Tom that he had been pessimistic about the outcome: 'Great news winning the case,' he wrote. 'I never anticipate success in cases like this for fear of disappointment, so the pleasure is all the keener.'[25]

In September, Clement, together with Bernard and Laurence, made a sentimental trip to Gallipoli. It was a moving experience for Clement, who described it to Tom on his return. The three brothers, together with 'some 200 of all ages and conditions', sailed from Marseille aboard the *Stella d'Italia*, cruised through the Straits of Messina, rounded the Peloponnese and sailed up to Salonika, the Dardanelles, and Constantinople, where 'Santa Sophia fully came up to its reputation'. At Gallipoli, Bernard 'had the joy of presiding at the community service'; Clement visited the battlefield and gave an explanatory talk to the group, mostly survivors of the campaign and relatives of those killed.[26] When he returned, Violet and the children were already on holiday at Weymouth, where he joined them for a week before returning to London.

In the following year MacDonald informed Attlee of the government's decision to send a statutory commission to India to review the position and propose constitutional reforms. He had decided that Attlee should be one of the two Labour members of the commission. Why MacDonald chose Attlee, no expert on Indian affairs, is unclear. The most plausible explanation is that he was unlikely to take an extremist position and commit the party to an unpopular policy on a controversial issue. He was prominent, but not so prominent that his opinions would become a mandate for Labour action.

The suggestion was not welcomed. Martin Attlee had been born on 10 August 1927 and promptly to leave Violet and three children for three months was inconvenient. The appointment could scarcely advance and might easily damage Attlee's career; moreover, he was concerned that his absence from the political centre at an important stage in Labour's evolution would be tactically unsound. He therefore sought and received an assurance from MacDonald that his membership of the commission 'would not in any way militate against [his] inclusion in the next Labour government should the next general election result in Labour's taking office'.[27]

Thus reassured, Attlee joined the commission which was to make two visits to India, the first an exploratory trip lasting three months, to be followed by a more extended trip between October 1928 and February 1929. In the company of Vernon Hartshorn, the second Labour member, a selection of diehard Tories, and the commission's chairman, Sir John Simon, an increasingly right-leaning Liberal, he sailed for Bombay on 19 January, arriving to a mixed reception on 3 February.

In 1919 the Government of India Act had introduced dyarchic government and undertaken to appoint a commission to recommend constitutional reform within ten years. Conservative opinion was that India was far from being able to govern itself. Concern that if a Labour government came to power in 1929 it would advocate withdrawal prompted Lord Birkenhead, Secretary of State for India, to appoint the commission while the Tories were still in power. The timing suggested to Indian politicians that the exercise was a mere placebo, that the British would maintain their grip on the Raj. There were some optimists who believed in the government's sincerity, and their welcome at Bombay leavened the ominous message of protesters brandishing placards and banners urging, 'Simon Go Home'.

The purpose of the trip was to gain a general impression of conditions and to make a detailed study of the Punjab and Madras provinces. Attlee felt that the inspection visit was useful but that British high-handedness in not including a single Indian on the commission was arrogant folly. Neither the Congress Party nor the Muslim League co-operated. Attlee, who had regarded the issue as 'particularly intractable and nearly insoluble',[28] learned a great deal about the country and the issues at stake. By the time the commission returned for a more extensive tour in October, visiting every province, he was better qualified to assess the task. He was also shrewd enough to recognise the value of investing time in an issue that would sooner or later demand deft handling.

On the second visit the commissioners were accompanied by their wives. Violet, believing this to be a once-in-a-lifetime chance to visit the subcontinent, arranged for the three children to be looked after by friends and sailed with Clement in October. She enjoyed the elegance of the Raj, the balls, the leisured life with plenty of golf and tennis, the reassuring meetings with Old Haileyburians or Oxford men serving in India.[29] She also recognised that they were being shown the glamour rather than the reality of British India. When the commission moved on to Burma in January 1929, she sailed home from Calcutta.

Attlee's impressions of India ranged from the romantic ('the streets redolent of the Arabian Nights') to wonder at the way of life in the Raj ('like a dream populated by people from Oxford. Tennis played every-where') to cold realism about the nature of the problems faced. He had, he wrote to Tom, become 'very sick of hearing the same old story'. He had been rereading Morley's life of Oliver Cromwell and compared the Montford scheme for a ten-year probationary period in India with Cromwellian experiments. 'A provisional government working within the limits of a fixed period inevitably works at a heavy disadvantage', Morley had written. People expected everything from it, but its author-ity was impaired. Corruption was rife as unscrupulous operators sought 'to make hay while the sun shines'. With shifting political parties and a restless populace, no governing body could be popular.

Cromwell himself, Attlee added, had believed that: 'It is not the manner of settling these constitutional things or the manner of your or another's doing it. There remains the grand question after that. The grand question lies in the acceptance of it by those who are concerned to yield obedience to it and accept it.'

Was this not exactly the problem that Britain faced in India, he asked Tom. People at home would not accept that in India they were 'not dealing with *tabula rasa* but a paper that has been much scribbled over … The risk is that people will try to fit a ready-made garment on India after some model used elsewhere without trying to see how far it will fit.'[30]

The differences between Hindu and Muslim he regarded as trivial and annoying. He wrote to Tom that 'The Hindu professes a belief in free and open competition because he is good at exams. The Muslim believes in adult suffrage because his is the poorer community.' By the time he arrived in Burma in February, it was 'rather a relief to be away from Hindu and Muslim squabbles and to discuss raising the question of the separation of India and Burma.' Overall he favoured decisive action – *'l'audace, l'audace, toujours l'audace'* – but he recognised that it was not simple, adding, 'I don't think one can devise effective safeguards. The real trouble is that India's disabilities are social and economic; we have to deal with political change.'

By the time the commission returned to England from Bombay on 13 April, Baldwin had called a general election. The Labour manifesto charged the Tory government with inaction on unemployment and disarmament, of hampering the work of the League of Nations. It was an uninspiring document, predictably partisan and largely concerned to reassure electors that it was not a Bolshevik or revolutionary party. This was the first election at which all women over the age of twenty-one could vote, and a section of the manifesto reaffirmed Labour's commitment to the fight for women's emancipation.

If the Labour manifesto was bland, it was exceeded in this quality by Baldwin's election address, which urged the electorate to return the Tories with a clear majority in order to avoid 'a state of political chaos and uncertainty'. 'I make no spectacular promises for a sudden transformation of our social or industrial conditions,' Baldwin declared, 'but I am resolved to maintain and consolidate the advance already made, to bring to fruition the schemes on which we are engaged, and to carry still further the solid work of reconstruction on which depend the unity of the Empire and the peace and well-being of its people.'[31]

The slogan of 'Safety First' that Baldwin adopted failed to stimulate, and the second Labour government was elected, once more without an absolute majority. With 287 seats, the new government benefited from a swing of 8.7 per cent against the Tories but garnered only 37 per cent of the popular vote. It was not the mandate that MacDonald sought.

In Limehouse Attlee faced three other candidates and, despite an increased Liberal vote in line with the national trend, he increased his total vote and was elected with a majority of 7,288 over Evan Morgan, the Tory candidate. Morgan complimented Attlee after the election, saying that 'No one could have had a more sporting fight than myself, or a more courteous opponent as was to be found in Major Attlee'.[32]

When MacDonald announced his ministerial appointments, both Attlee and Hartshorn found themselves excluded, despite assurances given to them when they agreed to serve on the Simon Commission. Of particular annoyance to Attlee was MacDonald's failure to notify them before announcing his appointments to the press. This, he wrote, was 'characteristic of MacDonald'.[33] In fairness, there is only Attlee's word that MacDonald promised him a post and such a promise may well have been couched in the vaguest terms.

The party's failure once more to secure a convincing mandate renewed internal dispute over the wisdom of taking office as a minority. The Labour Party was faced by the conundrum that it would depend on Liberal support for any divisive measures, but in its attitude to radical reform the Liberal Party was closer to the Tories than to Labour. Inevitably, the government's programme would have to be diluted. During the debate on the Address, MacDonald openly reflected on the absence of a majority, speculating that, while retaining party principles, the government might be considered more a Council of State than as 'arrayed regiments facing each other in battle'.[34]

MacDonald's critics point to this speech as early evidence of determination to cling to power, to surrender as many items of party principle as necessary in order to stay in Downing Street.[35] That judgement, dismissed as malicious and *ex post facto* by Roy Jenkins,[36] was substantially the opinion that Attlee developed later. For the moment, however, he was content to have saved his seat and preoccupied with the business of preparing the report of the Simon Commission.

Between May 1929 and June 1930, the commission members wrestled with the question of India. Attlee made several contributions, principally on the question of central and local government, which he addressed in a practical manner. No overall philosophy unites his thinking. As he wrote to Tom when the report was eventually published, it had defects. 'The real difference in dealing with the central government is that there is no feasible transitional stage between [the Raj] and a government sympathetic to the Indian people.'[37]

From the comments and recommendations that Attlee made to the Simon Commission one can extract certain threads of his thinking, most of which were reflected in the commission's report, published in June 1930. Underpinning them all is the view that dominion status was 'an impossibility'; dyarchy, however, should be abandoned and a federal union to embrace all India should be the long-term goal. As he expressed to Tom, the stages of such transfer of power, with particular attention to law and order and the interests of minorities, were unclear. The establishment of such stages was delicate, and the relations between central government and a British Governor-General could not reflect the systems in other dominions.

By the end of the process Attlee had confirmed the truth of his original premise, that the issue was 'intractable' and his practical contribution to the report was slight. The report offered no uniform plan, no timetable, no solid proposals beyond accepting that movement towards federal union would evolve naturally. The entire exercise was anyway rendered peripheral by the recommendation already made by Lord Irwin, the Viceroy, in October 1929: that dominion status should be the goal. Once that principle was accepted by MacDonald and, more reluctantly, by Baldwin, the report could be conveniently shelved and the problems it purported to address, for the moment at least, ignored.

During the preparation of the report the principal problem addressed in the 1929 manifesto – unemployment – had become acute, exacerbated by the Wall Street crash that saw the market lose $14 billion on 'Black Tuesday', 29 October. In a steadily widening gyre over the next eighteen months, the interconnectedness of world economies became clear as not only the United States but the industrialised world was plunged into the Great Depression and unemployment rose to three million in Britain. MacDonald appointed a committee of four ministers under J. H. Thomas, Lord Privy Seal, to propose a new employment policy.

Thomas proposed a set of mild measures, palliatives described as 'trivial absurdities' by Oswald Mosley, Chancellor of the Duchy of Lancaster.[38] Mosley proposed instead a massive injection of public funds to create a comprehensive public works programme, strict import controls – a vigorous, albeit risky, approach to replace the government's inertia. When his proposals were rejected by the Cabinet, Mosley resigned. In May 1930, tardily fulfilling his promise of 1927, MacDonald appointed Attlee to replace Mosley at the Duchy of Lancaster, a post without portfolio outside the Cabinet.

That lack of portfolio grated with Attlee, who felt that MacDonald had done no more than grant him a token appointment. He was impatient to have the responsibility for a department and demonstrate his ability as a minister. That opportunity came in March 1931, when Hastings Lees-Smith was moved from the Post Office to the Board of Education and Attlee succeeded him. In what was to be his one experience of running a department in a Labour government, he applied himself with characteristic objectivity and zeal.

Because the office of Postmaster General was regarded as little more than a foothold for an ambitious politician, there had been little attempt on the part of his predecessors to put their stamp on the department. As a result, an efficient and profitable business had become conservative in outlook, run by its civil servants, and a 'milch cow' for the Treasury, who appropriated its revenues as part of its annual Budget. Attlee discovered the Post Office to be 'a collection of varied business enterprises' and decided that its first priority was to 'gain the utmost goodwill of the users of the service and to get proper publicity'.[39]

His approach to running the Post Office was novel and typical of the man: identify short-term aims and long-term goals, decide on the best method of implementing them and create effective committees to report to one executive responsible for overall policy. In this way he broke down the centralised autocratic control of Sir Evelyn Murray, the Secretary at the Post Office since 1914. Having been told by Baldwin that 'your real difficulty will be Murray'[40] and having discovered this to be the case, he neatly outmanoeuvred opposition and improved efficiency by a commercial rather than a bureaucratic approach.

Attlee immediately saw that the Post Office could contribute significantly to solving the unemployment problem by maximising revenue from the revolutionary new product over which it enjoyed a monopoly – the telephone. To be effective, particularly during a depression, it would need to operate as an efficient business, concentrating on increasing revenue by driving up sales, for which an extensive advertising campaign would be required. In other words, unlike other government departments, the Post Office should be run along commercial, capitalist lines. Completely ignorant of commercial management techniques, Attlee arranged for 'tutorials' from Harold Whitehead, a successful business consultant.

Using newspapers for extensive advertising, confident that careful use of a small investment could produce dramatic increases in sales, he studied business methods of the private sector and prepared a set of recommendations that were implemented wholesale by his successor, Sir Kingsley Wood. Attlee wrote with some pride to Tom that the Bridgman Committee, a 1932 inquiry into the status and organisation of the Post Office, had closely followed the proposals that he made to it.[41]

Attlee thoroughly enjoyed his time at the Post Office, which came to an end abruptly in August. One of the last letters that Attlee wrote on the letterhead of the Postmaster General was written to Tom during the family's summer holiday in Frinton, deploring the state of the government. 'The political scene is full of alarums and excursions', he wrote, 'and what will be the upshot God knows. I have been summoned to see the PM tomorrow but whether on certain GPO matters or the general situation I know not.'[42]

The summons to Downing Street was the prelude to the final breakdown of relations between MacDonald and Attlee. The Economy Committee, chaired by Sir George May of the Prudential Insurance Company, proposed orthodox Tory solutions to the economic crisis, remedies that would 'cut down the purchasing power of the masses'. Unsurprisingly, these proposals were unacceptable to the party; MacDonald's response was to abandon the Labour Party and accept the King's commission to form a 'national' government, a solution that he had hinted at for some months. Arriving at Downing Street, with other ministers outside the Cabinet, Attlee was requested to offer his resignation.

In Attlee's later account of his eighteen months in MacDonald's second government, it is easy to trace the disillusion that led to the irreparable break between them. For a Labour Prime Minister to be insensitive to unemployment on the scale that followed the Wall Street crash was reprehensible. The leader who had appeared dynamic and inspiring had become supine. When Attlee submitted a paper on the re-equipment and redeployment of industry, a paper that he considered 'within the terms of reference … useful and constructive', it was never discussed, 'as was not uncommon in the MacDonald government'.[43] When Attlee and Hartshorn, who had joined the government as Lord Privy Seal, were asked to wind up debates, they 'both replied that until [they] saw signs of a more vigorous policy [they] would not speak'.[44]

MacDonald had apparently decided to throw his lot in with the Tories and his inertia over unemployment was incipient 'Tory creep';

it was certainly divisive. Mosley's resignation and the revolt of the ILP damaged the party; the conversion of the Chancellor of the Exchequer, Philip Snowden, to orthodox Tory economic policy further alienated his Labour colleagues. Gradually, Attlee realised that he was witnessing not mere inertia but an irreparable breach between MacDonald and socialism. He later admitted that until MacDonald took office a second time, he had been blind to his defects. Even when he recognised his vanity and snobbery and his habitual indiscretion,[45] he did not 'expect that he would perpetrate the biggest betrayal in British political history'.[46]

That permissible hyperbole, prompted by MacDonald's abandonment of the Labour Party and his formation of a 'national' government without consultation with his colleagues, belonged to the following year, but there were doubts in Attlee's mind early in 1930. He and G. D. H. (Douglas) Cole[47] planned to reanimate the Fabian Society and its original goal, the 'reconstruction of society in accordance with the highest moral possibilities'. This led to the foundation of the New Fabian Research Bureau (NFRB) with Attlee as its first chairman. The presence of Attlee, a government minister, as a doctrinal watchdog underscored growing doubts about the Prime Minister's commitment to socialist principles.

Through the NFRB, Attlee came into contact with two young economists with backgrounds similar to his own middle-class origins. Hugh Gaitskell and Evan Durbin had met as freshmen at New College in 1924. Gaitskell's parents were 'greatly shocked by his conversion to socialism', while Durbin's mother, married to a Baptist minister, 'never really recovered from her sorrow that her beloved son had renounced his belief in the Lord Jesus'. Close friends, they were nicknamed Rosencrantz and Guildenstern by Lady Longford.[48] Both were rising stars, and by them and their friend Douglas Jay, Attlee was introduced to Keynsian economic theory. They were to rise together in the party until Durbin drowned, rescuing his daughter from a dangerous undertow on a Cornish beach in 1948.

Meanwhile, Attlee had a job to do and he added to his experience, working with MacDonald on the Imperial Conference, sitting on the Prime Minister's Economic Advisory Committee, and working with Christopher Addison, the Minister of Agriculture, preparing a number of Bills and sitting on the committees that considered them. Addison, a medical doctor thirteen years older than Attlee, had come to politics through the belief that only government action could effect improvements in public health, a position identical with Attlee's beliefs. The congruence of their attitudes to the role of government launched a close friendship and an intellectual partnership in which Addison played a mentor's role until his death in 1951.

Unelected, the 'national' government illustrated how radically MacDonald's position had shifted. He and Snowden were expelled from the party amid violent mutual recrimination. The government, 'formed to maintain that gold standard which it declared in panic-stricken accents to be the indispensable condition of national safety, within less than three weeks ... abandoned that standard with the insolent explanation that industry would benefit by its change'.[49] For six weeks there was an air of unreality in the Commons as Labour Members vehemently attacked their former leaders now on the government front bench. 'Things are pretty damnable,' Attlee wrote to Tom. 'I fear we are in for a regime of false economy and a general attack on the workers' standard of life.' Snowden, he believed, had failed to face the financial situation, while MacDonald had been 'far too prone to take his views from business – big business'.[50]

In such an atmosphere, an election could not be long postponed and in October Parliament was dissolved. After its triumph of 1929, the Labour Party faced the reality that a socialist Prime Minister had abandoned socialist principles in favour of bankers' orthodoxy. It was very possible that the electorate would interpret this as an admission that Labour could not govern, that the great socialist experiment was over.

ENDNOTES

1   *As It Happened*, p. 75.
2   Harris, *Attlee*, p. 50.
3   Ibid., p. 52.
4   Beckett, *Clem Attlee*, p. 67. From a conversation with Attlee's daughter Felicity.
5   Remarks at the dinner table by Edric Millar, June 1960.
6   *As It Happened*, p. 77.
7   CAC: ATLE 1/12.
8   Roy Jenkins, *Mr Attlee*, p. 102.
9   W. Golant, 'The Early Political Thought of C. R. Attlee', *Politics Quarterly* 40.3, July–September 1969.
10   *Hansard*, HC Deb, 23 November 1923, cols. 92–6.
11   *As It Happened*, p. 81.
12   *Hansard*, HC Deb, 15 March 1923, cols. 1870–1900.
13   *As It Happened*, p. 87.

14 Ibid.
15 J. T. Murphy, *Labour's Big Three*, p. 109.
16 *As It Happened*, p. 88.
17 Cited by Jenkins, *Mr Attlee*, p. 106.
18 *Workers Weekly*, 25 July 1924.
19 For the Cabinet's assessment in 1924, TNA: CAB 27/254.
20 *As It Happened*, p. 91.
21 *As It Happened*, p. 83.
22 *As It Happened*, p. 84.
23 *As It Happened*, p. 86.
24 Letter to Tom Attlee, 9 November 1928.
25 Letter to Tom Attlee, 23 November 1928.
26 Letter to Tom Attlee, 19 September 1926; CAC: ATLE 1/18.
27 *As It Happened*, p. 95; CAC: ATLE 1/13.
28 Jenkins, *Mr Attlee*, p. 118.
29 Letters to Tom Attlee, 7 December 1928 and 4 February 1929, for example.
30 This and the surrounding comments on India and Burma are included in letters to Tom Attlee on 14 November 1928, 23 November 1928, 7 December 1928, 4 February 1929 and 20 March 1929.
31 1929 Conservative election manifesto, para. 1.
32 *East London Advertiser*, 8 June 1929.
33 *As It Happened*, p. 96.
34 Granada Historical Records, *Clem Attlee*, p. 9.
35 For example, MacNeill Weir, *The Tragedy of Ramsay MacDonald*.
36 Jenkins, *Mr Attlee*, p. 128.
37 Letter to Tom Attlee, 27 June 1930.
38 Oswald Mosley, *My Life*, p. 232.
39 *As It Happened*, p. 101.
40 Ibid.
41 Letter to Tom Attlee, 1 September 1932.
42 Letter to Tom Attlee, 23 August 1931.
43 *As It Happened*, p. 99.
44 *As It Happened*, p. 100.
45 Granada Historical Records, *Clem Attlee*, p. 9.
46 *As It Happened*, p. 107.
47 Cole, a protégé of Sidney Webb, was a leading light in the Fabians. Attlee respected his socialist principles, but found him impractical, calling him 'a permanent undergraduate'. Durbin, *New Jerusalems*, p. 81.
48 Elizabeth Durbin, *New Jerusalems*, pp. 2–4.
49 Labour Party general election manifesto of 1931, section 2, para 2.
50 Letter to Tom Attlee, 2 September 1931.

CHAPTER FIVE

IN OPPOSITION, 1931–1935

The election of October 1931 was, from the outset, a hopeless cause for Labour. Placed in the position of arguing that the previous government had failed to solve Britain's problems, the party wrestled with the conundrum that it was a Labour government whose record they needed to attack. Moreover, if the Labour leader had concluded that socialism could not offer a remedy without the participation of other parties, how was it tenable to argue that more socialism, rather than less, was the rational approach? Yet this was precisely the tack that the Labour Party took.

Under the heading *Labour's Call to Action: the Nation's Opportunity* the Labour manifesto produced the same arguments that they had adduced in every election since 1918: broadly, that capitalism had failed worldwide and that this was the moment to rebuild the foundations of society. To reaffirm that 'socialism provides the only solution for the evils resulting from unregulated competition and the domination of vested interests'[1] was to repeat doctrine that the charismatic orator MacDonald himself had rejected. To pronounce the party's 'faith in the considered principles of its programme of 1929 … when … it made a substantial beginning'[2] was to prescribe that although a large dose of the medicine had nearly killed the patient, a larger dose would provide the remedy.

The election was a disaster for Labour. Again led by Henderson, it lost 241 seats including those of all its former Cabinet ministers except Lansbury. The extent of the rout was a shock to Attlee, whose own majority was reduced to just 551. Henderson was defeated and once more the Parliamentary Party needed to elect a new chairman. Attlee, one of the few remaining Members with any government experience, was proposed as Lansbury's deputy; both nominations were ratified without opposition; Henderson, outside Parliament, briefly continued as party leader. The rump of forty-six Members was left with the task of opposing 554 Members loosely united in the national government. As Raymond Postgate described it, 'The Nabobs had vanished never to return'. The old guard was gone, 'as though a huge tide had smashed through a breakwater, sweeping it away and carrying the timber far out into the sea, leaving standing only one tall, stout and solitary stanchion.'[3]

Attlee's elevation was a collateral result of Labour's immolation in the election. Apart from the old guard of Henderson, Clynes and Greenwood, there were younger men with at least equal qualifications. Morrison, Minister of Transport, was the obvious candidate. Hugh Dalton, Under-Secretary of State at the Foreign Office, A. V. Alexander, First Lord of the Admiralty, Tom Johnston, Lord Privy Seal and Tom Shaw, Secretary of State for War all might have staked a claim, had they been re-elected. In the event, Lansbury was the only realistic choice, and Attlee and Cripps the only others with significant experience. Once more, Fortune had smiled at a critical point in Attlee's career. He now had a unique, though possibly brief, opportunity to capitalise on his windfall.

Aware of both the challenge and the opportunity, he adopted the mood of St Crispin's Day and wrote to Tom in the vein of 'We happy few'. 'We put up a fair show on the address,' he wrote.

> *Cripps did very well. He is a tower of strength and such a good fellow. We are a very happy family in the party and some of our fellows will now get their opportunity ... We intend to push ahead with the New Fabian and SSIP.*[4] *We want to get the party away from immediates and on to basic socialism. I think the shake-up will be the salvation of the party.*[5]

Lansbury made his room in the House of Commons available to Attlee and Cripps, and this served as a beleaguered headquarters for the Parliamentary Party. After two months in opposition Attlee wrote to Tom, endorsing Lansbury's leadership, repeating the 'happy family' motif and ending with contempt for MacDonald. 'I fear J. R. M. has completely gone', he wrote. 'He revels in titled friends. He will have a rude awakening soon, I think.'[6]

To demonise MacDonald was mandatory, but Attlee recognised that his 'betrayal' of the party was preceded by genuine belief that socialism could not provide solutions to the crisis. Attlee had identified this dilemma when he spoke to Cole before the 'betrayal'. As chairman of the New Fabian he aimed for 'constant expansion and adaptation of policy in the light of changing conditions'.[7] It is a measure of his quiet competence that over the following decade he was able to re-shape party policy into a close approximation of the manifesto of 1945, a feat that required considerable agility. It also brought about greater visibility for Attlee and a remarkable increase in his stature that could hardly have been predicted in 1931. At no stage was he unaware of the opportunity and at no stage did he fail to capitalise on it.

Francis Williams, Attlee's press adviser during the Downing Street years, had no illusions about his realistic grasp of the nature of power. 'He had in fact great self-confidence and a streak of ruthlessness', he recalled, 'and although he was an administrator of ideas rather than a creative political thinker he knew exactly what he wanted to do.' Anyone who assumed that his lack of vanity was due to self-doubt had 'a rude awakening'.[8]

The position in which he found himself had a certain irony. At a local level his pre-war work had brought its reward, loyalty from the voters of Limehouse. On the national level his sudden prominence was due to the misfortunes of others. His job in 1931 was to help provide an effective Opposition in the knowledge that if he and his colleagues were successful, it would lead to the return of the very people whose absence had enabled his elevation. Lansbury, twenty-four years older than Attlee, would clearly not be leader for long; Attlee needed to expend maximum effort on behalf of the party while consolidating his position as Lansbury's natural successor. This called for diplomacy and tact, as well as considerable energy.

As second-in-command in the Parliamentary Party he had stature, but he sought wider visibility in the party as a whole, for which his work with the New Fabianism provided the stage. Between 1932 and 1938 the group published forty-two research pamphlets on subjects ranging from 'The Machinery of Socialist Planning' to 'Studies in Capital and Investment' and 'Twelve Studies in Soviet Russia'. During the same period Attlee wrote *The Will and the Way to Socialism* (1935), *The Labour*

Party in Perspective (1937)[9] and *Britain's Shame and Danger* (1938). Although no more than 'a reasonably well-read layman'[10] in the field of economics, he became the Opposition spokesman on economic matters, leading for Labour on the debate on Snowden's emergency Budget in October 1931, criticising the Chancellor for 'going back' and for discriminatory taxation. The load was not being evenly shared. Why was there a tax increase on beer but not on imported wine? 'The country', he charged, 'is carrying an inflated *rentier* class, which it cannot afford.'[11]

Maintaining a credible presence in the House placed enormous demands on the three leaders. Attlee recalled that 'The whole work of debate in the House and in committee had to be sustained by scarcely more than thirty men', as the older members who held safe seats in the mining areas were loyal voters but infrequent speakers.[12] He wrote to Tom that he had 'made ninety-three speeches in this session, second only to Cripps'. He remained remarkably optimistic, confident that the artificial make-up of the anti-Labour coalition would be its undoing. The government had no constructive ideas; the PM was worn out, the government clinging to the 'miserable economy stunt'. He predicted that 'as we get deeper into the mire, a change of leadership of the coalition will be called for, and [Lloyd George and Churchill] will come in'.[13]

Not only did Attlee speak frequently, his speeches filled the columns of *Hansard*, which, as he pointed out, was remarkable, 'as I am generally considered to be rather a laconic speaker'.[14] He was also required to speak on subjects previously outside his brief: on foreign affairs, on economics, tariffs, on any subject being debated. In the 1931–32 session of the Commons he made 125 speeches, occupying 352 columns in *Hansard*. For four years his approach was to reject 'MacDonaldism' and position himself as spokesman for the speedy return of socialism, fashioning policy and remaining loyal to party doctrine. He imposed a rigorous discipline on himself, handling an almost crippling workload. Lansbury's daughter, working in her father's office, dubbed him 'The White Rabbit'. His industry later received a compliment from an unexpected source in the Commons. In May 1935 Baldwin commented that, after being 'nearly wiped out at the polls', the Opposition had 'equipped themselves for debate after debate and held their own and put their case'.[15]

Nor was his activity confined to the Commons. He supported Labour candidates at by-elections, made several broadcasts on *The Week in Westminster* for the BBC, wrote copiously and established contacts with socialist organisations across Europe. In May 1932 he attended a conference in Zürich where he 'for the last time saw the German Social Democratic party in its full strength'. A year later, at an International Conference of League of Nations Socialists, he commented that the 'Germans were represented by some very tough-looking Nazis, the first of the breed that I had seen'.[16]

Lansbury was seventy-two when he became chairman. A pacifist, he could never have survived as Prime Minister in the climate of the 1930s. While Attlee recognised the temporary nature of Lansbury's position, he had no wish to remain a critic of the government on the Opposition benches. He might have very little time in which to replace Lansbury, particularly if a by-election brought Morrison, Dalton or Alexander back to the Commons. Mindful of the lesson learned in 1923 about the dangers of moving ahead of the party, he needed to be seen as the architect of socialist policy while reinforcing the image of the party as an electable body. The first Labour government had been rendered ineffective by a dearth of ideas of how to govern. There were few policies waiting to be implemented.[17] Attlee needed to bring about rapid change.

In October the Labour Party conference was held at Leicester. This was a defining point in the party's move to the left. In August he had predicted to Tom that the Independent Labour Party would go their own way and lose a big proportion of their membership. The trouble, he felt, was that they had no real ideas on which to work. 'They talk revolution but Brockway[18] has the phrases and Maxton[19] the appearance of revolutionaries but nothing more', he wrote. 'We anticipate an accession of strength to the SSIP.'[20] It required nifty footwork for Attlee to accept a rejection of gradualism and to maintain a centrist position in the eyes of the electorate.

The withdrawal of the ILP from the mainstream led to the creation of the Socialist League at the conference. The adoption of a more radical programme left Lansbury and Attlee as leaders of a party committed to the nationalisation of the Bank of England and determined never again to allow doctrine to be compromised by politics.

Lansbury was at the height of his popularity with the party and much of this popularity accrued to his industrious deputy. Early in the following year Attlee described the mood of the party at a demonstration in Hyde Park. Lansbury was hailed as 'almost a Gandhi', while 'Old JRM [MacDonald] is ... completely shameless in these days.'[21]

By the end of 1932 Attlee's position within the party had altered dramatically. From the status of worthy but unexceptional junior minister he had evolved into a deputy leader, charting the strategic direction of the party. As deputy to Lansbury, whose prestige had never stood higher, he represented progressiveness, mixed with a link to the roots of the early Labour Party. Lansbury already belonged to another era, while Attlee projected a more modern, more worldly approach.

Attlee opened the year of 1933 with a statement of fundamental principles in a letter to his brother. Working from proposals for internationalising civil aviation, he drew an idealistic picture of his vision of international relations. Only a world state, he believed, would be 'really effective in preventing war'. The question, of course, was who would 'bell the cat' in case of need. He proposed first a united navy, later an international air force and an organisation that included the USA, Britain and France. This would bring in Russia and, when they realised they could not compete, Germany and Japan would follow. 'This may sound very visionary', he concluded, 'but I am convinced that unless we see the world we want it is vain to try to build a permanent habitation for Peace and that temporary structures will catch fire very soon if we wait any longer.'[22]

Visionary it certainly was; it was also prescient. At a time when the Labour Party was looking back at the errors of 1929–31, Attlee was looking forward to the role of a socialist government in Europe of the 1930s. The party was feeling its way toward the overall plan that was ultimately implemented in 1945.

Despite the enormous burden of work – or, perhaps, because of it – this was a thrilling period for Attlee. It was easy to blame MacDonald and Snowden for 'betraying' the party, but there was a far wider question to address: if Labour were ever to regain power, what would be their guiding principles? Attlee was taken to task by Lord Eustace Percy in the Commons after one assault on the Prime Minister. 'I think the hon.

Member would have to think out his measures a great deal more,' Percy reproved him, 'before he could be said to have an alternative policy, whatever he may be said to have of alternative sentiments.'[23]

The Leicester conference had demonstrated the determination of the National Executive to prevent another 'Trojan Horse' leadership; there would now be more accountability of the PLP to the wider membership. It was incumbent on the parliamentary leaders to tailor the party's message to fit with the aspirations of both the left and the middle-of-the-road voters that Labour would need to pry from the Liberals if they were to be electable. Thus, while 'the White Rabbit' dashed hither and thither to keep the PLP in line, he needed to ensure that the left did not 'go off the reservation'.

The role was perfect for Attlee. As when in 1918 he had discussed with Tom the direction Britain would take after the war, so now he saw that the party needed to rebuild itself by consensus. It would need both theoretical discussion and swift action to implement decisions in order to be effective. Naturally, he saw himself as central to both establishing policy and the translation of policy into action. Equally naturally, he found time to write to his brother to seek his thoughts.

'I have just been reviewing Laski's latest, *The Crisis of Democracy*,' he wrote. 'Amazingly good.' Discounting MacDonald completely ('His mind is mainly fog now'), he remarked on the wily Lloyd George moving into the void that Attlee wanted Labour to occupy, and commented on the affection in which Lansbury was held by the masses and in the House of Commons.[24] This revealing paragraph, loosely interpreted, sets out Attlee's immediate goals: to be as influential on party doctrine as Laski; to emulate MacDonald by becoming leader, but to remain faithful; to prevent Lloyd George detaching Liberals from the mainstream Liberal Party and pre-empting Labour; to be held in the same affection as Lansbury. It was an ambitious agenda.

During the next three years the 'rather diffident committee man'[25] increased his stature within the party, in the country, and on the international stage. His untiring work made him indispensable and his increasing personal stamp on policy established his position as a party intellectual. Although he frequently refused to accept that label,[26] that perception was a central element of his ascent.

In 1933, however, he was still far from being Lansbury's obvious successor. Cripps had equal stature within the party; Morrison had enormous, though overwhelmingly local, influence as leader of the Labour Group in the London County Council; Dalton's credentials as an economist and former Under-Secretary at the Foreign Office were congruent with a contemporary profile of a party leader. Yet each had qualities that mitigated against their becoming the party's standard bearer. None had a broadly based constituency – and two of them had no seat in the House.

Cripps, with whom Attlee had established a close friendship, was increasingly regarded with suspicion by Dalton and Morrison as he inched to the left. Accused of wanting to introduce what amounted to a socialist dictatorship, he alarmed colleagues at the party conference at Hastings in October. Morrison in particular was doubtful that Cripps would be acceptable to the middle-class voter, the renegade Liberal that the Labour Party needed to capture.[27]

Cripps came to politics at the age of forty-one after a highly success-ful career at the Bar, where he was the youngest King's Counsel of his generation. Appointed Solicitor-General by MacDonald in 1930, he entered Parliament as MP for East Bristol, a safe Labour seat, and declined to join the national government in 1931. Although a brilliant debater – Morrison considered him invincible in private discussions – he had a childlike innocence of politics and was considered by his aunt Beatrice Webb to be 'oddly immature in intellect and unbalanced in judgment'.[28] Nonetheless, for the left wing of the party, convinced that they had been done down by a capitalist conspiracy, Cripps was a worthy champion. Although such a controversial figure might not have been able to lead Labour to victory in a general election, Attlee needed first to ensure that he, not Cripps, had that opportunity.

Fortune once more intervened on Attlee's behalf in 1933, this time in macabre fashion. Lansbury's wife Betty, to whom he was devoted, died in March 1933. Lansbury described his loss as 'inexpressible' and turned to working intolerable hours, attending meetings up and down the country. At Gainsborough in December, exhausted by his schedule, he fell badly and broke his thigh. He spent the following eight months in hospital in constant pain.[29]

He was replaced *pro tempore* by Attlee for nine months. On domestic issues Attlee continued his assault on the government's handling of unemployment. On foreign affairs he became more vocal, criticising the Tories, particularly Simon, for hypocrisy over the role of the League of Nations and the lack of progress at the Disarmament Conference that had dragged on since 1932. He watched with mounting alarm the rise of the Nazis in Germany. 'There is so much loose powder lying about', he reflected, 'and one cannot tell where the match will be applied.' Social democracy had been destroyed for a generation in Germany. 'It raises most difficult problems of policy for our movement. How are we to frame a world plan for socialism with these conditions on the continent?'[30]

He continued to travel to conferences. In 1934 he was in Prague and Geneva, the latter at the invitation of Konni Zilliacus,[31] where he spoke on the need to establish a police force as an arm of the League of Nations. In the face of the growing power of the European dictators he continued to support disarmament in debates in the House, although the party was divided on the issue. That division became clear at the 1934 party conference in Southport when Cripps inveighed against the League, urging withdrawal and the forging of alliances with socialist governments of other countries. Attlee spoke persuasively in favour of collective security and for sanctions in a speech that further established his authority. At this conference he was elected to the National Executive Council, a mixed accolade as he polled substantially fewer votes than Morrison and took third place behind Morrison and Dalton. While he maintained a strong position at Westminster, he still needed to win acceptance as leader from the wider party.

During the early 1930s Gandhi's campaign of civil disobedience in India laid bare the need to reach some agreement on the future status of the subcontinent. In March 1933 the government published a White Paper with proposals for a new constitution. Attlee, the Opposition member with the greatest experience of conditions in India, led the offensive against the proposals. There was, he charged, no provision for eventual dominion status, no suggestion that the powers of the Governor General be attenuated, no proposals for the 'Indianisation' of the Army. There were, moreover, exacting demands for financial prerequisites for federation, demands that 'no modern state at the present time could possibly get through'. The government, he said, was 'tied to the forces of privilege and reaction'. Unless the White Paper were substantially revised, he was not optimistic about future peace in India.[32]

In May 1933 Attlee was appointed to a joint select committee, which in November 1934 presented its recommendations to Parliament. In a broadcast in January 1935 he spoke out for gradual granting of dominion status, stressing the need to ensure that genuine progress was made to improve the quality of Indian life. His principal concern was that the government was behaving hypocritically, substituting Indian vested interests for British vested interests and putting it about that this was reform.[33] The proposals in the report, the basis of the 1935 Government of India Act, were essentially the recommendations of the Simon Commission. He was clear in his determination that dominion status was the goal – more than a mere doffing of the cap to the left – but, in terms of tangible achievement, this *intermezzo* achieved little for India. It did, however, position Attlee as a statesmanlike advocate for Indian democracy in the eyes of both the party and the electorate.

The dominant issue in foreign relations in the first half of the decade was that of disarmament, on which the party was predictably divided. Leslie Hore-Belisha, Minister of Transport,[34] commented that the mood of the people until 1935 was such that 'a parliamentary candidate who advocated increased defence expenditure ran the risk of finishing at the bottom of the poll, if he did not actually lose his deposit'.[35] This was borne out by the East Fulham by-election of October 1933. During the campaign Lansbury vowed that he 'would close every recruiting station, disband the Army, dismiss the Air Force'. The enthusiastic reception of his speech was reflected in the transformation of the Tory majority of 14,521 to a Labour majority of 4,840.

In March 1935 the government published a White Paper on Imperial Defence to 'establish peace on a permanent footing'. Even before it was presented to the House there was dissent within the Tory Party that it was 'mealy-mouthed', shying away from telling the truth for fear of upsetting Hitler.[36] After it was presented on 4 March Hitler, contracting a 'diplomatic cold', cancelled a meeting with Foreign Secretary Simon in Berlin.[37]

As Hitler re-armed, Britain looked the other way. Sir Robert Vansittart, Head of the Foreign Office, commented that 'we had to feel our way with the British, while the Germans strode ahead with their Führer'.[38] Moving a Vote of Censure on 11 March, Attlee spoke out against the proposal to increase defence expenditure by £11,000,000, describing it as 'rattling back to war'.[39] Vansittart recorded that it was 'a rattling bad speech'. Of Cripps he was equally damning, commenting that 'Stafford Cripps, a grave and ascetic offender against sense, played with the idea of a general strike if we sought to defend ourselves'.[40] Austen Chamberlain was more savage:

> *If war breaks out ... and if the hon. Member for Limehouse and his friends be*
> *sitting on the government bench while London is bombed, do you think he will hold*
> *the language that he held to-day? Do you think that that is the defence he will make?*
> *If he does, he will be one of the first victims of the war, for he will be strung up by*
> *an angry, and a justifiably angry, populace to the nearest lamp-post.*[41]

Attlee, seeing the issue in purely party parliamentary light, wrote to Tom that the debate had been 'pretty good', adding that he thought that the Opposition had the best of it.[42] That may have been so, and it may have been that he could have said little else or little more, given the constraints of party loyalty. Just two years later, however, his posture of 1935 was one he would happily have disowned.

In May 1935 George V celebrated his Silver Jubilee and Baldwin, now Prime Minister, requested Lansbury to recommend three names for awards of honours. Lansbury, who disapproved of the honours system, declined, but privately requested that Attlee, who had led the party for most of 1934, should become a Privy Counsellor.[43] The congratulations he received from both sides of the House were a source of pleasure and pride. For the Labour Party, however, the Jubilee, inducing a mood of jingoism, was ill timed.

In December 1934 a confrontation occurred at Walwal, close to the Abyssinian border, involving Abyssinian, Somali and Italian forces. The League of Nations failed to achieve settlement; Eden went to Rome to broker a peace agreement with Mussolini but returned empty-handed. The Italian dictator 'was determined to have his Abyssinian adventure'[44]. On 3 October Italian forces invaded Abyssinia.

The crisis dominated the news and, when the Labour Party conference opened in Brighton on 1 October, the party's foreign policy was put to the test. A resolution was proposed to the conference that immediate sanctions should be applied to Italy and that the government should use all necessary measures provided by the League. This provoked furious and divisive debate, culminating in a virulent attack on Lansbury by Bevin.[45] Lansbury's impassioned speech, stating his Christian principles of pacifism, roused Bevin to accuse him of 'hawking your conscience round from body to body asking to be told what to do with it'.[46] The resolution was carried by a margin of over two million votes.

Attlee was pleased by the outcome of the vote; to him a policy of non-resistance was morally indefensible, but was appalled by the chasm that the debate opened in the party. He was certain that this would be exploited by the government and that a general election would be called while the Labour Party was split over so significant an issue.

The Tories correctly assessed that Labour was vulnerable; Abyssinia took attention away from domestic issues. Unemployment had at last fallen below two million. Neville Chamberlain recorded that 'Labour is torn with dissensions' and resolved to stress the Tories' support of the League, the new Conservative defence programme 'to enable us to perform our task of peace preserver', and 'the dangers of a socialist administration'.[47] Attlee was right; Baldwin called an election for 14 November.

As soon as Parliament reassembled on 8 October Lansbury offered his resignation and, despite spirited attempts to dissuade him, insisted that in view of the party vote in conference he could not continue as leader. The names of Greenwood, who had re-entered Parliament as Member for Wakefield, and Attlee were considered as Lansbury's successor. With little hope of winning the impending election, the support of the Parliamentary Party for Attlee was a deciding factor and a motion was put that he be elected temporary leader to shepherd the party through the election. Attlee accepted; Lansbury commented that 'Clem is well able to handle anything that comes up'.[48]

ENDNOTES

1   Labour Party general election manifesto, 1931, section 3, para 1.
2   Ibid, section 4, paras 1–2.
3   Raymond Postgate, *George Lansbury*, p. 276.
4   The Society for Socialist Information and Propaganda, formed in January 1931 and later merged into the Socialist League.
5   Letter to Tom Attlee, 16 November 1931.

6   Letter to Tom Attlee, 18 December 1931.
7   New Fabian Research Bureau manifesto, 1930.
8   Lord Francis-Williams, *Nothing So Strange*, p. 219. He added that Attlee had 'a polite ruthlessness in getting what he wanted'. (p. 221).
9   It is notable as an indication of his increased status that this was written at the invitation of Victor Gollancz.
10   Swift, *Labour in Crisis*, p. 13.
11   *Hansard*, HC Deb, 2 October 1931, cols. 705–712.
12   *As It Happened*, p. 109.
13   Letter to Tom Attlee, 15 July 1932.
14   *As It Happened*, p. 112.
15   *Hansard*, HC Deb, 22 May 1935, col. 371.
16   *As It Happened*, p. 126.
17   See Golant, 'The Early Political Thought of C. R. Attlee', *Politics Quarterly* 40.3, July–September 1969.
18   Former MP for Leyton East, defeated at the 1931 election.
19   MP for Glasgow Bridgton since 1922 and chairman of the ILP from 1926 to 1931.
20   Letter to Tom Attlee, 8 August 1932.
21   Letter to Tom Attlee, 7 February 1933.
22   Letter to Tom Attlee, 1 January 1933.
23   *Hansard*, HC Deb, 25 November 1932, col. 382.
24   Letter to Tom Attlee, 15 February 1933.
25   Lansbury's comment on Attlee, quoted by Harris, *Attlee*, p. 109.
26   Granada Historical Records, *Clem Attlee*, p. 12.
27   Donoughue and Jones, *Herbert Morrison: Portrait of a Politician*, p. 187.
28   Both Morrison's and Webb's comments are at Pimlott, *Labour and the Left in the 1930s*, p. 35.
29   Bessie Lansbury's death and its effect on Lansbury are described sympathetically at Postgate, *The Life of George Lansbury*, pp. 289–290.
30   Letter to Tom Attlee, 3 April 1933.
31   A left-wing Labour politician who worked for the League of Nations Secretariat until Hitler's invasion of Czechoslovakia. Later MP for Gateshead.
32   *Hansard*, HC Deb, 27 March 1933, cols 723–732.
33   *Hansard*, HC Deb, 10 December 1934, cols. 61–72.
34   Later Secretary of State for War under Neville Chamberlain, 1937–40.
35   Minney, *The Private Papers of Hore-Belisha*, p. 33.
36   Young, *Stanley Baldwin*, pp. 193–194.
37   Young, *Stanley Baldwin*, p. 194.
38   Vansittart, *The Mist Procession*, p. 508.
39   *Hansard*, HC Deb, 11 March 1935, cols 35–46.
40   Vansittart, *The Mist Procession*, p. 509.
41   *Hansard*, HC Deb, 11 March 1935, col. 77.
42   Letter to Tom Attlee, 12 March 1935.
43   CAC: ATLE 1/14.
44   Jenkins, *Mr Attlee*, p. 158.
45   Described as of a 'virulence distasteful to many delegates'. *News Chronicle*, 2 October 1935.
46   Postgate, *The Life of George Lansbury*, p. 303. There is uncertainty whether Bevin said 'hawking' or 'taking'.
47   Diary entry for 19 October 1935, quoted at Feiling, *Neville Chamberlain*, pp. 268–269.
48   Jenkins, *Mr Attlee*, p. 163.

CHAPTER SIX

PARTY LEADER, 1935–1940

Reaction in the press to Attlee's accession split along predictable lines. Harold Laski, writing in the *Manchester Guardian*, likened him to Henry Campbell-Bannerman, approved his position as a left-centre socialist and presciently predicted that 'if the new session lasts long enough for Mr Attlee to prove himself, experience will show that the Labour Party has found a permanent and not a temporary leader.'[1] By contrast, a *Daily Mail* editorial predicted, 'So the leader of the socialist Opposition is to be Major Attlee. I am afraid he will not be so for long, but he deserves the success that is his momentarily.'[2]

Stability and security, interlaced with vague promises of future social reform, were the basis of the national government's manifesto. The Labour Party, in a manifesto notable for its brevity, criticised the government, arguing that it had 'wrecked the Disarmament Conference by resisting all the constructive proposals made by other States';[3] it had 'helped to restart the arms race' and 'ranged itself at the eleventh hour behind the Covenant at Geneva. Even so, its action has been slow and half-hearted'.[4]

Labour recovered significantly from the catastrophe of 1931, winning over eight million votes. It regained status as a credible second party, but the national government, dominated by 386 Conservative Members, gave Baldwin a comfortable majority. The resounding mandate was, *The Times* declared, 'a splendid result' and 'a triumph of steadiness'.[5] Devoting three columns to its summary of the results, its eulogy does not mention the name 'Attlee' once. In contrast, the local paper in the East End trumpeted that 'Poplar and Stepney [are] now all red' after Labour gains in Mile End and Whitechapel.[6]

It was an active campaign for Attlee, who spoke extensively to support candidates. He hammered away at the same themes: unemployment, the bankers 'ramp', the need to avoid an armaments race and the inevitable results of rearmament. His purpose was twofold – to establish himself as leader and to ensure that Labour avoided the catastrophe of 1931. In both endeavours he succeeded, confounding the judgement of the *Daily Mail*. During the campaign he was able to land some solid punches on MacDonald, referring to him as 'a political nudist' and 'a voice out of the fog', accusing him of 'sheer, unmitigated mendacity'. 'Who is to rule this country?' he demanded. 'There never was a government more subservient to the interests of the rentier class. Labour says money is to be the servant of Man, not his master.'[7]

When the Parliamentary Party met to elect their new leader the field was very different from that of four years before. Greenwood, Morrison, Clynes, Alexander and Dalton – all senior to Attlee in common perception – were among the possible contenders. According to Attlee, Greenwood was the choice of Transport House; Morrison 'of the intelligentsia and the press', while he himself counted on his parliamentary colleagues.[8] Had Members been faced with *tabula rasa*, Attlee might not have been their first choice. The slate, however, was not blank. The 'happy few' who had worked with Attlee during the lean years had seen his quality, his energy and his dependability. When Clynes decided not to stand, and Alexander and Dalton kept their powder dry, Greenwood, Morrison and Attlee emerged as the three candidates. Each had different assets to offer.

Greenwood most embodied the traditions of the party. A *protégé* of Henderson, he was a warm-hearted intellectual of modest political skills with wide support in the north of the country. He was also known to enjoy a few drinks. Morrison had a great following in London but was relatively unknown elsewhere. Attlee, as it emerged, had solid support of the Members who had seen him at work over the past four years. That support was enough to put him ahead in the first ballot, in which he led with fifty-eight votes. Morrison polled forty-four votes and Greenwood thirty-two. When Greenwood withdrew, almost all his supporters moved to Attlee on the second ballot, while Morrison's vote held steady. A. L. Rowse commented that the result was inevitable as 'The election of either Morrison or Greenwood would have alienated one-third of the party. Attlee alienated none.'[9]

With a decisive majority Attlee dispelled the image of himself as a caretaker while the 'real' leaders were outside Parliament. Morrison blamed the result on Freemasons, adding that Attlee 'stressed that it was just for a single session and that then a change could come'.[10] With breathtaking disingenuousness he wrote in his autobiography that 'he declined to accept the invitation to become the deputy leader as I thought my leadership of the LCC Labour Party ... more important to the party'.[11] Dalton's reaction was sour and ungenerous. It was, he wrote, 'a wretched, disheartening result', for now 'a little mouse shall lead them.'[12] He was not alone in failing to see the spine within the slight stature. Oswald Mosley, Attlee's predecessor at the Duchy of Lancaster, sneeringly referred to him as competent to preserve the balance between conflicting forces within the party; 'a quality which the Labour Party always prefers in its leader either to vision or to dynamism'.[13] All three underestimated the new leader; Attlee was to retain the position for twenty years.[14]

The first opportunity to stimulate Tory defection occurred soon after Parliament reassembled. In April MacDonald, Pierre Laval, the French Foreign Minister, and Mussolini signed an agreement in Stresa, guaranteeing Austria's independence. This agreement, 'The Stresa Front', encouraged Mussolini that France and Britain would turn a blind eye to his imperial ambitions in Abyssinia. In December Sir Samuel Hoare and Laval had proposed ending the fighting in Abyssinia by granting Mussolini a partition of Abyssinia that allowed the Abyssinians a corridor to the sea at Assab. When details of the secret pact were leaked there was an outcry in Britain. A leader in *The Times* echoed public opinion, denouncing the agreement that granted 'a corridor for camels'[15]; in a debate in the House on 19 December Attlee moved a Vote of Censure.

In a coda to his attack on Hoare, Attlee made a tactical error in questioning Baldwin's *bona fides*. 'There are two issues raised today', he said. 'There is the question of the honour of this country, and there is the question of the honour of the Prime Minister.' Accusing Baldwin of winning an election on one policy and pursuing another, he continued accusingly: 'If you turn and run away from the aggressor, you kill the

League, and you do worse than that ... you kill all faith in the word of honour of this country.'[16]

Once the Prime Minister's honour was questioned, Attlee's critics maintain, it was certain that the government's ranks would close and that potential rebels would fall into line. Had he not overstepped that mark, he might have combined with Austen Chamberlain to bring the government down.[17] Chamberlain, in reproving Attlee, suggested that potential Tory abstainers, not outright rebels, were persuaded to vote with the government.[18] Chamberlain's argument that Tories critical of the government and resolved to bring about its downfall on a matter of principle would be restrained by a breach of parliamentary etiquette was self-serving Tory cant. Attlee had fixed his eyes on a longer strategy than parliamentary debate. His goal was to erode public confidence in the ethical stance of both Baldwin and his government as the international situation worsened.

The government's basic policy was clear: Italy's invasion of Abyssinia was a *fait accompli*. Britain and France would go to any lengths to avoid bringing Mussolini and Hitler together; the enmity of Italy would threaten Britain's entire maritime strategy. The editor of *The Times* even suggested that, if Germany was as powerful as was rumoured, perhaps Britain should ally with Hitler.[19] To avoid a European war, the sacrifice of Abyssinian territory, never a prime consideration in Tory policy, was a small price to pay.

Baldwin's policy over Abyssinia laid bare its weakness. Sanctions were defensible only if Britain were prepared to stand behind them with force. Once sanctions were imposed, Britain alienated Italy. When the government failed to take the next step it sent a message to Hitler that collective security would not be used to check German aggression. As a side effect, Baldwin's policy succeeded in achieving what Britain had striven to avoid – the creation of a Rome-Berlin Axis.

Observing the success of Mussolini's bluster, Hitler became increasingly vocal in condemnation of the Franco-Soviet pact of May 1935, concluded in violation of the Treaty of Locarno.[20] In November André François-Poncet, the French Ambassador in Berlin, warned Paris that Hitler's protests were being made to justify a planned aggressive action. By 10 January he was certain that Hitler's objective was the reoccupation of the Rhineland.[21] When the French Senate ratified the Franco-Soviet pact on 27 February 1936 Hitler brushed aside the concerns of his generals and diplomats that France would immediately mobilise. Convinced that there would be no resistance from either Britain or France, he ordered General von Blomberg to make necessary preparations, and on 7 March a force of just one division and three battalions crossed the Rhine.[22] Hitler's confidence was justified. Paris and London conferred; the Council of the League of Nations met. Germany's action was roundly condemned, but Hitler was not challenged. He later said that the two days after the reoccupation were 'the most nerve-wracking in my life'. If the French had marched into the Rhineland, then 'we would have had to withdraw with our tails between our legs'.[23]

Instead, the government accepted Hitler's action, weakly maintaining that Germany was merely righting one of the punitive wrongs of Versailles.

In the Commons Attlee spoke out vehemently against inaction. 'In the last five years we have had quite enough of dodging difficulties, of using forms of words to avoid facing up to realities,' he said prophetically. 'I am afraid that you may get a patched-up peace and then another crisis next year.'[24]

Events had moved rapidly in six months and the next crisis came sooner than Attlee predicted. In July General Franco led a revolt against the Popular Front government in Spain, at first apparently a purely local affair of little international concern. Attlee had been invited to visit the Soviet Union by Ivan Maisky, the Russian ambassador in London, with whom he had established a friendship. It was a short trip, visiting only Moscow and Leningrad, and Attlee recognised that he was able to see only what the Soviet government wished him to see. He did not meet Stalin but was everywhere conscious of the personality cult surrounding him. All the Soviet Union's successes, he learned, were the work of Stalin; all its failures were the fault of Trotsky. Propaganda aside, he was impressed by the commitment to building society that the Russian people shared. 'They were not working for landlords or capitalists', he wrote. 'Their work was for the good of all and was worth doing. The attitude of the workers struck me as quite different from that of most workers under capitalism.'[25]

During his visit to the Soviet Union the local trouble in Spain developed into civil war, liable to involve the European powers in a proxy left versus right battle. Baldwin's government took the disingenuous position that a local squabble did not concern Britain, and urged non-intervention. During August a Non-Intervention Agreement was signed and systematically ignored by Germany and Italy. Since Mussolini and Hitler were supporting Franco, non-intervention meant standing aside while the constitutional government of Spain was overrun.

Against this background the Labour Party met for its annual conference in Edinburgh. The war in Spain compelled the party to define its position on non-intervention and rearmament generally, while behind the Spanish question lurked the bogey of Germany and the greater bogey of how a capitalist government would deal with Nazi aggression in Europe. From the left of the party came the familiar argument that the League of Nations was a capitalist tool and that Labour policy should be to oppose rearmament and stimulate international socialist co-operation to avoid a capitalist war. From the right came the proposition that the party must support rearmament to defend freedom and democracy and do everything to endorse the authority of the League. It fell to Attlee to sum up and arrive at a policy that the conference could adopt.

In his closing speech he succeeded in 'lowering the temperature' and gave the lead for rearmament 'consistent with our country's responsibilities', while advocating continued opposition to the National Government. It was a worthy attempt to achieve consensus that defined neither the nature of the country's responsibilities nor the party's policy on non-intervention. Nonetheless, there had been a fundamental shift in party policy: rearmament, consistent with Britain's needs to defend herself against other rearming nations, became accepted policy.

The government's policy of consistently maintaining that non-intervention was effective was, to Attlee, utter dishonesty. In a debate in October Alfred Danville, a far-right conservative and supporter of Franco, blandly stated that neither side could obtain armaments, that it was 'six of one and half a dozen of the other'.[26] Philip Noel-Baker denied this. The Republicans, he said, were receiving nothing while Italy was supplying the Nationalists.[27] Attlee, in an impassioned speech, described the war as 'a fight for the soul of Europe', charging that non-intervention had become 'a farce'. For the first time he stated that the government was guilty of incremental steps of appeasement. If Britain had stood firm earlier there would have been no Abyssinian crisis; if she had stood firm over Abyssinia there would not have been this trouble in Spain. 'We had Locarno', he said, 'but where is Locarno now? It has gone, because there has been no policy in foreign affairs except the policy of giving way. The result of that is a world in anarchy.' The government's policy, he maintained 'is disastrous for world peace and … the government has not brought us nearer peace but has brought us closer and closer to the danger of war.'[28]

Attention was diverted from the drift to war by a domestic crisis. King George V had been succeeded by his eldest son David, who took the title Edward VIII. A charismatic and popular figure, he combined 'genuine solicitude for the unemployed'[29] with what Attlee considered instability and poor judgement.[30] During the summer and autumn it had become an open secret in London society that he was conducting a love affair with Mrs Wallis Simpson. Gossip turned to scandal when Mrs Simpson divorced her husband and the King determined to marry her, now a twice-divorced woman. Baldwin informed the King that any such marriage, whether morganatic or not, would be unacceptable to the King's subjects in Britain and the Commonwealth, and that, if he married Mrs Simpson, the government would resign. If no other party were prepared to form a government, this would cause a constitutional crisis. In short, the King would be forced to abdicate.

During November Baldwin briefed Attlee in confidence on the impending crisis, a confidence that Attlee respected. Before presenting the King with what amounted to an ultimatum, Baldwin consulted Attlee, Archibald Sinclair, the Liberal leader, and Churchill, a known supporter of the King, to ascertain their reaction if the King proceeded with his plan to marry Mrs Simpson. Baldwin believed that Sinclair would support him but was less sure of Attlee.[31] He misjudged his man. Attlee was adamant that, while the Labour Party would not object to an American queen, the twice-divorced Mrs Simpson and a morganatic marriage were unacceptable. Walter Citrine, the TUC General Secretary, confirmed to Baldwin at Chequers that Attlee spoke for the Labour movement. 'Most people were prepared to smile indulgently while the King was Prince of Wales, but now ... it was a different matter'.[32] Attlee was proved right when MPs returned from their constituencies after the weekend of 4–6 December. The mood in the country had shifted in favour of Baldwin.[33]

Much has been made of the opportunity presented to Attlee to exploit the crisis to Labour's advantage. If Baldwin's government had refused to serve, then the Labour Party, adducing the King's concern for the unemployed, could reasonably have agreed to form an administration. In rejecting this course and supporting Baldwin, Attlee, his critics argued, showed too great a concern for the monarchy and too little for his party. Such a view fails to take into account the public's respect for the institution of monarchy. Bevin expressed this succinctly. 'Our people won't 'ave it,' he declared.[34]

To have exploited the King's distress would have been abhorrent to Attlee. He saw his duty as clear: to support the constitutional position taken by Baldwin; to fight an election on the issue would be manifestly opportunistic. Nonetheless, the Labour left, particularly Bevan, saw his action as reactionary pandering to the irrelevant institution of monarchy. More widespread, however, was the feeling that he 'showed sensitive consideration for Mr Baldwin's repugnant duty'.[35] There was an additional valuable outcome for Attlee. For some time he and Ernest Bevin had increasingly found themselves on the same side within the party, but a certain distance remained between them. When he gave Bevin the details of his conversations with Baldwin, Bevin recognised him as a leader of firm principle and supported his position. It launched a remarkable co-operation.

As to Edward VIII, subsequently the Duke of Windsor, both Attlee and Bevin remained opposed to finding any diplomatic role for him when this was mooted by George VI in 1946. 'I have used all my persuasive powers with both of them to make them see our point of view,' the King wrote to his brother. 'I know this will be a blow to you and I am sorry that I have not been able to arrange it for you.'[36]

In 1936 Attlee was invited by Victor Gollancz, founder of The Left Book Club, to write a book outlining the history and mission of modern socialism. This was published in 1937 as *The Labour Party in Perspective*. It is an important book, central not only to the author's own 'enthusiastic' conversion to socialism but also as a broad road map to the direction the party was taking as contemporary tensions mounted in Europe. He drew a distinction between the Tory policy of treating the League of Nations as an adjunct to national defence and socialist policy to which the League was central, while being realistic concerning the need for armed forces as a last resort for maintaining world order. The League must be adequately strong to deter aggression so that an attack against one nation is treated as an attack against all.[37] As at the party conference, however, while he had fundamentally modified his views on the need for rearmament, the practical implications were unclear.

The book also aimed to reassure voters that the Labour Party was not bent on revolution. Nor was the party doctrinaire; carefully explaining the roles of the NEC, the trade unions and the Parliamentary Party, he drew a clear line between areas where state control was necessary – finance, land, coal and fuel, transport – and the rights of minorities within a socialist economy.[38] Yet the reader is left in no doubt about the author's resolve that 'a Labour government should make it quite plain that it will suffer nothing to hinder it in carrying out the popular will'.[39]

It is an authoritative, not authoritarian, document. It conveys both the clarity of Attlee's perception of socialism's purpose and his role in expounding it. If, at times, it is less than definitive, it honestly reflects the differences of opinion on tactics. In terms of strategy, it is the forthright declaration of a leader. The book was well reviewed overall and sold 50,000 copies.

In January 1937 the Socialist League, the ILP and the CPGB collaborated to produce a 'Unity Manifesto', an extreme left-wing document urging aggressive revolutionary measures to impose socialism, and criticising Attlee for not exploiting Baldwin's difficulties over the abdication. Its extremist positions angered Attlee and caused the NEC to expel the Socialist League from the party. Two months later the NEC released 'Labour's Immediate Programme', a restatement of decisions taken at Edinburgh.[40] It counteracted both the woolly policies of the National Government and extremist calls for revolution from the left of the party. At a time when social democracy was hard pressed throughout Europe, it provided a clear blueprint for action and denied that Labour in power would shrink from socialist measures. When the party met for its conference in Bournemouth it was adopted as the party's manifesto for the next election. It stood the test of time, for, as could not have been predicted in 1937, the manifesto endured as the basis for Labour policy when it eventually came to power.

In December Attlee led a fraternal delegation from the party to Spanish Republicans. They visited Barcelona and Madrid, experienced bombing in Barcelona ('a very mild prelude to what was to come a few years later'),[41] inspected the British contingent of the International Brigade, where Attlee consented to a company being named the 'Major Attlee Company', and were pursued between Valencia and Barcelona by three Nationalist planes. On his return to England Attlee was pleasantly surprised to learn that a clenched-fist salute he had given in support of the Republicans had won approval from the left. Thus 1937 came to an end with the party apparently more united than would have been thought possible fifteen months before and with 'Major Attlee' greatly more secure in the saddle. He also received financial reward for his efforts for the first time, as the Ministers of the Crown Act provided for an annual salary of £2,000 for the Leader of the Opposition.

Any euphoria that Attlee may have felt at the end of 1937 was soon dissipated in the first months of 1938. President Roosevelt contacted Chamberlain, who had succeeded Baldwin as Prime Minister, to propose an international conference. Chamberlain, who expected nothing but words from Americans, ignored the offer.[42] Foreign Secretary Anthony Eden resigned, protesting that 'the diplomatic floor was littered with Mussolini's earlier broken promises'.[43] Attlee, although cannily suspicious of Eden's professed motives for resigning, supported his criticism of Chamberlain's policy of separating Mussolini from Hitler, commenting that Eden's resignation would be seen as a victory for Mussolini. In a coruscating attack on Chamberlain in the House he predicted that the government's policy would sooner or later lead to war.[44]

In the following month Hitler annexed Austria to the Reich. Mussolini, who had undertaken to defend Austria against German invasion, did nothing. Chamberlain's hopes of separating the dictators were revealed as worthless when they met four days later at Brennero to co-ordinate strategy. In the Commons Attlee vigorously attacked Chamberlain's policy, stressing the futility of dealing with dictators 'on the assumptions that usually prevail in the intercourse of states'. Chamberlain, he said, yielded to force at every point.[45]

When, one month later, Chamberlain and Lord Halifax, now Foreign Secretary, concluded the Anglo-Italian Agreement, Attlee poured scorn on Chamberlain's naïve policy. He was now convinced that appeasement of the dictators could lead only to a war for which Britain was unprepared. He confided his fears in a letter to Tom, lamenting that 'Chamberlain is just an imperialist of the old school but without much knowledge of foreign affairs or appreciation of the forces at work. It is a pretty gloomy outlook.'[46]

At the end of April Hitler confirmed the fears of Locarno's critics – as well as Attlee's gloomy forecast – by demanding, through his puppet Konrad Heinlein, autonomy for the three and a half million Sudeten Germans in Czechoslovakia. This, however, was mere sabre rattling; Hitler resolved to acquire the Sudetenland by the end of September.

After a short visit with Violet to Denmark, a trip arranged by Bevin and financed by the Workers Travel Organisation, Attlee watched with mounting dismay as Germany increased pressure on Czechoslovakia to cede the Sudetenland. In July he spent a weekend with Stafford Cripps and his wife in Gloucestershire. The other guest was Pandit Nehru; the three men discussed the future of India, reaching conclusions that formed the basis of Labour policy in 1947. A family holiday in South Wales ended the summer, effectively the last summer of European peace for seven years.

Keeping to his schedule for invading Czechoslovakia, Hitler maintained pressure on Beneš to yield to Heinlein's demands. Chamberlain increased that pressure by sending Lord Runciman to broker agreement between Prague and the Sudeten Germans. Subjected to a blitz of propaganda, Runciman concluded that Prague should yield. Chamberlain, belatedly aware of the risk of war, flew to Berchtesgaden to meet Hitler, who demanded the right of total self-determination for Sudeten Germans. Britain and France pressured Prague to accept; Chamberlain flew to Bad Godesberg to communicate to Hitler the Czech acceptance of his demands. Hitler promptly raised them. Chamberlain, Attlee claimed, was out of his depth.

He seemed convinced that he was so clever that he could manage everything. But if you suggested it needed a pretty long spoon to sup with the devil he always thought he could pull it off. He thought so right up to the end, first with the Nazis and then with the Russians.[47]

When the Czech government rejected Hitler's latest demands, Parliament was recalled early. In a sombre speech Chamberlain held out hope that an invasion might yet be avoided; he had sent a message to the Führer via Mussolini, hoping to arrange a further conference. As he spoke, a note was passed to him, notifying him of Hitler's agreement to a third conference. The relief in the House was universal; Hitler was yielding to Chamberlain's diplomacy. War would yet be avoided.

Attlee, without doubt prepared to lambast the Prime Minister for sacrificing another country to Germany, was faced with a dilemma. To attack Chamberlain amid this mood of jubilation would be unwise. Confining himself to ninety-seven words, he had little option but to encourage him in his definitive act of appeasement, wishing 'to give the Prime Minister every opportunity of following up this new move, and we ... hope that when the House reassembles in a short time the war clouds may have lifted.'[48]

Five days later, after Chamberlain returned from Munich proclaiming 'Peace for our Time' and Duff Cooper resigned in protest, Attlee delivered his deferred attack on Chamberlain. He compared his emotions before Munich with those he had experienced at Gallipoli – mixed emotions combining relief that one was leaving the fighting and certainty that one would soon be embroiled again. Munich represented one of the greatest diplomatic defeats that Britain and France had ever sustained. 'If the Prime Minister wants to walk with the dictators,' he charged, 'he will have to conform with their wishes ... Seven years of National Government have brought us to a day of humiliation, to a more dangerous and humiliating position than any we have occupied since the days of Charles II.'[49]

He explained his shift of position from that of five days before with a 'ship of state' metaphor:

> *The Prime Minister has given us an account of his actions. Everybody recognises the great exertions he has made in the cause of peace. When the captain of a ship by disregarding all rules of navigation has gone right off his course and run the ship into great danger, watchers from the shore, naturally impressed with the captain's frantic efforts to try to save something from the shipwreck, cheer him*

when he comes ashore and even want to give him a testimonial, but there follows
an inquiry, an inquest, on the victims, and the question will be asked how the
vessel got so far off its course, how and why it was so hazarded?[50]

Inevitably, support for the government's motion was overwhelming, but
there was a growing group of Tories opposed to Chamberlain's policy
who abstained. Determined opposition to the policy of appeasement
was stifled by an impregnable Tory majority; moreover, Tory rebels
were reluctant to alienate their party. Hence opposition led not to votes
against the government but to abstentions. For as long as the Tory-led
National Government remained in power, Labour's and Attlee's options
were circumscribed.

In 1960 Attlee recorded his recollections of his years as Labour leader
and Prime Minister. The first issue addressed in that series of interviews
was the question of Labour's culpability for the drift to war. While he
regretted Labour's opposition to rearmament before 1935, he insisted
that there was little that the party could do against a government with an
overwhelming majority unless at least fifty Tories were prepared to vote
to bring Chamberlain down. Once the government turned its back on
Czechoslovakia, he maintained, war was inevitable. Most of the Tories,
Churchill included, were content to allow Italy to take over Abyssinia;
during the Spanish Civil War fear of communism deterred them from
intervention. Chamberlain, whom he characterised as a 'peace-at-any-price
man', was 'prepared to throw anyone to the wolves'. Ultimately, responsibility for a weak British policy lay with those who formulated it – MacDonald,
Baldwin, Simon and Chamberlain. When the Tories did eventually reject
Chamberlain's policy and march into Labour's lobbies in 1940, Britain was
already at war. He conceded that an earlier alliance of Labour and dissident Tories might have achieved the same result but that, even when Eden
resigned, Tory opposition to Chamberlain never crystallised.[51]

In the year that elapsed before Britain eventually slipped into war there were
milestones, points at which Attlee vigorously proclaimed Labour's opposition.
His critics maintain that he failed to make the best use of those moments –
when a united front with disaffected Tories was discussed after Munich; when
conscription in peacetime was introduced in March 1939; when Hitler occupied the rump of Czechoslovakia in April; when the government pursued a

treaty with the Soviet Union and ultimately saw Stalin turn aside and deal with Germany; when Labour refused to join the national coalition. Could Labour – or, more precisely, could a leader other than Attlee, a more dynamic demagogue – have prevented the slide into war?

After the 1935 election the Conservatives held 387 seats before adding the other supporters of the national coalition. It required eighty Tory abstentions to erode that absolute majority. It would, additionally, have required every Liberal Member and every Nationalist, Independent and Communist MP to join Labour in a vote of No Confidence. Those conditions could not have been achieved in the climate prevailing between 1935 and 1939. Attlee consistently argued that Baldwin's and Chamberlain's policy was leading to war, but Baldwin and Chamberlain argued – and probably sincerely believed – that the opposite was true, that if the dictators could be separated, Hitler would shrink from aggression in the West. In retrospect one may imagine a groundswell of support for Churchill and Eden, which could have been exploited to advantage. This was decidedly not the case. Churchill had lost considerable ground over the abdication and was regarded as an outdated liability within his own party. As for Eden, his replacement by Halifax was seen as adding experience and stability to a government committed to avoid war at any cost. For as long as the cost seemed worth paying – the sacrifice of Austria, Czechoslovakia and Albania – there would be no wholesale rebellion in the Tory ranks.

Nor was Attlee's policy congruent with all shades of opinion within his own party. Labour had a long tradition of pacifism; the belligerence of Bevin at the 1935 Party conference was a radical departure from the conventional party line that Lansbury represented. By the time that Attlee could overcome the knee-jerk response to a 'capitalist' war and seek more than collective security through the League, Hitler had, as Attlee himself pointed out, achieved in a few months more than the territorial gains that had eluded Germany over four years between 1914 and 1918.[52]

It is difficult, after 1939, to understand that the term 'appeasement' carried none of the pejorative slant that it has since acquired. Appeasing a defeated enemy with justifiable complaints was considered right and proper; yielding to Hitler's demands, however savagely conveyed, was seen as correcting the punitive terms of Versailles. Nor was Attlee entirely fair in accusing the government of 'playing one dictator off against another'. Overtures to Mussolini by the Western powers were defensible as attempts to keep the two dictators apart. The government made its mistake in not following through on sanctions, making it clear to both Hitler and Mussolini that Britain could not be depended upon.

Hitler and his generals confirmed that firm action in March 1936 would have prevented the occupation of the Rhineland.[53] If we continue the contrafactual sequence, however, there is no indication that the Sudetenland, vastly more difficult for France and Britain to protect, would not have replaced the Rhineland on Hitler's agenda. Had events followed that course, Attlee, who did accept rearmament as inevitable once Hitler moved outside Germany, would probably have attacked the government in the same manner with the same lack of result. The only course of action open to Britain and France to prevent the rape of Czechoslovakia would have been prompt invasion of the Ruhr through the Rhineland. There is little to suggest that either country would have taken up arms for the Sudetenland. Particularly after January 1937 when Mussolini and Hitler had reached agreement over Austria.[54]

Attlee saw his role as to establish the majority view among dissenting opinions and to pursue vigorously the resultant policy. This he did to perfection. Yet the charge remains that he 'led from behind'.[55] He was consistent in his belief that dictatorships were inherently unstable and would crumble from within. After the Abyssinian crisis demonstrated that Western democracy was more prone to crumble, his policy of collective security backed by controlled rearmament gradually became more bellicose. The combination of a 'Safety First' policy, an overwhelming government majority, an electorate desperate to avoid war and brilliantly managed totalitarian aggression, however, rendered such logic powerless.

ENDNOTES

1   *Manchester Guardian*, 9 October 1935.
2   *Daily Mail*, 14 October 1935. Attlee was unconcerned. 'I just go ahead'. Granada Historical Records, *Clem Attlee*, p. 13.
3   Labour Party election manifesto, 1935, section 3, para 2.
4   Ibid, paras 3–4.
5   *The Times*, 16 November 1935, p. 12. Geoffrey Dawson, editor of *The Times*, and Baldwin were friends. Dawson was a Fellow of All Souls and Vansittart comments that 'Baldwin liked a Fellow of All Souls better than other fellows (*The Mist Procession*, p. 352).
6   *East London Advertiser*, 16 November 1935, p. 5.

7   Speech at Southampton, 30 October 1935. *The Manchester Guardian*, 31 October 1935.
8   CAC: ATLE 1/14.
9   From a conversation with William Golant, cited in 'The Emergence of C. R. Attlee as Leader of the Parliamentary Labour Party', *The Historical Journal*, xiii, 2 (1970), p. 330.
10 Morrison, *An Autobiography*, p. 164.
11 Morrison, *An Autobiography*, pp. 164–165. Morrison's disingenuousness is at least matched by Attlee's, when he later commented that 'he didn't realise that the poor little man was full of seething ambition'. Granada Historical Records, *Clem Attlee*, p. 53.
12 Pimlott, *The Political Diary of Hugh Dalton 1918–1940*, Entry for 26 November 1935, p. 196.
13 Sir Oswald Mosely, *My Life*, p. 222.
14 There were challenges, but they tended to be grumbles about lack of dynamism rather than either / or confrontations. The most overt challenge came from Cripps in 1947. See Chapter 14, 'Annus Horrendus'.
15 *The Times*, 16 December 1935.
16 *Hansard*, HC Deb, 19 December 1935, col. 2029.
17 Young, *Stanley Baldwin*, p. 218.
18 Jenkins, *Mr Attlee*, pp. 172–173.
19 Rowse, *Appeasement*, p. 28.
20 The Locarno Treaty of 1926 between Britain, France, Germany, Belgium and Italy was a mutual non-aggression pact that defined national borders and was hailed as a guarantee of peace in the pre-Hitler years.
21 François-Poncet, *Souvenirs d'une Ambassade à Berlin, Septembre 1931–Octobre 1938*, p. 249.
22 General Jodl's estimate of the German force is from his post-war interrogation, cited by Bullock, *Hitler: A Study in Tyranny*, p. 313.
23 Bullock, *Hitler: A Study in Tyranny*, p. 315.
24 *Hansard*, HC Deb, 26 March 1936, cols. 1535–36.
25 Jenkins, *Mr Attlee*, p. 176.
26 *Hansard*, HC Deb, 29 October 1936, col. 126.
27 *Hansard*, HC Deb, 29 October 1936, col. 128.
28 *Hansard*, HC Deb, 29 October 1936, cols. 137–142.
29 *As It Happened*, p. 122.
30 Granada Historical Records, *Clem Attlee*, p. 14.
31 Philip Ziegler, *King Edward VIII*, p. 304.
32 Lord Citrine, *Men and Work*, p. 327.
33 Frances Donaldson, *Edward VIII: A Biography of the Duke of Windsor*, p. 300.
34 Francis Williams, *Nothing So Strange*, p. 141.
35 Hector Bolitho, *Edward VIII*, p. 274.
36 Letter of 28 January 1946. Royal Archives/Duke of Windsor, 6151. Cited by Ziegler, *King Edward VIII*, p. 507.
37 Attlee, *The Labour Party in Perspective*, pp. 248–254.
38 Attlee, *The Labour Party in Perspective*, pp. 170 ff.
39 Attlee, *The Labour Party in Perspective*, p. 286.
40 *Labour's Immediate Programme* was based on *For Socialism and Peace*, the comprehensive party programme, approved by the 1934 conference in Southport. This was the first major policy document issued by the party since the catastrophe of 1931.
41 *As It Happened*, p. 133.
42 Feiling, *The Life of Neville Chamberlain*, p. 325.
43 Eden, *Memoirs*, vol. 1, 'Facing the Dictators', pp. 586–587.
44 *Hansard*, HC Deb, 21 February 1938, cols 69–72.
45 *Hansard*, HC Deb, 14 March 1938, cols 53–56.
46 Letter to Tom Attlee, 29 April 1938.
47 Williams, *A Prime Minister Remembers*, p. 15.
48 *Hansard*, HC Deb, 28 September 1938, col. 26.
49 *Hansard*, HC Deb, 3 October 1938, cols 51–66.
50 *Hansard*, HC Deb, 3 October 1938, col. 52.
51 This series of recollections was published by his interlocutor, Francis Williams as *A Prime Minister Remembers*.
52 *Hansard*, HC Deb, 3 October 1938, col. 52.
53 See notes 22 and 23 above.
54 von Hassell to Goering, 30 January 1937. Cited at Bullock, *Hitler: A Study in Tyranny*, p. 329 n.
55 For example, Rowse, *Appeasement*, p. 52.

CHAPTER SEVEN

LORD PRIVY SEAL, 1940–1942

Attlee's progress from critical outsider to dedicated insider began on 10 May 1940 when the beleaguered Neville Chamberlain, compelled to form a coalition government, summoned Attlee and Greenwood to Downing Street to sound them out on the possibility of the Labour Party's joining a coalition either under his leadership or under that of someone else. The party was in conference in Bournemouth; Attlee agreed to consult the Executive and give the Prime Minister an answer on the following day.

Predictably, the response was a unanimous 'No' to serving under Chamberlain and a 'Yes' to the second possibility. Attlee telephoned the responses to the Prime Minister and caught a train back to London. By the time he arrived at Waterloo Chamberlain had resigned and Churchill had accepted the King's commission.[1] The new Prime Minister, he was informed, wished him to go immediately to the Admiralty to help him form a government.[2]

In May 1940 Attlee had scant experience of running a government department. By the time of the German surrender five years later he alone had served with Churchill throughout in the War Cabinet; he had become Britain's first Deputy Prime Minister and sat on the three committees central to the direction of the war. Most importantly, he had ceased to be a remote leader of a minority party; he had become highly visible, with proven Cabinet experience, widely respected for his integrity and readiness to tell unvarnished truth without platitude. It was a remarkable transformation in public perception.

Even more remarkable was that he achieved this while remaining loyal to ostensibly mutually exclusive principles. Without once challenging Churchill, whom he regarded as Britain's greatest war leader – not her greatest strategist, an accolade he reserved for his hero Cromwell[3] – he emerged from the coalition as a viable alternative leader, more fitted than Churchill in the view of the electorate to the task of rebuilding Britain in 1945.

Throughout those years he was obliged to restrain the demands of the left wing of his party for overt challenge to the coalition. Time and again, particularly after November 1942, he enjoined his party and the electorate to be patient. First the war must be won; only then could the party and the country turn to the more challenging task of rebuilding the country. With deft assurance he remained loyal to his Cabinet colleagues, loyal to the principles of socialism, making no promises on which he could not deliver. As Churchill had offered blood, toil, tears and sweat in wartime, so Attlee stressed the vastness of the post-war task, the privations that Britons would suffer to 'win the peace'. As Britain's military success waxed, so did his confidence in his future role. From 1941 until the German surrender his speeches grew in assurance until he inspired his listeners with the challenge of the crusade that he would undertake with them.

In May 1940 the new Prime Minister created the machinery for strategic decisions, machinery that remained substantially unchanged throughout the war. It was, in his own words, part adaptation and part innovation and it evolved into a lean and efficient system for waging war.[4] While mercurial and unpredictable, Churchill was a highly competent administrator who insisted on accountability; his determination to translate policy into action appealed greatly to Attlee, who served as his deputy chair in the War Cabinet and the Defence Committee. The third central element, the Lord President's Committee, chaired by Attlee, ran the civil side of Britain at war. From the outset, therefore, Attlee was effectively Deputy Prime Minister, a title officially conferred on him in February 1942.[5]

His actual if unofficial status was demonstrated by his physical proximity to Churchill. The Prime Minister wanted him close at hand and Attlee, at his request, moved into 11 Downing Street, normally the official residence of the Chancellor of the Exchequer. Throughout the week, away from home, his life was lived in a triangle bounded by Downing

Street, Parliament Square and the Oxford and Cambridge Club, where he generally took breakfast and, absent any official engagements, dinner. He returned to Downing Street after the evening round of Cabinet and committees and dealt with his 'boxes' before going to sleep after the midnight news bulletin. At weekends, if his schedule allowed, he would escape to spend time with Violet and the children at Stanmore. More often than not, however, as the war progressed, his weekends involved visits and speeches outside London.

Sharing Churchill's view that a small Cabinet was essential – initially it comprised just five members – Attlee, with help from Greenwood, streamlined the workings of the machinery. As he later described it to Francis Williams, they found 'a mass of committees'. Each had two branches, and all seemed to have 'that fellow, Neville's man (Sir Horace Wilson) on it'. With some satisfaction, Attlee told Williams that 'we pushed him off the whole lot of them and started afresh'.[6]

From that bald account of Wilson's removal it is easy to grasp how Churchill and Attlee, *prima facie* incompatible, worked so well together for the duration of the war. They shared the same relentless determination. That one was a showman and the other the very opposite was irrelevant; each was a shrewd and pragmatic operator. For both men the objective of victory at almost any cost was paramount – as Attlee demonstrated when he moved the Emergency Powers (Defence) Bill in the Commons;[7] the lives and property of every Briton were placed at the government's disposal, should they be required for the waging of the war. To the public he sounded a reassuring note to avoid popular panic: 'Don't worry', he urged them. 'No one is going to seize your property.'[8]

From the first day the coalition faced crisis. The invasion of the Netherlands was followed by the invasion of France. On 13 May, the day that Attlee attended his first War Cabinet meeting, German Panzer divisions crossed the Meuse and, defying orders to pause, turned west towards the Channel. Two days later Paul Reynaud informed Churchill that the French armies were defeated and requested him to supply air support, an action that would have left Britain defenceless. Attlee agreed with Churchill that this would be irresponsible folly; attention turned to the evacuation of British troops from France. As General Brooke retreated towards Dunkirk the War Cabinet discussed the option of

making peace with Germany. On 26 May Reynaud flew to London
to urge a joint Anglo-French approach to Italy to persuade Mussolini
to stay out of the war. Halifax saw this as an opportunity to reach an
accord with Hitler and proposed that an offer be made to Mussolini on
condition that he exercise his influence with Hitler to obtain fair and
lasting peace terms.

To this suggestion Attlee was viscerally opposed.[9] He and his
colleagues had agreed to serve under Churchill precisely because he
would fight rather than appease Hitler. To be immediately confronted
by a modified plan for appeasement undermined the basis of Labour's
joining the coalition.

In opposing Halifax, Attlee, veteran of the Gallipoli campaign,
believed that the British Expeditionary Force could be successfully
evacuated, a point of view challenged by the Chiefs of Staff. Churchill,
moreover, maintained that terms obtained at that point would not be
significantly different from terms obtainable later if Britain fought on.
Attlee agreed, pointing out that any approach to Hitler at that juncture
would reveal the weakness of the British position. On 28 May the War
Cabinet rejected Halifax's proposal.

Three days later, on 31 May, Churchill and Attlee flew to Paris for
discussions with Général Weygand. Belgium fell that day and Weygand
saw little chance of France's being able to continue. It was a sobering day
for Churchill, who strove in vain to animate the French High Command,
and for Attlee, who was shocked by the 'utter hopelessness' he saw around
the city. Léon Blum, the French socialist leader friendly with Attlee, failed
to make any impact on the French commanders who, in Attlee's eyes, with
the exception of de Gaulle, were 'a hopeless lot'.[10] Convinced that France
was already defeated, the British party returned to London.[11]

Within a month of the formation of the coalition Britain stood at
the brink of disaster. By good fortune, with the assistance of conflicting German orders, the British Expeditionary Force was evacuated
from Dunkirk between 27 May and 4 June in what Churchill termed
'a miracle of deliverance'. Desperate attempts were made to salvage
something from the 'colossal military disaster in France'.[12]

Churchill's efforts now aimed at preventing French collapse. On
11 June he was back in Paris, leaving Attlee to deliver a summary of

the military situation, a statement that was disheartening without relief. Worse followed four days later when France requested release from the agreement with Britain that neither country would surrender unilaterally. With Churchill once more in France, at Attlee's urging, a document was produced by Sir Robert Vansittart, Lord Halifax, Jean Monnet and Général de Gaulle providing for indissoluble union between France and Britain. This, Churchill and Attlee hoped, would stiffen Reynaud's will to fight on; he alone among the French political leaders showed any such inclination. De Gaulle took a copy of the document and hurried to Bordeaux, where the French government had decamped after the fall of Paris. Churchill, Attlee and Sir Archibald Sinclair prepared to travel to Southampton and by destroyer to Concarneau. As they waited for their train to leave London a message came from Downing Street that Reynaud had been overruled; no French Minister would meet the British delegation. France had fallen. Britain stood alone.

For sheer drama Attlee's first month in the War Cabinet was unsurpassed. The Battle of France was over; the Battle of Britain raged. As spring yielded to summer and summer to early autumn, the Defence Committee met frequently – forty times in the last seven months of 1940. This group included Churchill as Minister of Defence, Chamberlain, still nominally Tory leader, Attlee and the three Service Ministers, with the Chiefs of Staff in attendance. Six other members of the Labour and National Labour Parties had been appointed to key posts in the government: Bevin at the Ministry of Labour and National Service, A. V. Alexander at the Admiralty, Morrison at the Ministry of Supply, Dalton as Minister of Economic Warfare, Malcolm Macdonald at the Ministry of Health, and Jowitt as Solicitor-General.

With the passing of the threat of imminent invasion after the climax of the Battle of Britain the focus of the coalition shifted. No longer was mere survival the dominant issue, but formulation of war aims revealed disunity of purpose. When Chamberlain, already a sick man, resigned in October Churchill seized the opportunity to reorganise the Cabinet. Anderson replaced Chamberlain as Lord President of the Council; Morrison became Home Secretary and Sir Kingsley Wood went to the Treasury. Bevin and Beaverbrook joined the War Cabinet; Greenwood, at Attlee's suggestion, was given responsibility for post-war reconstruction.

When, in December, Halifax was appointed Ambassador to the United States, Eden, replacing him as Foreign Secretary, joined the Cabinet.

Looking back on this reorganisation in an interview with Francis Williams, Attlee felt that it had all worked smoothly as no one agitated about their political status. Instead they worked as a team. Beaverbrook, he admitted, was an annoyance, particularly to Bevin. 'Beaverbrook thought he could take what he wanted without consulting anybody. He was mistaken.'[13]

While there was general harmony within the Cabinet, there were fissures in the Labour Party. From late 1940 until the end of the war in Europe Attlee faced consistent pressure to impose Labour Party policy on the coalition, even to bring pressure to end the war with a negotiated peace. Maintaining loyalty both to Churchill and to the left wing of his own party required tact and diplomacy. He consistently repeated the mantra that 'first we must win the war; then we can win the peace'.[14]

The period from the declaration of war until the invasion of France has acquired the name 'the Phony War'. From September 1940 until the Japanese bombing of Pearl Harbor in December 1941 there was a similar unreality to Britain's position. With the Western Desert Force Britain resisted the Italian invasion of Egypt and, when Italy invaded Greece – to the annoyance of Hitler – Churchill, after some hesitation, decided to send an expeditionary force. A short-lived campaign of less than three weeks ensued in April 1941; the British force was evacuated amid violent criticism of the apparently pointless venture. Neither campaign appeared to be contributing to the downfall of Hitler.

Labour's commitment to the coalition came under increasing attack from within the party. An electoral truce had been agreed between the members of the coalition, whereby, for the duration of the war, neither party would challenge the other in a by-election. As successive military disasters undermined British morale and faith in the War Cabinet, Attlee endured mounting criticism within the party for his loyalty to the Churchill government. In August 1940 he responded in a balanced analysis of the strategic situation, free of propaganda, simply stating that Hitler was bent on destroying the basis of British civilisation. In a broadcast to the Empire at the end of 1940 he repeated this assertion. Hitler had won immense victories, but as long as Britain remained undefeated, Hitler's essential aim was thwarted. Britain, he said, had no quarrel with the common people of Germany and Italy, but was fighting for their liberation as well as for her own survival.[15]

Attlee was concerned that by co-operating with the hated Tories he and his Labour colleagues in the coalition would incur the charge of 'MacDonaldism'. The liberation of 'the common people of Germany and Italy' was congruent with *Labour's Peace Aims*, but little was being achieved towards that lofty goal. Attlee, Bevin and Morrison might be invaluable to the coalition, but that loyalty was not improving the electoral chances of the Labour Party. Attlee, moreover, an invaluable administrator within the government, was not, at this stage of the war, enhancing his public image. If the war were to end in victory for the Allies – at that point a distant prospect – credit for the victory would accrue to Churchill and Eden. The Labour Party might face an election with similar results to those of 1931. Chuter Ede drew that comparison when, following an aggressive speech by Bevan in the House,[16] he wrote to Attlee in February 1941 that 'a minority of the party are trying to recreate the position of 1929 and 1931 when those members of the party who were in the government were treated as if they had no real connection with the party'. It was vital, Ede wrote, that party members were loyal to party decisions.[17]

In a speech in Glasgow in March, Attlee set out his position bluntly. Unity in the face of the enemy demanded suspension of party political strife, but people should not give up considering and discussing social, political and economic questions. It was folly to think that Britain could or should seek to restore everything to the same condition as it was in 1939. 'We shall have moved into a new world,' he said. 'We have already moved from the old.'[18]

In November 1939 Morrison had raised the fundamental question of 'What are we fighting for?' Attlee never doubted that the struggle was for the survival of civilisation, a notion distinct from his faith in the eventual triumph of socialism. His basic premise was that the old world of capitalism and spheres of influence was defunct, amply demonstrated by the failure of the Baldwin and Chamberlain governments. He was equally certain on two points: that it was morally incumbent on everyone, socialist or not, to unite in the effort to defeat Nazism and, once that had been achieved, the shift to socialism and a supra-national collective security was inevitable. The commitment to the one should not exclude the commitment to planning the other. This theme, consistently repeated, assumed that the demise of the Old Order was proven. Moreover, it provides clear empirical evidence for his claim in 1945 that, while there had been an electoral truce, there had never been a political truce between the Labour and Conservative Parties.

In June he expanded that message in a speech at Chesterfield. Strongly supportive of Churchill's determination to fight wherever possible, he pointed out that losses were minimal compared with those suffered in France in the last war. Britain, he said, was fighting a ruthless enemy and must smash or be smashed. The world, he said, had become a jungle and but for Britain's isolated position, she too might have fallen. Had Europe been united in spirit, 'the Nazi monster would have been strangled at birth'.[19]

He was not disingenuous. His support for Churchill, the unique and irreplaceable war leader, was absolute. His conviction that, absent a war, Churchill was an anachronism is equally certain. He pointed at disunity among nations as responsible for the success of Nazi Germany for, had there been unity, there would have been no war. From that proposition it is a short step to maintaining that the only way to ensure unity is to have it imposed by an organisation that transcends national interests. Such an organisation, he argued plausibly and consistently, could only exist in a world where capitalist advantage was banished – in short, a socialist world.

The strategic situation was radically altered on 22 June when Hitler turned east. On the following day Attlee renewed the theme of disunity providing Hitler the opportunity to defeat countries in detail. 'If there is still anyone in this country who believes it is possible to get a negotiated peace with the Nazis,' he said, 'he must be an absolute fool'. This, of course, is exactly what Labour had been condemning the Tories for believing in the 1930s. The invasion of Russia should not cause people to relax, he warned. 'We are resolved to destroy Hitler and every vestige of the Nazi regime. As the Prime Minister said, we will never parley.'[20]

This support for Churchill was not only political good sense; Attlee was also utterly sincere. He knew that Churchill alone could provide the visage of determined, warlike resistance that was essential to the nation's will to fight. During the summer he repeated that belief, answering his critics while steadily increasing his own visibility.

In July he repeated the caution that there must be no relaxation of effort because Hitler had turned to the east. Hitler wants to prove that he is greater than Napoleon, he said. Hence his attack on the Soviet Union and his determination to overcome Britain. The danger at this juncture was that Hitler would appeal to those who advocated peace at any price. The responsibility for defeating Hitler lay with Britain. The world had changed since the days when one would hear of a faraway battle and go about one's business. The battles were 'in North Africa and at the same time all around us in the Battle of Britain, the Battle of the Atlantic.'[21]

Four days later the BBC sent out a broadcast in German, a paean in praise of Attlee. Hitler consistently branded Churchill as a war criminal who deceived Britons by prolonging a war that the majority would reject. The BBC's portrait of Attlee, Churchill's political opponent, calmly and steadfastly helping to lead Britain through the war while planning for a better post-war world, was designed to encourage anti-Hitler groups inside Germany.

> It was his quality of quiet resolution that made his general give Attlee that dangerous task at Gallipoli a quarter of a century ago. By the same quiet resolution, backed by manifold experience, unbending courage and tireless energy, Attlee has done very much to lead the people of London through Germany's great bombardment from the air; he has made and he will make an immense personal contribution to the destruction of the Fascists and Nazis and to the building of a better world for Britain, for Germany and for all mankind.[22]

By characterising Attlee as an unbending, tireless patriot the broadcast defused Hitler's claims that Churchill was a wild, lone warmonger. By reviving the image of 'Major Attlee' the BBC underscored his commitment to Britain's war effort and by highlighting his dedication to creating a more egalitarian post-war world painted him as a humanist who would abhor exacting penance from Germans duped by Hitler. It was a fine piece of propaganda and, if it was an accurate picture of how he was viewed by the majority of Britons, then Attlee was indeed polishing his public persona.

In August Churchill left for the Atlantic Conference with Roosevelt in Placentia Bay. Just before leaving he wrote to Attlee regarding a statement on the war situation in the Commons. He urged him to put off delivering the statement until after the recess but added, 'However, I leave the matter entirely to your judgment, as I am sure you would make a very excellent survey.'

Attlee, in character, did not defer the address but immediately set about drafting his statement and by the following day this was ready. Things have improved since a year ago, he assured the House.[23] Germany was now fighting on two fronts. But we must not relax. The House was aware that everything possible was being done to aid the USSR. Meanwhile, he added, the Battle of the Atlantic was taking a smaller toll on shipping. It was a lucid and factual statement of the strategic position, to which Attlee had given great thought, as he described it to Tom: 'I had to take the place of the PM last week as the reviewer of the war situation, no easy thing to follow such an artist. I eschewed embroidery and stuck to a plain statement. It is no use trying to stretch the bow of Ulysses.'[24]

The meeting between Roosevelt and Churchill at Placentia Bay marked a milestone in relations between the two leaders. It was important for Attlee too for several reasons. First, he was demonstrably competent to act as Churchill's *locum* during a longish absence. He described this experience as well in a letter to Tom. 'I addressed yesterday my biggest audience to date in blowing the gaff on the PM's meeting with FDR', he wrote. 'You will have realised that I have for some time been running the show here which means a bit of extra work. One is a bit tired as telegrams of importance come in at any time so I have not been home except for the inside of last Sunday.'[25]

Second, as exchanges between Churchill and Attlee show,[26] he impressed Churchill with his ability to roust Cabinet Members from their beds at midnight and chair a meeting to approve the proposed Joint Declaration (which became the Atlantic Charter) in an expeditious manner. Churchill's description of the sequence of events in *The Grand Alliance* reveals a growing mutual confidence between the two. His initial cable is greatly less bombastic, more intimate in tone, than many of his memoranda. He talks freely of FDR's likely reaction before saying, 'You should summon the full War Cabinet, with any others you may think necessary, to meet tonight and please let me have your views without the slightest delay'. Churchill finished dictating the telegrams at about 2.00 p.m. and had the War Cabinet's 'most helpful reply' in his hands within twelve hours. This had been achieved by Attlee's gathering members of the War Cabinet for a meeting at 1.45 a.m., at which there was full attendance.

The response of the War Cabinet made certain minor suggestions of wording and emphasis, which Churchill acknowledged in a cable to Attlee.[27] He was clearly impressed at Attlee's speed and efficiency in handling the matter; for this he thanked him as it enabled him to leave Placentia Bay a day earlier than planned. On the same day he cabled, 'Many thanks for your kind message. I am delighted you will broadcast statement and declaration yourself … I read with much pleasure your admirable war statement at end of session.'[28]

Third, after persistently reassuring his party colleagues that Labour was faithful to socialist principles in its handling of the war, Attlee announced the Atlantic Charter, giving substance to his claim. At the TUC conference in Edinburgh in September he stressed the Charter's significance. It gave expression to the desire of ordinary people to live in freedom. 'For this we must keep fighting', he urged. 'This war will not be won for us by anyone else.'[29] For the first time he linked the continued fighting with a tangible step towards the extension of socialism.

In spite of the enormous sense of anticipation aroused by the Placentia Bay meeting, Britain still stood alone on the Western Front. The country had been at war for two years with no sign of relief; there was still austerity; wartime controls continued to irk. It fell to Attlee to reassure the public that their sacrifices were worthwhile. In October he spoke in Cambridge, balancing current problems with optimism for the future.[30] Increasingly, Attlee became the medium through which the strategic situation was communicated.

Such speeches underscore the importance of Attlee's position in the coalition. For the bulldog spirit, the defiant, never-say-die challenge to Nazism, Churchill could not be bettered. But as the war dragged on with no evidence of breakthrough, the country needed reassurance as well as rhetoric. This was Attlee's strength, his ability to breathe life into the Home Front, to continue to buoy up flagging enthusiasm, to reiterate that the struggle was worthwhile, that ultimately Britain would emerge from the war as a better, more egalitarian country. He will have been well aware of the electoral advantages this offered; it is beyond doubt that he emerged as a national leader from this unceasing round of addresses.[31]

In October he escaped the treadmill of London and attended the conference of the International Labour Organisation in New York. He enjoyed New York and was pleasantly surprised by Washington. He had two meetings with Roosevelt, which confirmed his and Churchill's view that the President would bring America into the war as soon as he could. Roosevelt impressed him profoundly as a determined leader; he was also greatly struck by Frances Perkins, the Secretary of Labor. Of the American trade unions, however, he was deeply suspicious, astounded by their materialism and lack of socialist doctrine. He summed up the visit in a letter to Tom, commenting that the 'supporters of the New Deal have the right idea'.[32] In a broadcast after his return he again emphasised his respect for FDR and the New Deal in words that went beyond the ritual propaganda required to woo America. Referring to FDR as 'that great champion of democracy', he assured listeners that, while there were many differences between Americans and Britons, they were united in the things that really mattered.[33]

Less than two months after this visit, on 7 December, aircraft launched from the Japanese Imperial Navy bombed the United States naval base at Pearl Harbor in Hawaii. Roosevelt promptly declared war on Japan; when Hitler declared war on the United States four days later, Churchill, reckoning that America was now 'in the harem', flew to Washington for consultation with Roosevelt. This was the first of the several wartime meetings between the Allies and it fell to Attlee to report on the war's progress. 'I'm sure that members would have liked an address from the Prime Minister in his own inimitable style', he began, 'but I'm equally certain they understand why he's in Washington.' There followed a very thorough and detailed analysis of the strategic situation.[34]

Churchill was absent for four weeks and Attlee 'held the baby'. During those weeks he came into closer contact with General Brooke, who replaced Sir John Dill as Chief of the Imperial General Staff (CIGS) before the Prime Minister's departure. Brooke found working with the mercurial Churchill difficult and he was pleased to have the chance to get through work while he was away; the amount he had to read was so great that his eyes suffered. He was greatly relieved to find that Attlee, whom he had initially discounted as Churchill's 'Yes Man',[35] was brisk and efficient in dealing with committee work, as expeditious as Brooke himself. On 15 December he recorded that there was an 'afternoon Cabinet at 5 p.m. and a Defence Committee meeting at 6 p.m. which lasted until 8 p.m., run by Attlee very efficiently and quickly'.[36]

Brooke's experience in December with Attlee in the chair contrasted starkly with Churchill's handling of meetings. In his first week as CIGS, before Churchill sailed to Washington, the Prime Minister, Attlee, Eden and the Chiefs of Staff met. Churchill used the meeting to berate the Chiefs when Air Chief Marshal Portal tried to prevent the transfer of ten squadrons from North Africa to Russia at the end of the Libyan offensive. Brooke recorded his impressions of the meeting, commenting that 'This produced the most awful outburst of temper. We were told that we did nothing but obstruct his intentions, we had no ideas of our own and, whenever he produced ideas, we produced nothing but objections etc. etc.' Attlee, he recalled, had pacified Churchill once, but Churchill later slammed his papers together and left the room. 'God knows where we should be without him', Brooke wondered, 'but God knows where we shall go with him.'[37]

In late 1941 and early 1942 Attlee gave a series of daily interviews to the socialist author-journalist Ritchie Calder, laying out Labour's plans for the future. In the first interview he set out what 'social security' meant in socialist policy:

An adequate and rising standard of living

Security against ill health, unemployment, old age

A well-equipped home in healthy surroundings for all families

Full and equal education for all

Complete medical care throughout one's life

A legal system accessible to all

High standards of working conditions

Abolition of privilege, economic inequality and wealth distinction.

These benefits, he stressed, involved reciprocal duties.

In the second interview Calder asked how that differed from the 'Homes Fit for Heroes' battle cry after the Great War that led to the 1919 Housing Act. Attlee responded that the standard of building must be higher than after the Great War: 'We want to see a better and brighter Britain. We want a spring cleaning that will not only sweep away the drab industrial areas, the legacy of nineteenth-century exploitation, and our deceptive rural slums, but will scour the very air itself.'[38]

As for 'Homes Fit for Heroes', everyone was a hero in the conditions the war had brought. To a populace that during the Second World War saw almost four million homes destroyed, this goal must have sounded Utopian. By stressing that 'everyone is a hero' Attlee offered a society that not merely applauded British grit but substantially rewarded it.

The third interview raised a more controversial issue when Calder asked about the Labour policy for ownership of the land. Attlee responded that 'without common ownership of the land there can be neither efficient planning nor efficient agriculture. To ensure lasting prosperity for agriculture, the state must act as the good landlord.' This was a departure from the principle that mines, the City and transport must be nationalised. The interview raised the possibility of collectivisation of agriculture, something that smacked of the Soviet experiment.

As so often, Attlee had the delicate task of balancing demands from the left of the Labour Party with policies that would not alarm the centrist voter. In the interviews with Calder he was successful.

The first two weeks of February marked the lowest point of Britain's military fortunes: the loss of two capital ships en route to Singapore, Japanese advances in Burma, Malaya and Borneo, a successful drive by Rommel in North Africa – these combined to erode Churchill's authority. This was further eroded on 15 February when Singapore, defended by 85,000 men, fell to a Japanese force of 35,000. There were calls from Tory backbenchers for the Prime Minister to relinquish some of his responsibilities and, faced with a possible revolt, Churchill summoned Attlee to discuss an immediate Cabinet reshuffle.

It is a measure of the rise of Attlee's star that in the reorganisation Churchill retained Bevin over Beaverbrook, appointed Cripps Lord Privy Seal and member of the War Cabinet, and officially gave Attlee the post that he had unofficially filled for two years, appointing him Deputy Prime Minister. This, Churchill later wrote, was 'a change in form rather than in fact' as Attlee's 'simple, steadfast loyalty amid such strains was invaluable'.[39] Not only had Attlee consolidated his own position, the importance of his and his Labour colleagues' contribution, already known to parliamentary and military insiders, was publicly recognised.

ENDNOTES

1   When Attlee had telephoned the party's response, he was unsure if Churchill or Halifax would replace Chamberlain. The Labour Party had a preference for Halifax, partly because of his more conciliatory attitude to India. (Gerhard Weinberg, *A World At Arms*, Cambridge University Press, 1994.)
2   *As It Happened*, pp. 158–9.
3   Attlee, 'The Churchill I Knew' in *Churchill by His Contemporaries*, p. 14.
4   *Hansard*, HC Deb, 24 February 1942, col. 42.
5   For Churchill's account of the formation and structure of the coalition see Churchill, *The Second World War*, vol. 2, 'Their Finest Hour', pp. 8–22.
6   *A Prime Minister Remembers*, p. 40. CAC: ATLE 1/16.
7   *Hansard*, HC Deb, 22 May 1940, cols 154–159.
8   Bodleian: MS. Attlee, dep. 1, Broadcast by Attlee, 22 May 1940.
9   Churchill, *The Second World War*, vol. 2, 'Their Finest Hour', pp. 123–124. Roy Jenkins, *Churchill*, p. 602; Gilbert, *Churchill: A Life*, p. 651; Andrew Roberts, *The Storm of War*. 2009, London: Allen Lane, p. 69.
10   For a full summary of the meeting, Spears, *Assignment to Catastrophe*, vol. 1, pp. 292–319.
11   *As It Happened*, p. 164.
12   Churchill, *The Second World War*, vol. 2, 'Their Finest Hour', chapter 5.
13   Williams, *A Prime Minister Remembers*, pp. 40–41.
14   The theme recurs throughout Attlee's speeches in the war years. See, for example, Broadcast of 28 November 1941. Bodleian: MS. Attlee, dep. 4.
15   Bodleian: MS. Attlee, dep. 1.
16   *Hansard*, HC Deb, 13 February 1941, cols. 1598–1605.
17   Bodleian: MS. Attlee, dep. 1, Ede to CRA, 14 February 1941.
18   Bodleian: MS. Attlee, dep. 2, 30 March 1941.
19   Bodleian: MS. Attlee, dep. 3, 13 June 1941.
20   Bodleian: MS. Attlee, dep. 3, 23 June 1941.
21   Bodleian: MS. Attlee, dep. 3, Speech at Neath, 13 July 1941.
22   Bodleian: MS. Attlee, dep. 3, BBC broadcast, 17 July 1941.
23   *Hansard*, HC Deb, 6 August 1941, cols 1973–81.
24   Letter to Tom Attlee, 9 August 1941.
25   Letter to Tom Attlee, 15 August 1941. The text of Attlee's address is at CAC: ATLE 2/2.
26   Churchill, *The Second World War*, Vol. 3, 'The Grand Alliance', pp. 442–447 and at several points in MS. Attlee, dep. 3.
27   PM to Lord Privy Seal, 12 Aug.1941. Churchill, *The Second World War*, v. 3, 'The Grand Alliance', pp. 446–7.
28   PM to Lord Privy Seal, 13 Aug.1941. Churchill, *The Second World War*, v. 3, 'The Grand Alliance', p. 448.
29   Bodleian: MS. Attlee, dep. 3, TUC conference, 1–4 September 1941.
30   Bodleian: MS. Attlee, dep. 4, Speech in Cambridge, 8 October 1941.
31   See, for example, his speech at the National Defence Public Interest Committee Luncheon on 15 October 1941. Bodleian: MS. Attlee dep. 4.
32   Letter to Tom Attlee, 21 November 1941.
33   Bodleian: MS. Attlee, dep. 4, Broadcast of 28 November 1941.
34   *Hansard*, HC Deb, 8 January 1942, cols 82–91.
35   Brooke later qualified his view, writing, 'Somehow the presence of these four 'colleagues' of Winston's at these discussions always infuriated me … It was so palpable that they were brought along by him to support him, which they proceeded to do irrespective of the degree of lunacy connected with some of Winston's proposals. It must be remembered that the war had been going on for several years and tempers were becoming distinctly frayed'. In retrospect, he revised his opinion of Attlee's role. (Danchev and Todman, *War Diaries*, Entry for 6 March 1944, p. 529.) Attlee always reposed the greatest confidence in Brooke and it was not until January 1946 that Brooke could gain Attlee's approval to hand over his position to Montgomery. David Fraser, *Alanbrooke*, p. 503.
36   Diary of Field Marshal Lord Alanbrooke, Entry for 15 December 1941, *War Diaries*, p. 211.
37   Ibid. pp. 238–239.
38   Bodleian: MS. Attlee, dep. 5, December 1941 and January 1942.
39   Churchill, *The Second World War*, vol. 4, 'The Hinge of Fate' pp. 79–80.

CHAPTER EIGHT

DEPUTY PRIME MINISTER, 1942–1945

In the Cabinet reorganisation of February 1942 Attlee was appointed Secretary of State for Dominion Affairs as well as Deputy Prime Minister. Four days later he spoke to his new constituency in a luncheon speech in the City of London. Highlighting the contribution made by Commonwealth countries fighting side-by-side with British units, he declared that Britain was not alone in the dark days of 1940 – because the Commonwealth was there. Unity was essential to victory. Together Britain and the Commonwealth would rebuild civilisation, 'discarding the evil and making more splendid the good.'[1]

There is a stark contrast between Churchill, aching to kill more Germans, to wreak terrible vengeance on the Nazis and their followers, and Attlee, referring once more to 'civilisation' and the need to improve conditions after the war. He was canny in never attempting to ape Churchill's bellicose rhetoric. With every speech he improved his standing as a credible peacetime leader, fixing the image of Churchill as an irreplaceable asset in wartime, but only while the fighting raged. In March, in a speech during Stepney Warship Week, he personified the new spirit of optimism since the United States had entered the war. 'If you had asked me in August 1940 whether in March 1942 we should still be holding Gibraltar, Malta and Egypt', he said, 'I could not have given you a very confident yes'.[2]

This was a rousing speech, once more not bellicose but positive. He had moved subtly but significantly from mere reporting to venturing strategic opinions. By linking August 1940 to March 1942 he associated himself with progress made. Without in any way attempting to remove credit from Churchill he underscored his position within the wartime team of rivals that had achieved this progress.

On the following day he made another ringing speech in Liverpool. After a lengthy *tour d'horizon* of the war he expanded a familiar theme. 'This fight is not just a fight on the material plane,' he said. 'It is a spiritual contest between good and evil. Hitler is the incarnation of the dark side of the character of the German people. In every nation as in every human being there is a dark and a light side.' Hitler aimed to destroy the civilisation 'built up through the centuries on the teaching of Christ.' The Führer and his followers hated freedom. Hitler, like Milton's Satan, had said, 'Evil, be thou my God'.[3]

He concluded with a rousing paragraph:

> *Every one of us has within him the Fifth Column of selfishness and indifference. If we wish to be worthy of the high duty to which this generation has been called we must purge our own souls and preserve in our everyday tasks the spirit of devotion and sacrifice displayed by so many of our fellow men and women in the days of the Blitz.*

This speech, filled with religious references, was both tailored for the audience – in the archdiocese with the largest Catholic population in England – and a statement of Attlee's ethical principles. In the struggle to preserve civilisation he explicitly linked civilisation with Christianity. If we accept Christian values, he often argued, then we will be led to socialism as the ethical successor to Christianity. Paying tribute to the courage of those who bore the hardships of the Blitz and appealing to them as the leader of the party that would reward that fortitude with a better life once the war was over, he grew from politician to moral leader.

As Leader of the Labour Party and Deputy Prime Minister, he sensed that power was almost within his grasp. Yet he never exploited his position to play party politics, despite pressure and suggestions that the Tories were less scrupulous.[4] He remained loyal to the spirit of the electoral truce throughout the war, even writing to the Labour MP for Rhondda West to seek his support in supporting Sir James Grigg, a non-party coalition candidate.[5]

After the fall of Singapore Churchill dismissed David Margesson, the Secretary of State for War, replacing him with Grigg, the Permanent Under-Secretary of State at the War Office. This unconventional move necessitated finding Grigg a seat in the House of Commons and, with the appointment of the Member for Cardiff East to the County Court bench, a vacancy became available. Grigg may have been non-party as Attlee suggests, but his value to the direction of the war would be enormous – as his smooth working with General Brooke was to demonstrate – and this, for Attlee, was the only issue that was relevant.

Despite the optimism that he displayed publicly, the first six months of Attlee's time as Deputy Prime Minister coincided with the low point of British morale. When Churchill replaced General Wavell with General Auchinleck as Commander-in-Chief Middle East in July 1941, the new C-in-C achieved initial success, relieving Tobruk and driving Rommel back to el Agheila. The apparent gains, however, were illusory as Rommel regrouped and routed the disorganised Eighth Army, forcing Auchinleck back into Egypt, where he established a defensive position at el Alamein.

In mid-June 1942 Churchill was in Washington for the Second Washington Conference and Attlee, once more 'holding the baby', reported on the situation to the House. He began his appraisal by reminding Members that three weeks before Churchill had predicted heavy fighting in Libya, but 'whatever may be the result, there is no shadow of doubt that Rommel's plans for his initial offensive have gone completely wrong and this failure has cost him dear in men and material.'[6]

To Attlee now fell the task of apprising the House of the reversal that Auchinleck had suffered. He read Auchinleck's report, which concluded with the passage, 'The garrison is still fighting hard and a gallant attempt to save what appears to be an impossible situation is being made. But the fall of Tobruk is imminent if it has not already fallen.' After a pause he continued, 'This is the end of General Auchinleck's statement. Since then we have received definite news of the fall of Tobruk.'[7]

Aware of the effect that this would have in Britain and of the renewed criticism of the direction of the war that it would fan, Attlee drafted and redrafted this speech, making many alterations of emphasis.[8] Ultimately, however, there was bad news to report and Attlee characteristically performed the task in a crisp and businesslike way.

Unspoken in his report, however, were profound doubts about the direction of the fighting in North Africa. Earlier in June he had submitted a report to the Defence Committee, concluding that the Crusader tank had been hurried into production before defects had been identified and corrected. Rapid production had been obtained at the cost of reliability and fighting efficiency, and Eighth Army was fighting with tanks inferior to German tanks both in the quality of their guns and in reliability.[9] On 6 July he sent a 'secret and personal' memorandum to Eden, detailing his concerns and suggesting that they might discuss them 'prior to bringing the matter up more formally'. The memorandum poses fundamental questions concerning the organisation of troops, essentially concluding that 'our military minds are establishment-bound' and that Rommel, commanding from the front, was repeatedly outpacing the Allied forces who were hampered by an elaborate and cumbersome chain of command. This, together with the lack of coordination between land and air forces, was, he argued, the root cause of Auchinleck's setbacks.[10]

During July 1942 Churchill became increasingly concerned about Auchinleck's lack of offensive drive and flew to Cairo on 2 August, having previously made arrangements to fly on to Moscow to meet Stalin. On 5 August, after a typical day of touring bases, asking questions, forming impressions, he cabled Attlee in a positively chatty manner, almost as if he was formulating his ideas as he wrote. He had no recommendations to make at that point but was giving Attlee notice that these would soon be forthcoming. On the following day came the cable with its 'drastic and immediate change ... in the High Command'. He requested Attlee to present proposals to the War Cabinet to divide the Middle East command, to replace Auchinleck with Alexander, to replace Alexander with Montgomery and to put General Gott in command of Eighth Army.

In asking Attlee to present these sweeping changes to the War Cabinet, the Prime Minister reposed considerable trust in him. With the exception of having doubts about the division of the two commands, the War Cabinet accepted the Prime Minister's proposals.

When Gott's plane was shot down, Churchill asked Attlee to arrange for Montgomery to be sent to Cairo as soon as possible by special plane. The War Cabinet had already assembled at 11.15 p.m. to discuss the day's cables; the Gott cable arrived during the meeting. The shocked Cabinet sat until dawn making necessary arrangements.[11]

From Cairo Churchill flew to Moscow with the unenviable task of informing Stalin that there would be no second front in Europe in 1942; he then returned to Cairo. From there he cabled Attlee with copies to Eden, Ismay and Portal concerning air support for the Soviet southern flank.[12] Coordination to authorise action was left to Attlee. This method was also employed with a cable to Attlee, Ismay 'and others concerned' on 21 August concerning American handling of the Trans-Persian railway. On 20–21 August Churchill toured the Western Desert and reported to Attlee on his observations. The note is fully informative, detailed and comprehensive; its style shows clearly the friendly terms on which Churchill and Attlee operated.

In July the Home Intelligence Division of the Ministry of Information submitted a Reconstruction Report from which five main points emerged:

> *Fear of unemployment was the main concern among those who think about the future.*
>
> *The second concern of general interest was about housing.*
>
> *Among the intelligent minority education took the place of housing and with everyone else it took a good third place.*
>
> *There was also great enthusiasm for a forward movement in the field of social security.*
>
> *The problem of the post-war political settlement aroused less interest among the general public than any other problem of reconstruction. Only on the treatment of Germany was feeling strongly and emphatically expressed.*[13]

It is clear, the Report concluded, that the public has some very definite and hopeful ideas about domestic reconstruction.

This must have been encouraging to the Labour Party as people's principal concerns were in areas where Labour had committed itself to action. International affairs, beyond the curbing of Germany, were of little interest. It must, however, have been disappointing to Attlee that, according to the report, the Atlantic Charter 'excites neither interest nor discussion' and was thought 'too nebulous'. On the other hand, Labour's domestic policy for the post-war was congruent with the concerns of the majority of Britons.

Again, it was Attlee's task to explain the dismal strategic situation. This involved a schedule of appearances in every corner of the country, designed to boost fading morale. In September he made a speech in Aberdeen that showed him at his most objective and direct. He firmly nailed his socialist colours to the mast of war aims and treated a Labour government as a natural sequel to wartime hardship.[14]

Patriotic in theme yet devoid of cliché, it was an inspiring address. He told the truth – and that directness was the basis of his appeal to both soldier and working man. The general lack of rhetorical flourish, moreover, ensured that when he did employ a rhetorical device it was effective. A response to the speech was printed in the local Aberdeen newspaper four days later:

> *To the Deputy Prime Minister who came on a weekend journey to this fair city:*
>   *We were glad to see you, sir, and glad to hear you. It is no news to you that you*
> *are not a Winston Churchill. When he was fashioned the mould was broken. But*
> *you have your own fine qualities, and one of them is a deep ingrained sincerity. That*
> *was the chief impression created by your speech, and it caused many of your hearers to*
> *revise the mental picture of you they had carried forward from the pre-war era.*[15]

Attlee had grown in stature since 1940, particularly during 1942 when he had a full programme of speechmaking. His addresses during this period have a number of central themes to which he returns frequently – the Atlantic Charter, Hitler as Satan, the British tendency to self-deprecation, the contribution of the dominions, and the need to win the peace as well as the war – but he scrupulously wove new material into each speech. He never delivered a set piece and clearly took seriously each invitation; every address went through several drafts and was subjected to small but significant alterations. For his speech to the Royal Empire Society in December, for example, he declined to commit himself to a particular subject in advance, preferring to make the speech topical and more appealing.[16]

Within his own party, however, he continued to face criticism for his and his colleagues' support of the coalition. Four days after the Aberdeen speech he defended that support to the NEC, bluntly reiterating party policy. There was individual criticism of Churchill, sometimes violent, he conceded. But the Labour Party still possessed confidence in his government and supported it, not blindly but fully and generously.[17]

At the end of October came the turning point in the Allies' fortunes. Montgomery, who after taking command of the Eighth Army had insisted on taking time to rebuild morale, launched his long-awaited offensive at el Alamein. During the first three days of November Eighth Army broke through the German lines, forcing Rommel's Desert Army to retreat. Over the next two weeks the Red Army first held Stalingrad, then launched an offensive to encircle the German Sixth Army. In the Pacific, American marines, after a three-month campaign, forced the Japanese onto the defensive on Guadalcanal and by the end of the year held the strategic initiative. In three different theatres victories, each of which proved to be a strategic milestone, had been achieved.

During the same period, three amphibious task forces under the command of General Eisenhower landed at Casablanca, Oran and Algiers. Apart from the military significance of the landings, the greater strategic importance had a massive rallying effect in Britain. The vast might of American industrial production was now committed to the defeat of Germany. Hitler's fall was now merely a matter of time.

Ironically, the surge in morale created a novel set of problems for Attlee and the Labour Party. Success on the battlefield, long awaited, enabled the Tories to distract attention from post-war problems, encouraging Britons to exult in their changed military fortunes. Bevan accurately identified this tactic and subjected the government to continuing criticism. Attlee, persistently loyal to Churchill, but inevitably his future political opponent, was equally concerned at the propaganda benefit accruing to the Tories but powerless to counter it. Churchill met Roosevelt at Casablanca; the American President issued a call for unconditional surrender.

Claiming to have been surprised by Roosevelt, Churchill cabled Attlee and Eden to seek their opinion as to whether Italy should be included in the demand.[18] They responded that 'the balance of advantage' was against excluding Italy as it would cause uncertainty in Turkey and the Balkans if Italy were not included; moreover, knowing that they would be forced to unconditionally surrender would have an adverse effect on Italian morale.[19] Attlee delivered a comprehensive analysis of the strategic situation to the House of Commons when Parliament reassembled in the New Year,[20] but he rightly assessed that it was Churchill and the Tory Party that would most benefit from the improved strategic situation.

He had few options. In a speech at Keighley in January he attempted to balance the books. For the first time, he told his audience, the United Nations held the initiative; the German war machine was no longer hurtling along from conquest to conquest. Victory, he said, would provide a great opportunity to rebuild Britain and the rest of the world. In Britain, however, there would be urgent problems in the fields of planning, reconstruction, physical rebuilding, land utilisation, location of industry, education, unification and extension of the social and allied services.[21] To a nation now brimming with confidence this litany of difficulties to be overcome was an unwelcome depressant.

Churchill had defined his aim in one word – 'Victory'. He had, in this blunt statement of ambition, limited his focus to the period it took to achieve that victory. Attlee, by contrast, repeatedly looked beyond the German surrender. This was not expressing a need to win at the Peace Conference but to ensure that the world was a better place once Nazism had been overcome. He identified with the common man. That identification was powerful, based on his recognition of what had preceded the war, the structural damage during the war and, as a result, the immense job of rebuilding from the ground up once it was over. But the constant reminder that the pre-war economy, already frail, would be immeasurably worse once the fighting was over was now less welcome.

During the first few months of 1943 Attlee and Eden, whom the Prime Minister used as his principal lieutenants, struck an informal but effective alliance when they combined in attempts to block Churchill's more exotic plans. The first confrontation came soon after the Casablanca Conference when Churchill persuaded Roosevelt to join him in Turkey and pressure President Inönü to bring the Turks into the war. Attlee and Eden jointly cabled the Prime Minister that this would court either 'a rebuff or a failure'.[22] The latter, however, was relentless and, after four days of cables to and fro, the War Cabinet agreed to the *démarche*.[23] In May, when Admirals Pound and King[24] urged occupation of the Azores, the buccaneering idea appealed to Churchill and once more Attlee and Eden strenuously urged delay.[25] Later in the war General

Brooke frequently observed this alliance at work, privately grateful that there were others apart from himself who were willing and capable of standing up to the mercurial Prime Minister.[26]

From 17 to 19 February, twenty months after Greenwood had announced the Beveridge Committee, the committee's report was debated in the House of Commons. Attlee was disappointed with the outcome of the debate, writing to Tom that, while Morrison had been first class, 'so many of our fellows, good men not mischief makers, tend to use their hearts to the exclusion of their heads.'[27]

In March he wrote to George Shepherd, the National Agent of the Labour Party, expressing his concern that the party was losing prestige and asking for suggestions on how it might be restored. Given that the economic transition from war to peace would be infinitely harder than that from peace to war and that all of Europe would be in a state of economic distress after the war, it was vital to know whether the party was respected or held in contempt. People, he believed, were no longer thrilled by the prospect of a Labour victory; 'the socialist case must be stated with positive vigour.' He candidly defined the problem that faced him personally. 'It is not easy to work with a man in the afternoon in the Cabinet Room' he wrote, 'and then in the evening appear to differ from him on the public platform.'[28] As Bevan and Attlee had feared, in March Churchill made a pre-emptive grab for the moral high ground, announcing the government's commitment to improve standards of living in Britain, the creation of a four-year plan of transition after Germany's defeat, and hinting at the continuation of 'a National Government comprising the best men of all parties who are willing to serve'.[29]

To a Labour Party meeting on 7 April Attlee restricted himself to a bland but firm statement: 'No one can tell now when or under what circumstances the war will end or what will be the situation when a general election takes place … Meanwhile the Labour Party, like other parties, is entirely uncommitted and remains free to take its own decision at the appropriate time.'[30]

Put simply, this was an injunction to the left to back off, to await the outcome of events and to trust the Labour members of the coalition to consolidate the party's position as Attlee had been consistently striving to do. Fears of a repetition of 1918, however, and memories of the catastrophic events of 1931 refused to evaporate. These concerns were intensified by successes of Independent Party and Common Wealth candidates in by-elections. Concern grew on the left that a unique opportunity was being squandered and that the electoral truce was a typical Tory trick. His only viable course, he reasoned, was to repeat the same message, associate Labour with the strategic successes, increase his visibility as a leader, and let events take their course.

Accordingly, he threw himself into an even busier round of appearances, spanning the widest possible social spectrum. In May a letter to Tom perfectly expressed his feelings:

> *I have had rather a strenuous bout of speech making lately with the crowding of events in North Africa which allowed but scant time for preparation. It is not easy to sub for the PM. It is obviously futile to try to put on Saul's armour, but I seek in a more pedestrian style to preserve a mean between dignity of language and dullness. I have too in rendering thanks to be careful to avoid sins of omission.*[31]

Nonetheless, he showed no inclination to slow down. During June a plethora of diverse organisations contacted Attlee to invite him as a speaker. These included the English Speaking Union, Divisional Labour Parties, Youth Committees, High Commissioners, Ambassadors, the Child Health Planning Group, the Harrow Youth Rally, Harrow Girls Pre-Service Organisation, the Institute for British-American Understanding, Yugoslav House, the Anglo-Soviet Committee, the Corporation of London, the Newspaper Proprietors Association, the Conference of the British Federation of Social Workers, the New Zealand Society, the Women's Temperance League, the Society of Labour Candidates, the Dunkirk Anniversary Concert, Wings for Victory Week – all requested his presence and 80 per cent of them were accepted. This shows a remarkable availability for a man of his commitments.[32]

Occasionally he paused to marvel at how his life had evolved; after nine years as party leader he remained modestly surprised at his success and wrote to Tom: 'Last week Vi and I went to lunch with Admiral Evans to meet King Haakon and quite unexpectedly found Olive and

Algy[33] among the guests. As we said, it is the sort of thing we should have thought unlikely twenty years ago.'[34]

In a speech at Alloa he responded head-on in public to the criticism that Labour was making too little of its opportunities. Recognising that members of the party felt frustrated by a 'government of all parties', he stressed that an electoral truce was not a political truce and reminded his audience how far socialism had advanced over four decades. Ideas once regarded as silly or, at best, visionary had become part of the ordinary make-up of the vast majority of citizens.

For examples of this progress he cited two dramatic shifts. During the 1920s unemployment was viewed as a malady caused by individual defects. Now it was accepted that it was society's duty to prevent unemployment. Second, apart from education and the Poor Law, there were practically no social services. With the Beveridge Report, Britain had come a long way from the Lloyd George Insurance Act.[35]

Labour Members of Parliament were demanding socialist solutions but the government must at the moment reflect the policy of all parties, he argued. Nothing will be achieved if all parties insist on partisan plans for the post-war period. Then, in a rousing finish, he restated his basic theme, the post-war problems. There would be difficulties, but he relied on people's courage and ability to recognise that 'we shall need all our energy if we are to win the peace.[36]

This was a stirring speech which, taken in conjunction with the speech at Greenock two days later, illustrates the changed war fortunes and, by association, the importance of a new government at war's end to win the peace. While he spoke at Alloa, Alexander's Fifteenth Army Group, comprising General Patton's Seventh Army and Montgomery's Eighth Army, were fighting their way inland from the landing beaches of Sicily. Operation HUSKY had been launched the night before and, for the first time, Allied forces were breaching the defences of Fortress Europe. Attlee assumed a new confidence, consistently hammering at the theme that the opportunities for reform offered by victory must not be squandered. The mistakes of 1918 must not be repeated. Without undermining Churchill's war leadership, he began to speak like a potential post-war Prime Minister.

In Greenock he addressed the nature of democracy, 'the cause for which we are fighting'. He looked back to people's hopes in 1918 and 'the period of disillusionment that followed'. Democracy could only survive if there was 'a constant and real desire for it'. With that desire Britain would, at the end of the war, 'offer to the world an example of how a nation can, without violence, adapt its social and economic life to the demands of a changing world and of new conceptions of social justice.'[37]

It was a splendid speech, delivered at a thrilling time as Anglo-American forces advanced in Sicily. The overarching themes are first that a socialist government had become more than a dream, that the opportunity for far-reaching social change will soon be a reality, and that together government and people could make it happen. Attlee's confidence – as an orator and future leader – had soared. Possibly he too, for the first time, had come face-to-face with the certainty of the defeat of Germany and the proximity and scale of his post-war responsibilities.

Invitations to speak continued to cross Attlee's desk in such volume that he decreed that none were to be accepted unless they were of direct concern to him.[38] This somewhat indistinct criterion helped little, however, as the invitations ranged from the Stanmore Horticultural Society (in his home town), to an invitation to meet General Wavell (Viceroy-designate of India) and a reception given by the Free French for Général d'Astier de la Vigerie. His activities and involvement were so broad that his edict did little to liberate him. He knew, moreover, that he and Bevin, the two most visible ambassadors of socialism, held a pivotal influence in the political balance.

Thus in September he was in Carmarthen, urging listeners that 'democracy is not an easy system. It may be destroyed from within as well as from without. It is not a method of government but an attitude towards life.' It demanded a constant active striving, and so the battle for the things of the spirit would not end with the defeat of Germany and Japan.[39]

In November he spoke to the same theme in Plymouth. The endless round continued as Attlee strove at the same time to pre-empt complacency among the public and disruptive criticism from inside his party. His greatest virtuosity, however, was reserved for his radio address to the nation on New Year's Eve.[40]

On that occasion, in one of his most moving addresses, Attlee spoke from his heart to the common man, stressing that everyone's war effort was vital, that it had brought success and now all needed to plan together for the future. Paying tribute to the British people, he stressed his consciousness of their hopes and fears for the future. He was mindful too of the 'great valour of the men and women serving the country'. It was, he said, a privilege to serve them.

It was an address, devoid of oratory or bombast, that struck a chord across the country. Attlee hit the right balance of confidence, optimism and humility. Sir John Simon and Edna Lloyd George were among the many that wrote to congratulate him. Letters of thanks flooded in. Even so, there was inevitably one complaint – from a farmer who was unhappy that he failed to give agriculture an adequate pat on the back.

He was gaining confidence as a speaker, both in person and on the radio. After a speech to the American Outpost on 26 January 1944 one of the group's members wrote to the president, Arthur Goodhart, praising Attlee's address as 'one of the most perfect short speeches I have ever heard'. Goodhart himself, a King's Counsel and no mean orator, added his opinion that 'I don't think you have done anything better'.[41]

Over the next three months Attlee continued to send the same message both within the Labour Party and around the country. The days of Dunkirk and the Blitz seemed to belong to history; the long-awaited invasion of north-west France was approaching; there was a growing complacency that the war was won and that Britain would soon enjoy the fruits of peace. Attlee was relentless in 'gingering up' the public and emphasising that there would be shortages and hardship in the aftermath of the war. In Sunderland and Hartlepool at the end of January, in Exeter in March, in Leeds in April he spoke with confidence of the need to continue to make sacrifices for some time yet in the knowledge that, in the long run, a socialist government would redress the ills of the 1930s and create a more just society. By then it was a familiar message, delivered with a realistic but not entirely welcome honesty, even as the coalition itself was beginning to divide along party lines.[42]

During the spring and summer of 1944 his schedule of engagements continued unabated; he was putting himself increasingly in the public eye in preparation for a post-war election. He was particularly active in speaking to youth groups – shades of Stepney – and he accepted a number of tickets for football matches at Wembley, occasions that enhanced his image as a 'man of the people'. He had played football, turning out on one occasion for Fleet FC while staying with his aunt in Hampshire, but football ranked far lower than cricket in his hierarchy of sports. Appearances at Wembley were chosen for their political value.

The crescendo of public speaking culminated shortly before the invasion of Normandy, when he spoke in Birmingham. When he reminded his audience that 'last Wednesday was the fourth anniversary of the formation of the present government', the implication was clear: the clock was now ticking towards the end of the government's five-year term. Suggesting, in an almost dramatic structure, that great changes were inevitable, he stressed the Labour Party's decision 'without hesitation to take responsibility and face all the difficulties of the situation'. But all that might count for little as 'the real criterion of social change is the change in the assumptions that are accepted by the community. Their translation into action may take time and may be incomplete, yet it is the change in ideas that counts.'[43]

Change was desirable, inevitable. Moreover, he concluded, the war had prepared Britain for change. War, he explained, breaks down little selfish opposition. The flood of new ideas mounts and passes over the last barrier and a great advance is achieved. Three weeks before D-Day, when the Allied armies would 'pass over the last barrier' and achieve that 'great advance', Attlee linked the advance of socialism with the progress of the Allies.

For his last speech before D-Day he played on his home field. He accepted an invitation from the Rev. E. F. Bonhote, the Master of Haileybury, to visit the Senior Literary Debating Society of which he had once been a member. He gave a talk on 'Parliament and Democracy' at 6.00 p.m. and by 9.30 was on his way back to Downing Street. The visit was a success and Bonhote wrote to him the following day, expressing his regret that rationing had restricted the number of guests for dinner. 'You must come again when you are Prime Minister,' the letter concluded.[44]

He was able to take a short break from London at the end of August, when he visited Italy and North Africa. It was a rapid trip but full of memories of his tour of Italy with Edric and Violet twenty-two years before. He reported to Tom that he had visited Algiers, Naples, Rome, Florence, Siena, back to Algiers and home from Rabat. He was ecstatic to be in Italy, apart from Naples whose 'lower orders' appalled him. He spoke with pride of an apt quotation from Dante that he made to a monk at Cassino, was breathless at the Blue Grotto, thrilled to have an audience with the Pope ('a gentle idealist'), impressed by the Colosseum in moonlight. He rhapsodises about the trip and seeing 'little towns' like Perugia from the air. 'I saw a good deal of Gen. Alexander whose guest I was', he concluded, 'a very fine man.'[45]

It is not surprising that he found Alexander congenial. Attlee, a pragmatic man who liked to get the job done and done quickly, had a liking for generals who decided on tactics and implemented them; he had a huge respect for Brooke, who personified that virtue. Among the battlefield generals Alexander appealed most to Attlee. Described by his rivals as 'wood from the neck up', 'Alex' was an officer who took his orders, acted on them, and reported bluntly that they had been carried out − in a message to Churchill from Tunis he informed him in two sentences that there were no Germans left in Tunisia and he awaited further orders. Wavell, on the other hand, intellectual, artistic and 'deep', was considered 'defeatist' by Attlee, a judgement that he would recall in 1946.

August and September marked a watershed in Attlee's public appearances. The war had entered a critical phase as the Allies converged on Berlin and the Japanese were driven back after the fall of Myitkyina. It was a thrilling month that gave the Allies hope that the German war would be over by the end of 1944. Operation DRAGOON landed a second force in southern France on 15 August and on the same day Alexander's Army Group reached the Gothic Line in northern Italy. By the end of the month Paris had been liberated and the Red Army had taken Bucharest. For two months Attlee refused invitations, accepting only those to Labour Party events.

One such was at Whitehaven, shortly after the government's proposals for social insurance were published. 'Complaint has been made that these proposals took a long time to formulate', Attlee commented. 'They did, but the work had to be done by ministers heavily engaged in the task of carrying on the administration of the offices of the nation in wartime, and with a great many other reconstruction plans.'[46]

Once again, Attlee was resisting attacks from his own party. In his book, the aggressive *Why Not Trust the Tories?*, Bevan savaged the Tories for delaying both the report and any implementation of its proposals, interpreting these as part of a dark Conservative plot to inflict 'death by words'.[47] Attlee showed statesmanship in understanding wartime pressures on ministers. He, after all, was a member of the War Cabinet, which Bevan was not. To attack Churchill, the immensely popular war leader, would have been electoral folly. To attack the Tory Party, pointing out – as Attlee did in 1945 – that the party's relations with Churchill were extremely ambivalent, was good politics.

The war did not end in 1944, but, with the collapse of German resistance on both fronts, as the Allied armies converged on Berlin, both British political parties squared off for the end of the coalition and the long-awaited general election. 'All political parties are now busy selecting candidates for the general election', Attlee declared at Woolwich in February.[48] The gloves were finally off.

Four days later, speaking to the Bradford Labour Party, he talked openly of a general election. By now Belgium had been completely cleared, Budapest taken, Dresden firebombed. The surrender of Germany was imminent and the electoral truce effectively suspended. Reconstruction could begin after an election held between the surrender of Germany and the defeat of Japan. The Labour Party was prepared to go into that election to ask for a mandate. He was not, he said, afraid of responsibility. He wanted 'to enter upon the task of ridding mankind from fear and want in the spirit of crusaders who set before themselves a lofty ideal towards which they strive.'[49]

This was a far cry from the pre-war Tory philosophy. Gone is Baldwin's 'Safety First'; banished are the tentative steps of Chamberlain. This is a strong, stirring call to join a crusade for the benefit of the human race. The coalition existed now in name alone. Both parties were making clandestine plans, preparing for what promised to be a fundamental clash of ideologies after five years of enforced cohabitation. There was no doubt that Attlee would lead the party at the imminent election, and even Churchill's loyal lieutenants Eden and Cranborne 'thought Labour would quite likely win'.[50]

Attlee had achieved an eminence that could hardly have been envisaged in May 1940. By unwavering loyalty to the wartime Prime Minister and by strict observance of the electoral truce he had established himself as a statesman of stature and ethical probity. By maintaining the position that only by national planning and socialist principles could the quality of life in Britain be improved he projected Labour as the inevitable post-war government; by efficient dispatch of government business in Cabinet he demonstrated that he could lead that government. All the pieces were in place; it remained only to display them to the electorate.

ENDNOTES

1   Bodleian: MS. Attlee, dep. 4, 23 February 1942.
2   Bodleian: MS. Attlee, dep. 5, 21 March 1942.
3   Bodleian: MS. Attlee, dep. 5, 22 March 1942.
4   For example, Jim Middleton, the General Secretary of the Labour Party, wrote to him, pointing out that since the transfer of Hugh Dalton to the Board of Trade (on 22 February) there was now no Labour representative involved in the direction of Political Warfare – it was now in the hands of Bracken and Eden. Bodleian: MS. Attlee, dep. 5, 3 April 1942.
5   Letter to William John MP, 3 April 1942. Bodleian: MS. Attlee, dep. 5.
6   *Hansard*, HC Deb, 23 June 1942, col. 1819.
7   *Hansard*, HC Deb, 23 June 1942, col. 1821
8   Bodleian: MS. Attlee, dep. 5.
9   Butler (ed.), *Grand Strategy*, volume 3, pp. 440–441.
10   Precisely the military tendencies that Attlee had complained of in 1923. See Chapter 4 above.
11   Churchill, *The Second World War*, vol. 4, 'The Hinge of Fate', pp. 464.
12   Ibid., pp. 511–512; for cable of 21 August, p. 513.
13   Bodleian: MS. Attlee, dep. 5, July 1942.
14   Bodleian: MS. Attlee, dep. 6, September 1942.
15   *Aberdeen Bon Accord*, in Bodleian: MS. Attlee, dep. 6, 10 September 1942
16   Bodleian: MS. Attlee, dep. 6, 15 December 1942.
17   Bodleian: MS. Attlee, dep. 6, 10 September 1942.
18   Churchill, *The Second World War*, vol. 4, 'The Hinge of Fate', p. 684. Prime Minister to Deputy Prime Minister and War Cabinet, para. 6, 20 January 1943.
19   Churchill, *The Second World War*, vol. 4, 'The Hinge of Fate', p. 686. Deputy Prime Minister and Foreign Secretary to Prime Minister, 21 January 1943.
20   *Hansard*, HC Deb, 19 January 1943, cols 92–102.
21   Bodleian: MS. Attlee, dep. 7, 27 January 1943.
22   Churchill, *The Second World War*, vol. 4, 'The Hinge of Fate', p. 700. Deputy Prime Minister and Foreign Secretary to Prime Minister, 21 January 1943.
23   Churchill, *The Second World War*, vol. 4, 'The Hinge of Fate', p. 703. Deputy Prime Minister and War Cabinet to Prime Minister, 25 January 1943.
24   Admiral Ernest King, the irascible American naval chief. His daughter, asked about her father's temper, replied, 'My father's the most even-tempered man in the world. He's always in a rage.'
25   Llewellyn Woodward, *British Foreign Policy in the Second World War*, p. 379.
26   Danchev and Todman (eds.), *War Diaries of Field Marshal Lord Alanbrooke*, Entry for 14 July 1944, p. 570.
27   Letter to Tom Attlee, 22 February 1943.
28   Bodleian: MS. Attlee, dep. 7, 10 March 1943.
29   *The Times*, 22 March 1943.
30   Bodleian: MS. Attlee, dep. 8.
31   Letter to Tom Attlee, 19 May 1943.
32   Bodleian: MS. Attlee, dep. 8.
33   Violet's twin sister Olive and her husband, Admiral (later Admiral of the Fleet) Sir Algernon Willis.
34   Letter to Tom Attlee, 8 May 1943.
35   The National Insurance Act of 1911.
36   Bodleian: MS. Attlee, dep. 9, Speech at Alloa, 10 July 1943.
37   Bodleian: MS. Attlee, dep. 9, Speech at Greenock, 12 April 1943.

38 Bodleian: MS. Attlee, dep. 9, August 1843.
39 Bodleian: MS. Attlee, dep. 10, 3 September 1943.
40 Bodleian: MS. Attlee, dep. 11, 31 December 1943.
41 Ibid.
42 The drafts and final versions of his speeches in the first four months of 1944 are in his papers,
    Bodleian: MS. Attlee, dep. 13.
43 Bodleian: MS. Attlee, dep. 14, 13 May 1944.
44 Bodleian: MS. Attlee, dep. 14, 2 June 1944.
45 Letter to Tom Attlee, 4 September 1944. He described Alexander as the man for a campaign, whereas
    Montgomery was the man for a battle. Williams, *Nothing So Strange*, p. 234.
46 Bodleian: MS. Attlee, dep. 15, 7 October 1944.
47 Bevan, *Why Not Trust the Tories*, Chapter 3, 'Death by Words'.
48 Bodleian: MS. Attlee, dep. 16, 11 February 1945.
49 Bodleian: MS. Attlee, dep. 17, 15 February 1945.
50 Eden, *Memoirs*, vol. 2 'The Reckoning', p. 551.

CHAPTER NINE

THE 1945 ELECTION

By the end of the war in Europe there were few of Attlee's colleagues who doubted his ability to handle business efficiently, to work tirelessly for party unity or to act swiftly and ruthlessly when occasion demanded. Within the Labour Party, however, doubts remained among opposing factions – doubts about his popular appeal as a leader and his commitment to press for far-reaching reform and a socialist foreign policy. Bevin and Morrison had both held important positions throughout the war; each had supporters prepared to promote his claim to lead the party.

Since 1935 Attlee had remained virtually unchallenged. Now the very need for change that Attlee had predicted when the war ended prompted movements to unseat him. Without prejudice to his patent strengths, there was concern that the end of the coalition would offer Labour a unique opportunity to gain power and that the occasion called for a man of greater stature – or more palpable socialist credentials – to defeat Churchill and seize it.

In 1944 *The Observer* had published a profile of the Labour leader that was perceptive, accurate and, on the whole, positive.[1] It did, however, focus on Attlee's capacity to serve as second man in government rather than as a charismatic leader. Employing passages such as 'sign of diffidence, a lack of confidence' and 'He is almost anonymous. Slight in figure, he does not stand out in a crowd', it fuelled the doubts of those who sought a change in the leadership.

For as long as the coalition continued, however, the doubters were powerless. Then, on 31 October, the Prime Minister himself moved the second reading of the Prolongation Bill, clearly doubtful that the Parliament would be required for another year.[2]

In truth, Churchill had been campaigning since he broadcast his Four Year Plan.[3] In that broadcast he attempted to hijack the Labour Party platform, associating himself with steps towards a welfare state. He described himself as a 'lieutenant' of Lloyd George, 'the prime parent of all national insurance schemes'; he painted himself as having been 'prominently connected' with them since he brought Sir William Beveridge into public service 'and when Sir Hubert Llewellyn Smith and I framed the first unemployment insurance scheme'.

The plan attempted two things: to associate the Conservative Party with the desire for real post-war reform and to suggest that the coalition – naturally headed by Churchill – would remain in power after the defeat of Germany. Greenwood described the second suggestion as 'staggering'.

By the end of the 1944 parliamentary session, with victory in Europe imminent, no one doubted that this was the last session of coalition government. But, since the date of the Nazi surrender could not be accurately foretold, there could be no definitive plan for the withdrawal of ministers from the coalition. As Churchill put it, the 'odour of dissolution was in the air'.[4]

Domestic politics were overshadowed by international events as the Allies closed on Berlin. Differences between the parties were apparent enough – private enterprise *versus* nationalisation – and these were highlighted by members of opposing parties. In March Attlee spoke in Nottingham, drawing the lines between them. 'We are now in the season of party conferences', he said. 'The Conservative Party have made it quite clear that they take their stand on what is called private enterprise.' In a deft thrust he rebuked the Tories for their 'optimistic doctrine that if everyone puts his own interests first, the interests of the community are served.' Labour, he told his audience, took a more realistic view based on experience.[5] A few days later, on 9 April, Bevin made a provocative speech, effectively his opening bid in the imminent contest.[6]

When the German surrender was signed and Churchill treated as a national hero, Attlee and Eden were in San Francisco on United Nations business. Clearly, announcement of an election needed to await their return. There was talk of an election in July, of an election in October. Surprisingly, Churchill forced the issue by writing to the leaders of other parties on 18 May, suggesting that either the coalition remain in power until the end of the Japanese war or it be disbanded forthwith and an election held in July. He also mooted the possibility of holding a referendum.

The former option came as a surprise, although Churchill maintained in his letter that he and Attlee had discussed this. Attlee, however, after discussion with the National Executive of the party, rejected it in a letter of 21 May.[7] Churchill's remarks at the second reading of the Prolongation Bill had indicated that an election would be held during the year and this should now take place. He did, however, assure the Prime Minister of Labour's support for the war against Japan, whatever the outcome of the election.

Concerning the election's timing, he argued that autumn would be more suitable as a more accurate electoral register would be completed, and this would give returning servicemen time to consider the issues. He rejected Churchill's suggestion that party politics were already harming the business of government. As to the suggestion of a referendum, he rejected it as un-British.

A certain disingenuousness suffuses this exchange. Churchill knew his prestige to be high at this point and that the notion of a government with continuity of leadership would have wide appeal. The Prime Minister had been the very persona of Britain's resistance to Hitler. He had promised a long struggle with victory at the end; now that victory had been achieved. The attractions of a Churchill-led government would never be higher than immediately after VE Day.

Attlee recognised this and needed to allow time to wear some of the shine from the Prime Minister's crown. It is hard to gauge to what extent either Churchill or Attlee was aware of the greatly enhanced prestige of the Deputy Prime Minister. Since 1940 he had served with conspicuous loyalty in the coalition. He had chaired the War Cabinet in Churchill's absence, an acting Prime Minister for a total of almost six months; he had spoken up and down the country, in measured, rational speeches that gave an honest statement of the strategic position, spiced with encouragement over the nation's achievements. Attlee was a leader in his own right; Churchill at first failed to appreciate that. The Liberals too failed to grasp the changed status of the Labour Party. Lord Rosebery, in a pamphlet 'Why Liberals Should Support Churchill', charged that Labour had 'deliberately chosen to seek power in its own right, entirely free from any kind of commitment to or co-operation with any other party.'[8] The impertinence of it!

Churchill responded to Attlee and Sinclair on the following day. It was a patently political letter, overtly drawing the lines between the parties and suggesting that Attlee had unilaterally rejected the possibility of working together – which he, Churchill, reluctantly had to accept. Dismissing the suggestion that an early election was proposed for party political reasons, he subtly laid the blame for the dissolution of the coalition on the Labour leader.

This was a neat piece of politics. If Churchill could smear the Labour Party as the saboteurs of the Four Year Plan that he had proposed in 1943, then he could – as he subsequently did – suggest that the measures proposed therein were not sufficiently extreme for Labour, that they were aiming at a far greater socialisation. It was the first step in the creation of a scenario in which Churchill was not being allowed to 'Finish the Job' purely as a result of political discord created by Labour, anxious to dissolve the successful coalition.

The Labour Party, however, having been bound by the electoral truce throughout the war, was now resolved to have not a referendum, but a full-scale general election fought on the issues concerning post-war Britain that divided the parties. The justification for the continuation of the coalition could only be to carry through the proposals of the Four Year Plan, yet it was precisely the party differences over the Plan that required an election. It was clear, then, that the coalition should be disbanded; the principal issue remaining was when this should take place.

Churchill's decision to request the King to dissolve Parliament in time for a July election infuriated Labour leaders who, quite accurately, saw this as a political decision and accused him of using his position as Prime Minister for purely party purposes. This was either remarkably naïve or utterly disingenuous as every party leader seeks to time his actions for the benefit of his party. Attlee understood that the Prime Minister would capitalise on his enormous stature in the aftermath of Germany's surrender. No realistic politician would have expected him to do otherwise. The party would simply have to make the best of the situation.

Attlee urged that the break-up of the coalition be postponed until various international issues were settled, but there was uncertainty if this would happen between July and October. Moreover, as Churchill responded, if the date of the dissolution of the coalition were fixed, then the government would be a 'lame duck' during the interim.

On 23 May Churchill offered King George VI his resignation and four hours later accepted the King's invitation to form a new government, whereupon he requested that His Majesty dissolve the Parliament on 15 June. He then set up a 'caretaker government', principally of members of the Conservative Party. National Liberals and Liberals were invited, but not Labour Members. Press reaction ranged from tributes to the coalition (*The Times* and the *News Chronicle*) to contempt (*Daily Herald* and *Daily Worker*) with many shades of opinion in between (*Daily Telegraph, Manchester Guardian, Daily Sketch*).[9]

Churchill chose to make the break-up of the coalition appear a selfish, political, even unpatriotic act – something that he, in his long-suffering role, must needs overcome. Thus the opening of the Conservative manifesto, 'Mr Churchill's Declaration of Policy to the Electors', regrets Labour's ingratitude and desertion of their posts. Churchill lamented the unwillingness of the Socialist and Sinclair Liberal Parties to agree to his proposal, noting that he had 'formed a new National Government, consisting of the best men in all parties who were willing to serve and some who are members of no party at all.' Many had helped him 'carry the burdens of state through the darkest days'.[10]

The balance of the Conservative manifesto was remarkable for its appropriation of Labour aims. The Conservatives claimed to 'seek the good of the whole nation, not that of one section or one faction', believing in 'the living unity of the British people, which transcends class or party differences'. The manifesto based its hopes for world peace upon 'the setting up of a World Organisation strong enough to prevent future wars of aggression whether by the weak or the strong'. Their 'prevailing hope' was that 'the foundations will be laid on the indissoluble agreement of Great Britain, the United States and Soviet Russia.'[11]

Concerning India, the Conservatives welcomed 'the framing of plans for granting India a fuller opportunity to achieve dominion status'. As to the rest of the Commonwealth they accepted responsibility 'to help them to raise their standards of life by agricultural advance, the application of science and the building up of local industries; to improve conditions of labour and of housing, to spread education, to stamp out disease and to sustain health, vigour and happiness'.

Concerning defence Churchill declared himself 'in agreement with Mr Bevin and other leaders of the Socialist Party that, until the end of the Japanese War and, I hope, until the World Security Organization has become a reality, all citizens under a democratic government should bear responsibility for defending their Country and its Cause'. On the issue of demobilisation too Churchill doffed his cap to Bevin, saying, 'The broad and properly considered lines of the demobilisation proposals, based on age and length of service, which Mr Bevin has elaborated with much wisdom, will be adhered to, and releases will be made as quickly as the condition of the tormented world permits.'[12]

Committing themselves to a plan to build 220,000 new homes and have 80,000 under way in the first two years, advocating a nationwide and compulsory scheme for national insurance, proposing a 'comprehensive health service covering the whole range of medical treatment from the general practitioner to the specialist', and vowing to 'guard against the abuses to which monopolies may give rise', the Conservatives strove to take ownership of the fundamental aims of the Labour Party. The complimentary references to Bevin enhanced the impression that a Conservative government, if elected, would embrace the same humanitarian, egalitarian principles as the Labour Party.

There was, however, one glaring difference between the manifestos of the two parties. The Labour Party manifesto opened with the confident declaration that the fighting was almost over and that 'Japanese barbarism would be defeated just as decisively as Nazi aggression and tyranny.' The men of the fighting services deserved a happier future than they had received after the last war. Their welfare was 'a sacred trust'.[13]

The Conservatives, by contrast, took the position that the future was still perilous. Britain was still at war, and even when all foreign enemies were utterly defeated, that would not be the end of their task. It would be the beginning of 'further opportunity – the opportunity which we snatched out of the jaws of disaster in 1940 – to save the world from tyranny and then to play our part in its wise, helpful guidance.'[14]

The underlying implication was clear. Whereas the Labour Party wanted to focus immediately on domestic issues, Churchill, war leader *par excellence*, was mindful of the military problems still to be overcome and proposed, in his wisdom, to 'take stock of our resources and plan how the energies of the British people can best be freed for the work that lies ahead'.[15]

This approach was carefully calculated to gain the maximum benefit from the Conservative Party's greatest asset, the Prime Minister. The use of the name 'National Government' for the caretaker government that contained not a single Labour member suggested a continuing emergency and Churchill, clearly, was the leader most fit to handle an unfinished war, to 'Finish the Job'. In time a Conservative government would apply itself to the several pressing domestic issues, but in the meantime there must be sensible circumspection with an experienced guiding hand to prevent over-enthusiastic untimely reform. The fact that Churchill was the Tory Party leader with a chequered history of relations with the Conservative Party was, naturally, not emphasised.

The choice for the voter was effectively between retaining Churchill – a decision that would temporarily freeze social change – or to look for immediate change, which involved removing from power the very symbol of Britain's continuing struggle. Change from the period of the 1930s was devoutly to be wished, but at what price? The choice could be made either on emotional or coldly logical grounds. It is easy in retrospect to judge Churchill a magnificent, indeed a unique, wartime leader and to argue that Britain needed another leader in 1945. It was not, however, an obvious truth at the time.

A people fighting a war needs to believe that it is fighting for a better world. A world without Hitler certainly, but in the light of wartime austerity, Britain needed also to believe that wartime measures were part of the risk:reward equation. Expectation grew and people believed that Labour was more likely to reward them. Hence the need for Labour to emphasise that the fighting was over – and the Tories' need to maintain that it was not.

The Labour Party drew a parallel between 1918 and 1945. Their message was clear and divisive along class lines: the Tories will look after the rich; ordinary folk have suffered during the war. Don't fall for that smooth talk about progress that was handed out dishonestly in 1918. Vote 'Straight Left'. Bevan, unsurprisingly, went further. In *Why Not Trust the Tories?*, published in 1944, he pointed out the parallels.[16]

In 1945, as in 1918, the country had changed Prime Minister during the war. In each case fighting morale had been sustained by promises of a better Britain after both wars – a fairer distribution of wealth, better social services, housing and employment. The Beveridge Committee had been formed in June 1941; in September 1943 it was announced that the government would soon pronounce on the committee's report. Now, in 1945 after Tory delaying tactics, with an election imminent, it was time to ask the Tories why they had withheld benefits for so long. 'Why should we trust you to do in the future what you would not use your power to do in the past?'

While ostensibly both parties campaigned on the battle cry of a better Britain, the Labour claim was that the Tories could not be trusted to deliver on their election promises. In 1918 when the government had promised 'Homes for Heroes', they had pledged to build 500,000 houses in three years. In 1919 they built 700 houses and it took the Wheatley Act of 1924 to improve the situation. Simply, for the Tories to make good their promises they would have to act against Tory interests. It was, Labour argued, 'Eyewash'.[17]

For the Labour Party the issue in 1945 was Britain, the kind of Britain that should 'win the peace'. For the Tories the thrust of argument was that Britain needed as never before experienced statesmen like Churchill and Eden to ensure that the country's international position was protected. Yet both parties proposed substantially the same foreign policy – the maintenance of the Big Three alliance and contribution to the United Nations for collective security.

The Labour Party manifesto emphasised that action, not mere words, was needed. The coming election would be 'the greatest test in our history of the judgment and common sense of our people'. To counter the Tories' appropriation of Labour programmes, the manifesto questioned the Conservative Party's commitment to reform:

The nation wants food, work and homes. It wants more than that – it wants
good food in plenty, useful work for all, and comfortable, labour-saving homes that
take full advantage of the resources of modern science and productive industry. It
wants a high and rising standard of living, security for all against a rainy day,
an educational system that will give every boy and girl a chance to develop the best
that is in them.[18]

On the issue of foreign policy the Labour Party was able to drive a wedge between Churchill and the Tories by quoting from a speech of Churchill from 5 October 1938 in which he had castigated the Tory Party for leaving Britain 'in the hour of trial without adequate national defence or effective international security'. Churchill may have been correct before the war, they suggested, but the Tory Party under Baldwin and Chamberlain assuredly had not been.

On the question of state control the two parties differed most fundamentally. The Conservative position, naturally, was that state control entailed 'excessive taxation'. The Labour Party argued that only by nationalising certain industries could industrial efficiency and full employment be achieved. Just a theory, countered the Conservatives. It had never been attempted and it would achieve the reverse of efficiency. This, retorted the Labour Party, was the traditional argument for 'sound' finance, the policy that led to unemployment in the 1930s. Ultimately, however, the appeal of the Conservatives was to the experience, essentially of one man, that they would bring to the task of restructuring Britain.

The Labour Party held its conference just before the election campaign. When Parliament reassembled the lines had been drawn. On 6 June in the House of Commons, Attlee criticised Churchill for rushing the election.[19]

Attlee was active in supporting local candidates and spent much of the period from 16 to 30 June in the Midlands and Yorkshire. Bevin spoke on the east coast, working down from Lincolnshire, the two meeting up at a huge Labour rally in the Albert Hall on 23 June. This organisation was in vivid contrast to the apparent lethargy of the Tories, other than Churchill who made an extensive election tour. Curiously, the most voluble speaker for the Conservatives was Beaverbrook, who made notable speeches at Bradford, Chatham, Streatham and Worcester.

For the Labour Party Bevin was most clearly visible in the front lines, answering Beaverbrook's thrusts. Attlee orchestrated a series of radio broadcasts by different Labour speakers, clearly and cogently setting out the three principal Labour programmes: public *versus* private, controls, nationalisation. Here we see the force of the partnership between Bevin and the Labour leader. Attlee had little of Bevin's pugnaciousness and Bevin could not have performed Attlee's job with the same efficiency and dispatch. Bevin became the most visible and charismatic of the Labour ministers and Attlee knew well enough to allow him all the space necessary to be effective. The partnership was central to Labour's success; without such a close working relationship between two prominent ministers, there could not have been the harmony that later characterised their working methods.

The successful co-operation of Conservative and Labour ministers during the wartime coalition guaranteed that the election would be a straight fight between the two leading parties. Within the grouping of the left, however, there were the Communist Party, the Common Wealth Party and the Independent Labour Party. All three were to the left of Labour; none differed greatly from Labour's domestic goals in principle, only in degree.

The broadcasts by Churchill and Attlee to open the contest set the tone for the rest of the campaign. Churchill's opening salvo on 4 June was a tirade against socialism. His Labour colleagues, he charged, had unpatriotically left the coalition, planning to subvert the British way of life. From this ungenerous opening he crossed the Rubicon of reasonable political debate:

> *My friends, I must tell you that a socialist policy is abhorrent to British ideas of freedom ... Socialism is inseparably interwoven with totalitarianism and the abject worship of the state ... Socialism is in its essence an attack not only on British enterprise, but on the right of an ordinary man or woman to breathe freely without having a harsh, clumsy, tyrannical hand clapped across their mouth and nostrils. [Labour] would have to fall back on some kind of Gestapo, no doubt very humanely in the first instance.*[20]

Attlee's response came in measured tones, totally in contrast to the hyperbole of the Prime Minister. He recognised that to criticise the

Colossus who had directed the war would be a gross tactical error and directed his counter-attack with subtlety:

> *When I listened to the Prime Minister's speech last night in which he gave such a travesty of the Labour party, I realised at once what was his object. He wanted the electors to understand how great was the difference between Winston Churchill the great leader in war of a united nation, and Mr Churchill the party leader of the Conservatives. He feared lest those who accepted his leadership in war might be tempted out of gratitude to follow him further. I thank him for having disillusioned them so thoroughly. The voice we heard last night was that of Mr Churchill, but the mind was that of Lord Beaverbrook.[21]*

He struck exactly the right note. The villain was not Churchill but Beaverbrook. It was not Churchill who would descend willingly to such outrageous accusations; it had to be the company that he was keeping – the Tories who would stop at nothing to win. Without overtly criticising Churchill, he drew a distinction between Churchill in wartime and Churchill in peacetime. Ironically, by continuing to insist that he could not have meant what he said, the Labour leaders were able to inflict even more damage. In a fine rhetorical flourish Morrison, in a speech on 19 June, wondered why, if he was likely to introduce a Gestapo to Britain, did Churchill give him the Home Office in 1940. In thoroughly devastating good humour he chuckled and suggested indulgently that 'Winston was having a night out'.[22] The Prime Minister's most violent criticism turned out to be his biggest blunder of the election.

The final Big Three conference of the war, appropriately named TERMINAL, was scheduled to take place in Potsdam, a suburb of Berlin, between 17 July and 2 August. Polling day was to be on 5 July, but, because of the difficulties in shipping back votes from those serving overseas, there was to be a delay of three weeks before the votes were counted and the results declared. Thus the results of the election would be known while the conference was taking place and it was possible that during the first week of meetings there would be one Prime Minister, replaced by another for the second week.

To ensure some continuity if this were to occur, Churchill invited Attlee to accompany him to Potsdam for the first week of the conference. Attlee accepted, whereupon Laski, the chairman of the Labour Party's NEC, called on him to attend the conference merely as an observer.[23] He argued that 'it was desirable that the leader of the party which may shortly be elected to govern the country should know what is said, discussed and agreed at this vitally important meeting'. The Labour Party, he said, 'cannot be committed to any decisions arrived at by the Three-Power Conference where matters will be discussed which have not been debated either in the party Executive or at meetings of the Parliamentary Labour Party.'

In the light of Churchill's suggestions that socialism would lead to totalitarianism, a suggestion gleefully adopted by Conservatives across the country, this was an unfortunate remark. While the Parliamentary Party consisted of Members of Parliament elected by voters, the National Executive Council had no such status. Thus Laski created the impression that, if elected, the Labour Party would be directed by an unelected body, a kind of Politburo that would erode the autonomy of a democratically elected Parliament. It also created the impression, exploited in subsequent elections by the Tories,[24] that Attlee was merely a 'front' for a more extreme leader who would replace him.

The potential damage caused by Laski was compounded by his response to a question in Newark on 16 June. His remark that 'If Labour did not obtain what it needed by general consent, we shall have to use violence even if it means revolution' was seized on by the press and widely reported. Laski filed a suit for libel against the *Daily Express*, a suit that he ultimately lost, but which mitigated the damage that his comments might have caused.

A British general election, unlike an American presidential election, allows no direct vote for the future Prime Minister. Were that not so, it is very likely that Churchill would have been returned in 1945, much like Roosevelt in 1944. The British electorate could have expressed their vast gratitude to the existing Prime Minister, while registering a desire for domestic reform through a vote for the local Labour candidate. As it was, Churchill was greeted by huge enthusiasm but 'he seemed strangely out of touch with the new mood, and was certainly misled – as were so many others – by the triumphal nature of his reception wherever he went.'[25] Later in life, when asked why the electorate had rejected

Churchill, Attlee replied simply and accurately that they had not. They had rejected the Tories.[26]

In this reply Attlee did himself less than justice. If the leader of the Labour Party had been an extreme radical, a Laski for example, then voters, aware that the leader of the majority party would be asked by the King to form a government, would have exercised more caution. As it was, Attlee was a familiar figure, a responsible statesman perfectly acceptable as a potential leader. A vote for Labour in a constituency did not run the risk of putting a firebrand in Downing Street. Voters could, therefore, vote for reform without opening the floodgates of revolution. They felt able to show their gratitude to Churchill while consigning him, as they thought, to a past era. They were enormously grateful, but the war was effectively over.

Attlee had a shrewd appreciation of the forces at work, recognising public gratitude for what it was and not believing that it would translate into votes for the Tory Party. As the campaign came to an end, he wrote to Tom: 'We are getting near the end of the election now. I can't find that my opponent is getting any support ... Winston keeps slugging away at the silly Laski business, but I don't think he gets the better of the exchanges with me.'[27]

Churchill unwisely 'slugged away at the Laski business' until the last days of the election. The *Manchester Guardian* reported that 'Mr Churchill in his letter to Mr Attlee tonight has so magnified the bogy of the Labour National Executive as to transform it into a new scare.' Attlee had 'wisely lost no time in ... demonstrating that the Labour Party is completely autonomous'.[28]

Newspapers also published the exchange of letters between the two leaders from which the impression emerges of a petulant Prime Minister being firmly dealt with by a reasonable and regretful Attlee, whose rejoinder ended simply, regretting that Churchill 'should have been so distressed owing to ... lack of acquaintance with the procedure of the democratic parties in general and of the Labour party in particular'.[29]

Remarkably, Churchill refused to let the matter rest and weighed in once more on the very eve of the election, concluding that 'the controversy on these very important issues [cannot] be satisfactorily cleared up until the public has a statement signed jointly by yourself and the chairman of the Executive Committee regarding the use of these powers in the future'. The tirade was a gift to Attlee who replied with a brisk dismissal, concluding with a stinging rebuke. 'Despite my very clear statement', he wrote, 'you proceed to exercise your imagination by importing into a right to be consulted a power to challenge actions and conduct ... I think that you underestimate the intelligence of the public, and I do not share your belief.'[30]

After this final exchange of fire Britain went to the polls in a somewhat unreal atmosphere pending the delayed counting of votes. Meanwhile the leaders of the two principal parties would travel together to Berlin to meet Stalin and the new American President, Harry Truman, to settle critical issues affecting the post-war world. They would both return to Britain to learn the results of the election; one of them would return to Potsdam to continue the conference. Attlee would have no *locus standi* during the first period. No longer Deputy Prime Minister, he was inevitably, as Laski had insisted he should be, a *de facto* observer.

Churchill, at this stage, was confident that his party would be returned to power. His invitation to Attlee to accompany him was a device, an apparent courtesy that would demonstrate his magnanimity to his former deputy. He expected a majority of about eighty in the House of Commons – a view with which, apparently, Attlee concurred, telling Chip Bohlen of the American State Department that 'he did not think the Labour Party had a chance of gaining a majority in Parliament. He hoped for gains sufficient to force the Churchill government to listen to Labour's views.'[31]

Throughout the first half of the conference these remained the stated positions of the British leaders. Churchill was back in his element, determining the fate of nations while Attlee modestly yielded primacy to him. It was clear that Stalin expected Churchill to remain in power, while Truman was greatly more interested in reaching agreement with Stalin on important issues than speculating about the outcome of the British election.

Attlee's position was far from easy. When he made his first general appearance he was cruelly described by Bohlen as 'a mechanical toy, which, when wound up and placed on the table by Churchill, would perform as predicted'.[32] For Bohlen, as for many people, it was unimaginable that Churchill should cease to be Britain's leader, certainly while the war was in progress and until the legacy of the war was settled. Yet here was Attlee, like some premature undertaker, ready to take over, a lean Cassius waiting to impale his chief.

On a different, unemotional level, however, it was Churchill who had his critics. Sir Alexander Cadogan, the waspish Permanent Under-Secretary at the Foreign Office, who was appalled at Churchill's handling of his position, had earlier confided to his diary: 'How have we conducted this war with the PM spending hours of his own and other people's time simply drivelling, welcoming every red herring so as only to have the pleasure of more irrelevant, redundant talk?'[33]

Of the Prime Minister's performance before and at the plenary session he was no less contemptuous. Churchill, Cadogan wrote to his wife,

> *since he left London has refused to do any work or read anything. That is probably quite right, but then he can't have it both ways: if he knows nothing of the subject under discussion, he should keep quiet or ask that his Foreign Secretary be heard. Instead of that, he butts in on every occasion and talks the most irrelevant rubbish and is giving away our case at every point.*[34]

One can easily imagine how these sessions must have affected Attlee. Churchill's rambling was anathema to Attlee even in a purely British setting. In January he had written formally to Churchill to complain of his inefficient use of time at Cabinet meetings. 'Not infrequently', he wrote, 'a phrase catches your eye which gives rise to a disquisition on an interesting point only slightly connected with the subject matter.'[35]

Now, as when a family member behaves badly outside the family, so must these ramblings have seemed when delivered in the presence of Stalin and Truman, both of whom were brisk and businesslike in their dealing with the agenda. Clearly harsh words were going to be exchanged between the Soviet Union and the United States and neither flinched from confronting issues. Churchill, by contrast, occupied the seat that Attlee would dearly have wished to occupy – the third no-nonsense negotiator at a top-level conference. Attlee, loyal to the last, could only sit, watch and shudder.

Towards the end of the first period of the conference Churchill dined with Stalin. 'I think that he wants me to win the election', he told Lord

Moran, his personal physician.[36] On the following evening he confessed to Moran that the uncertainty about the election results 'hovers over me like a vulture of uncertainty in the sky.'[37] Away from the hustings, from the adoring crowds, aware perhaps that the *realpolitik* of a world of two 'Superpowers' was now passing him by, he confronted for the first time the reality of his position. Despite his popularity, he might have lost the election. As Truman and Stalin marginalised him at Potsdam, so, he began to fear, might he have been marginalised in Britain.

At the end of the plenary session on 23 July Churchill joked that he and Attlee had some business in London on 26 July and that they would leave on the afternoon of the 25th. 'But we shall be back by the afternoon sitting on 27 July. Or at least some of us will.'[38] All those present assured the Prime Minister that he would win. He had been a fixture in wartime conferences since Casablanca. He had shuttled the Atlantic to persuade and cajole Roosevelt. Yet now the war was over and some premonition was telling him that his government too was finished. The moment must have been bitter-sweet for him; for Attlee, if he is to be believed when he says that he did not imagine that Labour would win, the experience of being very much a No. 2, a minor actor who had a brief scene on stage, must have been humiliating. The curtain would come down and only the Big Three would be remembered. Photographs of him at TERMINAL seem to reflect this. He fades into his seat while Truman and Stalin expand. He appears not to belong among such exalted company, yet he had as grand and clear a vision of the future as either of the other principals. Sadly, it is for his lack of grandeur in such company that Cadogan characterised him when he spoke of the 'Big Two and a Half'.[39]

Nor was Attlee's irritation confined to the conference. Morrison, encouraged and supported by Ellen Wilkinson, informed him in a letter opening 'My dear Clem' that, if he were elected to Parliament, he would stand for the leadership of the party. Such action, he assured Attlee, would be solely in the interests of the party.[40]

On 25 July Churchill and Attlee returned to London. By the following evening the Labour Party led convincingly in the cities, but the votes from the rural constituencies, traditionally Tory strongholds, were not yet in. By the following afternoon the extent of the landslide was clear.

Labour won 393 seats (up from 154 in 1935) while the Tories won 197 (down from 386). For the Liberal Party it had been a disaster, a mere twelve seats completing their demise as a national party. As a percentage of votes cast, however, the Labour Party's mandate was less overwhelming; they captured 47.7 per cent of the popular vote, against 36.2 per cent cast for the Tories. In retrospect, the indications throughout the war were that Labour would win a post-war election. The British Institute of Public Opinion had concluded that from June 1943 onward Labour held a lead in voting intentions, rising from 7 per cent in June 1943 to a dominant 16 per cent superiority in April 1945. Polling was less scientific – and less slavishly respected – in 1945, however, and the result came as a thunderclap to the majority of Britons.

In typically matter-of-fact style, Attlee records the events of the day. A summons came from the Palace. Bevin openly supported Attlee over Morrison's machinations and urged him to go to the Palace immediately. Violet drove him there and he received the King's commission to form a government. After a Victory Rally at Westminster Central Hall, he 'looked in at a Fabian Society gathering, and then returned to Stanmore after an exciting day.'[41]

ENDNOTES

1   *The Observer*, 5 May 1944.
2   *Hansard*, HC Deb, 31 October 1944, cols 662–668.
3   Broadcast speech of 22 March 1943, outlining the post-war social programme of the Conservative Party.
4   *Hansard*, HC Deb, 31 October 1944, col. 667.
5   Bodleian: MS. Attlee, dep. 17, 25 March 1945.
6   *The Times*, 10 April 1945.
7   Bodleian: MS. Attlee, dep. 18.
8   Bodleian: MS Simon, 96, folio 39.
9   McCallum and Readman, *The British General Election of 1945*, p. 22.
10   Conservative Party, 1945 general election manifesto, *Mr Churchill's Declaration of Policy to the Electors*, paras 1–2.
11   Ibid. 'Britain and the World', para 4.
12   Ibid., 'Defence', para 2.
13   1945 Labour Party general election manifesto, *Let Us Face the Future: A Declaration of Labour Policy for the Consideration of the Nation*, para 1.
14   Conservative Party, 1945 general election manifesto, para. 4.
15   Ibid, para 5.
16   Bevan, *Why Not Trust the Tories*, Chapter 1, '1918, After the Armistice'.
17   One Labour Party election poster depicts a medicine bottle labelled 'National Eyewash: Poison. Tory Mixture as before' and quotes a Churchill speech in 1908, in which he attacked the Tories.
18   Labour Party general election manifesto, 1945, '*What the Election will be About*', paras 2–3.
19   *Hansard*, HC Deb, 6 June 1945, cols 921–923.

20 *The Listener*, 7 June 1945. This became a popular, if unworthy theme of the election. See, for example, *Daily Express*, 5 June 1945. Tony Benn commented, 'If I was establishing a Gestapo I wouldn't have picked Clem to run it.' Attlee Lecture 1998, Royal Overseas League, 9 February 1998.

21 Bodleian: MS. Attlee, dep. 18, 5 June 1945. According to A. J. P. Taylor, however, the Gestapo *bon mot* was not Beaverbrook's but Churchill's own. He discussed it only with his son Randolph and with James Stuart, the Tory Chief Whip. Taylor, *Beaverbrook*, p. 515. Beaverbrook and Attlee disliked each other intensely. Attlee found 'the Beaver' bombastic and dishonest. Beaverbrook referred to Attlee, sitting next to Churchill on the coalition front bench as 'a sparrow perched beside the glittering bird of Paradise'. *Beaverbrook*, p. 469.

22 See *The Times*, 20 June 1945. Sir Winston's fondness for the stimulus of alcohol was an open secret. While many of his close associates denied that they had ever seen him adversely affected by the quantities he consumed, his fondness for champagne and brandy and his tendency to accompany breakfast with a bottle of Chablis were well known. Attlee compounded the impression of the Prime Minister as irresponsible with the comment 'I am aware that he has rather old-fashioned views about fighting an election.' *The Times*, 3 July 1945. See also Maudling, *Memoirs*, pp. 48–49 for Churchill and alcohol.

23 For reports and comment on Laski's intervention see Churchill College, CHAR 2/557. For Attlee's comments, *As It Happened*, p. 203. Churchill wrote to Attlee that 'Merely to come as a mute observer would be derogatory to your position as the leader of your party and I should not have a right to throw this burden on you in such circumstances. I hope however that I may have your assurance that you accept my invitation.' *Manchester Guardian*, 16 June 1945.

24 This became a theme of the Conservatives in the 1950 election, as Bevan pointed out.

25 Rhodes James, *Anthony Eden*, p. 305.

26 Williams, *A Prime Minister Remembers*, pp. 8–9.; Granada Historical Records, *Clem Attlee*, p. 27.

27 Letter to Tom Attlee, 3 July 1945.

28 *Manchester Guardian*, 3 July 1945.

29 The text of the lengthy letter from Churchill to Attlee on 2 July and Attlee's response on the same evening are printed under the sub-headline 'No New Situation has Arisen' in the *Manchester Guardian* of 3 July 1945.

30 Once again the *Manchester Guardian* and other newspapers printed the exchange of letters in full. The contrast between the almost hysterical tone of Churchill's accusations and the calm response of the Labour leader can only have damaged the Conservative Party. *Manchester Guardian*, 4 July 1945.

31 Charles E. ('Chip') Bohlen, *Witness to History*, p. 250.

32 Ibid., loc. cit.

33 *The Diaries of Sir Alexander Cadogan, 1938–1945*, Entry for 22 February 1945, pp. 719–720.

34 A. C. to T. C., 18 July 1945, *The Diaries of Sir Alexander Cadogan, 1938–1945*, p. 765.

35 Attlee to Churchill, 19 January 1945. The Prime Minister sulked for most of the day before rousing himself and saying to Jock Colville, 'Let us think no more of Hitlee or Attler; let us go and see a film.' On 22 January he responded, 'My dear Lord President, I have to thank you for your Private and Personal letter of January 19. You may be sure I shall always endeavour to profit by your counsels.' Both letters are at CAC: ATLE 2/2. According to Colville, Churchill, outraged, asked Beaverbrook and Brendan Bracken their opinion of Attlee's letter, Both agreed with Attlee; Clementine Churchill applauded Attlee's frankness. Wheeler-Bennett, *Action This Day*, p. 117.

36 Lord Moran, *Churchill*, Diary entry for 19 July 1945, p. 295.

37 Ibid., Diary entry for 20 July 1945, p. 297.

38 Charles L. Mee, *Meeting at Potsdam*, p. 163.

39 Cadogan, *op. cit.*, p. 778. Cadogan was scathing about Attlee's lack of presence at Potsdam (entries for 24 July, 29 July and 31 July, for example).

40 Bodleian: MS. Attlee, dep. 18, Morrison to CRA, 24 July 1945.

41 *As It Happened*, p. 207. Equally matter-of-fact was his conversation with the King. After their brief exchange the King said to his Private Secretary, 'I gather they call him "Clem". "Clam" would be more appropriate.'

CHAPTER TEN

DISILLUSION: FOREIGN POLICY, 1945–1946

RELATIONS WITH THE USA

Readers of Winston Churchill's six-volume work, *The Second World War*, may be forgiven for imagining that American entry into the war was inevitable, that relations between Britain and the United States were free of tension, and that the Anglo-American alliance would continue unaltered into the post-war years. All this, the reader might be persuaded, was due to excellent relations between Roosevelt and Churchill. Together they had signed the Atlantic Charter which clearly, in Churchill's view, did not apply to the British Empire. This *entente*, he supposed, would remain unchanged once the war was over.

The first indication that post-war relations between the Allies would be altered came at the Tehran Conference of November–December 1943. Churchill felt that he was the one realistic leader among the three, later expressing his thoughts to Violet Bonham Carter,

> *There I sat with the great Russian bear on one side of me, with paws outstretched, and on the other the great American buffalo, and between the two sat the poor little British donkey, who was the only one, the only one of the three who knew the right way home.*[1]

Confidence that relations between the United States and Britain, further eroded at Yalta, would now improve evaporated in Potsdam. Roosevelt was dead and Truman had just received news from Alamagordo that would radically change America's position in the post-war balance of power. When Attlee and Bevin[2] returned to Potsdam it soon became clear that Truman sought to establish a *modus vivendi* with Stalin and return to Washington as soon as he decently could. During Attlee's absence Joseph Davies, Truman's Special Envoy, and James Byrnes, the American Secretary of State, had put together a 'package deal' for Stalin and Molotov. This was designed to solve the three issues over which the USA and the USSR were haggling: reparations, recognition of Soviet-sponsored regimes in Hungary, Romania and Bulgaria, and the western Polish frontier. Byrnes proposed to offer the package on a 'take-it-or-leave-it' basis. British agreement to the deal would, Attlee and Bevin rapidly realised, be welcome but far from essential.[3]

The changing of the American guard was patent at Potsdam. The suave Roosevelt had been replaced by the blunt Truman, Stettinius by the abrasive Byrnes. Truman was to be his own strategist, a role for which, according to Admiral Leahy, he was every bit as fitted as Roosevelt, being 'amazingly well read on military history, from the campaigns of the ancients such as Hannibal and Caesar down to the great global conflict into which he had suddenly been thrust in virtual supreme command.'[4]

Both Truman and Stalin were surprised by the Labour Party victory. Molotov complained that, after saying the election would be a close thing, Labour now had a big majority. Attlee was sure that Molotov thought that Churchill would have 'fixed' the election. 'The changeover by democratic process shocked him.'[5] Stalin, who in Eden's opinion had learned how to handle Churchill, contracted a diplomatic cold, stalling for time to discuss the new situation with Moscow and to prepare his position. As Leahy commented, 'There was a notable coolness in their attitude after Attlee took over.'[6]

Truman, a plain-speaking man replacing the devious Roosevelt, and Attlee, a man of few words succeeding the bombastic Churchill, would seem natural colleagues. Both were veterans of the Great War; neither was as glamorous as his predecessor. Truman sent his daughter Margaret his impressions of Attlee and Bevin. They were, he wrote 'sourpusses'. After Eden, 'a perfect striped pants boy', and Churchill, 'as windy as Langer'[7], he was unimpressed by their replacements. 'Bevin is sort of the John L. Lewis[8] type.' and Attlee was 'an Oxford graduate and talks with that deep-throated swallowing enunciation same as Eden does. But

I understand him reasonably well. Bevin is a tough guy.'[9] According to Roy Jenkins, Truman never warmed to Attlee as he had to Churchill.[10] Churchill, he thought, had Roosevelt's greatness without the pretension. Politically, at least, he should have favoured Attlee, but he never developed respect for him as a statesman.

Attlee was already in 'the loser's corner' when he and Bevin returned to Potsdam. Despite Bevin's assertion to General Ismay that he was not going to allow Britain to be barged about,[11] British *desiderata* were already unattainable. In every substantive negotiation at Potsdam Churchill had either been ignored or circumvented. Plans for British presence in the final stages of the war with Japan had been brushed aside by Truman, as had the suggestion that American aid might restore Britain's greatness; the sharing of bases worldwide had been treated by the President as too chummy, an arrangement that would be better decided by the United Nations. Depressed at the erosion of the Empire, the economic plight of Britain, the new realities of Atlantic co-operation and the encroachment of the Soviet Union into Western Europe – and, above all, by the peripheral nature of his own position – Churchill later subtly laid the responsibility for Britain's post-Potsdam status on Attlee and Bevin. He wrote that he had planned to 'have a showdown' with Stalin at the end of the conference and insist that nothing beyond the Oder and the eastern Neisse be ceded to Poland.[12]

At the first plenary session attended by Attlee and Bevin little was achieved. Bohlen commented that Stalin appeared to have lost all interest once Churchill left; despite their mutual combativeness, he had provided an ideological foil for Stalin. Or perhaps, with the change of cast, the unreality of the theatre of the Potsdam conference suffused the entire production. Decisions were no longer made in plenary session; Truman and Stalin reached agreement in private and there was nothing that any third statesman – Churchill or Attlee – could have done about it. This became clear on the following day, Sunday 29 July.

At that meeting the crux of the conference discussions was revealed. Byrnes opened, stating that there remained only two issues to settle – the western border of Poland and the question of reparations to be exacted from Germany. Once these were disposed of, they could 'wind up' the conference. This became a bargaining session in which all parties understood what was taking place. An agreement in principle was to be reached, reviewed separately by Stalin, and then returned for the final hammering out of details. Decisions would be made by Molotov and Byrnes; before the plenary session all essentials would have been agreed. Attlee was effectively excluded, merely informed of decisions taken. His contributions to the final plenary session were uninspiring, largely because there was nothing left to discuss. Churchill's insistence that Poland not extend to the western Neisse had been ignored. As to recognition of Romania, Hungary, Finland and Bulgaria, another issue that had exercised Churchill, careful phrasing would appease the British while allowing the United States and the Soviet Union to proceed as they wished. Any semblance of tripartite agreement had by now been dispensed with; whether or not Churchill would have been able to impose his wishes is moot.

As to Churchill's later claim that he was planning to 'have a show-down' with Stalin when the moment was right, there is little room for discussion.[13] Even if he did have a 'silver bullet' that he planned to use, it is unlikely that it could have reversed the determination of Truman and Stalin to end the conference quickly. If Churchill did have a negotiating point that would have preserved Britain's interests, it is unclear why he chose not to keep Attlee abreast of his intentions or to brief him on them once the election results were known.

Instead, at the final plenary session Bevin proposed that the joint communiqué state that 'the three governments consider it desirable that the present anomalous position of Italy, Bulgaria, Finland, Hungary and Romania should be terminated by the conclusion of peace treaties. They trust that the other interested Allied governments will share these views.' Not only had no agreement been reached, but the final communiqué was so vague as to indicate that none of the powers present really cared.

Attlee had at first hoped to maintain the wartime triple alliance. By the time he left Potsdam he was deeply suspicious of Soviet intentions and cognisant of the need to buttress the Atlantic alliance. Events of the next few months, however, were to test the basis of Anglo-American co-operation.

Another subject of discussion between Attlee and Truman early in the life of the government began in August 1945, when the first atomic bomb was dropped on Hiroshima. Truman had learned at Potsdam of the successful test of the first nuclear weapon in New Mexico. He informed Churchill and they discussed whether Stalin should be told of the new weapon. Churchill advised against this, but Truman mentioned it almost casually at the end of a plenary session. Stalin gave no visible reaction; knowing more than Truman about the development of the bomb from his spies, he was neither shocked nor surprised.[14]

Truman kept the knowledge from Attlee until after the general election, whereupon he shared details of the test on the day before the conference ended. Attlee agreed with the President that, if the use of the bomb would shorten the war by six months and save several hundred thousand lives, then it should be used. For him at this stage, as for Truman, it was a mathematical, not a moral consideration.

Once the effects of the attack on Hiroshima on 6 August became evident, however, he cabled Truman to express his anxiety at the destructive capacity of nuclear weapons and the need to make the attitude of both countries towards its use clear to the world. Britain and America were, as he expressed it, 'trustees for humanity'.

When the second bomb was dropped on Nagasaki on 9 August, prompting the Japanese surrender five days later, Attlee immediately proposed that a committee be set up to examine potential uses of this new weapon. Truman had announced the formation of an American committee to study the question. It was agreed that a similar British committee should be established under the chairmanship of Sir John Anderson, as it was important that Britain should not be left behind in the industrial and military applications of the new discovery.[15]

Although increasingly convinced that the United States and Britain should reassure all nations of their understanding of the moral issues in the nuclear age, Attlee agreed to allow time for the Americans to settle matters in Japan. He did, however, begin to press for an early meeting with Truman at which a declaration of intent could be issued.

Attlee spoke of Truman and himself as 'heads of the governments which have control of this great force', referring to a secret agreement signed by Churchill and Roosevelt at Quebec in August 1943. This provided, *inter alia*, for 'full and effective interchange of information and ideas between those in the two countries engaged in the same sections of the field'. This agreement was an embarrassment to Truman who could neither admit its existence nor propose to Congress that the USA should share what they saw as the fruits of their own research and development. The United States alone was in possession of a uniquely destructive weapon; Truman recognised that Congress would fiercely resist sharing it with any other nation.

Attlee, accepting the logic, if not the morality, of that position, was concerned that the bomb had rendered all existing strategy out-of-date. He made his views clear in a memorandum to the Cabinet committee on Atomic Energy. Britain, he argued, must decide on an atomic policy. Britain was vulnerable to an attack from 'the Continental power'. (He tactfully avoided the use of the word 'Russia'.) Bomb shelters and the ARP were pointless, considerations of strategic bases in the Mediterranean and the East Indies obsolete. The security of the heart of the Empire was all that counted; all else was peripheral. At Potsdam people talked in terms of obsolete strategy; even the latest strategy had become outdated. Bombing must be answered by counter-bombing. An atomic bomb must be answered by an atomic bomb. A Geneva Convention would not be effective – witness the use of gas in the First World War. It was only a matter of time before the atomic secrets were discovered by another country; the USA and Britain had at best a few years' start. Those two nations might attempt to establish an Anglo-American hegemony, using their power to enforce worldwide inspection, but that was not desirable or practicable.

> To attempt to penetrate the curtain that concealed the vast area of Russia would be to invite a war that might destroy civilisation. There must be a decision by the three powers and all nations to avoid war. The USSR should abandon its hopes for worldwide communist revolution; the West should abandon plans to overturn socialist governments. All nations should look forward to a peaceful future rather than to a warlike past. What was previously considered Utopian was now the key to survival. The United States and Britain had unprecedented responsibility for the future of the human race. Only a bold course could save civilisation and Britain must decide on it before the UN met.[16]

At the following day's meeting of the committee he stressed the need to make fundamental decisions and to meet urgently with Truman and

Stalin. Britain could either maintain the Anglo-American lead as an element of the balance of power or be ready to give information freely as part of an effort to establish world security. Bevin argued that the issue should not be treated in isolation by the Big Three but should arise as an aspect of policy as part of the Foreign Ministers' meetings.[17]

Attlee opposed this view and resolved to meet Truman as soon as possible. On 25 September, he sent a much redrafted letter to Truman stating his view that the atomic bomb had altered for ever the basis of international relations and had wrought not a quantitative but a qualitative change in the nature of warfare. It was infinitely more destructive than its predecessors, would be developed to greater power, and was impossible to defend against. If mankind continued to develop nuclear bombs, then sooner or later there would be mutual annihilation. Only the USA and the UK had the secrets and only in the USA could the weapon be produced, but neither country could guarantee exclusive possession of that knowledge nor control supply of necessary raw materials. They had at best a temporary lead and needed to decide how to employ it. His thoughts, he wrote, were both focused on the need to prevent nuclear capability spreading as well as on the future nature of international relations. The framework of the United Nations, laid at San Francisco, must be developed. 'I am anxious', he wrote, 'to know how your mind is working and I believe it essential that we meet to discuss this monstrous problem together before the fears and suspicions that are developing elsewhere (again, he avoided the word 'Russia') harden enough to make any solution difficult.'[18]

On 13 October Truman responded, thanking Attlee for his 'thoughtful letter' and agreeing that 'there can be no division of opinion regarding the gravity of the problem which presses for a solution'.[19] He agreed to a meeting in the near future to discuss the question. Attlee replied on 16 October suggesting that he fly to Washington soon for talks. Truman replied the next day suggesting a meeting either before 27 October or between 5 and 14 November.

Truman, agreeing with the Prime Minister in principle, was unsure how he should handle the question with Congress. He sent a message to Congress in which he proposed to commit the United States to the principle of international control of the bomb.[20] Stimson, his Secretary of War, had already proposed in Cabinet that basic scientific data should be shared with the Soviet Union.[21] When the essence of this was leaked, a firestorm ensued. Truman was forced to distinguish at a press conference between scientific knowledge, which might be shared, and technical knowledge about the manufacture and use of atomic energy, which would not.[22] Then, in his Navy Day speech, he set out twelve principles of American foreign policy before turning to the issue of nuclear weapons. Talk of the atomic bomb scrapping all navies, armies, and air forces was, Truman stated, 100 per cent wrong. The atomic bomb did not alter the basic foreign policy of the United States but made its development and application more urgent. Discussion of the bomb with Great Britain and Canada and later with other nations could not wait upon the formal organisation of the United Nations, but would begin in the near future.[23]

At the end of the speech he used language similar to Attlee's, pledging that America's possession of the bomb posed no threat to any nation. That possession was a sacred trust which 'the thoughtful people of the world' knew would not be violated.

Reaction to the speech was mixed. The more optimistic accepted the concept of 'sacred trust'; the more cynical saw the linkage between the possession of the weapon and the 'control of the seas' as an alarming statement of American dominance. One analysis of the speech commented that the President had assumed the ambitious task of conducting American foreign policy simultaneously according to the principles of Theodore Roosevelt and Saint Francis of Assisi.[24]

Against this background of scepticism about his real intentions – as unclear to Attlee as they were to the American public – Truman invited the British and Canadian Prime Ministers to Washington 'to effect agreement on the conditions under which co-operation might displace rivalry'. Churchill was sceptical of Truman's statement and, in a debate on 7 November, restated his view that only an Anglo-American alliance could guarantee world peace, applauding Truman's reluctance to share atomic secrets with the Soviet Union.[25] Bevin's response, not at all what his party wanted to hear, endorsed Churchill's comments and underlined the difficulties of reaching agreement with the USSR.[26]

On 9 November Attlee flew from London to Washington. He had a dual purpose in making the trip: first to reach a satisfactory agreement with Truman and Mackenzie King on atomic research, principally observance of the 1943 Quebec agreement which, despite his commitment to the United Nations, he saw as vital to British security. Second, partially linked with the first goal, he wanted to reassure the American public that Britain had not 'gone communist'. If there were to be co-operation between nations over the bomb, it was vital that the American Congress and public not believe that anything shared with London would promptly be handed to Moscow. On 10 November the tripartite talks opened and on the following day the three leaders and their advisers continued talks during a cruise on the Potomac. The talks fell into two sections: first, proposals to minimise the possibility of nuclear war; second the agreement between the three nations on their mutual relations in the context of the atomic bomb. On the first issue Attlee relentlessly pursued the notion of the obligation that the United States, Britain and Canada bore for the role of atomic weapons in an altered world. That responsibility would in time become a global obligation. With the discovery of nuclear fission the world had changed for ever and it behoved the powers who possessed atomic secrets to search for means to ensure that the bomb was never used. Power politics were not only outdated, they were potentially catastrophic. He was shocked at the time spent at Yalta and Potsdam in defining the western border of Poland, as the bomber had already rendered rivers obsolete as national boundaries. How much more was it the case that atomic weapons had rendered all previous considerations of national security irrelevant?[27]

The tenacity with which he continued to press on Truman the urgency of avoiding the future use of the bomb by, if necessary, sharing nuclear secrets was emblematic of his approach to creating a more morally sound society. It was practical and realistic. Other nations would learn how to make atomic bombs soon enough; the time to redefine international relations was already upon the powers that possessed the secrets, not to use that knowledge in the outdated game of pressure but to work to create an international environment that would ensure they were never used. Since future wars would almost certainly involve the use of atomic bombs – not to mention weapons not yet devised – it was incumbent on the United States and Britain to cede to the United Nations the means to ensure that war itself was made obsolete, but until the United Nations was empowered to act as supra-national arbiter, the United States and Britain had a unique trust.

This involved sacrifice of national independence, and Attlee's subsequent frustration in his dealings with Washington can be traced to his belief that, in spite of all his attempts to convince him to act as a world statesman, Truman could not be counted on to act in accordance with principles greater than national interest. Attlee was a fierce patriot but he saw the limitations of pursuing national goals when there were greater issues at stake. Just as the abolition of poverty and the introduction of a clearly delineated basket of reforms embodied his domestic policy, transcending party politics, so the greater vision of avoiding mutually assured destruction transcended national interests.

On 15 November the three leaders announced the results. The Agreed Declaration called for extending between all nations the exchange of basic scientific information for peaceful ends and the control of atomic energy to the extent necessary to ensure its use only for peaceful purposes. Atomic weapons and all other weapons of mass destruction would be eliminated from national armaments and there would be 'effective safeguards ... to protect complying states against the ... violations and evasions'. They favoured availability and free interchange of the 'fruits of scientific research' but not of 'detailed information concerning the practical industrial application of atomic energy' or of its 'military exploitation'. This must await 'effective, reciprocal and enforceable safeguards acceptable to all nations'. The United Nations should set up a commission to prepare recommendations for the Security Council.[28] Dean Acheson noted that it was the opposite of what Stimson had urged.[29]

This was hardly a breakthrough and it was disappointing for Attlee as it provided for no foreseeable relinquishment of the American atomic monopoly. Vandevar Bush, one of three American representatives on the Combined Policy Committee established at Quebec in 1943, approved of the agreement, although the slipshod manner of its formulation shocked him. 'I have never participated in anything that was so completely unorganized or so irregular,' he wrote to Stimson. I have had experiences in the last week that would make a chapter in *Alice in Wonderland*.'[30]

Attlee was concerned about American opinion not only to quieten the furore over sharing atomic secrets, but also because negotiations for an American loan were still in progress during his Washington visit. He worked long and hard on his address to a Joint Session of Congress, in which he explained the nature of the British Labour Party, how and why it attracted middle-class voters – people like Attlee himself – and a cross-section of the population. There was, he argued, no reason to be alarmed by socialism. His government was not 'out to destroy freedom, freedom of the individual, freedom of speech, freedom of religion, and the freedom of the press'. Indeed, was socialism not based on the same principles as American liberty, on Magna Carta and *habeas corpus*?

Then, turning to the purpose of the tripartite talks and, by implication, the obligations of moral leadership facing America:

> *Man's material discoveries have outpaced his moral progress. The greatest task that faces us today is to bring home to all people before it is too late that our civilisation can only survive by the acceptance and practice in international relations and in our national life of the Christian principle that we are members of one another.*[31]

It was a passionate speech, praised by Bevin, Laski and Morrison – and by John Winant, the American ambassador – and successful in allaying American fears over what had seemed Britain's inexplicable lurch to the left. The American public was stunned and alarmed by the results of the British election, a fact that had an amusing and profitable by-product for Attlee. Emery Reves of Co-operation Publishing in New York wrote to Attlee in August, enclosing a cheque for $820, being 50 per cent of the proceeds from an article that Attlee had written in June and which was published in nineteen newspapers across the USA. Initially Reves had been unable to sell the article to more than five newspapers, but when the election results were known, he wrote, 'My office was transformed into a madhouse as one paper after another asked for telegraphic transmission of the article.'[32]

Attlee returned to London, believing that he had achieved all that he could have done and that Truman, within the political constraints imposed on him, was generally supportive of the British position. He was logically correct to base his position on the 1943 Quebec agreement but, since Truman could not publicly speak of that agreement, the logic did not alter the President's public posture. On his return Attlee reported to the House of Commons on the talks, similarly concealing the nub of his private conversations with Truman.[33] As Vandevar Bush had written to Stimson, there was an air of unreality in the results of talks that had been ostensibly positive.

Truman was under pressure on several fronts on the issue of the bomb.[34] The 'fear and awe' surrounding the new weapon had given rise to demands that all atomic energy be placed under civilian rather than military control, a proposal vehemently opposed by General Groves, architect of the Manhattan Project. As pressure mounted within Congress, Senator McMahon of Connecticut, chairman of the US Senate Special Committee of Atomic Energy, held a series of hearings that led to the introduction of the Atomic Energy Act. Truman, determined that atomic energy be under civilian control, recognised the need to endorse an American monopoly of atomic secrets in order to achieve this.

In late 1945 and early 1946 Attlee continued to press Truman for what he considered Britain's agreed rights. Each had a defensible position. Truman argued that to extend the scope of collaboration would be unwise while the Atomic Energy Act of 1946 and the establishment of international control through the United Nations were pending. Attlee argued that American assistance on a British plant had always been contemplated and that Britain, by virtue of its help to the USA in the development of radar and jet engines, was entitled to such assistance. The fundamental issue was that the United States was resolved to 'go it alone' with atomic energy but there remained this wartime agreement that stipulated an unwelcome degree of collaboration, no longer contemplated in American strategy. While Attlee understood Truman's position, he felt that the President was ignoring a more cogent moral imperative – to do all he could to honour the Quebec agreement.[35]

The exchange of cables between Attlee and Truman brings into focus a significant difference between the wartime collaboration of Churchill and Roosevelt and the styles of their successors. Attlee, believing that it was futile 'to have a good dog and bark yourself', left the handling of foreign policy – with the notable exception of India – to Bevin.[36] Churchill would surely have seen the disagreement over atomic research as a matter that could only be resolved between principals and would have been a frequent visitor to Washington, badgering the President to respect the British position. Whether or not he would have achieved much is moot. The fact remains, however, that, during six years as Prime Minister, Attlee visited Washington on only two occasions, each time in connection with the atomic bomb. While the grandstanding involved in a summit conference was anathema to him and totally at variance with his approach to reaching measured decisions, it is a valid criticism that he allowed the initiative to pass to Senator McMahon. When the Atomic Energy Act was signed by Truman on 1 August 1946, it contained a clause that specifically forbade any sharing of nuclear technology with America's allies.

Attlee's attention to detail throughout the 1945–46 discussions reveals the importance that he placed on his having control of the implementation and conduct of Britain's nuclear strategy.[37] No longer do we see scrawled notes such as 'Yes' or 'Agreed' at the foot of memoranda; instead his responses are detailed and painstaking in the forceful presentation of his principles to Truman, Byrnes and Groves. He was determined that co-operation with the USA should be absolute and equally determined that the absolute nature of that alliance should not be a stimulus to Soviet paranoia. In October 1945 he had informed Stalin of his intention to fly to Washington for talks with Truman and received an icy acknowledgment in return.[38]

Before Attlee left London for Washington, Churchill had informed him that he had been invited to spend time with a Canadian friend at his Florida home and that, if he was known to be in the United States, he would doubtless be called on for a number of public appearances, as well as a courtesy visit to the White House. Truman had already suggested that he make a speech at Westminster College at Fulton in Truman's home state of Missouri. If he were to accept, Churchill asked, would he have access to American dollars and would there be any objection to his speaking at Fulton?[39]

The answer to the first question reflects the austerity of the time. The Treasury informed Downing Street that he would be allowed to take

£10 in dollars for each day he was away, the allowance for a representative visit by a Member of Parliament. All unused dollars would have to be returned by Churchill in due course. As to the second question, Halifax told Attlee that he could see no objection. 'If, as he doubtless would, Winston said the right sort of thing, I think it might have a very good effect.' He ended the message, 'There passes through my mind the hope that he will not bring Max (Beaverbrook).'[40]

On 5 March Churchill delivered at Westminster College the speech that has become one of his most famous and quoted addresses. Declaring that 'From Stettin in the Baltic to Trieste in the Adriatic an iron curtain has descended across the Continent', the former Prime Minister intoned that 'if all British moral and material forces and convictions are joined with your own in fraternal association, the highroads of the future will be clear, not only for our time, but for a century to come.'[41]

After returning to England Churchill reported to Attlee and Bevin that he felt Truman and his advisers were moving towards confronting Soviet ambitions more forcefully. In fact, Churchill's judgement was premature, as it took longer for the Truman Doctrine to coalesce. Both Attlee and Truman were nervous about the effect that the call for a permanent Anglo-American alliance might have had.[42] In the event, however, the American press seized on the phrase 'Iron Curtain', which dominated American dialogue on the subject. It was from the left of the Labour Party rather than from American isolationists that objections flowed.

It had been fear of American isolationism, concern at the speed with which the United States had withdrawn forces from Europe, and, above all, alarm at the voracious rapidity with which the Soviet Union had consolidated its gains in Eastern Europe that posed a mass of interlocking problems for Attlee and Bevin. Retention of British forces in potential trouble spots in Europe and the Middle East severely taxed the country's depleted financial resources. Yet Attlee was adamant that he should not withdraw troops, leaving areas vulnerable to Soviet influence, until he was assured that the United States would share the burden. During 1945 and 1946, however, this was far from clear. Indeed, British policy in relation to the USSR was far more surefooted than that of the Americans, who initially appeared indecisive.

Attlee could afford no time to wait for American policy to harden. With the signing into law of the Atomic Energy Act in August 1946 came the decision that Britain would build her own independent nuclear deterrent.[43] On the surface, it was one of the most extraordinary decisions taken by a Prime Minister in the twentieth century. Yet for Attlee, as for Truman, problems that *prima facie* appeared complex often had a simple, utterly logical solution. To understand the logic, however, requires an analysis of British relations with the Soviet Union in the two years following the end of the war.

RELATIONS WITH THE SOVIET UNION

On 14 February 1945 Churchill cabled Attlee from Yalta that he was 'profoundly impressed with the friendly spirit of Stalin and Molotov. It is a different Russian world to any that I have seen hitherto.'[44] Whether Churchill believed this or whether he was privately flattered by the toast that Stalin had proposed at dinner, praising him in the most fulsome manner, is moot. Certainly he had revised his assessment of Soviet ambitions three months later. Appalled at Roosevelt's decision to halt Patton's Third Army at Plsen, allowing the Red Army to occupy Prague and to grasp the greatest prize of all, Berlin, he approached Potsdam with considerable pessimism.[45]

Attlee, the legatee of Churchill's and Roosevelt's war policy, faced internal party problems unique to the Labour Party. While Churchill never had to justify within his own party any aggressive position towards the Soviet Union, almost all of Attlee's Cabinet had firm, though fundamentally differing, views on foreign policy. Dalton was a vehement anti-communist. Addison thought that the post-war situation with the Soviet Union was as disturbing as the pre-war situation with Germany. On the other hand there were calls from the left wing of his party for closer ties with Russia. These came not from outlying, quasi-communist elements but from the respected figures of Cripps, Bevan, and Laski. The British Communist Party attempted on several occasions to become affiliated with the Labour Party; Attlee continually resisted on the grounds that 'the aims and methods of the Communist Party are substantially different from those of the Labour Party. They aim at "Dictatorship of the Proletariat". There is obviously no room in Britain for two mass working class parties. One or the other must go.'[46]

By Potsdam there was ample evidence that Stalin felt the same way – that within a communist sphere of influence there was no room for social democrat parties. For that reason Stalin and Molotov were greatly more comfortable confronting 'imperialists' like Churchill and Eden than having to deal with Attlee and Bevin.

Thus at Potsdam, Britain, the country that traditionally had fought to achieve a balance of power in Europe, now incapable of offering any resistance to any policy agreed between the two 'Superpowers', was faced with the spectre of the USSR gliding effortlessly into the position of power that Germany had occupied, which the war had been fought to dismantle. Armed with a new atomic weapon, the new President felt no compulsion to justify his position to Britain. Byrnes, convinced that Roosevelt's desire to co-operate with Stalin was the *sine qua non* of any European settlement, had little time for the impotent squawks of British doubters.[47]

Potsdam became the first public test of the Labour government. Attlee and Bevin needed to return to London with an agreement. Yet by the time they returned to the conference the eventual agreement had already been essentially hammered out by their wartime allies. Although Bevin impressed Cadogan with his ability to grasp the most complex problems with rapidity, he and Attlee were compelled to subscribe to a joint communiqué that expressed the very opposite of the truth. Although the future unity of Germany was loudly proclaimed, Potsdam had guaranteed its division.

At Yalta Stalin demanded reparations from Germany amounting to $20 billion, of which 50 per cent should go to Russia. Now occupying 20 per cent of German territory, Stalin began to ship to the Soviet Union whatever material could be moved. Russian occupation, moreover, set in motion a huge westward flow of refugees, all of whom needed to be fed in the British and American zones of occupation.

During the 1930s Attlee believed that a socialist foreign policy would be the hallmark of a post-war Labour government. During the war, however, his views changed and it became clear at Potsdam that he and Bevin wanted continuity in Britain's policy. Indeed, Bevin shocked Truman and Byrnes with the vehemence with which he resisted Stalin's demands for the Polish western frontier. In his memoirs Byrnes recounts a story of a woman who followed foreign policy watching Bevin speak in the House of Commons. She turned to her American companion and commented, 'Anthony Eden is making a good speech, but he seems to have gotten a little stout.'[48]

Stalin had one important advantage over the Western Allies: since 1929 he had been in unchallenged control in Moscow. He knew exactly what his post-war aims were, while Truman and Attlee appeared far less certain. Roosevelt described himself as 'a juggler', claiming that he never let his right hand know what his left hand was doing.[49] He certainly perfected that opacity as far as his Vice-President was concerned; Truman succeeded him with the flimsiest grasp of American policy. Attlee, at least, had been an active and informed deputy to Churchill.

Attlee was concerned that Truman, under pressure to 'bring the boys home', would be reluctant to be drawn into what he saw as essentially European problems for Europe to resolve.[50] Stalin meanwhile, having successfully driven a wedge between Roosevelt and Churchill at Tehran, saw Potsdam as a vastly simpler proposition.

Initially keen to preserve the wartime alliance between the Big Three, Attlee realised that there was no substantial alliance to preserve, and that Britain, alone of the Big Three, was dangerously exposed; Red Army strength at the end of the European war totalled over 11 million. Despite Attlee's long-term commitment to collective security, stark facts indicated that, as Britain withdrew forces from Greece, Turkey and the Middle East, those areas might be swiftly occupied by the Soviet Union. If, in another Doomsday scenario, the Red Army continued its westward advance, there would be little to prevent them reaching the Channel; the sole deterrent would be America's nuclear capability.

General Brooke had observed with incredulity the blind faith that Churchill placed in the West's nuclear superiority. 'He had absorbed all the minor American exaggerations,' he recalled,

> *and, as a result, was completely carried away. It was now no longer necessary for the Russians to come into the Japanese war; the new explosive alone was sufficient to settle the matter ... He had at once painted a picture of himself as the sole possessor of these bombs and capable of dumping them where he wished. Thus all-powerful and capable of dictating to Stalin!*[51]

Attlee had no such illusions, certainly not after his discussions with Truman in November 1945.

Several conflicting pressures influenced British policy. Despite her crippled economic position, strategic considerations dictated that British forces be retained in key areas until the United States could be persuaded to assist or replace them. At home, meanwhile, demand for accelerated demobilisation was becoming more vocal. The government's ability to make good on its election promises, moreover, was being eroded by expenditure on defence commitments. This expenditure, in turn, reduced Britain's ability to pay for badly needed foodstuffs. An export drive, therefore, was vital to earn necessary dollars; but there was a manpower shortage, owing to the large numbers still in uniform, necessary to show a British presence in areas considered strategically vital. It is easy to see how Stalin was confident that time was on his side.

Between the announcement of the election results and his return to Potsdam Attlee had announced six vital Cabinet appointments. One of those, undoubtedly the most important, was that of Bevin to the Foreign Office. His initial plan had been to send Bevin to the Treasury, the post that Bevin most wanted, and to appoint Dalton Foreign Secretary. According to Alan ('Tommy') Lascelles, Private Secretary to George VI, the King objected strongly to Dalton's appointment and, in deference to his monarch's wishes, Attlee switched the two. Attlee himself later wrote that he was doubtful of the wisdom of appointing Morrison to the Home Office and Bevin to the Treasury, two sworn enemies in control of domestic affairs.[52]

A contributing factor was that, after observing the tactics of Molotov at Potsdam, it was clear to him that the Labour minister best equipped to stand up to Molotov was the equally abrasive Bevin, schooled in trade union battles and quite able to hold his own with the Soviet Foreign Minister. It turned out to be an inspired choice; he and Bevin worked closely together, mutually supportive, colleagues with a close understanding of each other and of the policy they pursued. To no other minister would Attlee have delegated so comprehensively. Bevin, he later wrote, was 'the soul of loyalty' and until his death in April 1951 he and Attlee spoke daily on matters of state. Kenneth Harris quotes an interview with Lord Franks in which the Ambassador said that on major issues Bevin 'would not move until he knew he had Attlee with him'.[53]

In Bevin's view, Attlee possessed a rare quality among politicians: he was a morally consistent colleague who accepted responsibility for his decisions. When a coup against Attlee was planned in 1947, Bevin, at least three times approached as a possible successor, vehemently refused to co-operate. Unlike other luminaries of the party – Cripps, Bevan and Morrison, for example – Bevin had no wish to be Prime Minister; that absence of ambition for the top job made him the perfect ally for Attlee. For those whose ambition was to replace Attlee his contempt was savage. Once, hearing Bevan described as 'his own worst enemy', Bevin chortled and commented 'Not while I'm alive, he ain't.'[54]

Since 1937, when he wrote in *The Labour Party in Perspective* that a socialist foreign policy would necessarily be different from a Tory policy, Attlee had changed his view and believed that parties should be united in defence and foreign policy, a view he expressed in the Commons in March 1945.[55] Once Labour came to power, to the dismay of the left wing of the party, Attlee and Bevin proceeded to observe that principle. Laski, attending the French Socialist Party conference in August, voiced his view that British foreign policy would now experience a dramatic shift to the left. Attlee reproved him acerbically on 20 August, emphasising that 'Foreign Affairs are in the capable hands of Ernest Bevin' and that there was 'widespread resentment in the party' at Laski's activities. He concluded, saying that 'a period of silence on your part would be welcome'.[56]

The first trial of strength was to come at the Council of Foreign Ministers which opened in London on 11 September. This council had been agreed upon at Potsdam and included the foreign ministers of the 'Big Three' and of France and China. A 'spirit of cordiality and co-operation' was optimistically envisaged.

The glow of that spirit, however, was tarnished by three weeks of bickering between the United States and Britain on one side and the Soviet Union on the other. The ostensible cause of the rift was the status at the conference of France and China whom Molotov, referring repeatedly to Stalin for instructions, demanded be excluded. The true cause was the determination of the Soviet Union to dispense with promised free elections and establish puppet regimes in Romania and Bulgaria. This, in turn, was precipitated by the unsettling speed with which the

United States had established its power in Asia after the destruction of Hiroshima and Nagasaki and the collapse of Japan.

Stalin employed for the first time what would become a familiar tactic in his negotiations with the West. Careful to avoid offering *casus belli*, he instructed Molotov to maintain an inflexible posture on the matter of how and in what capacity the French and Chinese ministers might attend. This would test the strength of Western resolve. If forced to yield – as he was – then Molotov should make a further unacceptable demand – in this case Soviet trusteeship of Tripolitania. Again challenged, Molotov should revert to the original position of excluding the French and Chinese, not simply from voting on the peace treaties in Eastern Europe but from the entire conference, thus diverting attention from the issue most central to Soviet policy, their determination to dominate Romania and Bulgaria. The declared cause of the inevitable breakdown of the talks would be the inflexible position taken by Britain and the USA in aligning four powers against the Soviet Union. Predictably, the conference came to an end, having resolved nothing.

Criticism from the left of the Labour Party became shrill after the London meeting. This period coincided with the uncertainty concerning American plans for atomic energy and, in the absence of a clear American policy for Europe and uncertainty about Russia's intentions, Attlee and Bevin were groping their way towards a plan for dealing with the Soviet Union. Bevin expressed this uncertainty in a memorandum to the Cabinet on 8 November, describing the situation as 'rapidly drifting into spheres of influence or what can be better described as three Monroes'. This, he said, was both American and Russian policy, and Britain, after two great wars, would have to take sides with one or the other.[57]

When Bevin, Byrnes and Molotov met in Moscow from 16 to 26 December there was less overt animosity than there had been in London. There was even progress towards settling the peace treaties scheduled for signature the following May, towards establishing a Far Eastern Council and Allied Council for Japan, and the setting up of a Joint Commission to enable Korea to move towards independence. Overall, however, the conference did little more than codify an agreement to agree. George Kennan of the US State Department, who was present at the meetings, recorded a cynical and probably accurate assessment of the conference. Byrnes, he believed, only wanted an agreement for its political effect in America. The Russians knew this and will 'see that for this superficial success he pays a heavy price in the things that are real.'[58]

Truman too was beginning to doubt Byrnes' motives and was particularly enraged after the Moscow conference, believing that his Secretary of State was pursuing his own agenda without reference to the President. Simply, Byrnes, to whom Roosevelt had originally promised the nomination for Vice-President in 1944, felt that he and not Truman should be President. The growing distance between the two encouraged Attlee and Bevin to the view that, given time, Truman would adopt a policy more congruent with their own.

In the meantime, however, their task was to defend an Atlantic policy while Truman appeared to be imposing harsh terms on Britain. It was not only with the left-wing press that the terms of the American loan rankled. The *Sunday Times* commented that 'as victors we are being asked to pay reparations'.[59] The feeling that Britain was being exploited by the United States increased pressure from the left of the party to reach accommodation with the Soviet Union. Attlee and Bevin remained deaf to such urging, certain that they would eventually arrive at a satisfactory accord with Washington. When Zilliacus, by now Member of Parliament for Gateshead, took the government to task for its Atlantic policy, Attlee responded in typically brusque fashion, 'Thank you for sending me your memorandum which seems to me to be based on an astonishing misunderstanding of the facts.'[60]

Before the Council of Foreign Ministers met again in Paris at the end of April 1946 Churchill spoke at Westminster College. Reaction in the Soviet press was violent, comparing Churchill with Hitler. Stalin denounced him as a warmonger. The speech has passed into history as the opening shot in the Cold War; such a description is grandiloquent, but it did crystallise doubts about Soviet intentions that many Americans and Britons were starting to feel, dispelling any lingering hopes for the continued life of the wartime alliance.

Throughout 1946 Attlee was compelled to rebut accusations that Britain was 'ganging up' with the United States against their former ally. When Stalin delayed the withdrawal of Soviet troops from Iran in

March Truman was enraged but cautiously avoided any open breach with Russia. The matter was referred to the United Nations and Stalin agreed to withdraw his troops – an undertaking that he was slow to honour.

Britain's Mediterranean policy – that bases in Gibraltar, Malta and Alexandria enabled control of the Mediterranean and safeguarded the Suez Canal, vital for the supply and defence of India – was an established cornerstone of British strategic thinking. Attlee challenged this concept as outdated in an era of air power, particularly in the atomic age. If India was to be offered independence, Britain was no longer a Mediterranean power with interests to safeguard to the East, but the eastern terminus of the American sphere of influence. This view, predictably, was resisted by the Chiefs of Staff, who had successfully opposed too rapid withdrawal from the Persian Gulf in the previous year. Neither the United States nor the Soviet Union had a coherent Middle East policy beyond wishing to reduce or remove British interests in the region. Kennan, in drafting a speech for Harriman in October 1945, had written simply that Russia 'looked on all advanced countries as Russia's ultimate enemies and all backward countries as pawns in a struggle for power.'[61] Frank Roberts, British Minister in Moscow, expressed the same sentiment in a more colourful manner, noting that the Soviet Union regarded the Middle East 'as an artichoke whose leaves are to be eaten one by one'.[62]

Bevin agreed strongly with Kennan and Roberts and argued that Britain, the last bastion of social democracy between capitalist America and communist Russia, needed to establish her base in Africa, possibly Kenya. The Chiefs of Staff, while sceptical about Bevin's grandiose plan for Africa, remained united in opposition to any concessions in the Mediterranean. Ultimately, however, Attlee, Bevin and the Chiefs of Staff were unanimous in their conviction that the Soviet Union would push at any weak spot that appeared and that this must be resisted at all costs.

None of this endeared Attlee and Bevin to the left of the Labour Party and Attlee incurred a barrage of criticism for allying Britain with America's economic ambitions. At the party conference in June Laski once more pressed for a socialist policy less antagonistic to the Soviet Union. This theme repeated itself at the TUC conference in October when a resolution condemning the government's policy for its alignment with the United States was tabled. While the resolution was defeated, it revealed strong opposition to the direction that Attlee and Bevin had taken.

Within the Parliamentary Party, too, a dissident group was forming. On 16 November, soon after the opening of the new session of Parliament, Hector McNeil, Minister of State at the Foreign Office, warned Attlee that Dick Crossman, spokesman for the dissidents, intended to raise four points in an amendment calling on the government to 'provide a democratic and constructive socialist alternative to an otherwise inevitable conflict between American capitalism and Soviet communism': Would the government disavow Churchill's Fulton speech? Why did the government support the American claim to air facilities in Iceland? Was it true that British and American military equipment was to be standardised as one? Why has the government held up credit to Czechoslovakia on a US initiative?

Attlee's immediate reaction, scribbled on McNeil's note, reads:

– *We are not pursuing an exclusive Anglo-American alliance*
– *Is it thought that this is the theme of Mr Churchill's speech?*[63]

When the amendment was moved on the next day the thrust of Crossman's attack was that Britain was acting as America's lackey in its growing conflict with the Soviet Union much as she had been her catspaw in the recent war with Germany. This in spite of its election claim that only a Labour government would be able to prevent East–West polarisation.[64] Attlee's response, measured, logical and precise, first commended Bevin and his 'services in the cause of Labour and social-ism'. The government's foreign policy, he continued, was not based on groupings or spheres of influence, nor was it a continuation of Tory policy. It was based on collective security, on the United Nations. It was unrealistic, moreover, he asserted, to treat domestic policy and foreign policy as comparable. Every statesman constantly had to decide between aggression and compromise.[65]

It was a sober but devastating reply. Even so, there was, if not outright support for Crossman, equivocal response from several dissident Labour members who abstained in the division. Attlee had won – for the moment at least.

In the eighteen months since the European war ended Attlee managed to keep several crises at bay. Aware of the cost of maintaining a British presence in regions vulnerable to Soviet pressure, he had persisted, not to maintain the British Empire, for he had no illusions about its sustainability. He was coming to believe that Britain's security was threatened by an expansionist Russia and that an alliance with Washington was essential. When Churchill spoke at Fulton he secretly applauded the sentiments expressed but, mindful of American public opinion, held his peace. It was no time to move ahead of Truman on the issue of an Anglo-American alliance.

Instead he needed to wait for the American climate to change, for recognition that the three-cornered wartime alliance could not be preserved. This was not, as was persistently charged, a decision to 'gang up' on the Soviet Union; it was an objective analysis that anticipated Truman's doctrine of 'containment'. From time to time, as he considered the cost of resisting Russian pressure in the several areas where it might be applied, he became downcast and questioned the return on human capital employed. But there was always support from Bevin, determined that Britain should not be 'barged about'.

As 1946 came to an end, he wrote to Tom that 'We are just ending a very good ten days Christmas holiday at Chequers.'[66] Since he had first visited the country home of the Prime Minister as Churchill's guest he had found it a haven of peace away from London and went there whenever pressure of business allowed. In August he had written to Tom, 'We stayed at Chequers for a fortnight with only occasional visits to town, papers taking only three or four hours a day … Public affairs grow no easier, but I suppose we shall get a ray of light sometime.'[67]

By the end of the year he must have wondered, as far as foreign affairs were concerned, if that ray of light would ever shine through.

ENDNOTES

1   John Wheeler-Bennett and Anthony Nicholls, *The Semblance of Peace*, p. 290. See also Keith Eubank, *Summit at Teheran*, pp. 488–489.

2   Eden, who had great admiration for both Attlee and Bevin, offered to accompany them to Potsdam if Attlee wished, but would not be at all hurt if he were not invited. Eden noted in his diary that Attlee 'seemed relieved'. Rhodes James, *Anthony Eden*, p. 309.

3   Byrnes recorded that he discussed the package deal with Attlee and Bevin, who promptly accepted it. *Speaking Frankly*, p. 84.

4   Charles L. Mee, Jr., *Meeting at Potsdam*, p. 6.
5   *As It Happened*, p. 208. Mee, *Meeting at Potsdam*, p. 201.
6   Margaret Truman, *Harry S. Truman*, p. 277.
7   Senator William Langer, controversial Republican Governor and later Senator from North Dakota, was described as 'a master of political theater'.
8   John L. Lewis, president of the United Mine Workers of America from 1920 to 1960, had strenuously opposed FDR's moves to involve the USA in the war.
9   Truman Library, HST to Margaret Truman, 29 July 1945. Cited by McCullough, *Truman*, pp. 447–448.
10   Roy Jenkins, *Truman*, p. 205. There might have been mutual sympathy for the position in which each found himself, following in the footsteps of a legend. In the same way as Attlee was derided by his critics (e.g. 'a modest man with much to be modest about'), so was Truman mocked in the USA (e.g. 'to err is Truman').
11   *The Memoirs of General Lord Ismay*, p. 403.
12   Churchill, *The Second World War*, vol. 6, 'Triumph and Tragedy', p. 672.
13   For Churchill's account see *The Second World War*, vol. 6, 'Triumph and Tragedy', pp. 671–674.
14   Bohlen, *Witness to History*, pp. 247–248.
15   TNA: CAB 130–2. GEN. 75/1st Meeting, 10 August 1945.
16   Memo from PM, TNA: CAB 130–3, GEN 75/1. 28 August 1945.
17   TNA: CAB 130–2, GEN. 75/2nd Meeting, 29 August 1945.
18   The first draft of the letter was written on 7 September. TNA: CAB 130–3, GEN. 75/2.
19   TNA: CAB 130–3, GEN 75/6. 13 October 1945.
20   *Public Papers of the Presidents, Harry S. Truman*, 1945/156. 3 October, 1945.
21   Stimson's Memorandum of 11 September 1945 to the President is reproduced in full at Henry L. Stimson and McGeorge Bundy, *On Active Service in Peace and War*, pp. 642–646.
22   *Public Papers of the Presidents, Harry S. Truman*, 1945/164. 8 October, 1945.
23   *Public Papers of the Presidents, Harry S. Truman*, 1945/178. 27 October, 1945.
24   *Nation*, Editorial, 3 November 1945
25   *Hansard*, HC Deb, 7 November 1945, cols 1290–1300.
26   *Hansard*, HC Deb, 7 November 1945, cols 1333–43.
27   TNA: CAB 130/3, 14 November 1945.
28   *The Public Papers of the Presidents, Harry S. Truman*, 1945/191. 15 November 1945. TNA: PREM 8/367/400, 16 November 1945.
29   Dean Acheson, *Present at the Creation*, pp. 131–132.
30   Bush to Stimson, 13 November 1945, Stimson MSS, Box 427. Cited by John Lewis Gaddis, *The United States and the Origins of the Cold War*, p. 272.
31   Bodleian: MS. Attlee, dep. 26, 13 November 1945.
32   Emery Reves, letter to CRA, 25 August 1945. Bodleian: MS. Attlee, dep. 20. There was, in fact, a sudden Attlee-mania in the USA and Attlee appeared on the cover of *TIME* magazine for 6 August 1945.
33   *Hansard*, HC Deb, 22 November 1945, cols. 601–609.
34   TNA: PREM 8/367, Makins to Ricketts, ANCAM 528, fol. 334, 4 February 1946.
35   TNA: PREM 8/367 between 5 March and 20 April 1946, fols. 98–177.
36   *As It Happened*, p. 237.
37   In multiple instances in TNA: PREM 8/367 and CAB 130–2.
38   Ministry of Foreign Affairs of the USSR, *Correspondence between Stalin, Churchill and Attlee During World War Two*, pp. 378–379, nos. 513 and 515, 30 October and 8 November 1945.
39   Correspondence between Churchill, Sir Leslie Rowan, Attlee and the Treasury in Bodleian: MS. Attlee, dep. 25.
40   Bodleian: MS. Attlee, dep. 25, 31 October 1945.
41   James Rhodes, *Winston S. Churchill: His Complete Speeches 1897–1963*, vol. 7, pp. 7285–93.
42   Bevin commented angrily that Churchill thought he was Prime Minister of the world. Sir Nicholas Henderson, *Private Office*, p. 27.
43   Bevin was completely in agreement with Attlee, saying to a 26 October meeting of GEN 75, 'We've got to have this thing over here whatever it costs ... We've got to have the bloody Union Jack flying on top of it.'
44   S. M. Plokhy, *Yalta: The Price of Peace*, p. 332.
45   For the correspondence between Churchill and Eisenhower on this strategic divergence see Churchill, *The Second World War*, vol. 6, 'Triumph and Tragedy', pp. 463–468.
46   Bodleian: MS. Attlee, dep. 33, 27 February 1946.
47   Mee, *Meeting at Potsdam*, pp. 204 ff.

48   Byrnes, *Speaking Frankly*, p. 79. Francis Beckett attributes the comment to 'Rab' Butler. *Clem Attlee*, p. 221.
49   Speaking to a Latin-America study group on 15 May 1942.
50   Granada Historical Records, *Clem Attlee*, pp. 34–35.
51   Danchev and Todman, *War Diaries*, p. 710.
52   CAC: ATLE 1/17.
53   Harris, *Attlee*, p. 294.
54   Bullock, *Ernest Bevin, Foreign Secretary*, p. 77.
55   *Hansard*, HC Deb, 1 March 1945, col. 1614.
56   Williams, *A Prime Minister Remembers*, p. 169.
57   Alan Bullock cites this memorandum in *Ernest Bevin: Foreign Secretary*, p. 193 and notes that the paper did not appear in the Cabinet agenda but is found in Bevin's papers, FO 800/478/MIS/45/14.
58   George Kennan, *Memoirs 1925–1950*, pp. 287–288.
59   *Sunday Times*, 16 December 1945.
60   Bodleian: MS. Attlee, dep. 31, 17 February 1946.
61   Hugh Thomas, *Armed, Truce*, p. 405.
62   Roberts, 20 March 1946, TNA. FO 371/56831 N35756/605/38 Cited by Thomas, *Armed Truce*, p. 406.
63   Bodleian: MS. Attlee, dep. 46, 16 November 1946.
64   *Hansard*, HC Deb, 18 November 1946, cols 526–531.
65   *Hansard*, HC Deb, 18 November 1946, col. 579.
66   Letter to Tom Attlee, 29 December 1946.
67   Letter to Tom Attlee, 30 August 1946.

CHAPTER ELEVEN

ANNUS MIRABILIS, 1945–1946

The Labour government of 1945 included men of solid experience. Morrison, described by Harold Macmillan as 'an almost Dickensian character',[1] had shown his worth as an accomplished, charismatic administrator. Bevin, the highly visible wartime Minister of Labour and, to quote Macmillan again, 'the strongest man in the Labour government',[2] was instantly recognisable to the public. It was, curiously, the new Prime Minister who was the least known of Labour's 'Big Three'. Peter Hennessy in a 1995 lecture described him aptly as 'decidedly *diminuendo*'.[3]

Attlee had constructed his Cabinet carefully, looking at his choices for offices from every angle, moving names about like a homeowner fitting furniture to a new house.[4] It was no easy task; the talent pool was well-stocked, but with many newcomers, few of whom he had yet been able to assess. In the ten years since the last election the reins of government had been tightly held and there had been no intake of promising Labour Members. As a result, his first Cabinet was made up of older men; its average age was sixty-one and a half. Only six of the twenty members were under sixty.

From the outset, however, Attlee drove his team with the vigour of a far younger man. Evidence of his preference for action over words abounds.[5] In a speech to an Oxford audience he later said that 'the great thing in the Cabinet was to stop people talking'.[6] Dalton recalled that he could name 'two, perhaps three, ministers … who lost their jobs, at least for a while, because they talked too much in Cabinet.'[7] Bevin was allowed some latitude as a raconteur, but members of Attlee's Cabinet quote examples of ministers being summarily silenced. Wilson recalled an occasion when the Prime Minister opened a Cabinet with 'Minutes of the last meeting'. A Scottish minister said, 'Well, Prime Minister, I don't disagree but I do remember a similar occasion three years ago.' … Attlee cut in brusquely and demanded, 'Do you disagree with the Minutes. No? All right. Agreed. Next item.'[8]

Roland Moyle, son of Arthur Moyle, Attlee's Parliamentary Private Secretary, told a similar story to illustrate Attlee's minimalist approach. After his secret decision to build an atomic bomb became known, Harold Davies, a Welsh backbench MP, subjected the Parliamentary Party to a ten-minute harangue on the horrors of nuclear warfare, describing in lurid detail the effects of radiation. Attlee paused a second before removing his pipe from his mouth. 'Yes', he nodded. 'We must watch it. Next item.'[9]

This brusqueness in meetings led junior colleagues to feel that their work was not appreciated. Invariably polite in his dealings on a human level, he rarely bothered to do more than acknowledge a job well done; he expected nothing less and would have been astonished if anyone had accused him of bad manners. Jim Callaghan commented that when Attlee did congratulate him, he 'blushed with pleasure, as it came from such an unaccustomed source.'[10]

Speedy and efficient dispatch of business required a small Cabinet with ministers who acted as 'overlords' for a number of policy areas, relying on committees to bring business to Cabinet. Morrison, after his success with London Transport in 1931, had overall responsibility for nationalisation; individual departmental ministers – Dalton, Shinwell, Bevan, Alfred Barnes, John Wilmot and James Griffith – had specific responsibility for preparing legislation for the transfer to public owner-ship and creation of plans for (e.g.) national insurance and the National Health Service.[11]

Committees, a central feature of the wartime coalition, proliferated in the post-war government, until 148 standing committees and 313 *ad hoc* committees had been created.[12] Every major issue spawned a Cabinet committee, distinguishing Attlee's style from the later fashion of central-ised control vested in the Prime Minister and special advisers.

From 1940 to 1945 Attlee had repeatedly emphasised the approaching need to win the peace. Winning the war entailed austerity, but behind wartime austerity was the ringing clarion call of Churchill's oratory, invoking Blenheim, Ramillies, Oudenarde and Malplaquet, Trafalgar and Waterloo. Behind Attlee's call for austerity there was coal rationing, bread rationing, an increasing, gnawing anxiety that there would be no peacetime El Alamein, no glorious victory to end austerity, no Sunday when church bells would ring. This was not what Britons felt they were owed; it was a puzzling kind of victory. Rationally, they understood the need for controls; emotionally, it was hard to accept that manufactured products must be kept from the home market in favour of an export drive, that Germany must be rebuilt while much of Britain was in ruins, that in a time of famine occupants of the British zone in Germany must be fed while Britons continued to suffer rationing. After initial euphoria, the question of who had won the war was on many lips.

The accuracy of Attlee's predictions was brought home in a Cabinet Paper presented by Dalton in August. A survey of 'Our Overseas Financial Prospects', it warned of 'almost desperate plight unless some … source of temporary assistance can be found to carry us over while we recover our breath – a plight far worse than most people, even in government departments, have yet realised.'[13]

On 16 August Attlee addressed the Commons on the subject of the dire economic situation facing Britain and all Europe, warning that 'we are going to face difficult years, and to get through them will require no less effort, no less unselfishness and no less hard work, than were needed to bring us through the war.'[14] Five days later, without warning, Truman cancelled Lend-Lease with effect from 2 September, explaining to the press that 'the bill passed by Congress defined Lend-Lease as a weapon of war and after we ceased to be at war it is no longer necessary'.[15]

Attlee commented that this was untrue and the decision had been taken without adequate consideration of its consequences. He informed the Commons of Truman's action and its implications. Britain was spending £2,000 million annually and receiving £350 million from exports and £450 million reimbursement from the dominions. 'Thus', he said, 'the initial deficit with which we start the task of re-establishing our overseas commitment is immense.'[16] To add to Attlee's distress, Canada cancelled Mutual Aid at the end of the Japanese war. Initially enraged at the lack of prior consultation, he was mollified to learn that Canada was merely performing 'a book-keeping operation' and that 'The end of Mutual Aid transfers will not end or delay the flow of essential civilian supplies to [Canada's] allies'.[17]

Nonetheless, Britain needed to take drastic steps, not only to fund reforms that Labour had promised, but simply to survive. This required immediate action to give export trade priority over domestic rehabilitation, to restrict imports, and radical pruning of government overseas expenditure. The first two courses would 'involve serious limitations on the restoration of civilian standards'. The third would impose 'serious limitations on the strategic and diplomatic part which we can play in the rest of the world.' It was far from certain that these steps would be adequate; they would, moreover, involve greater austerity than in wartime. Financial assistance would be needed and this could only come from the USA. To obtain a loan from Washington would necessitate 'positive action to reduce obstacles to international trade in conformity with Article VII of the Mutual Aid Agreement.'[18]

Keynes, commenting that 'The country was facing a financial Dunkirk',[19] was confident that a loan of five billion dollars would be forthcoming from Washington, part in the form of grant-in-aid and part as an interest-free loan.[20] When the State Department insisted that credits to Britain were conditional on Britain's readiness to forswear imperial preference, Bevin commented that, when he listened to Keynes and his 'winged words', 'I seem to hear those coins jingling in my pocket; but I am not so sure they're really there.'[21] Further doubt was generated when loading of American supplies for Britain was suspended, pending agreement on credit terms. When Attlee acidly told Truman that 'it is hardly necessary for me to assure you that if these supplies for the next month come forward to us as I have suggested, they will be paid for',[22] Bevin's scepticism seemed justified.

Keynes and his delegation left for Washington in early September and encountered grave disquiet at Britain's direction among Republicans in Congress. This was sharpened by anti-American articles and comments from Laski, giving the impression that Britain was governed by quasi-communists. During Keynes' mission Attlee received letters, postcards and telegrams from concerned American anglophiles urging him to muzzle Laski.[23]

As the talks progressed, Dalton observed, the British team 'retreated with a bad grace and with increasing irritation, from a free gift to an interest-free loan and from this to a loan bearing interest.'[24] The amount of the loan was reduced, strings were attached and tightened; the conditions attached seemed 'so tight that they might strangle our trade and, indeed, our whole economic life', but the government had little option. Throughout September, October and November the Washington talks inched towards accord. Dalton and the Treasury continued to believe that some form of grant or interest-free loan was possible[25], despite Keynes' recognition that 'we must substitute prose for poetry'.[26]

Keynes described the American attitude as 'ruthless'[27] but by early December terms were finalised and Attlee announced details in the Commons.[28] There would be a line of credit for $3,750 million to facilitate Britain's purchase of goods and services from the USA, to meet transitional balance-of-payment deficits, to help the UK maintain gold reserves, and to assist her multilateral trade. Further, there had been agreed a settlement of Lend-Lease and reciprocal aid with Britain owing the United States $650 million. The total amount loaned was $4,400 million for a fifty-year term at 2 per cent interest from 31 December 1951. A condition was that sterling be made convertible into dollars by July 1947.

Attlee took little part in Cabinet and committee discussions of the loan, involving himself far less than he did in negotiations with Ben Chifley of Australia or Mackenzie King of Canada. This is curious as the American loan was of vastly greater immediate importance. As Harold Wilson observed, Attlee was 'tone deaf' on economic matters[29] and relied on Douglas Jay for analyses of the implications of American proposals.[30] It is arguable that, had Attlee interceded with Truman, better terms might have been obtained more rapidly, but he allowed events to run their course.

The unreality of American expectations that their boys could be brought home immediately after VE Day was matched only by the naïve British expectations that the twenty-seven months that she had stood alone against Germany would be liberally rewarded once the war was won. That Britain could approach only America for a loan while that country was systematically dismantling the British Empire was

ironic. The effect within the Labour Party was to drive a wedge between
the Atlanticists and Crossman's group that became 'Keep Left'. This
posed particular problems for Attlee, whose style of Cabinet management was to obtain consensus. Consensus is generally absent in times
of crisis, particularly a novel form of crisis that has no tried, effective
response. Not only were the Welfare State and the entire nationalisation
programme threatened, but the ability of the country to survive at even
wartime levels of austerity was doubtful.

Even before the American loan was secured, however, even while the
issue of demobilisation was acute, Attlee decided to proceed immediately with plans for public ownership and control of vital elements of
the economic system. In general, the extent of wartime controls, which
the public had come to accept, greatly facilitated the process of nationalisation, the central feature of the election manifesto. As Attlee stresses
in his autobiography, nationalisation was not an end in itself but an
essential element in creating a society based on social justice.[31]

Attlee himself assumed the responsibility for prioritising the various
initiatives in the sequence most likely to succeed. Figuring that most
Tories, including Churchill, his most vociferous opponent, had already
accepted the inevitability of the nationalisation of the Bank of England,
he placed that at the top of his list. Between the wars, under the control
of Montagu Norman, the Bank had moved closer to fulfilling the role
of a central bank and thus the process was relatively straightforward.
When Dalton spoke at the second reading of the Bill, he referred to its
simplicity, pointing out that Churchill had already professed to having
no objection to the move. It was, he argued, a model that would, 'in due
course, make a streamlined socialist statute.' With only five clauses and
three schedules, 'it does the job which we intend to do'.[32]

The tone of the debate on the Bill confirmed that there was no
concerted objection in principle; on the Tory benches there was a
resigned acceptance of the inevitable. Dalton spoke with assurance; to
Tory rearguard action Glenvil Hall, Financial Secretary to the Treasury,
responded, pointing out that the Bank recognised that, in all matters of
major policy, the Treasury had the last word. It was 'a logical step that
the relationship which has existed between the Treasury and the Bank,
should be given something more than informal recognition, and should

be put into statutory form, which ... should give the Treasury the ultimate responsibility for saying what the policy should be.'[33] The Tories
baulked at that single issue, possibly a foretaste of more sinister control
to come. A majority of 200 in the vote, however, ensured the ultimate
outcome; on 14 February 1946 the Bank of England Act became law.

Attlee had chosen his first sortie well, but he expected no easy passage
of his entire legislative programme. If he had any doubts, these were
dispelled on 6 December, when the Opposition tabled a Motion of
Censure, criticising the government for the 'formulation of long-term
schemes for nationalisation creating uncertainty over the whole field of
industrial and economic activity, in direct opposition to the best interest
of the nation, which demands food, work and homes.'[34]

Churchill, speaking first on the second day of the debate, made a
spirited and wide-ranging attack on the government, concluding with
the extraordinary claim that the government, not he, was partisan. Had
the Tories won the election, he claimed, 'my first thought would have
been to seek the co-operation of the minority, and gather together the
widest and strongest measure of agreement over the largest possible
area.' Instead Labour had introduced 'party antagonism, bitter as
anything I have seen in my long life of political conflict'. He charged
the government with 'trying to exalt their partisan and faction interests
at the cost not only of the national unity but of our recovery and of our
vital interest.'[35]

In response Attlee offered a powerful rebuttal, not merely of the
charge but also of its motivation. Recently returned from Washington,
he stood taller in the Parliamentary Party than ever. As Prime Minister
responding to the Leader of the Opposition, he addressed Churchill
very differently from his wartime manner as the latter's deputy. In four
months of office he had established himself as a vigorous leader and,
according to Jim Callaghan, he 'began to demonstrate his supremacy
over his party and a growing mastery of the House'.[36]

There was no secret about plans to proceed with nationalisation, he
said; it was central to the party's manifesto. Why should Churchill be
surprised at the government doing what it had pledged to do? As for
bitter party antagonism, Churchill's objections amounted to asking
'Why, when you were elected to carry out a socialist programme, did

you not carry out a Conservative programme?' The government did not accept that when Churchill 'suggested we should carry on the good old Conservative policies, he was speaking for the nation.'[37]

In a single speech Attlee, while paying tribute to Churchill's war leadership, stripped away whatever remained of the Churchill mystique. He, the Prime Minister, was statesmanlike. His opponent was a mere party politician. It is not over-dramatic to treat the speech, which Roy Jenkins quotes as one of Attlee's most accomplished,[38] as one that consolidated his colleagues' respect for him as leader.

Almost all retrospective analyses of Attlee's leadership focus on the contrast between his retiring demeanour and the more charismatic style of his senior colleagues. One history of the Labour leaders contrasts the 'tortoise' with the four 'hares' – Bevin, Cripps, Dalton and Morrison – in his Cabinet.[39] There was, of course, a fifth hare, the Leader of the Opposition. Attlee achieved ascendancy over all five by the simple expedient of being himself, specifically being the man he was at the time he lived. Of the four Labour hares, each had a characteristic that stood in the way of his being a successful leader.

Morrison was a magnificent No. 2, an attack dog able to implement the wishes of the chief executive. Like many able seconds-in-command, he did not see why he should not be No. 1. His strength in the Attlee Cabinet was as Leader of the House of Commons, in which role he excelled, driving colleagues relentlessly to keep legislation on track.

Dalton, larger than life, bombastic, though far from stupid, had a battery of things he hated – Germans, Americans, Tories, all were grist to his mill. He was also an inveterate plotter. Francis Williams believed that if Dalton had become Labour's leader 'he would have started intriguing against himself out of sheer habit'.[40] If the key to negotiation is to be able to put oneself in the position of one's opponent – a quality of critical importance for a chief executive – Dalton would have failed. He would have failed with great panache, but failed nonetheless.

Cripps was briefly viewed as a future leader when he returned from the Moscow embassy in 1942. But he owed his sudden popularity to the Russian struggle more than to his own talents for leadership. By the end of World War II his time had passed; by the beginning of the Cold War the basis for his wartime ascendancy was removed.

Bevin was the only Attlee lieutenant who could have won and held the leadership. He had the opportunity in July 1945 and twice in 1947, but, like Julius Caesar on the Lupercal, he did thrice refuse. Instead, his unswerving support allowed Attlee to do what Bevin readily admitted he did best – keeping the diverse and mutually antagonistic Labour Cabinet ministers harnessed to the same waggon.

As to Churchill, the fifth hare, Attlee was savvy enough to separate the image of the wartime leader from the reality of the leader of the Opposition, now under fire from his own party for lack of peacetime leadership and frequent absences from the Commons.[41]

In an article for *The Observer* in 1960 Attlee described his concept of leadership. In writing the article, 'What Sort of Man Gets to the Top', he may have had these months of 1946 in mind. To lead effectively, he wrote, a man should display 'such things as moral or physical courage, sympathy, self-discipline, altruism and superior capacity for hard work.' Leadership was not a prize to be grabbed, for: 'Men who lobby their way forward into leadership are most likely to be lobbied back out of it. The man who has most control of his followers is the man who shows no fear. And a man cannot be a leader if he is afraid of losing his job.'[42]

In three sentences he neatly expressed the relative virtues and status of himself and Herbert Morrison.

In April 1945 the coalition government passed the Civil Aviation Act which established a Ministry of Civil Aviation. From there it was a short step, via a Labour government White Paper, to pass the 1946 Civil Aviation Bill. The cost of constructing Heathrow, purchasing land and building road and rail access would amount to £30 million, a figure that alarmed the Cabinet. Dalton suggested consideration of a site further from Central London.[43] In the event, Heathrow was adopted.

The Bill established three separate companies, British Overseas Airways Corporation (BOAC), British European Airways (BEA), and British South American Airways Corporation (BSAA), which was absorbed into BOAC in 1949.[44] As with the Bank of England Bill, this met with little opposition from the Opposition benches.

As an ironic footnote to the Bill it is amusing to read an exchange between Lord Winster, Minister of Civil Aviation, and the Prime Minister. Winster sent Attlee a report about requirements at Heathrow for an

LEFT Chancellor of the Duchy of Lancaster, 1930. Attlee was appointed to replace Sir Oswald Mosley when he resigned after the rejection of his economic proposals. Although this was not a Cabinet post, Attlee did at last have his foot in the door.
Courtesy of Anne, Countess Attlee

Haileybury Boys Club on a visit to Haileybury College, 1911. Courtesy of Anne, Countess Attlee

Leader and deputy leader, c. 1933: Attlee with George Lansbury. Courtesy of Anne, Countess Attlee

MIDDLE Toynbee Hall, 1910. Clement, aged twenty-seven, is first from the left in the back row.
Courtesy of Anne, Countess Attlee

BELOW The Simon Commission with dignitaries in Karachi, 1928. Attlee is first from the left in the second standing row.
Courtesy of Anne, Countess Attlee

Armistice Day, 1937 (*l. to r.*) With Captain Fitzroy, the Speaker of the House, and Lord Hailsham as well as Neville Chamberlain (far right), a Tory with whom Attlee had a personal as well as political enmity.

© Alpha Press

Deputy Prime Minister, 1944.

Courtesy of Anne, Countess Attlee

BELOW The Labour Cabinet, 1945. Flanking Attlee are (*to left*) Cripps, Greenwood, Bevin; (*to right*) Morrison, Dalton, Alexander.

Courtesy of Anne, Countess Attlee

At Buckingham Palace, 15 August 1945. (*l. to r.*) Morrison, Attlee, HM King George VI, Greenwood, Bevin, Alexander.

© Mirror Press

Potsdam, July 1945, with President Harry S. Truman and Marshal Stalin.

Courtesy of Anne, Countess Attlee

On a train from Montreal, November 1945, after the Washington meetings between Truman, Attlee and Canadian Prime Minister Mackenzie King.

Courtesy of Anne, Countess Attlee

Leaving the United Nations Association Service at St Paul's, 1946. Attlee and Violet are followed by Janet and Martin.
© Alpha Press

Outside 10 Downing Street, September 1951. Once again Clement and Violet covered the country over the next few weeks as Violet drove him to election rallies the length and breadth of Britain.
Courtesy of Anne, Countess Attlee

At Chequers, 1949. Both Clement and Violet enjoyed Chequers greatly and would spend weekends and holidays there whenever possible.
Courtesy of Anne, Countess Attlee

With the Chairman of Scripps-Howard Newspapers, Washington, 1950. Attlee made only two trips to Washington as Prime Minister. In 1945 and 1950 he was at pains to reassure Congress and the media that Britain was not 'going Communist' and that the Atlantic alliance was alive and well.
Courtesy of Anne, Countess Attlee

With the Mayor
of Bridlington on
a visit in 1949.
Courtesy of Anne, Countess Attlee

Clement's grandson
John, 3rd Earl Attlee,
at the unveiling of a
plaque at Clement's
birthplace in
Portinscale Road,
Putney in 2009.
Courtesy of Wandsworth Council

Campaigning in
Walthamstow,
February 1950.
When the constituency
of Limehouse was
absorbed into Stepney,
the Walthamstow
Labour Party invited
the Prime Minister
to represent them.
He was elected
with a majority
of over 12,000.
© Topham PicturePoint

An appalling typist, he would type secret memos himself.
Courtesy of Anne, Countess Attlee

Commonwealth Conference, 1949. Clement and Violet, together with Sir Stafford and Lady Cripps, host Commonwealth leaders at the London conference.
© Mirror Press

At the Yorkshire Miners' Gala, 1954.
Courtesy of Anne, Countess Attlee

The Labour Party's elder statesman, 1960. Courtesy of Anne, Countess Attlee

international airport, runways, access by rail and road, and the airports that could accommodate converted Lancasters. Three runways were envisaged as well as access by rail.[45] Attlee responded that 'possible' road and rail access was not good enough.[46] Transport should be phased to fit with the development of the airport. Nearly seventy years after that exchange rail access remains limited and the third runway is still under discussion.

During February 1946 the National Insurance Bill, which also had broad bipartisan support, had its second reading. Attlee pointed out, however, that the Bill needed to be seen in the context of broader reform, and that its success depended on full employment and a high level of national production. Both at the second reading of the Bill and in a debate on manpower he stressed the broad themes of the government policy. In the latter debate he returned to the familiar refrain that he had never promised immediate and spectacular results. He had made about fifty or sixty speeches, he said, and in every one of them stressed that the period was going to be difficult. The government needed to rebuild battered homes, schools and factories and to restore the normal peace-time life of industry. It needed to refill shops and homes which had been depleted of reserves, to create an export trade on a greater scale than ever before and to fulfil essential requirements abroad. It was, as well, he stressed, to remember that there were unavoidable responsibilities abroad. After six years of war and many years of neglect this would be a long process. Meanwhile 100,000 personnel were being demobilised each week and the government expected, barring external disturbances, to reach its target for reduction by the end of 1946.[47]

The issue of demobilisation became the weapon most used by the Opposition to discredit the government. This was not an abstract issue but one that affected the majority of families in Britain and, therefore, had immediate appeal.

The most important feature of Labour's first-year programme was the Bill for the nationalisation of the coal industry. From the outset it was handled at speed; when Gaitskell moved the third reading of the Bill, he admitted that it had been hastily prepared.[48]

As early as October 1945 the Lord President's Committee had resolved that speed was vital in order to demonstrate the government's determination to the miners. The Bill was to be as short as possible and with terms sufficiently wide to avoid the necessity of legislation to amend it later. For example, to keep the Bill simple, there was no intention at this stage to provide for the nationalisation of distribution.[49] Shinwell hoped to introduce the Bill before the Christmas recess and before the end of November he submitted a Bill, 'substantially in its completed form'.[50]

Throughout the deliberations of Morrison's committee Attlee was kept in the picture by Douglas Jay, who wrote incisive analyses of the Bill's virtues and perceived shortcomings. The extent to which Attlee trusted Jay is clear from the simple manner of acceptance of Jay's suggestions, normally 'Yes – CRA' scrawled at the foot of the page. Jay was a brilliant economist and a Prize Fellow of All Souls. At the end of his time at All Souls in 1937 he published *The Socialist Case*, for which Attlee wrote a foreword to the second edition in 1946. Jay's analytical, humane and common-sense approach to economic issues appealed greatly to the Prime Minister. As a result the notation 'Mr Jay to comment' appears frequently on memoranda dealing with economic questions.

Jay was favoured by Attlee principally because he was not afraid to be the bearer of unwelcome news. Late in November he sent the Prime Minister an unsparing analysis of the problems facing the coalmining industry. 'On present policy and prospects', he wrote, 'we seem threatened with a chronic shortage at home, and no exports whatsoever for some years, if not the lifetime of the present parliament.' He questioned the committee's assumptions about recruitment, pointing out that mining was the one industry in which the labour force was still falling. This he believed to be the root cause of low production. The fundamental question to be asked was, 'Shall we raise earnings to the level necessary to restore coal exports? Or shall we abandon our coal export trade in order to adhere to a wage level which is really only an accidental survival from quite different conditions?' There was a danger of 'drifting into nationalisation while averting our eyes from this awkward problem'.[51] It took some courage to speak out so critically of the handling of a central plank of the government's programme, and it is to his credit that he did – and to Attlee's that he continued to seek Jay's advice.

The difficulties in the 'speedily prepared' Bill were ironed out by 393 amendments and the third reading was eventually moved in May 1946. Gaitskell commented that in discussions of the question of coal nine out of ten Tories had expressed the view to him that 'There is nothing to be done about coal except nationalise it.'[52] As he predicted, there was acceptance of the principle on both sides of the House and the third reading was passed by 324 votes to 143.

The 45th Labour Party Conference met in Bournemouth in early June. On the second day Attlee addressed the conference to report on the government's ten months in office. The first steps of nationalisation had been completed; the Cable and Wireless Bill and the Civil Aviation Bill were in committee. He spoke with confidence, assuring the delegates that the government was proceeding at a reasonable pace, not overloading the machinery but planning ahead. Seventy-three Bills had been introduced and fifty-five had already received the Royal Assent.

The Opposition, he said disparagingly, had gone to the country with a five-year plan. It would have taken them five years, he said, to have done what the Labour government had done in ten months. He credited the Parliamentary Party, saying 'I have never known a Parliamentary Party with so many Members so capable of putting Labour's point across.'

There were, he admitted, problems that were less easy to solve: demobilisation and housing. The building programme was moving forward, Attlee assured his audience, but it could only advance if the materials and manpower were available. There had been progress, and this would continue steadily.

Steadiness was the central theme of his address. Many difficulties at home had been foreseen; many, equally, were unforeseeable. Britain's responsibilities, he continued to maintain in 1946, were both to Britons and to other countries. Food shortages, coal and transport shortages were foreign problems as much as home problems.

We are holding a firm balance between our responsibilities to our own people and our responsibilities to peoples of the world, and we are striving, and with success, to get the world food problem viewed not as that of a scramble for every country to get its own, but for all of us to overcome these years of dearth and, in the future, to have a world that is free from want.[53]

It was a difficult balance. Attlee's insistence on ensuring adequate food in other countries led directly to shortages at home. In May he sent

Morrison to Washington to request the Americans, whose food was not rationed, to ship grain to avoid famine in Germany and India. Washington agreed, provided Britain would forego 200,000 tons of her wheat allocation in September. A less than attractive deal threatened to cause a furore when Morrison announced the result of his negotiations in the House.[54] He succeeded in provoking Tory anger, American concern – as they claimed that this was a proposal not a commitment – and the resignation of Sir Ben Smith, the Minister for Food, furious that Morrison, and not he, had been made responsible for solving the shortage. As an added demerit, the shortfall of 200,000 tons of wheat guaranteed that bread rationing would be introduced.

Appointing John Strachey to succeed Smith and accepting that bread rationing, while unpopular, was another necessary hardship for the time being, Attlee refused to be pressured, even when the Opposition seized on this as another example of lack of planning. Morrison, by contrast, perhaps perceiving another opportunity for him to replace Attlee, certainly aware of the adverse effect on popular opinion that bread rationing would cause, on 19 July demanded a Cabinet meeting the following day. Attlee, in Durham with four other Cabinet members, brushed this aside, refusing to allow the bread crisis, despite its dramatic symbolism, to divert him from his course. Bread rationing was introduced on 22 July and remained in force for two years.

The alarm generated by the crisis, however, convinced him that several of his ministers were finding it hard to stay the course. Morrison, he felt, had broken ranks in fuelling the mood of alarm; there were signs that Bevin and Cripps were suffering from overwork. The Cabinet suddenly had the air of a group of tired old men and he was impatient to promote younger men. Much encouraged by Gaitskell's handling of the coal nationalisation and, after a year, having had time to assess the new talent at his disposal, he decided that the time was right for a Cabinet reshuffle. At the same time he would implement two changes that had long been in his mind: to reduce the size of the Cabinet and to subordinate the three service ministers to a Minister of Defence.

Two speeches from 1946 illustrate Attlee's resolve in the first seventeen months of the Labour government. Speaking in Newcastle in May he told his listeners:

I remember some of our opponents saying to me before the election, 'Don't you hope you don't win? Any government that has to deal with the post-war situation will have a very hard time,' and I invariably replied, 'I know that, but I believe these difficulties can be met and surmounted by the application of the principles in which we of the Labour Party believe.'[55]

In November, in a speech at the Mansion House, he again spelled out HMG's refusal to be diverted. He had always warned that hard times lay ahead, but the government recognised the problems and was competent to solve them. Demobilisation was on track with 4,000,000 already released; exports were surging but it would take longer than fifteen months to undo the damage of six years. The target was 175 per cent of the pre-war level and the balance of payments was a problem. Food remained a challenge, as did reconstruction, particularly given the shortages of timber, iron, coal and steel.[56]

It had been a remarkable year and Attlee had patiently tackled issues as they arose. He remained steadfastly loyal to Labour's election promises while many around him wavered. He ended 1946 with his hands firmly on the levers of power, having greatly improved his personal standing in the country.

ENDNOTES

1   Macmillan, *Tides of Fortune* 1945–55, p. 54.
2   Macmillan, *Tides of Fortune* 1945–55, p. 55.
3   Peter Hennessy, 'A Sense of Architrechtonics: Clement Attlee, 1945–1951.' Lecture at Gresham College, 7 November 1995.
4   MS. Attlee dep. 18. Also CAC: ATLE 1/17 for a detailed list of appointments and committees. He also described the process as similar to selecting a cricket team. Morrison was an all-rounder, Cripps and Bevin could score a century on a good day. Bevan was a fast bowler ('There's no one to touch Nye when he's got his length. Doesn't always find it though.') Williams, *Nothing So Strange*, p. 233.
5   TNA: PREM 8/432, Memorandum of 8 October 1947 illustrates his views on brevity and the best use of time.
6   *The Times*, 15 June 1957.
7   Dalton, *High Tide and After*, pp. 17–18.
8   Lord Wilson, 'Attlee, the Reasonable Revolutionary'. Cited by Hennessy, Lecture at Gresham College.
9   Dellar, *Attlee As I Knew Him*, p. 36.
10   Dellar, *Attlee As I Knew Him*, p. 21.
11   The PM's concept of 'overlords' is set out in a memorandum after a Cabinet reshuffle in a Note on 'Cabinet Business and Procedure', 18 October 1947, TNA: PREM 8/432, CP (47) 288.
12   Morgan, *Labour People*, p. 139.
13   TNA: PREM 8/35, fol. 448, CP (45) 112, 14 August 1945.
14   *Hansard*, HC Deb, 16 August 1945, col. 101.
15   *The Public Papers of the Presidents, Harry S. Truman, 1945*, 107, p. 235.

16   *Hansard*, HC Deb, 24 August 1945, cols. 956–957.
17   Cable traffic between CRA and Mackenzie King, TNA: PREM 8/35 fols. 27*ff*, 25, 17–31 August
      1945.
18   Sir Norman Brook to CRA, TNA: PREM 8/35, fol. 432*ff*, 23 August 1945.
19   Keynes, 'Our Overseas Financial Prospects', cited by Radice, *The Tortoise and the Hares*, p. 136.
20   TNA: PREM 8/35, fols 427*ff*, 23 August 1945.
21   TNA: PREM 8/35, fols 422*ff*, 31 August 1945. Harrod, *The Life of John Maynard Keynes*, p. 596.
22   TNA: PREM 8/35, fol. 403, T.77/45, 1 September 1945.
23   Bodleian: MS. Attlee, dep. 22.
24   Dalton, *High Tide and After*, pp. 74–75.
25   TNA: PREM 8/35 *passim*, especially fols. 334, 254–258, 250, 194–198. Only on 22 November (folio
      113) did Dalton grasp that Britain would receive no interest-free loan.
26   TNA: PREM 8/35, fol. 295, NABOB 177, Keynes to Dalton, 18 October 1945.
27   TNA: PREM 8/35, fol. 318, NABOB 132, Keynes to Dalton, 9 October 1945.
28   *Hansard*, HC Deb, 6 December 1945, cols 2662–70.
29   Harold Wilson, *A Prime Minister on Prime Ministers*, p. 297.
30   TNA: PREM 8/35 fols. 259–262, 208, 77. Compared with Dalton's wishful thinking, Jay's memoranda
      are models of clarity.
31   *As It Happened*, pp. 228–229.
32   *Hansard*, HC Deb, 29 October 1945, cols. 44–50.
33   *Hansard*, HC Deb, 29 October 1945, col. 153.
34   *Hansard*, HC Deb, 6 December 1945, col 2530.
35   *Hansard*, HC Deb, 6 December 1945, col 2534.
36   Harris, *Attlee*, p. 317. From a conversation between Harris and Callaghan.
37   *Hansard*, HC Deb, 6 December 1945, cols. 2551–52.
38   Roy Jenkins, *Purpose and Policy*, pp. 27*ff*.
39   Giles Radice's portrait of the Labour leaders, *The Tortoise and the Hares*.
40   Williams, '*Nothing So Strange*', p. 135.
41   Attlee later charged Churchill with treating the House of Commons as a place where he went to make
      speeches.
42   *The Observer*, 9 February 1960.
43   TNA: PREM 8/136, Cabinet Meeting, CM (46) 4th Conclusions, 10 January 1946.
44   TNA: PREM 8/136, CP (46) 110, 14 March 1946.
45   TNA: PREM 8/136, Winster to CRA, 4 January 1946.
46   TNA: PREM 8/136, CRA to Winster, 7 January 1946.
47   *Hansard*, HC Deb, 27 February 1946, cols 1953–54.
48   *Hansard*, HC Deb, 20 May 1946, col 45.
49   TNA: PREM 8/295, LP (45) 35th Meeting, 2 October 1945.
50   TNA: PREM 8/295, LP (45) 238, 21 November 1945.
51   TNA: PREM 8/295, Jay to CRA, 26 November 1945. He also took a view diametrically opposed to
      that of Dalton when he argued that directors of nationalised industries should be paid on the same
      scale as their counterparts in private industry. It was irrelevant that the chairman of a nationalised
      concern would earn £10,000 a year, as against £5,000 for a Cabinet minister. The alternative to
      paying competitive salaries would be 'the failure of the government's general policy of nationalisation'.
      TNA: PREM 8/295, Jay to CRA, 10 December 1945.
52   *Hansard*, HC Deb, 20 May 1946, col 57.
53   Bodleian: MS. Attlee, dep. 38.
54   *Hansard*, HC Deb, 23 May 1946, col. 549.
55   Bodleian: MS. Attlee, dep. 36, 27 April 1946.
56   Bodleian: MS. Attlee, dep. 44, 9 November 1946.

CHAPTER TWELVE

WITHDRAWAL FROM INDIA, 1945–1947

Attlee's experience with the Simon Commission[1] stimulated his interest in Indian independence. In 1942 and 1943 Leo Amery, Secretary of State for India, proposed to Churchill that, on Lord Linlithgow's retirement, Attlee should succeed him as Viceroy. 'He knows the India problem and has no sentimental illusions as to any dramatic short cut to its solution', Amery wrote. 'He also has a good shrewd understanding of military matters.' The appointment would have political benefits as 'there are not many of the Labour Party suitable for Empire posts. This would meet Labour criticism on that score.'[2]

In the event, Churchill was guided by military considerations. He achieved a neat solution to the Middle East command, replacing Auchinleck with Alexander and sending 'the Auk' back to India to succeed Wavell as Commander-in-Chief. Wavell, already on the spot, was appointed Viceroy. By the time Labour came to power he had been immersed in Indian politics for two years and was sceptical about the ability and intentions of the government. 'I am afraid there will be a lot of foolish, inexperienced and rather wild legislators amongst the 400 odd of Labour', he reflected.[3] Wavell also doubted his own suitability for his office and yearned to retire.[4] He feared that Lord Pethick Lawrence, the new Secretary of State, 'may have fixed and old-fashioned ideas derived mainly from Congress contacts',[5] but, despite his fears, he was impressed that 'the present government certainly moves quicker than its predecessor'[6] when he was summoned to London on 22 August.[7]

Since his tour of India in 1927–28 Attlee had not substantially changed his attitude towards the subcontinent. The greatest problem, he believed, would be to find an interim solution during transition from the Raj to independent government. If one could be implemented, then reason would prevail and a peaceful transition could be achieved.

By the time the Labour government came to power, however, the situation in India had altered. Three round-table conferences in London between 1930 and 1932 achieved nothing, but led to the 1935 Government of India Act, whose central thrust was the Federation of India. As the Act promised, elections were held in 1937, and the Congress Party emerged with clear majorities in six provinces while the Muslim League failed to win a single province. Pandit Jawarharlal Nehru, the Congress leader, rejected a coalition with the League, declaring that the only parties that mattered in India were Congress and the British Raj. This rebuff set Muhammed Ali Jinnah, the League president, on the path towards demanding a separate Muslim state that he called 'Pakistan', the land of the pure.

Early in the war Jinnah won favour with the British government as a supporter of the Allied effort. Congress, by contrast, opposed the war and saw its leaders imprisoned by the British for their obduracy. Once Singapore fell in February 1942, however, the prospect of Japanese forces invading while the dominant Indian party was acting against British interests raised alarming possibilities. Cripps was sent to meet with all parties in India and, against the promise of dominion status after the war, obtain support from Congress as well as the League. When his mission failed, Congress launched a 'Quit India' campaign; the Viceroy responded by incarcerating Congress leaders for the balance of the war.

Between 1942 and 1945, with 'Congress Fascists' out of circulation, Jinnah's position was strengthened and the League grew in Muslim communities. Churchill rejoiced to see the socialists of Congress losing ground but he and the British Cabinet failed to see that the widening gulf between Congress and the League created insurmountable problems. Against this background, fearful that the new government planned to resurrect the Cripps offer,[8] Wavell arrived in London on 26 August.

The two weeks that the Viceroy spent in London reinforced his view that the Cabinet had little grasp of reality. He returned to Delhi with instructions to implement the Cripps proposals and to broadcast the government's intention to create a Constitution Making Body and hold elections without delay.[9] Despite his scepticism that 'words, however skilfully chosen, will not solve fundamental differences',[10] Wavell characteristically obeyed orders and made the broadcast on 19 September.

His principal concern was that the government failed to appreciate the growing mood of anti-Europeanism and that the chasm between Congress and the Muslim League had widened, differences being expressed as much in religious as in political language. Fusion between freedom for a united, Congress-dominated India and Hinduism on the one hand and between Islam and the vague, undefined notion of 'Pakistan' on the other had created an atmosphere in which the *status quo* was universally resented. The Governor of the Central Provinces wrote to Wavell in October saying that he could not 'recollect any period in which there have been such venomous and unbridled attacks against government and government officers.'[11]

On 5 November the CIGS,[12] Viscount Alanbrooke, arrived in Delhi for talks with Wavell. He found him 'depressed about the state of India and expecting serious trouble within the next six months'. 'As we sat on the terrace outside the Viceroy's house, surrounded by Viceregal pomp,' he wrote, 'one felt that the British days in India were numbered.'[13] Wavell showed Alanbrooke the note he proposed to send to London, warning of a grave situation in which Congress leaders fomented violence, and stressing the need for troops to maintain order. Alanbrooke agreed that it should be sent but 'had no idea where the troops would come from if we wanted them'.[14]

Pethick-Lawrence circulated Wavell's report to the Cabinet[15] and, when the India and Burma Committee met five days later, it was agreed that a Cabinet delegation should be sent to India.[16] Pethick-Lawrence eventually replied to Wavell on 21 November; in the following days riots broke out in Calcutta and Bombay before the government announced the plan to send a delegation.

The lack of urgency in the light of the apocalyptic picture painted by Wavell is remarkable. On 26 November, twenty days since Wavell's message had been received, Norman Brook, the Cabinet Secretary, informed Attlee that the Chiefs of Staff were awaiting a requested appreciation of British forces from Auchinleck.[17] At a Cabinet meeting on 27 November it was decided only that the India and Burma Committee should prepare a revised draft statement for Pethick-Lawrence. Bevan urged that this statement should focus less on the need to restore law and order than on the government's intention to take steps to improve conditions in India. This was recorded but, apparently, not discussed.[18]

Despite the immediacy with which Attlee and his colleagues had addressed India in August, by the end of the year no new initiative beyond a visit by a Cabinet committee had been proposed. Wavell viewed the future despondently, noting on New Year's Day, 'I am not much looking forward to 1946 and shall be surprised and pleased if we get through without serious trouble.'[19]

On 27 December Wavell sent Pethick-Lawrence a 'political appreciation for the Cabinet'.[20] This was a detailed document that described his plan to institute a new central government, emphasising the need to maintain order. As a document presented by the C-in-C of an occupying power, it was comprehensive, reflecting considerable thought and preparation. At no stage did it refer to an independent India.

The Viceroy's plan was superseded by the formation of the Cabinet Mission to visit India at the end of March. Wavell had recommended that if Muslims insisted on self-determination in primarily Muslim areas, this should be conceded, but that there should be no compulsion of non-Muslim areas, such as Punjab and Bengal, to join Pakistan against their will. The committee agreed that if Jinnah and Congress could not work out a solution, then the Viceroy should dictate one. Somewhat optimistically, they felt that economic and defence difficulties might bring Congress and the Muslim League together to agree some form of federal solution.[21]

Attlee was conscious that he needed to act and be seen to be acting. Wavell's gloomy forecasts, however, were rapidly realised. On 18 February a naval mutiny broke out in Bombay. Industrial disputes erupted everywhere; a national railway strike in the summer was barely avoided. Police mutinies in Bihar and Delhi, protests against the suppression of the naval mutiny – all combined in unprecedented fashion to harry overworked officials.

Before any meaningful discussions could take place an election was needed, and between December 1945 and March 1946 staggered elections took place across the country. Congress claimed to represent all Indians, whatever their religion; the League claimed to represent all Indian Muslims; neither brooked any dispute. Initially both leading parties ran on the battle cry of economic hardship but soon they became divided by the issue of 'Pakistan'. The claims of each party outdid the other as they strove to demonstrate to the British their right to govern. Religion was increasingly politicised; all parties competed to win the Muslim vote. While Congress emerged as the leading party, the League, winning 446 of the 495 Muslim seats, garnered support with widely different roots in different regions. The unifying element was the undefined but hugely emotive concept of an Islamic state. After the elections Sir Penderell Moon commented, 'It is now abundantly clear that the Pakistan issue has got to be faced fairly and squarely. There is no longer the slightest chance of dodging it.'[22] Moon's forecast was shrewd. Muslim separatism and new nationalism were fuelled by success in the elections. Jinnah became a popular hero, hailed as a saviour by his supporters. 'Pakistan' became more than a notional country; it became identified with the essence of being a member of the Muslim League. Even Jinnah was unclear exactly what 'Pakistan' meant in practical terms; the ratcheting of emotion was designed to extract the best possible terms from Britain in the transfer of power. Many Muslims envisaged a simple division between North and South, with a Pakistan that stretched from Afghanistan to East Bengal. Naturally, they assumed, the highly symbolic new capital, Delhi, would fall into Pakistan.[23]

The elections gave unprecedented power to local governments of both parties. With access to political power came a radical shift in behaviour. Organisations were formed – sports clubs and the like – which also served as defence groups. Football teams were co-opted to patrol the streets after matches. *Ad hoc* groups were turned into private militias. Religious and moral tenets were at the centre of many such politically charged groups, moving into the void allowed by the weakness of the Raj.[24] Gangs of volunteers became quasi-police groups, performing tasks that the British Raj, reluctant to spend more money on India, no longer performed. The lackeys of imperialism were replaced by volunteer groups, all with political beliefs at their centre. Gandhi's non-violence was almost universally rejected. Politicians incited loyalist groups to defend themselves against – in other words, to attack – rival forces. Congress declared, 'Pakistan is not in the hands of the British government. If Pakistan is to be achieved, Hindus and Muslims will have to fight. There will be civil war.'[25]

Against this background of anti-European feeling and sudden polarisation along religious lines, Pethick-Lawrence, Cripps and A. V. Alexander arrived in India on 25 March with a brief to establish an interim government and to facilitate an early and smooth transfer of power to a democratically elected government. HMG might speak easily of granting independence to India but by the time the Cabinet Mission arrived in India this was meaningless. To whom would Britain grant what and over what area? A mission of three key ministers so soon after Labour's coming to power demonstrated the importance that Attlee placed on the Indian question, but changes had taken place with such bewildering speed that the 'Three Magi' (as Wavell referred to them[26]) were blind to the nuances of India in 1946.

Once the Cabinet had resolved to send a Cabinet Mission[27] they invested all confidence in that decision, further marginalising Wavell. When the Viceroy asked Pethick-Lawrence whether the delegation members approved of his 'breakdown' plan, the Secretary of State dodged the question, almost as if Wavell had no right to ask.[28] When Wavell, having received a copy of the terms of reference of the Mission, was given no indication of their attitude to Pakistan, his frustration grew.[29] This was reinforced by a cable in which Wavell spent an entire page pleading that he be allowed to discuss the Cabinet Mission with Sir John Thorne, the Home Member.[30] This was a relatively trifling matter; the larger issue was that Cabinet allowed the Viceroy no freedom of action. Wavell again stressed his need to know the Cabinet's inclinations in order to govern effectively, and with foresight asking to be informed how the Cabinet regarded Pakistan and the partition of Kashmir and Punjab.[31] In theory, the Cabinet Mission was led by Pethick-Lawrence. In fact, Attlee and Cripps determined British policy in India, and Cripps took control of negotiations. Wavell saw Cripps as 'much the ablest of the party'. Noting that he was ambitious and determined not to fail a second time, he wrote that, according to Linlithgow, 'Cripps was not quite straight under pressure, and he was right'.[32]

Attlee deplored the halting nature of negotiations and, once Pethick-Lawrence was safely away from the India Office, took firmer personal control, making the India and Burma Committee the sole mouthpiece for communication. He also enhanced the committee by adding the Lord President, the Foreign Secretary, the Dominions Secretary and the Parliamentary Under-Secretary of State for India, enabling swifter action without the need to refer to the Cabinet at every stage.[33]

Delay now gave way to decision, vacillation to firmer control. In the first half of April 1946 we see the process by which the idea of partition was accepted. A cable from the Mission in Delhi on 30 March spoke of 'an interim government or governments;'[34] at a Cabinet Meeting on 11 April Attlee brushed aside the objection that partition would leave Pakistan weak as not Britain's problem.[35] He made clear his *desiderata*. A united India (Scheme A) was the primary goal but the Mission was authorised to discuss the future on the basis of two states (Scheme B), but, in that event, every effort should be made to secure a central defence to include Hindustan, Pakistan, the Indian States, Burma and Ceylon.[36] The Cabinet Mission met with all political parties and invited suggestions for framing a constitution. When this was greeted with no response, Cripps put together a draft outline and sent it to all groups. The draft had four basic principles. First, a central government would deal with foreign affairs, defence and communications. Second, provinces would be divided into two groups, one of predominantly Muslim, the other of predominantly Hindu provinces to handle matters that could be sensibly dealt with on a collective basis. Third, individual provincial governments would continue to handle all other matters, while preserving the sovereign status of provinces within a federal structure. Fourth, the 'princely' states, bound by separate treaties to Britain, would eventually take their place within the federal structure on terms to be agreed.

Congress immediately objected to the grouping of provinces on a religious or communal basis, claiming that this would weaken the central government. In truth, they objected to any proposal that had a suggestion of a separate group of entities superior to a single province, for that smacked of 'Pakistan'. Congress and the League each sent four members to discuss the proposals at Simla[37] but no agreement was reached.

By the end of the month the Mission began to grasp the difficulties that besieged Wavell. They cabled London that they had 'been working on the draft of a statement ... in the event of failure to reach agreement'.[38] A 500-word statement was drafted and agreed in Cabinet[39] before Gandhi raised questions of detail and Jinnah requested time to resolve problems among League members.[40] With added demands from Congress that British troops be withdrawn immediately and that the proposed Constituent Assembly be sovereign, prospects of an agreement evaporated. The Delegation had been naïvely optimistic. Congress had insisted from the start that independence be immediately effective and that all Europeans be excluded from the governance of India. This naïveté became clear with the publication of letters between all parties in the discussions.[41]

The Cabinet Mission and the Viceroy fashioned a constitution for independent India and announced it on 16 May.[42] Designed to appeal to all groups, it succeeded in satisfying none. Independent Pakistan consisting of six provinces, as demanded by Jinnah, was rejected. A smaller Pakistan, containing only Muslim areas and entailing the division of Bengal and Punjab, was also considered impractical. The original three-tiered government was proposed with the proviso that any province could request revision of its status after ten years. To settle the constitution a Constituent Assembly would be elected by members of provincial legislatures, grouped into three combinations: the five Hindu-majority provinces; Punjab, Northwest Frontier Province, Sind, Bengal and Assam. Each province would have the right to opt out only after the new arrangement was introduced.

While Jinnah was not offered an independent Pakistan, there was provision for a group of provinces that ensured protection of Muslim interests – an arrangement that might lead to partition. Congress set up a working party to study the proposals, which Gandhi had applauded, but could not agree to parity between the League and Congress. Additionally, the Sikhs, critically important to a peaceful settlement of Punjab, were resentful that their interests were ignored.

Attlee's seizing of the reins had been only partial. Wavell had been right to be pessimistic. The Cabinet had unrealistic hopes; once these were dashed, Attlee was no closer to agreement than he had been six months before, as became clear from cables received from both Wavell and the Mission on 3 June. Wavell offered an excellent *tour d'horizon* of India from a military perspective[43] but no solution to fundamental problems. The delegation discussed the military plan for withdrawal should

Congress resort to direct action – to hold the ports and strong points, then withdraw all Europeans who wished to leave. For the first time came the notion of a deadline and talk of using the intervening period to arrange phased withdrawal. It was a message from a mission that knew it had failed and was seeking to safeguard European lives and its reputation for impartiality.[44]

Attlee, under increasing pressure to show evidence of progress, proposed a meeting with Tory and Liberal leaders in an attempt to postpone a full debate until the interim government was settled. In the meantime he instructed Wavell to reopen negotiations with Congress and the League and to emphasise that the government did not regard the issue of the League's nominating all Muslims to be a valid objection.[45] Wavell agreed to do so but stated firmly, 'I wish it, however, to be clearly understood that this will be done contrary to my advice and wishes'[46] – the clearest indication yet of growing disagreement between Attlee and the Viceroy.

For almost a year Wavell had watched the situation deteriorate. He wrote to the King comparing Indian politics with 'one of my childhood puzzles – a little glass-covered box with three or four different coloured marbles which one had to manipulate into their respective pens ... Just as the last one seemed on the point of moving in ... all the others invariably ran out.'[47] Now, vindicated over the Cabinet Mission's tactics, he was in the ascendant. Attlee might at this point have recognised the impossibility of continuing to work with a Viceroy whom he considered 'defeatist'.[48] Instead, he issued instructions which Wavell openly challenged, and accepted Pethick-Lawrence's suggestion that if the Muslim League boycotted the Constituent Assembly, Wavell should proceed without them. This would, he admitted, create problems as the Hindu majority would totally dominate the government.[49] A frustrated Attlee wrote to Lord Simon on 21 April that the Cabinet Mission was experiencing the same problems as the Commission had experienced eighteen years before.[50] Simon, while well disposed to his former colleague, was outraged by the plan to govern with only Congress participation. He compared it to a football match where only one side turned up. Could that, he asked in a letter to Eden, be properly termed a match?[51]

Jinnah was adamant that only the Muslim League should appoint Muslims to the interim government, a demand unacceptable to Congress, whose president Maulana Azad was a Muslim. Wavell announced the abandonment of negotiations and his intention to nominate fourteen people – six Hindu members, five Muslims, one Sikh, one Parsee and one Indian Christian – to serve in an interim government. Clutching at straws to maintain the appearance of progress, the Mission seized on the ambiguous phrase 'accept your proposals' in a letter from Azad to Wavell, treated this as acceptance and announced that 'constitution-making can now proceed with the consent of the two major parties'.[52] No interim government could be formed, but the Viceroy would address that issue; the Mission could return to London having ostensibly achieved its purpose. Jinnah quickly torpedoed this by having the League working party accept the proposals for an interim government. Now, he argued, since Congress had rejected these, the British were committed to work exclusively with the League, who had accepted the 16 May proposals. The Mission members had been dishonest, he maintained, in saying that both sides had accepted them. The Cabinet Mission departed, having achieved nothing.

Attlee was intolerant of discussions that covered and recovered the same ground with no decisions. However open-minded he may have been until this point, the outcome of the Cabinet Mission marked a turning point in his attitude. Jinnah's wrecking of any semblance of accord and the spectacle of three British Cabinet ministers being treated with disdain undoubtedly influenced his perception of the Muslim League. When the League met in Bombay at the end of June and voted to embrace a policy of 'direct action', in Jinnah's words, bidding 'goodbye to constitutional methods', it is not difficult to imagine Attlee's reaction.[53]

He accepted that civil war was likely, maintaining that it was the responsibility of the Indian leaders to avoid it. If it was unavoidable, Britain should extricate herself sooner rather than later; the sequel would be the same whenever that came to pass. Once Jinnah announced his departure from constitutional methods, this was the moral *Schwerpunkt* that altered the rules fundamentally. The issue of the 'ingratitude' of the Indian people, a theme stressed frequently in the British press, was not motive with Attlee. Simply, he felt that the Indian leaders had brought this deadlocked situation on their people and they, not Great Britain, must resolve the issues.[54] Once the League had rejected the proposals, Congress accepted Wavell's invitation to form an interim government.[55] When, on 16 August the League instituted 'Direct Action Day' resulting in rioting that left 5,000 dead and 15,000 injured in Calcutta,[56] Hindus retaliated against Muslim aggression and massacred Muslims in Bihar. Civil war, Gandhi proclaimed, was imminent. Wavell cabled the India Office that he saw no hope of avoiding more serious rioting unless there was 'some settlement at centre' and he could change Jinnah's attitude.[57]

Three weeks later Jinnah issued a direct challenge to Attlee. 'The wound is too deep', he said, and the negotiations had caused so much rancour that discussions were pointless. Declaring that he was prepared to travel to London and participate in a new series of conferences, he accused Britain of supporting the existing government with bayonets. If the British wished to arrest him, he was ready to go to prison.[58]

Still Wavell strove to include the League in the Constituent Assembly in the teeth of London's objections.[59] Jinnah agreed that five members should join the government. Initial delight was soon dissipated when it became clear that League members had accepted the invitation not to collaborate with Congress but to impede them.[60]

Attlee invited leaders of Congress and the League, as well as Baldev Singh, the Sikh representative, to London for talks.[61] Congress leaders promptly refused the invitation as 'a brief visit to England cannot bear fruit'; Jinnah agreed to think about it; Baldev Singh, the Sikh representative, has said that since there would not be representatives of both Congress and the League, there was no point in his going.[62] Attlee intervened and twice requested Nehru to attend talks.[63] Jinnah promptly cabled Attlee to complain that the Prime Minister had created a new situation by corresponding with Nehru and that, therefore, the League members would not join any discussions. After further intervention from Attlee, however, he agreed to attend.[64]

The area of disagreement between the two main parties seemed relatively small – whether voting in the Sections should be by provinces or by majority of those present – but the gulf between the parties was greater. Each accused the other of bad faith; Gandhi urged Assam and the Sikhs to withdraw from the Assembly; Jinnah refused to rescind the Bombay resolution.[65] If Congress members withdrew from the Assembly, Britain

might be forced to maintain order throughout Hindu regions; if the
League members refused to work with Congress, there might be civil
war. In either case it would be difficult for Britain to withdraw with
any claim to have settled matters. In this unpromising atmosphere the
London talks opened on 6 December.

On behalf of the government Attlee made a grandiloquent opening
statement. Britain's resolution to allow India to determine its constitution had attracted the support of the world, he said. Now the world
was surprised that objections from Indians were preventing agreement.
He maintained that the statement of 16 May had not been substantially altered and denied that HMG was applying pressure. They were
merely trying to gain agreement on the 16 May principles so that the
Constituent Assembly could move forward.[66]

After four days of meetings Attlee commented to Cabinet that there
was no will among the parties to reach agreement.[67] Nehru seemed determined to extend Congress' power over the whole country and that would
be unacceptable to the League. The time for imposing order from without
had passed as British forces in India were no longer adequate for the task.
Withdrawal might become necessary but to withdraw in haste would
be regarded as scuttle. Cabinet agreed in principle, but offered no real
proposals to break the deadlock. The paucity of ideas was demonstrated
at a Cabinet meeting at which Wavell's breakdown plan was reconsidered.
Two and a half months had passed since Wavell produced the plan; the
government was no further forward. Once again the same arguments
were batted to and fro; once again the meeting was inconclusive.[68]

For a further twelve days before his return to Delhi Wavell urged
a phased withdrawal on the India and Burma Committee.[69] By
20 December, when somewhat grudgingly the committee seemed to
accept his advice, he pressed his point with Attlee, asking for confirmation of four points – that Britain would quit India by 31 March 1948,
that the government accepted his breakdown plan, that legislation would
speedily be placed before Parliament and that the Secretary of State's
services would be wound up.[70] Attlee responded from Chequers on the
following day, saying that the committee's recommendation to be placed
before Cabinet 'covers the broad decisions that [Wavell] asked for'. By
any standards, it was a brusque reply.[71]

Understandably so, for Attlee was now thoroughly frustrated by the intransigence of the Indian leaders, by Wavell's 'defeatist' plans for a military withdrawal and by his Cabinet's inability to propose any alternative. On 18 December in a meeting with Admiral Viscount Mountbatten, and in the strictest confidence, Attlee mooted the idea that he succeed Wavell as Viceroy. According to Mountbatten's later account, he was horrified, knowing how complex and intractable the situation had become. Where the Cabinet Mission and Wavell had failed, he asked, what hope remained of anyone else satisfying the Indian leaders? The only hope was to present the Indians with a definite time limit.[72]

Mountbatten's rise during the war had been remarkable, if controversial. Field Marshal Brooke regarded him with caution; aware of his ability, he confided to his diary when Mountbatten was appointed Supreme Commander, South-east Asia, that 'he lacked balance for such a job'.[73] Later, commenting on the appointment, Brooke noted that what he lacked in experience he made up in self-confidence. He had boundless energy and drive, but 'would require a steadying influence in the nature of a very carefully selected Chief of Staff'.[74] After initial doubts, Attlee believed that Mountbatten's disdain for conventional methods might be of value in India. The young admiral already had a friendly, though unconventional, acquaintance with Nehru, dating from January 1946 when Nehru visited Singapore. The Civil Governor of Burma 'emphatically refused' to invite Nehru, who had recently been released from prison, whereupon Mountbatten invited him to Singapore. He 'ordered military transport to be provided into the city to enable the Indian soldiers to see their political leader'. He lent Nehru one of his own cars and invited him to call at Government House on arrival.[75]

This iconoclastic approach appealed to Attlee, who later recorded that 'I had what I now think was an inspiration. I thought of Mountbatten.'[76] At their meeting he agreed to grant the new Viceroy unprecedented authority to act independently of the Secretary of State – as the absence of such power had crippled Wavell's authority – and, subject to certain conditions, Mountbatten, not without considerable qualms, inclined to accept the offer. His acceptance, he emphasised, was conditional on Attlee's linking the announcement of the new Viceroy with a definite date for transfer of power. Otherwise, he would not be able to do the job.[77] Ismay, whom Mountbatten appointed his Chief of Staff, accurately commented that Attlee 'had taken a very great risk' in imposing a time limit before there was a successor-authority to take over.[78]

While Attlee waited for Mountbatten's formal acceptance of the post he allowed his frustration to show in an exchange with Bevin, who deplored the negativism that had pervaded a Cabinet meeting. 'I cannot help feeling that the defeatist attitude adopted both by the Cabinet and Field Marshal Wavell is just completely letting us down', he wrote. Cripps was too pro-Congress; Alexander was too pro-Muslim. After listening to the discussion he was despondent. The government should hand over India 'as a going concern' and place responsibility on the shoulders of the Indian leaders.[79]

In a response quite out of character – for he valued Bevin's counsel above all others – Attlee allowed his frustration to show. 'We are seeking to fulfil the pledges of this country with dignity and avoid an ignominious scuttle. But a scuttle it will be if things are allowed to drift', he wrote. Somewhat acidly he ended the letter saying, 'If you disagree with what is proposed you must offer a practical alternative. I fail to find one in your letter.'[80] His irritation is understandable. Bevin had identified the flaw in the government's attitude but, in common with everyone else who had addressed the problem, saw no solution. Clearly, Attlee had not yet informed Bevin of his talks with Mountbatten and, while he waited for Mountbatten's acceptance, he resented the impotence of his own position.

He guarded that secret for a further frustrating month, during which Mountbatten assembled his staff, and the unfortunate Wavell was kept in the dark.[81] On 8 January 1947 Attlee wrote to Wavell, informing him bluntly that the Cabinet had rejected the breakdown plan.[82] Wavell, in fact, had already learned this and commented that 'I thought they well might run out after I left, they seem quite unable to face an awkward decision'.[83] On receipt of official notification from Attlee, he wrote sourly that Attlee's letter was 'cold, ungracious and indefinite, the letter of a small man'. He could see no point in agreeing to go to London for discussions, surmising that the invitation was intended to force his resignation.[84]

Resignation was by then redundant. On 31 January, after consulting Cripps, Attlee wrote to Wavell, pointing out that his appointment as

Viceroy was a wartime appointment for three years, which had now expired; since there was a policy difference between them, it was time for Wavell to resign. He concluded by saying that he was recommending him for an earldom which he hoped he would accept.[85] Wavell devoted two lines in his diary to acknowledging this, commenting that it was 'not very courteously done'.[86]

After an acid response[87] and having learned that Mountbatten was to succeed him, Wavell requested Attlee to delay the announcement until after his daughter's wedding on 20 February, at which he was expecting 800 guests.[88] Attlee readily agreed.[89] Wavell then showed great magnanimity, offering to assist Mountbatten in any way possible, a gesture that Attlee acknowledged.[90]

It is hard not to sympathise with Wavell, a devotedly loyal Army officer placed in a highly inflammable political situation and held in 'abject and humiliating thralldom' by the Cabinet.[91]. A Wykehamist, erudite lover of poetry, greatly more 'civilised' than most of his peers, he remained a soldier, appointed to the Viceroyalty as a wartime solution to a military problem. Yet, while politicians manoeuvred to acquit themselves with credit, Wavell remained constant, if unimaginative. His assessments of Pethick-Lawrence and Cripps were justified by later events; his contempt for Attlee's handling of his relief, dismissing him with a month's notice, rather than the customary six months, was not unjustified.

Attlee emerges without credit from his relations with the Viceroy. His brusque manner was typical, but his ungenerous treatment of Wavell was uncharacteristic. Under the circumstances, his frustration is understandable; at every turn initiatives were thwarted. Once the Cabinet Mission failed, he might profitably have taken stock and decided in June 1946, rather than six months later, that a different Viceroy was needed. He did not, and that hesitation led to drift until the appearance of Mountbatten, *deus ex machina* with a radical solution.

It is also questionable whether he made a wise choice of Pethick-Lawrence as Secretary of State. Aged seventy-three when Labour came to power, he was neither flexible nor dynamic. As relations between Secretary of State and Viceroy deteriorated, we see Pethick-Lawrence taking care to prove Wavell wrong more often than making constructive suggestions.

As early as April 1946 Attlee had decided that India was as divided as it had been in 1928; that civil war had, if anything, become more likely. India posed a problem that Attlee's style of management failed to solve when the consensus of Cabinet was to shuffle responsibility and do nothing. Ultimately, he provided the decisive solution but his lack of decisiveness before December 1946 – the legacy of his belief in collective responsibility – contributed to the drift.

Establishing British authority to suppress chaos was politically unacceptable. Any such move would suggest an intention to prolong the Raj; harmony was unreachable. Attlee decided to announce the British intention to withdraw not later than June 1948, to which Cabinet agreed on 13 February 1947.[92] He made it clear that the absence of agreement between parties would not delay the handover. His Majesty's government would decide to which authority it would transfer power. This tacitly accepted the inevitability of partition, now an open secret throughout India. Responsibility for this was not attributable to one or the other party – although Gandhi's and Nehru's occasional fits of arrogance contributed – but to fundamentally different goals. Congress wanted a strong united country; the League wanted a divisible one. Jinnah had established his leadership of Muslims and Jinnah wanted Pakistan. Congress realised that the price he would require for unity would be too high. Better, Nehru finally accepted, to suffer the loss of certain peripheral territory.

After Mountbatten's appointment was announced[93] events moved at a very different pace. Wavell, considered the appointment 'unexpected but a clever one from their point of view',[94] noting that 'Dickie's personality may perhaps accomplish what I have failed to do.' Attlee spoke to the King, estimating the chance of success at six to four, somewhat optimistically as Sir George Abell set them at ten to one against, and, 'rather unexpectedly', the King approved.[95]

On 5 March Cripps opened the debate on India (Government Policy) in the House of Commons. Speaking for over an hour, he traced recent events – the 1935 Act, his 1942 mission, the Cabinet Mission of the previous year – before emphasising the need for decisive action and a time limit if the initiative were to be retained and any progress made.

Cripps acknowledged that this involved 'a tremendous experiment in the methods of peaceful progress', but stressed that 'we must not fail ourselves or India through lack of decision at a critical moment. In giving up our control in India, we want to do our utmost to co-operate with the Indians of all parties and communities through these final stages of the realisation of their freedom.'[96]

Sir John Anderson led for the Opposition, arguing against a fixed date, maintaining that the government had erred in handing over power to representative Indians without certainty of a constitutional settlement. In allowing British military control of India to be diminished to the point that it could no longer keep order, the government had exacerbated the present crisis.[97] The debate ranged to and fro for a further five hours. The differences between government and Opposition were plainly stated, but the debate was little more than a curtain raiser for the following day's passage of arms.

This was opened, unsurprisingly, by Churchill who claimed that the government had departed from the principles of the Cripps mission of 1942 and compounded its errors by recent actions. It would be impossible in fourteen months to bridge the gap between Hindu and Muslim that had existed for a thousand years. It would merely provide time for each side to prepare for civil war. Studded with gems of Churchillian oratory, it reflected nonetheless an archaic view of India, a feature that Attlee seized on. When Churchill spoke of 'these people, in many cases, of the same race, charming people, lightly clad, crowded together in all the streets and bazaars and so forth,' the picture he drew was more akin to *Ali Baba* than to India of 1947. India, he concluded, 'is to be subjected not merely to partition, but to … haphazard fragmentation. A time limit is imposed – a kind of guillotine – which will certainly prevent the full, fair and reasonable discussion of the great complicated issues that are involved.'[98]

After several skirmishes, it was left to Attlee to sum up. The House had been sitting for five and a half hours when he rose to speak and Members were treated to a classic Attleean treatment of the subject. First, however, he needed to point out that Churchill was out of date even with thinking within his own party. He referred to 'the great work' that had been done in India and closed on a high note, wishing Mountbatten 'God speed' and success in his 'great mission'.[99]

Over two days the House had watched a characteristic drama play out. Act One had opened with the cerebral, carefully accurate presentation from Cripps. Lesser but important players had batted the question to and fro, a *diminuendo* closing the first set of skirmishes. Act Two had been introduced by the massive figure of Churchill, as it emerged, a tragically outdated character whose central premise could not be anything but cannon fodder for his principal opponent. Then, in a brisk and businesslike finale lasting a mere thirty minutes, Attlee brought the dialogue to a polished closure. The vote, a foregone conclusion, saw the government defeat the Conservative amendment by 337 to 185. The new Viceroy was set to depart for Delhi to bring to an end in fourteen months the era of the British Raj.

On 22 March, Mountbatten arrived in Delhi. His instructions from Attlee were simple and direct – 'to obtain a unitary government for British India and the Indian States, if possible within the British Commonwealth'. Mountbatten's biographer succinctly summarised that directive as 'Keep India united if you can; if not, try to save something from the wreck. Whatever happens, get Britain out.'[100] Less sensitive to grassroots problems than Wavell, who had spent his childhood in India, he adopted a pragmatic approach and, if partition was in the air, he was easier to persuade than his predecessor.

From the outset Mountbatten inclined to the Congress position. He had already established a friendship with Nehru and, as he admits, '[as he had] been educated at Harrow and Trinity, and ... lived so many of his formative years in England, I found communication with him particularly easy and pleasant'.[101] He had great respect for Liaquat Ali Khan, Jinnah's deputy in the Muslim League and Nehru's deputy in the fragile interim government. 'He was a very different personality from Jinnah', Mountbatten recalled, 'tough but far less abrasive, a highly competent loyal follower, but not a leader. He was man with whom it was possible for Nehru to achieve more effective intellectual rapport than with Jinnah.'[102]

The new Viceroy's aim was to reach a swift conclusion, precisely what Jinnah was determined to resist. Very soon, therefore, Jinnah was perceived as 'remote' and as the principal obstacle to be overcome. Mountbatten strove to find the means to obtain any measure of agreement from him. He soon realised that this would come through partition alone, even with its potentially catastrophic consequences in divided provinces, as he recalled,

> *I tried to tempt Jinnah by offering him Bengal and the Punjab unpartitioned provided he would agree that, though the Provinces with Muslim majorities would have self-government, they must be within an overall federal government at the centre. However, he said he would sooner have a moth-eaten Pakistan that owed no allegiance to a central government than a larger and more important area which came under it.*[103]

Mountbatten swiftly concluded that, in the tinder-box climate, it would be folly to wait until June 1948; a solution must be found as soon as possible. By the end of March he was proposing partition into Hindustan, Pakistan and the Princely States.[104] On 11 April he told his staff to make it clear that he had been impartial from the outset and that, if it became clear that a united India would result in civil war, only then would he accept partition as an option.[105]

On 17 April Mountbatten told Lord Listowel, who had succeeded Pethick-Lawrence as Secretary of State, that a decision must be made quickly to avoid civil war, that he had a plan and that Ismay would return to London with it. By 1 May he had decided that partition was inevitable and he prescribed a comprehensive procedure for achieving it. He admitted that the problems were 'complex and considerable' but that he would pursue that policy.[106]

When Ismay and Abell attended the India and Burma Committee meeting on 5 May, Ismay reported that Mountbatten had encountered unexpected bitterness and opposition and had determined that the chances of co-operation between Congress and the League were 'negligible'. He was determined that responsibility for partition should be seen as entirely the responsibility of Indian leaders. He would hold a meeting on 20 May and inform the leaders that the results of the meeting would be announced immediately.[107] The need for speed was stressed in the draft announcement of the proposed transfer of power.[108]

There followed a month of breathtaking activity as both Congress and the League jockeyed for position before 20 May. Mountbatten reported that he had received a letter from Gandhi, effectively saying that the business of partition was not the responsibility of the British. Britain's job was to maintain order, transfer power and quit. As to the States, he argued that paramountcy automatically devolved to the Indian government.[109] Gandhi had now realised that Mountbatten and, therefore, the British Cabinet, saw partition as the only viable course and he attempted to ensure Congress domination of the putative government without interference from London. Mountbatten's tactic had worked.

On the following day Mountbatten revealed his hand, arguing that, for the best chance of success, the transfer of power should take place during 1947.[110] His arguments were somewhat specious but high on the list was enhancement of British prestige, which he knew would appeal to London. It is improbable that he reached this conclusion over the twenty-four hours since his previous cable. He simply timed his telegrams to stimulate a progression of thought from 10 to 11 May along lines that he had already formulated. His dexterity was confirmed when Nehru wrote to him on 12 May, commenting that 'HMG seems to function in an ivory tower of their own isolated from realities in India. They proceed apparently on certain assumptions which have little relevance and ignore the basic factors of the situation.'[111] This was an inspired ploy by Mountbatten, creating the impression that he and Nehru were working together with only bureaucratic red tape being contributed by Whitehall. Perhaps sensing this, Leslie Rowan, Attlee's Principal Private Secretary, suggested to Attlee that he go to India to negotiate the details of the transfer. If he pulled it off, Rowan argued, it would be a 'master stroke'.[112] Attlee, unsurprisingly, did not take the bait.

Just ten days after Ismay had presented Mountbatten's plan to the committee Attlee reported in Cabinet that, after meetings with Indian leaders, the plan had been altered. Mountbatten would present new proposals to the Cabinet in person.[113] Four days later the Viceroy gave the committee his opinion that unless Pakistan were created there would be civil war. Nehru objected to the 'Balkanisation' of India, confident that Pakistan would ultimately revert. Both Pakistan and India could, Mountbatten believed, remain part of the Commonwealth only if independence were granted 'well before the end of 1947'.[114]

At first the new proposal was ill received by the Cabinet, who had rushed to approve the original plan. Now they were being asked to approve a new proposal almost instantly. In truth, however, they could not reject a plan agreed to by Congress, the Muslim League and the Viceroy. Attlee praised the remarkable skill and initiative which the Viceroy had shown in the conduct of these difficult negotiations, urging that he 'be given a large measure of discretion to amend the details of the plan, without prior consultation with His Majesty's government.'[115] It remained only to obtain the approval of the Opposition, which the proposal that both countries become members of the Commonwealth facilitated.

On 31 May Mountbatten and Ismay returned to Delhi and on 2 June the Viceroy presented the government's statement of 'Immediate Transfer of Power', to which Mountbatten required leaders to respond before midnight. On 3 June all parties accepted the revised plan. Attlee announced this in the Commons, expressing 'the gratitude and appreciation of His Majesty's government for the great services which the Viceroy has rendered'.[116] It is revealing that in none of the statements was the word 'Pakistan' mentioned. Attlee was deliberately imprecise.

On the following day Mountbatten held a press conference at which he sparkled. Indians had wanted independence and made partition inevitable. 'I am quite sincere when I say that you have got to make up your own minds.'[117] Most remarkable was the statement that he planned for the transfer of power on about 15 August, a date that he claimed had been agreed with Indian leaders. No record of such agreement exists. Nehru reacted with incredulity. Rowan noted that it would be very hard to get legislation through in so short a time. 'Accept Viceroy's proposal,' Attlee minuted in his own hand in response.[118]

The announcement was greeted hysterically among Muslims. For Jinnah, however, partition of Bengal and Punjab posed problems. Who would live where? Should Muslims left in India migrate? Above all, the idea of India, a continent more than a country, was disintegrating. The proposed division of the Army also came as a shock.[119] Moreover, it weakened the Army at the time it was most needed. Sikhs realised with horror that their land would be divided; they lobbied for pushing the border west. Asked if he foresaw transfers of population, Mountbatten disowned responsibility, saying that this was a matter for local rather than central government.[120] A callous acceptance of the cost of withdrawal was thus laid at India's door. A slow trickle of refugees began while the plan was being discussed, as people realised that their religion not political beliefs would turn them into minorities within the new state. The wealthy moved their capital out of Pakistan before partition. Concern that communities should be protected from outsiders spawned armed camps.

Attlee said 'he was hopeful that there would be no bloodshed but feared that there would be'.[121] Effectively, British politicians, to the horror of those who had devoted their lives to India, had decided that their responsibility to South Asians had ended.

Having settled the issues between Congress and the League to his satis-faction, Mountbatten turned to the princely states. He was determined to persuade them to affiliate with either India or Pakistan, applying salesmanship and outright pressure until he succeeded. Hyderabad and Kashmir, however, continued to elude him; their princes felt betrayed by the Viceroy's pressure. This feeling was shared by Sir Walter Monckton, adviser to the Nizam of Hyderabad, who wrote to Leo Amery, 'It is horrible that we should have encouraged the Rulers to believe in our promises up to such a short time ago and should then leave them without the resources to stand comfortably on their own feet.'[122] Mountbatten granted an extension of two months for their accession and so was able to declare independence without having resolved their status.

As Independence Day approached Mountbatten drove himself as crisis after crisis arose. Some issues he dealt with; others he sidestepped. In the case of the boundaries it was clear that both sides would be unhappy; Mountbatten hoped that the distress of the other side would reassure each leader that his side had not been badly treated. Playing safe, he postponed announcement of Sir Cyril Radcliffe's boundary awards until 17 August. Discord over boundaries would not be allowed to mar the optimistic fanfare of Independence Day.

From all quarters, Indian and British, came tributes to Mountbatten's dexterity in brokering the agreement. Attlee cabled him, 'Your short tenure of Viceroyalty has been one of the most memorable in a long list.'[123] One of Attlee's goals was achieved when American columnist Walter Lippmann wrote in earnest praise of the achievement. 'Perhaps Britain's finest hour is not in the past. Attlee and Mountbatten have done a service to all mankind by showing what statesmen can do not with force and money but with lucidity, resolution and sincerity.'[124]

In the massacres that followed Independence many died – how many is not known, but figures between 250,000 and a million were widely accepted. At a speech at India House in November 1947 Mountbatten suggested that 'only' 100,000 had been killed, a statement whose callousness shocked Ismay.[125] At his first meeting with Attlee it had been common ground that in achieving self-government India would suffer 'further grave communal disorders'.[126] The extent of disorder, combined with the massive movements of population, came as a shock, not only to Mountbatten but also to Nehru and Congress leaders.

Wavell and Mountbatten shared the view that immediate action was necessary if civil war was to be prevented. Penderel Moon believes that the damage would have been worse had there been less decisive action by Attlee and Mountbatten. 'The vigour and speed with which Lord Mountbatten acted had at least the merit of confining it to the Punjab.'[127] 'All things considered', it was a mercy, he wrote, that Mountbatten did not foresee more clearly the magnitude of the calamity that threatened the Punjab. He might have faltered, desperate to avoid it while the whole country drifted into civil war. By driving at top speed he divided the country and the armed forces before strife spread beyond the Punjab.[128]

Attlee continued to maintain that rapid disengagement reduced the ensuing slaughter. In his later interview with Francis Williams he bordered on cynicism when he spoke of the massacres. They'd been brewing for some time, he said. 'They started with one lot killing the other in Bengal.' Then they spread until the Sikhs, a 'very undependable and a rough people', were involved.[129]

That Attlee was determined to bring the Raj to an end is beyond doubt. Equally certain is that, at the outset, he wanted to transfer power to a monument of British achievement – to a united India. It was the very lack of unity that had allowed Britain to divide and rule the country, yet the notion of Mother India had gained such credence under Gandhi's influence[130] that partition was at first unthinkable. Moreover, the affinity between Labour and Congress set the course of government policy and demonised Jinnah for his determination to create a separate Muslim state. Mountbatten had no difficulty in expressing his affinity for Nehru, a Harrow and Trinity man.[131] Neither Attlee nor Mountbatten was open-handed in dealing with the two Indian parties. Mountbatten arrived in

Delhi, disposed to partition but careful not to give the impression that he had reached a decision.[132] As to partiality, Nehru became a 'family friend'; whether or not his relations with Lady Mountbatten were intimate, they were certainly closer than Foreign Office guidelines for officials overseas.

As to the communal violence that followed hasty partition, the Maharaja of Bhopal told Mountbatten that the June 1948 deadline was 'quite impossible and if enforced must involve bloodshed and chaos'.[133] A week later, Gandhi added that the British system of Divide and Rule had created a situation where either the British remained to enforce law and order or there would be a bloodbath.[134] Sir Evan Jenkins, Governor of Punjab, referred to the proposed division of Punjab as Operation Solomon,[135] the very name of the operation connoting unnatural division and violence.

Beyond the facts, everything is contrafactual speculation. Could Wavell's Breakdown Plan have saved lives? Could the massacres have been avoided if Attlee had appointed Mountbatten earlier – in October 1946, when Wavell's term ended? Mountbatten himself thought that if he had taken on the task eighteen months earlier his job would have been greatly easier. Christopher Mayhew recorded that Bevin, on first meeting Wavell in August 1945, had 'gone straight off to the PM and demanded his removal. The man was a hopeless defeatist, he said.'[136] Should not Attlee have replaced Wavell then? Mountbatten has admirers and his fair share of detractors but, setting aside his colossal vanity and ruthless ambition, the fact remains that he achieved what Attlee asked of him. What, then, were Attlee's objectives?

The most obvious clue is to be found in the announcement of 20 February 1947 in which the handing over of power is treated as the culmination of British policy. That Britain had the chance to make a virtue of necessity and present its actions as other than a 'scuttle' is remarkable. That India's independence was declared before the national boundary lines were known, before the accession of Kashmir and Hyderabad had been decided, is evidence of haste rather than orderly transfer. In those circumstances it is easy to see why India's – and, if possible, Pakistan's – membership of the Commonwealth was symbolically so important. Attlee was able to present a national humiliation as a triumph of statesmanship.

After a slow start Attlee took control of a problem that was fast becoming intractable. To find a solution he was compelled to grant unprecedented power to a man whose vanity alone would ensure some kind of solution. Whatever his faults, Mountbatten was uniquely equipped to bring the Raj to an end in a manner that reflected best on him – and, therefore, on Britain. Possessed of great charm, massive ambition, royal blood to impress the princes, and a competent press attaché, he was able to achieve what was widely considered impossible.

As to the massacres, violence was inevitable; quantifying it in different scenarios is impossible. Penderel Moon believes that by localising the slaughter hasty withdrawal contained the bloodshed. Attlee's and Mountbatten's critics maintain that haste – a 'scuttle' – widened the slaughter unnecessarily. Both opinions are speculative.

In the two years between the 1945 election and Independence Day Attlee became fatalistic about India's future. In a speech in September 1945, in the first flush of optimism, he spoke of solving the country's problems with a little co-operation from all sides. Speaking of India's contribution to the Allied war effort, he appealed to reason.

> *I would ask all Indians to ... join together in a united effort to work out a consti-*
> *tution which the majority and minority communities will accept as just and fair*
> *... The British government will do their utmost to give every assistance in their*
> *power, and India can be assured of the sympathy of the British people.*[137]

With his eyes on India post-independence he gravely underestimated the problems of transition. By early 1947, when he took firm control, replaced Pethick-Lawrence,[138] and appointed Mountbatten, Britain had lost the initiative. It needed the Mountbatten treatment to portray rapid disengagement as a settlement, and assiduous public relations work restored Britain's prestige. The other side of that coin, however, is that Attlee's originally uncertain leadership contributed to the drift.

ENDNOTES

1   See Chapter 4.
2   Amery to PM, 13 November 1942 and 16 April 1943. TNA: PREM 5/532.
3   Moon, *The Viceroy's Journal.* Entry for 26 July 1945, p. 159.
4   Ibid., Entry for 31 July 1945, p. 159.
5   Ibid., Entry for 6 August 1945, p. 161.
6   Ibid., Entry for 22 August 1945, p. 164.

7   TNA: PREM 8/541, Part 1, CM(45) 24th, folio 61 for the Cabinet decision to invite Wavell to London.

8   *The Viceroy's Journal*. Entry for 22 August 1945, p. 164.

9   TNA: PREM 8/541, Part 1. CP (45) 155, folio 53.

10   *The Viceroy's Journal*, Entry for 11 September 1945, p. 171.

11   *Transfer of Power*, VI, p. 393, 25 October 1945.

12   Chief of the Imperial General Staff, the head of the British professional Army. Previously Sir Alan Brooke.

13   Bryant, *Triumph in the West*, p. 382.

14   *The Viceroy's Journal*. Entry for 5 November 1945, p. 181,

15   TNA: PREM 8/541, Part 1. CP (45) 281, folio 44, 14 November 1945.

16   TNA: PREM 8/541, Part 1. I. B. (45) 7th Meeting, folio 41.

17   TNA: PREM 8/541, Part 1. Brook to Attlee, folio 12.

18   TNA: PREM 8/541, Part 1. C. M. (45) 56th Meeting, Conclusions Minute 3, folio 5.

19   *The Viceroy's Journal*, January 1946, p. 202.

20   TNA: PREM 8/541, Part 2. I. B. (46) 4, folios 185–195.

21   TNA: PREM 8/541, Part 2. I. B. (46) 1st Meeting, folio 176.

22   *Transfer of Power*, VI, p. 771.

23   Yasmin Khan, *The Great Partition*, pp. 44–45.

24   Yasmin Khan, *The Great Partition*, pp. 47–52.

25   *The Times of India*, 15 January 1946

26   Adrian Fort, *Archibald Wavell: The Life and Times of an Imperial Servant*, p. 391.

27   TNA: PREM 8/541, Part 2. C. M. (46) 14th, Conclusions Minute 3, folio 126.

28   Exchange of telegrams Wavell and Pethick-Lawrence. TNA: PREM 8/541, Part 2, folios 114 and 116.

29   TNA: PREM 8/541, Part 2. Cable Wavell to Pethick-Lawrence, 3 March 1946, folio 72.

30   TNA: PREM 8/541, Part 2. Cable Wavell to Pethick-Lawrence, 6 March 1946, folio 56. (Mountbatten, of course, recognised this and insisted on greater autonomy.)

31   TNA: PREM 8/541, Part 2. Cable Wavell to Pethick-Lawrence, 10 March 1946, folios 45–46.

32   *The Viceroy's Journal*, Entry for 30 June 1946, p. 310.

33   TNA: PREM 8/541, Part 3. C. M. (46) 28th Conclusions, folio 261.

34   TNA: PREM 8/541, Part 3, folio 255.

35   TNA: PREM 8/541, Part 3. C. M. (46) 33rd Conclusions, folio 244.

36   I. B. Committee to Cabinet Mission, 13 April 1946. TNA: PREM 8/541, folio 228.

37   The summer capital of the Raj and site of the Viceregal Lodge.

38   Mission to I. B. Committee, 30 April 1946. TNA: PREM 8/541, Part 3, folios 211–215.

39   Cabinet 14 May 1946, TNA: PREM 8/541, Part 3. C. M. (46) 46th, folios 106–110.

40   Mission to I. B. Committee, 18 May 1946. TNA: PREM 8/541, Part 3, folios 65–66.

41   TNA: PREM 8/541, Part 3, folios 26–49.

42   *The Viceroy's Journal*, Entry for 16 May, pp. 270–272. (The text of the statement is in Appendix II.)

43   TNA: PREM 8/541, Part 4, folios 158–163.

44   TNA: PREM 8/541, Part 4, folios 144–152.

45   TNA: PREM 8/541, Part 4. C. M. (46) 69th, folio 151.

46   Viceroy to India Office, 18 July 1946. TNA: PREM 8/541, Part 4, folio 136.

47   *Transfer of Power*, VIII, p. 770.

48   He also felt that Wavell was too 'silent'. The Indians, said Attlee, 'are very loquacious. Silent people can't make much of a relationship with them.' Williams, *Nothing So Strange*, p. 251.

49   TNA: PREM 8/541, Part 4, folios 67–69, 31 July 1946.

50   Bodleian: MS. dep. Simon 96/206.

51   Bodleian: MS. dep. Simon 97/15.

52   TNA: PREM 8/541, Part 4, folio 15, 26 June 1946.

53   Cripps had produced a lucid, if one-sided, summary of the Mission's activities, squarely blaming Jinnah for the deadlock. TNA: PREM 8/541, Part 5, folios 173–192, 5 July 1946.

54   Attlee's resolve to make Indian politicians take responsibility is illustrated by his comments in Williams, *A Prime Minister Remembers*, p. 208.

55   TNA: PREM 8/541, Part 5, folio 46.

56   A British official described the riots as a cross between the worst of London air raids and the Great Plague. Suranjan Das, *Communal Riots in Bengal, 1905–1947*, p. 171, cited at Khan, *The Great Partition*, p. 63.

57   TNA: PREM 8/541, Part 5, folio 31.

58   *Daily Mail*, 9 September 1946.

59   Wavell to India Office, 23 October 1946. TNA: PREM 8/541, Part 7, folios 270–275. In this cable Wavell stated that if HMG persisted in urging a one-party interim government dominated by Congress, he would have to reconsider his position. This was his first threat to resign.

60   Wavell to India Office, 11 November 1946. TNA: PREM 8/541, Part 7, folio 265.
61   25 November 1946. TNA: PREM 8/541, Part 7. C. M. (46) 100th, folios 165–166.
62   Wavell to India Office, 26 November 1946. TNA: PREM 8/541, Part 7, folios 162–164.
63   Attlee to Nehru, 28 November 1946. TNA: PREM 8/541, Part 7, folio 158.
64   Jinnah to Attlee, 30 November 1946. TNA: PREM 8/541, Part 7, folio 148.
65   He commented that Nehru's assurance that the door was open meant that the door was open for
      Muslim surrender. *The Times*, 19 August 1946.
66   TNA: PREM 8/541, Part 7. I. C. L. (46) 12, folio 55.
67   Cabinet, 10 December 1946. TNA: PREM 8/541, Part 7. C. M. (46) 104th, folio 47.
68   11 December 1946. TNA: PREM 8/541, Part 7. I. B. (46) 8th Meeting, folios 23–28.
69   TNA: PREM 8/541, Part 8, folios 204–207, 202–203,.
70   Wavell to CRA, 20 December 1946. TNA: PREM 8/541, Part 8, folio 169.
71   CRA to Wavell, 21 December 1946. TNA: PREM 8/541, Part 8, folio 166.
72   Reflections on the Transfer of Power and Jawaharlal Nehru, Admiral of the Fleet Earl Mountbatten of
      Burma, Trinity College, Cambridge – 14 November 1968, para 7.
73   The Diaries of Field Marshal Viscount Alanbrooke, Entry for 15 August 1943. *War Diaries*, p. 441.
74   Arthur Bryant, *The Turn of the Tide*, p. 567; *War Diaries*, Entry for 6 August 1943, p. 437.
75   Reflections on the Transfer of Power and Jawaharlal Nehru, Admiral of the Fleet The Earl
      Mountbatten of Burma, Trinity College, Cambridge – 14th November 1968, para 4.
76   Williams, *A Prime Minister Remembers*, p. 209. Mountbatten had been on the shortlist of candidates to
      replace Lord Linlithgow in 1943.
77   This condition was specified by Mountbatten in a letter to CRA on 17 February 1947. TNA: PREM
      8/563, folios 3–5. The question of who first thought of imposing a time limit has been endlessly
      discussed but is relatively unimportant.
78   *The Memoirs of General Lord Ismay*, p. 413.
79   Bevin to CRA, 1 January 1947. TNA: PREM 8/564, folios 10–15.
80   CRA, to Bevin 2 January 1947. TNA: PREM 8/564, folios 2–5.
81   For the aura of secrecy surrounding preparations see *The Memoirs of General Lord Ismay*, pp. 409–411.
82   CRA to Viceroy, TNA: PREM 8/554, folios 54–6.
83   *The Viceroy's Journal*, Entry for 8 January 1947, p. 408.
84   *The Viceroy's Journal*, Entry for 12 January 1947, p. 410.
85   CRA to Viceroy, 31 January 1947. TNA: PREM 8/554, folios 39–41.
86   *The Viceroy's Journal*. Entry for 4 February 1947, p. 417.
87   Viceroy to CRA, 5 February 1947. TNA: PREM 8/554, folios 37–8.
88   Viceroy to CRA, 14 February 1947. TNA: PREM 8/554, T34/47, folio 28.
89   CRA to Viceroy, 14 February 1947. TNA: PREM 8/554, T35/47, folio 25.
90   CRA to Viceroy, 21 February 1947. TNA: PREM 8/554, T59/47, folio 19.
91   Lord Listowel, Nehru Memorial Lecture, 24 June 1980. Listowel continued, '… it was not until
      Mountbatten went out as Viceroy that the tight rein of ministers was loosened.'
92   TNA: PREM 8/541, Part 9. CM (47) 21st Conclusions, folios 114–115.
93   By Attlee (*Hansard*, HC Deb, 20 February 1947, cols 1395–98) and, in the House of Lords by Pethick-
      Lawrence, *Hansard*, Lords, 20 February 1947, cols. 835–839.
94   *The Viceroy's Journal*, 13 February 1947, p. 419.
95   Williams, *A Prime Minister Remembers*, p. 210.
96   *Hansard*, HC Deb, 5 March 1947, cols 494–512.
97   *Hansard*, HC Deb, 5 March 1947, cols 512–525.
98   *Hansard*, HC Deb, 6 March 1947, cols 663–678.
99   *Hansard*, HC Deb, 6 March 1947, cols 763–772.
100   Ziegler, *Mountbatten* p. 359.
101   Reflections on the Transfer of Power and Jawaharlal Nehru, Admiral of the Fleet The Earl
      Mountbatten of Burma, Trinity College, Cambridge – 14th November 1968, para 41.
102   Ibid, para 28.
103   Ibid, para 54.
104   *Transfer of Power*, X, p. 49.
105   *Transfer of Power*, X, p. 192.
106   Viceroy to India Office, 1 May 1947. TNA: PREM 8/541, Part 10, Cable 954–S, folio 342.
107   TNA: PREM 8/541, Part 10. I. B. (47) 31st Meeting, folio 321.
108   TNA: PREM 8/541, Part 10, folio 311, 6 May 1947.
109   Viceroy to India Office, 10 May 1947. TNA: PREM 8/541, Part 10, folios 260–261.
110   Viceroy to India Office, 11 May 1947. TNA: PREM 8/541, Part 10, cable 57–SC, folio 249.
111   Viceroy to India Office, 12 May 1947. TNA: PREM 8/541, Part 10, cable 57–SC, folio 249.

112 Rowan to PM, 15 May 1947. TNA: PREM 8/541, Part 10, folios 247–248.
113 TNA: PREM 8/541, Part 10. CM (47) 47th meeting, folio 239.
114 TNA: PREM 8/541, Part 10. IB (47) 25th meeting, folio 210.
115 TNA: PREM 8/541, Part 10. CM (47) 50th, folios 114–118. CAB 128/10.
116 *Hansard*, HC Deb, 3 June 1947, vol. 438, column 35.
117 *Transfer of Power*, X, pp. 115–122.
118 Harris, *Attlee*, pp. 383–384.
119 In March 1947 Auchinleck had estimated that it would take between five and ten years to divide the Army into two forces. This now had to be achieved in a few months at the very time that an impartial military force was needed in several cities and at the boundary line.
120 *The Times of India*, 5 June 1947.
121 From a private conversation cited by Yasmin Khan, *The Great Partition*, pp. 102–103.
122 Monckton Papers, Box 41, 186. Cited by Ziegler, *Mountbatten*, p. 415.
123 Broadlands Archive, S147, cited by Ziegler, *Mountbatten*, p. 427.
124 *Washington Post*, 7 June 1947.
125 Ismay Papers, III/8/22b, cited by Ziegler, *Mountbatten*, p. 437.
126 *Transfer of Power*, IX, p. 741.
127 Moon, *Divide and Quit*, p. 277.
128 Ibid. p. 283.
129 Williams, *A Prime Minister Remembers*, p. 211.
130 Perry Anderson, 'Gandhi Centre Stage', *London Review of Books*, 5 July 2012.
131 Reflections on the Transfer of Power and Jawaharlal Nehru, Admiral of the Fleet The Earl Mountbatten of Burma, Trinity College, Cambridge – 14th November 1968, para 41.
132 Campbell-Johnson, *Mission with Mountbatten*, Entries for 16 April and 25 April 1947, pp. 65 and 71.
133 Campbell-Johnson, *Mission with Mountbatten*, Entry for 25 March 1947, p. 44.
134 Campbell-Johnson, *Mission with Mountbatten*, Entry for 1 April 1947, p. 52.
135 Campbell-Johnson, *Mission with Mountbatten*, Entry for 16 April 1947, p. 65.
136 Mayhew, *Time to Explain*, p. 103.
137 Bodleian: MS. Attlee. dep. 22, 19 September 1945.
138 Pethick-Lawrence wrote to Attlee on 2 April 1947, saying that he was 'more than ever convinced that the increasingly heavy responsibilities falling upon the holder of my office and in particular the framing and piloting through Parliament of the legislation necessary to effect the transfer of power in India and Burma require to be undertaken by a younger man, and the sooner he is in the saddle the better.' Pethick-Lawrence was 75 at this point. On 17 April he was succeeded by Lord Listowel, aged 40. Bodleian: MS. Attlee. dep. 51.

CHAPTER THIRTEEN

PALESTINE, 1945–1948

If Attlee became resolute in ending British rule in India, he was less sure-footed in reaching decisions concerning Palestine, where the interlocking problems, strategic and economic, that dictated policy immediately after the war were uppermost. There was one additional element, moreover, to the Gordian knot. Whereas his policy in India was welcomed by the United States, whose economic support was vital to Britain, in Palestine every attempt to find a solution was complicated by the influence that American Zionist organisations – and concern about the 1946 and 1948 American elections – were able to exercise on Truman. International opinion was almost universally shaped by the recent Nazi extermination policy and by the existence of a quarter of a million Jewish refugees in Europe. Attlee and Bevin were thus under pressure to resolve the Jewish refugee problem without regard to the issue of dispossessed Arabs that would follow either creation of a Jewish homeland or the partition of Palestine.

The idea of a Jewish homeland was endorsed by the Balfour Declaration in November 1917, when Foreign Secretary Arthur Balfour announced that the British government '[viewed] with favour the establishment in Palestine of a national home for the Jewish people, and [would] use their best endeavours to facilitate the achievement of this object'.[1] The Declaration was immediately denounced by Arab leaders and provoked the accusation that Britain intended to make Palestine 'as Jewish as England is English'. The British government denied this intention in a White Paper of June 1922 and clarified its interpretation of the Balfour Declaration as proposing to create a Jewish homeland within Palestine, rather than to turn Palestine into a Jewish homeland.[2]

In the following month a League of Nations Mandate decreed that Britain 'shall be responsible for placing the country under such political, administrative and economic conditions as will secure the establishment of the Jewish national home ... and the development of self-governing institutions, and also for safeguarding the civil and religious rights of all the inhabitants of Palestine, irrespective of race and religion.'[3] The Mandate charged the British government with the responsibility of consulting with the Zionist organisation to secure the co-operation of all Jews willing to assist in the establishment of the Jewish national home[4] while ensuring that the rights and position of other sections of the population were not prejudiced.[5]

During the early 1930s, as German racial policies caused a surge of Jewish emigration to Palestine, Arab leaders became increasingly concerned that Arabs would become a minority; the Black Hand, an anti-Zionist group founded in 1930, orchestrated a campaign of terror. When its leader Sheikh Izz ad-Din-al-Qassam was killed by British police in November 1935 the Arab population organised a six-month general strike and acts of violence against Jewish settlers. In November 1936 the Palestine Royal Commission ('The Peel Commission') arrived in Palestine to investigate and report on the state of affairs. Members spent two months there before issuing a comprehensive report in July 1937.

The report narrated the history of Palestine since earliest times, recording that under the Mandate the Jewish population rose from about 55,000 to about 108,000 by March 1925.[6] A quite unusual number, they commented, were young and highly educated. The great majority was almost passionately conscious of a national mission.[7]

The report concluded that the co-existence of two separate communities, to each of whom Britain had made certain promises, was not feasible and recommended partition into the north and mid-west of the country, which would be awarded to the Jews, and the south and mid-east, which would be awarded to the Arabs. The Mandate should be terminated, except in the area surrounding Jerusalem and a corridor from Jerusalem to the sea at Jaffa. It added somewhat pessimistically, but not without hope, that 'To both Arabs and Jews Partition offers a prospect – and we see no prospect in any other policy – of obtaining the inestimable boon of peace.'[8]

Arab leaders condemned the report unequivocally as a breach of the British promise to grant them independence; 'the very presence of Jews enjoying rights was a betrayal of the British word'.[9] Jewish leader David Ben-Gurion was more pragmatic, believing that this was an undreamed of opportunity. It was, he said, a national consolidation in a free homeland. If through weakness, neglect or negligence, it was not seized, Zionists would have lost a chance that they might never have again.[10]

The Woodhead Commission, convened to examine the Peel plan in 1938, rejected partition as unworkable, and the Peel recommendations were abandoned. A White Paper of 1939 distinguished carefully between making all of Palestine a Jewish homeland and creating a Jewish homeland 'in Palestine', declaring that British policy was to pursue the latter. It proposed that, after the restoration of order, Palestine should become independent within ten years. In the meantime, 50,000 Jewish immigrants would be admitted over five years and 25,000 would be admitted as soon as the High Commissioner was satisfied that there was adequate provision for their maintenance.[11]

Both Arab and Jewish communities were disappointed with these conclusions. An inchoate Jewish campaign of violence was set aside when war broke out in 1939. Twenty years later Ben-Gurion reflected bitterly on the rejection of partition. Had partition been carried out, he said, six million Jews in Europe would not have been killed, as most of them would have been in Israel.[12]

British policy in 1945, established between Attlee and Bevin, was to retain British influence in the Middle East, a difficult task as Britain was committed to remove its forces from Egypt. Adjacent Palestine, therefore, assumed greater strategic importance. Both Attlee and Bevin were determined to prevent the Soviet Union from occupying any void created by British withdrawal. They were equally concerned that the United States, whose policy in the region was uncertain and inconsistent, might once again become isolationist and that Britain would be faced with the task of military occupation without American support. Truman had assumed that Churchill would win the election and wrote to him on 24 July appealing to Churchill's 'deep and sympathetic interest in Jewish settlement in Palestine' and urging the lifting of immigration restrictions.[13] That letter was delivered to Attlee, who responded, requesting time to consider the matter and undertaking to 'give early and careful consideration to [the] memorandum'.[14]

Attlee believed that Truman's concern was motivated principally by domestic politics. He later maintained to Francis Williams that 'There's no Arab vote in America, but there's a very heavy Jewish vote and the Americans are always having elections.[15] Bevin too expressed his belief that Truman's concern to settle Jews in Palestine was to avoid having more of them in New York. Both views were only partially true. Dean Acheson, Assistant Secretary of State, recognised Truman's deep commitment to the Jewish homeland, born from his long-standing friendship with Eddie Jacobson, formed when both served in France in 1917. Jacobson, the owner of Westport Men's Wear in Kansas City, was a passionate Zionist from whom Truman had acquired sympathy for Zionist claims in Palestine.[16]

Attlee needed time to be briefed on the issue but Truman, ever suspicious of advice from 'the clannish and snooty bunch'[17] in the State Department and not unlike the Prime Minister in his desire for immediate implementation of decisions, took personal control of American policy. He distinguished between long-term and short-term plans, confident that 'the long-range fate of Palestine was the kind of problem we had the UN for; some immediate aid, however, was needed for the Jews in Europe'.[18] He accordingly assured Arabs that 'no decision should be taken regarding the basic situation in Palestine without full consultation with Arabs and Jews'. Somewhat disingenuously, Truman later wrote that 'to assure the Arabs that they would be consulted was by no means inconsistent with my generally sympathetic attitude toward Jewish aspirations.'[19]

Having allowed Attlee one month to study the problem, Truman renewed pressure for action and wrote to Attlee on 31 August. He noted that 'the available certificates for immigration into Palestine will be exhausted in the near future' and proposed that an additional 100,000 certificates be granted. This would 'contribute greatly to a sound solution for the future of Jews still in Germany and Austria, and for other Jewish refugees who do not wish to remain where they are or who for understandable reasons do not desire to return to their countries of origin.' If this were to be effective, he maintained, it should not be delayed.[20]

Failing to recognise the strength of the President's determination to reach early resolution of the problem, Attlee again requested time to study the question, urging Truman to take no action 'in the interval'. His concern was that he was being pressured into action for which the President refused to take responsibility. Whatever course Britain took, it was certain to inflame the passions of one, or the other, or both of the groups in Palestine. He therefore decided to move the USA from 'being a private exhorter to a publicly responsible partner in Palestine affairs'.[21] While formally declining to refashion immigration policy, he proposed to Truman a suggestion of Bevin's that an Anglo-American Committee of Inquiry be established. Truman promptly announced at a press conference the establishment of the committee under a rotating chairmanship.[22] At the same time he released the content of his letter to Attlee of 31 August. When this failed to produce the desired result, he opened the New Year with a follow-up cable: 'Would appreciate your advising me how many certificates per month are now being issued for admission of Jews into Palestine. I understood that there were to be three thousand but news dispatches are confusing. There is, as you know, great interest in this subject in the United States.'[23]

Attlee responded on 4 January, informing Truman (as he doubtless knew) that 'the quota of 75,000 authorised under the White Paper of 1939 [was] virtually exhausted' and that immigration was being maintained 'at present rate of 1,500 (repeat 1,500) persons per month pending consideration of report of the Anglo-American Committee.'[24]

The committee submitted its report to the British and the American governments on 22 April. This was agreed to, and on 1 May the report and the ten recommendations of the committee were made known. These were that:

- *There was no country other than Palestine that could find the necessary homes to accommodate displaced persons;*
- *100,000 certificates should be issued immediately to victims of Nazis and Fascists, and immigration should be 'pushed forward as rapidly as conditions will permit';*
- *it must be made clear that Jew shall not dominate Arab and Arab shall not dominate Jew in Palestine and all rights of Christians, Jews and Muslims will be protected;*

- *because any attempt to establish an independent Palestinian state or states would result in civil war the Mandate should continue 'pending the execution of a trusteeship agreement under the United Nations';*
- *the 'mandatory or trustee should proclaim the principle that Arab economic, educational and political advancement in Palestine is of equal importance with that of the Jews and should at once prepare measures designed to bridge the gap which now exists and raise the Arab standard of living to that of the Jews';*
- *that Jewish immigration should be facilitated 'under suitable conditions';*
- *that there should be freedom of sale of land, without regard to 'race, community or creed', and the government should exercise close supervision of all holy places;*
- *plans for agricultural development should be implemented to raise the living standard of both Arabs and Jews;*
- *educational standards should be reformed and, in due course, compulsory education be introduced; and*
- *it should be made clear to all parties that terrorism, violence and the formation of private armies would be resolutely suppressed.*[25]

The report contained equitable recommendations to which no impartial reader could object. It also had no chance of being implemented, essentially voicing Utopian principles that neither side, in entrenched positions, would accept. As Acheson succinctly summarised, 'Unfortunately, the only significant omissions were how those goals, so unanimously desired, were to be achieved'.[26]

Bevin cabled Halifax in Washington on 22 April and, anticipating a violent reaction to the report, requested that it be released simultaneously in London and Washington the following week.[27] Attlee and Bevin were irked by Truman's wish to release at least part of the report immediately[28] and repeated their request on 24 April. Eventually a release date of 1 May was agreed on.[29]

When the Cabinet discussed the recommendations, Bevin was confident that a reasonable settlement could be reached. It was an Anglo-American committee, he stressed, and the two nations should handle the problems jointly. He resisted any suggestion of referral to the UN as that would be regarded as an admission of British failure. The first step must be to approach the American government, a task that he could undertake at the Foreign Ministers' meeting in Paris.[30] Dalton estimated that the cost of settling 100,000 Jews in Palestine would be £100 million and recurrent expenditure of between £5 million and £10 million. This was no small sum for Britain to undertake. The United States must be pressed to share in this expenditure; the committee's report had, after all, stressed the responsibility of the whole world for the Jewish victims of Nazi persecution.[31]

At the time that the committee's report was released the Cabinet Mission in India was having its first taste of how difficult it was to reach agreement between rival groups for whom politics and religion were one. Although circumstances in India and Palestine were radically different, Attlee must have drawn parallels between the difficulties presented by the two countries. Even if he did not at first do so, Churchill was ever willing to use the House of Commons to attack the government for its handling of either or both situations.[32]

Churchill was not alone in his criticism of the government's apparent indecision. Field Marshal Montgomery visited Palestine shortly after the release of the report and was 'much perturbed' by what he observed, concluding that the High Commissioner was unable to make up his mind what to do. Indecision and hesitation were in evidence everywhere, emanating from Whitehall. Policy and decisions were required.[33]

It is baffling that Attlee, whose eventual handling of the deadlock in India was firm and decisive, incurring criticism for its very decisiveness, could be so unsure of his footing in Palestine. The most likely explanation is that, recognising Britain's need for both political and material support from the United States, he continued to believe that joint action was a possibility. In this he was naïve. Truman continued to meet subtle implications of American responsibility with a straight bat. In May Harriman, American Ambassador in London, delivered a curtly elusive message from President to Prime Minister: 'In view of the urgency surrounding the question of the admission to Palestine of the 100,000 Jews whose entry is recommended by the committee, I sincerely hope that it will be possible to initiate and complete the consultations with Arabs and Jews at the earliest possible moment.'[34]

Attlee responded graciously to Truman, mentioning that Bevin and Byrnes had spoken and referred to the need to discuss military and financial implications. This was the first anniversary of VE Day and he spoke of the 'heartfelt gratitude of the people and government of this country for the outstanding part you played in the common victory', concluding, 'I trust that our comradeship in war will continue in the days of peace.'[35] Attlee wondered what else he could do to flush the President out. The Foreign Office and the Colonial Office discussed this and advised him on 11 May that they could see little else that he could do at that stage. Truman had neatly stonewalled the approach, discussing Palestine as though the only issue at stake was the granting of 100,000 entry certificates.

Exchanges along these lines continued as Attlee pressed the President gently about sharing military and financial responsibilities.[36] Truman responded on 17 May, agreeing to discussions between US and British experts and asking Attlee what subjects he thought they might discuss, quite ignoring Attlee's reference to military and financial matters.[37] Finally he stated terms. On 5 June he sent a cleverly constructed cable stating the *quid pro quo* in connection with a proposed meeting of British and American experts. He was, he said, organising the American group as quickly as possible, continuing,

> As we doubt however that our plans will be sufficiently advanced for our side to begin the discussions on the Report as a whole at the time you suggest, namely one week prior to June 20, we are planning to send to London by that time one or more experts to discuss the urgent physical problems arising out of the transfer of Palestine of the 100,000 Jews mentioned in the Report.[38]

The implication is clear: before any discussion of military or financial assistance can take place, not only must Britain contact Jewish and Arab organisations, there must also be firm arrangements in place for the 100,000 Jews whose admission to Palestine the Report advocated. In case Attlee had not grasped the interconnection, Truman returned to the subject later, saying, 'we feel it would be highly desirable that we begin immediately consideration of the hundred thousand Jews whose situation continues to cause grave concern' and commits the USA to responsibility for their transport to Palestine.

Truman had 'named the price of the papers'. Attlee could not afford to attract the world's odium as grotesque evidence of Nazi racial policy emerged after the occupation of Germany. Montgomery alluded to this, commenting that 'British rule existed only in name; the true rulers seemed to me to be the Jews, whose unspoken slogan was "You dare not touch us".'[39] Both Attlee and Bevin, to whom the Prime Minister entrusted British policy in Palestine, belonged to a generation for whom racial profiling and jokes, that today would be considered offensive, were common. Attlee wrote to Tom about American attitudes to Jewish immigration, jesting that in America Zionism had become a profitable racket. 'A Zionist is defined as a Jew who collects money from another Jew to send another Jew to Palestine. The collector, I gather, takes a good percentage of his collections.'[40]

Yet neither Attlee nor Bevin, whose comments on Jewish immigration aroused such hatred that he was pelted with eggs in New York, was fundamentally anti-Semitic.[41] Certainly Bevin was anti-Zionist and he was ever conscious that Arabs were under-represented in Parliament and Congress.[42] It would be false to see Attlee's hesitation over Palestine in counterpoint to Truman's pro-Zionist sympathies. For India Attlee had an 'inspiration' that led to a conclusion; in Palestine he had no such enlightenment. All he could envisage was world opinion, led by Truman, coalescing to present Britain as the villain, while it was Britain that continued to pay for maintenance of order in a rapidly deteriorating situation. Exactly as he feared, Truman took 'the plum out of the pudding',[43] seizing on the committee's recommendation that 100,000 entry visas be granted immediately; once again Attlee was faced with a crisis to which he had no solution.

By now, perhaps, he had come to realise that Truman's motivation was not purely political, that he was genuinely pro-Zionist. That realisation did nothing to stem mounting bad feeling between the two, however, as Attlee was thoroughly exasperated with the President's pressure. Neither Attlee nor Truman was 'of a leaning disposition'[44] and Truman was personally applying the tourniquet, overruling suggestions from Acheson and Loy Henderson at the State Department.[45] That pressure came closer than anything else to erode goodwill between London and Washington.

Truman also kept up diplomatic pressure; Harriman wrote to Bevin on 10 June, informing him that a group of State Department officials and US military officers would come to London on 12 June to discuss the 100,000 Jews and their movement to Palestine.

Effectively painted into a corner, Attlee replied, expressing delight at the proposed talks in London but repeating that the transfer of 100,000 people to Palestine was something that required careful planning.[46] Truman maintained the pressure, responding immediately and, in a four-paragraph cable, mentioning the 100,000 Jews three times.[47] As Sir Orme Sargent, Permanent Under-Secretary of State for Foreign Affairs, put it in diplomatic language to Attlee, 'It is evident from President Truman's latest telegram to you on this subject that the two governments still have different ideas as to the purpose of the talks about to begin in London.'[48]

By 28 June the first phase of the talks was complete and Truman informed Attlee that the American Cabinet committee on Palestine would leave for London after the return of 'the American experts who have been discussing in London the technical aspects of the early immigration of 100,000 Jews into Palestine.'[49] There was more bad news for the Prime Minister as George Hall, Secretary of State for the Colonies, warned that the Arabs were preparing to resist any increased immigration quotas and to 'fight with all the means in their power'.[50] In the following week the Chiefs of Staff warned of the importance of preventing Soviet influence in the region and that there would be a breakdown of trust between Britain and Arabs and renewed violence from Zionists if Britain attempted to implement the report's conclusions. There would be a need for an additional two infantry divisions, one armoured brigade and three infantry battalions, as well as additional air and naval forces. The annual cost of these reinforcements would be £96 million; it would be necessary to ask the USA to assist, but American public opinion was demanding immediate and total demobilisation.[51]

Almost a year had now passed since Truman urged Attlee to 'give early and careful consideration' to the question of immigration, yet despite the President's repeated plea for the granting of 100,000 visas, no progress had been made beyond agreement to hold another conference. Meanwhile Zionist terrorism was mounting, and Attlee authorised military action, arresting the Zionist leaders. This provided the background for the London meeting of British and American experts (known as the Morrison-Grady group), chaired by Cabinet Secretary Norman Brook and the President's emissary, Henry Grady. On 22 July, soon after the American team arrived, the Jewish Irgun group blew up the King David Hotel in Jerusalem, where the British Secretariat was housed, killing ninety-one people.

The attack increased pressure on the experts; three days later the contents of the Morrison-Grady plan were leaked. These incorporated most elements of Attlee's proposals, with the added principle of Truman's distinction between short-term and long-term measures. It urged the admission of 100,000 Jews but stressed that this must be conditional on Arab agreement. For the long-term it recommended federalisation, Jewish and Arab provinces with local powers, and American economic aid for Palestinian Arabs, amounting to $50 million.[52] In a masterly piece of litotes the statement added,

> *We recognise that, in view of the existing situation in Palestine, any policy*
> *... will probably have to be introduced without the willing consent of either*
> *community. On the other hand, we agree that no policy should be enforced against*
> *sustained and determined resistance by either Jews or Arabs. An effort to obtain*
> *at least a measure of acquiescence from the Arabs and Jews would therefore be*
> *an essential preliminary to the introduction of the above proposals ... We are not*
> *able at this stage to make recommendations regarding the course to be adopted if*
> *the conference with Arab and Jewish representatives led to the conclusion that the*
> *introduction of the policy proposed would be violently resisted by one or both of*
> *the two peoples in Palestine. In that situation further consultation between our two*
> *governments would be necessary.*[53]

One wonders why the American delegation bothered to cross the Atlantic. Nonetheless, Attlee cabled Truman on 25 July, paying tribute to Grady and his team and urging that the committee's recommendations be implemented without delay.[54]

Within days the plan had been rejected by Jews, Arabs and by Congressional leaders. The United States now acquired the mantle, handed off by Attlee, of the most hated power in the Middle East.[55] Recriminations flowed across the Atlantic as Truman informed Attlee that the US could not accept the report and Churchill proposed in the

Commons that Britain relinquish its mandate if the United States was not prepared to assist. Inevitably, the report languished and died.

Attlee can rarely have felt Britain's diminished position more acutely than at this point. Dependent on American financial and moral support, he believed that Truman, with his eye on public opinion, paid too little regard to the danger of Soviet penetration of the Middle East. This concern grew when he received a cable from the Moscow Embassy. Sir Maurice Peterson cabled the Foreign Office with a summary of a lecture by Lutski, the Soviet expert on Palestine.[56] Lutski's principal target had been British imperialism in the Middle East and, secondly, American interest in the strategic position and oil resources in the region. He came out strongly in favour of the Arabs – the first Soviet spokesman to do so – and attacked the Zionist goal of a Jewish bourgeois state in Palestine. Reports in *Pravda* and *Izvestia*, however, stressed the attacks on Britain and the United States but avoided any condemnation of Zionism.[57] Peterson took this as Soviet reluctance to express their long-standing disapproval of Zionism while being prepared to condemn the traditional targets, Britain and America. This added urgency to Attlee's conviction that the United States must be compelled to take a firm stand in the Middle East.

Truman's priorities, however, were more domestic than global. Attlee sent him a statement that he proposed to make on Morrison-Grady and eagerly awaited a reply.[58] When this was received, it confirmed Attlee's fears. Acheson informed Lord Inverchapel that the President was unable to make an announcement along the lines suggested, having received from the Cabinet 'the strongest opposition, which had been fully shared by the leaders of the Democratic Party in Congress'. Moreover, Senator Taft and the Jewish leaders also condemned the plan. According to Acheson, the President felt that 'so far as Palestine is concerned all the support he had in the country was falling away from under him' and that any statement from him would produce a kind of 'Donnybrook Fair'.[59] Two and a half hours later another telegram arrived from Washington with further news from Acheson: Truman was proposing to announce that he was recalling the Grady Mission to discuss the whole matter in detail.[60] A cable from Inverchapel later that morning was scathing about Truman's motives, attributing 'this deplorable display of weakness' to 'reasons of domestic politics which, it will be recalled, caused the Administration last year to use every artifice of persuasion to defer the announcement about the establishment of the Anglo-American Committee until after the New York elections.'[61]

It is worth examining the correspondence between Attlee and Truman in detail as it provides a key to understanding Britain's subsequent relations with the USA. Among many of Attlee's colleagues there was resentment at the eclipse of British power; more fundamentally, the basic disagreements over Palestine in 1946 led to mistrust that was never quite overcome. For Attlee, Britain's duty under the Mandate was cardinal. While he understood that Truman was not so obligated, he felt betrayed by Britain's principal ally and this led him to question American motives and to doubt whether he could depend on Washington. Some questions were 'political'; he understood the nature of diplomacy and pursuit of national advantage. But Truman's refusal to consider Britain's obligations and his persistent pressing for 100,000 entry permits influenced his attitude thereafter. It reeked of abnegation of duty for political advantage. He was able to compartmentalise relations between the two countries; on the other hand he was forced to recognise that he could not depend on Truman for what he considered fundamental moral support.

While Inverchapel in Washington was outspoken on the perceived enormity of Truman's posture, Attlee kept silent, conscious that he was more dependent on the goodwill of the President than he would wish. He suppressed his frustration, discussed the position with Harriman and proceeded to fulfil what he saw as Britain's obligation. The Cabinet agreed that Morrison should present the experts' conclusions in a comprehensive statement to the Commons, despite a hint from Acheson that this would be seen as undermining Truman's position.

Attlee still believed that a round-table conference of Zionist and Arab leaders and British and American representatives might bear fruit, but this hope was dashed when Zionist leaders refused to negotiate with the British. At one point he showed his teeth by stating that, without American support, there would be modifications which would 'relate particularly to the tempo and extent of Jewish immigration and Arab development'.[62] In short, he was telling Truman, if you want to see those 100,000 entry certificates, it would be best to support us. Truman, himself no stranger to political pressure, had more cards to play. When he needed to squeeze Attlee in the following year, he instructed Lew Douglas, the US Ambassador in London, to call on Bevin with the message that admission of the 100,000 to Palestine would enable Marshall Aid funds to be processed through Congress.[63]

Truman remained determined to facilitate the migration, yet the prospect of achieving this had waned between 1945 and 1946. Accordingly, on 4 October, the day of Yom Kippur, he announced that he was continuing his efforts on behalf of the 100,000 and was liberalising entry into the United States.[64] He added that a plan for Palestine, based on the partition of the country between Arabs and Jews, 'would command the support of public opinion in the United States'.[65]

Attlee, alerted that Truman was going to speak thus, cabled the President to ask him to delay his announcement until he had a chance to speak to Bevin. Truman ignored the request and Attlee, appalled at the President's precipitate statement, cabled him:

> *I have received with great regret your letter refusing even a few hours grace to the Prime Minister of the country which has the actual responsibility for the government of Palestine in order that he might acquaint you with the actual situation and the probable results of your action. These may well include the frustration of the patient efforts to achieve a settlement and the loss of still more lives in Palestine.*[66]

After an interval of six days Truman responded. He was not unaware, he told Attlee, of Britain's position, but his concern – and that of the American people – was with the displaced Jews facing another winter, eighteen months after their liberation. It was a grim prospect that was undermining his government. His obligation was to speak up without further delay.[67] It was not a dishonest letter as Truman was not a dishonest man. But he was a politician and he was aware that the proposed date for the conference of Arab and Jewish leaders came well after the mid-term elections and that, with the approval ratings of his administration badly damaged, he needed to inject some optimism before 5 November.

Attlee was too angry to reply. He wrote to Bevin that he had not replied to Truman and did not intend to do so immediately. He would consider his reply after the Cabinet meeting on 22 October. Bevin drafted a reply to Truman for the Prime Minister's approval.[68] Attlee scrawled on it with more than normal pressure 'NO answer to President required. CRA'.

Truman, however, – and more crucially, public opinion worldwide – was not interested in niceties of diplomacy. The President was advocating liberalised immigration policies which Attlee was apparently resisting. Zionist confidence that Jewish *desiderata* could be attained prompted an outright demand for all Palestine to become a Jewish state. This, commented *The Times*, was 'apparently on the principle that it is necessary to ask for a yard to get a foot'.[69]

At the end of January 1947 the second phase of the round-table conference ended in failure and Bevin informed General Marshall, now Secretary of State, that Britain would refer the whole problem to the United Nations.[70] Attempts by Marshall to keep the responsibility for Palestine firmly in Bevin's hands failed when Britain announced that she could no longer meet commitments in Greece.[71] Bevin attacked American policy towards Palestine in the Commons and was cheered.

Partition was now the favoured solution but, as Bevin advised the Cabinet, Arabs were implacably opposed to partition and the Jews demanded a sovereign Jewish state.[72] Bevin and Creech Jones[73] had proposed a solution, whose object was self-government in Palestine, incorporating most of the *desiderata* of both sides, including admission of 100,000 Jews at the rate of 4,000 monthly for two years.[74] If the Cabinet approved and if the plan had some chance of being accepted by both sides, then they should proceed; if not, then the matter should be referred immediately to the United Nations. Creech Jones said that he and General Sir Alan Cunningham, the High Commissioner, had believed that partition was the only solution, but that he now doubted its practical application. Wherever the frontiers were drawn, many Arabs would be left as minorities under Jewish rule. He now agreed with Bevin on the solution proposed, provided the period of trusteeship was increased from five to ten years.

When Bevin and Creech Jones reported to Cabinet that the British proposals had been rejected by both Arabs and Jews,[75] the Cabinet agreed that the matter should be referred to the UN. They clung to the possibility that notice of HMG's intention to do so – something that neither the Jews nor the Arabs wanted – might stimulate a desire to agree before this happened.[76] Bevin announced that decision in the House on 18 February, simply stating the government's inability to influence events.[77]

British resentment of American leadership was matched by American distrust of imagined British imperialism, and this, to Attlee's fury, was enhanced during June and July by an incident that suggested deep-rooted anti-semitism in the British High Command. Alexander Rubinowitz, a sixteen-year-old activist with Lehi, a Jewish resistance organisation, disappeared. There was suspicion that he had been murdered by a Palestine police squad under the command of a wartime SAS hero. Roy Farran, a swashbuckling operator, a 24-year-old major with a DSO and three Military Crosses to his name at the end of the war, had volunteered for service with the Palestine police when, after the destruction of the King David Hotel, more robust methods of anti-terrorism were adopted. His appointment rapidly became a public relations disaster. The British press – and, more importantly, the American press – were not slow to exploit the potential of the story: talk of officially sanctioned death squads, commanded by an officer with a record of savage violence and insubordination, were an embarrassment to the government. Farran meanwhile, claiming that he was being framed, fled to Syria.

Attlee was incensed, principally because he had not been informed of the incident, and pressed Creech Jones for details of the affair.[78] Creech Jones demanded explanations from Cunningham.[79] The press, he said, were linking the officers involved in the affair with the British Union of Fascists. When Attlee saw a copy of Creech Jones' cable on 19 June he sent the Colonial Secretary a minute pointing out that 'it is almost impossible for the government to abandon the defensive and to put the official statement across convincingly'.[80] He was acutely conscious that the government's credibility in Washington would be badly damaged. When, after terminating his position with the Palestine police and being arrested by the British Army on suspicion of murder, Farran escaped from the Army's custody, that tattered credibility was irrevocably destroyed. As Creech Jones, now the target of Attlee's severe displeasure, commented to Cunningham, 'this is a most unfortunate occurrence as the case has already aroused considerable notice and speculation.'[81] Farran had been awarded the American Legion of Merit for wartime exploits but the war was over and the image of a post-war Lawrence of Arabia, moving 'among Jewish civilians in Jewish clothing', was not at all appealing to American public opinion.

In the event, the case against Farran was dismissed for lack of evidence. The damage done to the British government, however, remained. The suspicion that the Army, following orders reflecting Montgomery's tougher stance on peace-keeping methods, had connived at Farran's escape would not go away; the effect of that suspicion on Truman's attitude was inevitable.

During the spring and the summer it became clear that no agreed settlement was possible. In July 4,500 illegal immigrants in Haifa were returned to Europe; on 29 November the United Nations passed a resolution that Britain's mandate would end not later than 1 August 1948 and Palestine would be partitioned. By the end of 1947 fighting had spread throughout Palestine.

Britain declared her intention to withdraw by 15 May 1948; on the day before that deadline the state of Israel came into being. Truman immediately recognised the new nation; on the following day the Arab-Israeli war was launched; concentrated attacks on Israel were orchestrated. The expected outcome, that the Arab coalition would drive the Israelis into the sea,[82] was dramatically reversed and in the armistice agreements with the separate Arab countries between February and July 1949 Israel obtained 30 per cent more territory than the United Nations had assigned her.

The four years between July 1945 and the final drawing of Israel's borders in July 1949 were punctuated by repeated demands by Truman for the granting of 100,000 entry visas for displaced Jews in Europe and by repeated refusals of those demands by Attlee. Critics of the British stance maintain that if Attlee had simply acquiesced to Truman's urging, the civil war and subsequent all-out conflict would have been avoided. Such an argument assumes that Zionist demands would immediately have ceased and discounts Britain's responsibility under the Mandate.

Attlee and Bevin misjudged Truman's reasons for repeated intervention; they, moreover, had British interests to protect in relations with several Arab states. It is as possible, therefore, that Attlee wore the Mandate as an ethical carapace to cover British interests as it is that Truman used humanitarian gestures to capture votes in the north-east United States. It is nonetheless puzzling that Attlee, normally flexible in his search for solutions and decisive in implementing them, was so resistant to Truman for so long. He was successful in manoeuvring the President into sharing some of the costs of increased immigration but singularly unsuccessful in sharing the moral responsibility at the bar of world opinion. As Gerald Kaufman commented, 'he betrayed the Jews without appeasing the Arabs'.[83]

The consequences of British policy in those four years were far-reaching, resulting in enormous human misery, and much of the responsibility must lie with Attlee's government. The lack of moral leadership, indeed the lack of perceptible policy beyond consistent refusal to accede to Truman's urgings, are untypical of Attlee. Moreover, his argumentative posture *vis-à-vis* the American President was dangerously at odds with his resolute determination to maintain a strong Atlantic alliance. His subsequent rationalisation that Truman throughout was merely courting votes is an astounding oversimplification.

He was determinedly correct in his interpretation of the Mandate, correct to the point of being stiff-necked. In the conditions of post-war Europe it would not have been impossible to justify increased allocation of entry visas. In his refusal to make the Arabs – or Britain – the residuary legatee of Hitler's policy of extermination, he was legally correct but he may be judged to have been somewhat short-sighted.

ENDNOTES

1　A. J. Balfour to Lord Rothschild, 2 November 1917, para 2.
2　British White Paper, June 1922, paras 2–3.
3　League of Nations Mandate, 4 July 1922, Article 2.
4　Ibid. Article 4.
5　Ibid. Article 6.
6　Report of the Palestine Royal Commission, 4 July 1937, p. 46.
7　Ibid. p. 49.
8　Ibid. pp. 394–395.
9　'British Policy in Palestine 1937–1938', *The Bulletin of International News*, vol. 15.no. 23, November 1938.
10　Shabtai Teveth, *Ben-Gurion and the Palestinian Arabs*, (OUP, 1985), pp. 180–182.
11　White Paper, May 1939 ('The MacDonald White Paper'), Section II, para. 9.
12　Tom Segev, *One Palestine Complete*, p. 414.
13　Cited by Williams, *A Prime Minister Remembers*, pp. 183–184.

14   Woodward, *British Foreign Policy in the Second World War*, pp. 394–395.

15   Williams, *A Prime Minister Remembers*, pp. 181.

16   McCullough, *Truman*, pp. 107–108; Dean Acheson, *Present at the Creation*, p. 169.

17   Robert H. Ferrell (editor), *Off The Record: The Private Papers of Harry S. Truman*, p. 235.

18   Harry S. Truman, *Years of Trial and Hope*, (Memoirs, volume II), p. 140.

19   Harry S. Truman, *Years of Trial and Hope*, (Memoirs, volume II), p. 135.

20   *The Public Papers of the Presidents, Harry S. Truman*, 1945, Document 188.

21   Acheson, *op. cit.* p. 171.

22   *The Public Papers of the Presidents, Harry S. Truman*, 1945, 13 November 1945, Document 187.

23   President to PM, 1 January 1946. TNA: PREM 8–350, T1/46.

24   PM to Truman, 4 January 1946. TNA: PREM 8/350, T6/46.

25   Anglo-American Committee of Inquiry, *Report to the United States Government and His Majesty's Government in the United Kingdom*, 20 April 1946, Chapter 1. See also TNA: PREM 8–627/2, fols 132–143.

26   Acheson, *op. cit.* p. 172.

27   TNA: PREM 8/627–2, T. 3475.

28   Halifax to FO, TNA: PREM 8/627–2, T2608.

29   Halifax to FO, TNA: PREM 8/627–2, T. 2614 and T. 2623.

30   TNA: PREM 8/627–2. CM (46) 38th Conclusions, 29 April 1946.

31   Ibid., loc. cit.

32   See, for example, *Hansard* HC Deb, 06 March 1947 vol. 434 col. 676.

33   *The Memoirs of Field Marshal Montgomery*, p. 423.

34   Truman to PM, 8 May 1946. TNA: PREM 8/627–2.

35   PM to Truman, 9 May 1946. TNA: PREM 8/627–2, T230/46.

36   PM to Truman, 11 May 1946. TNA: PREM 8/627–2, T245/46.

37   Truman to PM, 17 May 1946. TNA: PREM 8/627–2, T265/46.

38   Truman to PM, 5 June 1946. TNA: PREM 8/627–2, T323/46.

39   *The Memoirs of Field Marshal Montgomery*, p. 423.

40   Letter to Tom Attlee, 29 December 1946.

41   Attlee later denied any anti-Semitism on Bevin's part. Granada Historical Records, *Clem Attlee*, pp. 38–39. Ian Mikardo notes that, according to Dalton, he was denied a junior post by Attlee because he was Jewish. *Back-Bencher*, p. 4.

42   Mayhew, *Time to Explain*, p. 119. Mayhew makes the point that Bevin allowed anti-Zionism to colour his view of Jews as a whole.

43   Acheson, *op. cit.* p. 173.

44   Ibid. loc. cit.

45   The State Department generally supported Britain in urging a UN trusteeship until Arab-Jew conflicts could be resolved. Truman's staff, however, with their eyes on the 1948 election, wanted division and migration. On one occasion Truman aide David Niles said sharply to Loy Henderson, head of the State Department's Office of Near Eastern Affairs, 'Look here, Loy, the most important thing for the United States is for the President to be reelected.' McCullough, *Truman*, p. 600,

46   PM to Truman, 14 June 1946. TNA: PREM 8/627–2, T331/46.

47   Truman to PM 14 June 1946. TNA: PREM 8/627–2, T332/46.

48   TNA: PREM 8/627–2. PM 46/103, 16 June 1946.

49   Truman to PM 2 July 1946. TNA: PREM 8/627–2, T369/46.

50   S. of S. to PM 4 July 1946. TNA: PREM 8/627–3.

51   COS to PM, 10 July 1946. TNA: PREM 8/627–3, COS (46) 188 (0).

52   25 July 1946, Statement of Policy, of the British and United States Delegations, TNA: PREM 8/627–3.

53   Ibid., paras 31–33.

54   PM to Truman, 25 July 1946. TNA: PREM 8/627–3, T393/46.

55   See Acheson, *Present at the Creation*, pp. 175–6.

56   Moscow to FO 22 July 1946. TNA: PREM 8/627–3, T2457.

57   This was taken to indicate a certain ambiguousness in Soviet policy. See Amikam Nachmani, *Great Power Discord in Palestine: The Anglo-American Committee of Inquiry*, p. 141.

58   PM to Truman, 29 July 1946. TNA: PREM 8/627–3, T406.

59   Inverchapel to FO 30 July 1946. TNA: PREM 8/627–3, T20.

60   Inverchapel to FO 30 July 1946. TNA: PREM 8/627–3, T21.

61   Inverchapel to FO 31 July 1946. TNA: PREM 8/627–3, T22.

62   PM to Truman, 9 August 1946. TNA: PREM 8/627–4, T406/46.

63   Mayhew, *Time to Explain*, p. 118.

64	*The Public Papers of the Presidents, Harry S. Truman, 1946*, p. 442 ff.
65	For relations between the US State Department and the British Embassy in Washington during this period, see Acheson, *op. cit.*, pp. 176–180.
66	PM to Truman, 4 October 1946. TNA: PREM 8/627–5, T460/46.
67	Truman to PM, 10 October 1946. TNA: PREM 8/627–5, T468/46.
68	Bevin to PM, 22 October 1946. TNA: PREM 8/627–5, PM/46/147.
69	*The Times*, 10 January 1947.
70	Acheson, *Present at the Creation*, p. 180.
71	See Chapter 15.
72	TNA: PREM 8/627–6, CM (47) 18th Conclusions, 7 February 1947.
73	Attlee had replaced George Hall with Creech Jones, more sympathetic to the Zionist cause, on 4 October 1946.
74	6 February 1947, TNA: PREM 8/627–6, CP (47) 49.
75	13 February 1947, TNA: PREM 8/627–6, CP (47) 59.
76	TNA: PREM 8/627–6, CM (47) 22nd Conclusions, 14 February 1947.
77	*Hansard*, HC Deb, 18 February 1947, col. 988.
78	TNA: CO 537–2302 Prime Minister's Minute no M247/47.
79	TNA: CO 537–2302, Telegram 1287.
80	TNA: CO 537–2302, Prime Minister's Minute no M252/47.
81	TNA: CO 537–2302, Telegram 1309.
82	Benny Morris, *1948: A History of the First Arab-Israeli War*, p. 81.
83	Gerald Kaufman, Review of *Clem Attlee* by Francis Beckett, *The Independent*, 1 November 1947.

CHAPTER FOURTEEN

ANNUS HORRENDUS, 1947

On 30 August 1947 Anthony Eden, in a speech at Carnoustie, referred scathingly to the 'internal differences as well as foolish complacency' of the government.[1] Such attacks always make for good politics, but Eden's attack had an eerie truth: things had gone well for the Labour government in 1945 and 1946; arguably, with a huge majority in the House of Commons, they had gone too easily; it would not have been surprising if there was a certain self-satisfaction among Cabinet ministers.

The year was, in retrospect, a watershed for Attlee and his government. It brought a fuel shortage during a savage winter; it brought a financial crisis, an attempt to remove Attlee from the party leadership, and, by the end of the year, after a Cabinet reshuffle, it established austerity as the continuing theme of British life. As one writer put it neatly, in 1945 'Labour sensed that it had a rendezvous with destiny; in 1947 it became aware that history is one damned thing after another'.[2]

Throughout the latter half of 1946 Attlee had spoken to the same theme: things had improved but there was still a period of sacrifice before wartime rationing could be removed. This thread permeated his speeches during November. There were shortages, especially in relation to the building industry and all manufacturing. There was a need to boost exports; we could not hope for spectacular improvement, but needed to soldier on. There were worldwide shortages which particularly affected the UK because of abnormally high demand and curtailed supplies caused by production difficulties and a serious shortfall in imports. He gave as examples items like prams and fountain pens which, if industries were given all the necessary materials, there would be no need to import.

Despite these problems, there was no serious industrial unrest – a very different situation from 1919–20. All basic foodstuffs – grains, fats and meat – were in short supply. Bread rationing had been prolonged by shipping strikes in the USA which delayed delivery, and by bad weather that had damaged the British harvest.[3]

There was an additional drain on the country's resources – the need to feed the population of occupied Germany. The *Manchester Guardian* was scathing in its criticism of the distribution of food, chiding the government that 'the prospects of maintaining our name as efficient and humane rulers are vanishing.' At a time when Britons were suffering serious privation the issue of feeding a defeated nation was divisive; a group of churchmen and public figures sent a petition to Attlee, demanding that the Germans be fed as well as the British. 'If thine enemy hunger, feed him', the Reverend Prebendary P. T. R. Kirk of the Industrial Christian Fellowship reminded the government.[4]

Demobilisation, moreover, continued to be an issue after fifteen months of peace. In several speeches in the last months of 1946 Attlee undertook to maintain the promised rate of release. In November he spoke in the House and reiterated that the rate of release planned for the first six months of 1947 was the maximum that could be expected. The progress in concluding peace treaties was much slower than he had hoped.[5]

In early summer 1946 Jay had warned Attlee that coal reserves were dangerously low and that Shinwell's confidence in being able to meet winter demand was misplaced.[6] Coal stocks, moreover, would be at their lowest at the very point that the National Coal Board took control of the industry. Attlee promptly sent a message to George Isaacs, Minister of Labour, stressing the need to build up stocks. 'Great difficulties will have to be overcome', he warned, 'if a serious shortage next winter is to be averted.' To Dalton he stressed the importance of building up stocks, referring to this as 'now the most urgent economic problem'.[7]

An accelerated rate of demobilisation created an increasing number of consumers and increased demand for power. Attlee continued to be concerned about stock levels; he recognised that it would be 'touch and go' unless Britain enjoyed a mild winter. Reassured by Shinwell that stocks were adequate and that production could be stepped up if necessary,

Attlee remained doubtful but uninvolved. Shinwell was described by Gaitskell as 'a good speaker of the platform type – at his best when he prepares nothing'.[8] In a situation where Shinwell needed to be certain of his facts and to trust less to his ability to improvise, his reliance on the *extempore* was dangerous – doubly dangerous in an industry that had been so recently nationalised.

In the event, 1947 brought a winter of legendary bitterness. At the end of January a massive blizzard swept the country and the inadequacy of stocks was rapidly revealed. Power stations closed and rationing of power was introduced for private users. For a three-week period more than two million were put out of work. The government appeared ill informed and, after Shinwell's comment of October 1946 that 'everyone knows there is going to be a crisis in the coal industry – except the Minister of Fuel and Power',[9] simply negligent. Attlee's appeal to the nation, broadcast on 11 February, alerted his listeners to 'a situation of the utmost gravity' and repeated the familiar hope that 'you will all do your bit as you did in the war in other emergencies'.[10] Despite grave discomfort for eight weeks, the crisis passed without undue damage to the government.

Eighteen months had passed since the end of the war. The British public had accepted shortages in wartime, had accepted stoically that these would continue for a period, but the climate of austerity was becoming oppressive. Soon after the 1945 election, as the Attlees were preparing to move into 10 Downing Street, the new Prime Minister wrote to Tom that 'we are still in the honeymoon period of a government and many people have been very kind to me but no doubt storms will come soon'.[11] He was over-pessimistic, it turned out, as Labour's appeal to the electorate remained strong. The mood of the electorate was congruent with Labour's aims: 'the wartime ethos that had brought Beveridge, full employment, social planning, and the idea of "fair shares".'[12] Labour continued to do well at by-elections and borough elections, maintaining a solid lead over the Tories in opinion polls.

Ironically, Attlee was less busy as Prime Minister than he had been from 1942 to 1945 and he was able to spend a further ten days at Chequers over Christmas.[13] Eden was, perhaps, playing politics when he accused the government of 'complacency', but there was certainly no hint of the succession of crises that was to beleaguer Attlee and his Cabinet in the New Year.

No one could have foreseen the scale of the storm that struck Britain at the end of January 1947, bringing the worst winter weather in memory. For eight weeks Britain suffered from a disastrous combination of weather and the results of shoddy planning. Bread rationing had damaged morale, giving Conservatives the taunt of 'Starve with Strachey'. Now 'Shiver with Shinwell' was added. 'It was not only Conservative politicians who were critical of the government. King George VI confided to his diary that he had asked Attlee three times if he was worried about the situation. He confessed that, even if Attlee was not, he was.'[14]

Within the Cabinet too there was serious concern for the first time. On 20 January Dalton wrote to Attlee that he, Morrison, Cripps and Isaacs had compiled the report on economic planning, which was treated by the Cabinet without the attention due to it. He had already stated, he said, that the money demanded by the Minister of Defence was not available. 'We are, I am afraid, drifting in a state of semi-consciousness towards the rapids.'[15] Looking back on this period later, Dalton recorded that the fuel crisis was 'certainly the first really heavy blow to confidence in the government and in our post-war plans ... Never glad, confident morning again.'[16]

Dalton, more than Attlee and more than any minister except Bevin, was the face of socialist confidence. He 'seemed to epitomise a radical government, confident in its priorities, at peace with itself and a wider world.'[17] A product of Eton and King's College, Cambridge with connections to the royal family, the ebullient Dalton radiated the confidence of privilege and was more visible than the retiring Attlee. As July and the date for convertibility of sterling drew closer, Dalton raged against the expenditures forced on the government by its commitments. Alexander's soldiers, Bevin's Germans – all became objects of the Chancellor's resentment. Faced by increasing criticism, principally of his economic policy, it was Dalton, the Chancellor of the Exchequer, whose star most waned.

Attlee continued to urge restraint and insist on 'fair dos for all'. In a speech to Yorkshire miners he described his principles most clearly. The aims of the Labour Party, he said, were to improve the standard of living for everyone. But all must hold fast to the moral principles on which the movement has been founded. Rights entail obligations. No one can carry on without depending on other members of the community.[18]

It was a message that he repeated frequently – and a principle by which he lived. While Cripps was the public face of austerity, Attlee was the greatest puritan in the Cabinet. Chequers was always cold in winter as he kept the heating low and, according to Sheila McNeil, the Attlees' sherry glasses were the smallest she had ever seen.[19] The antithesis of the swashbuckling Churchill whose enormous Havana cigars added to his wartime persona, Attlee was studiously economical in both official and personal expenditure.

On 30 May, planning a rail trip to Durham, he discovered that the cost would be £55, of which staff and meals accounted for £22. Attlee told the Ministry of Transport that he required no special staff or special services to be provided when he travelled by train. No special meals, just a cup of tea brought to his carriage, which should be a normal carriage. If that was not possible, he said, he was quite capable of walking to the restaurant car. He would like a cup of tea in the morning, but not if it required a special attendant. This created difficulties with the railway company, who did not want the Prime Minister to be compelled to walk along the corridor of a moving train. The exchange became absurdly complex and much time was consumed in keeping things 'simple'. After four days of memoranda to and fro, the matter was resolved on 4 June to Attlee's satisfaction.[20]

On at least one occasion, however, he did make certain allowances for notables. In June Field Marshal Montgomery, the new CIGS, wrote, requesting his help in obtaining a licence to convert a Hampshire mill to a house at a cost of £6,000. He had already written to Bevan, who turned down the request. He pointed out that, although he was able to use a flat in London when he was there in his capacity as CIGS, he was, in fact, homeless, apart from his caravans. He commented that 'having led the Armies of the Empire to victory in the war, it is not suitable that I should have to go on living a caravan life.'[21]

Bevan maintained that it was a matter for the local authority and that, if he intervened, it would do no one any good. He suggested that

Montgomery wait 'until the edge has been taken off the housing shortage a little further'. After Attlee's intervention Bevan permitted Montgomery to proceed, provided that he spend no more than £1,500 as an initial outlay and that the balance of building be paid for in stages.[22]

The principal fear of the government's critics was that the oft-repeated mantra of austerity and short-term sacrifice, while well-intentioned, was inadequate to overcome the balance of payments shortfall and the steady outflow of dollars. In April Churchill attacked the government for living on the American dole. Attlee defused the attack, demanding what Churchill would do in his place. Moreover, he argued, the Opposition leader's attitude was 'dead and damned' and Churchill's posture was damaging to his party.[23]

Churchill's sources within the Treasury were reliable and his attack echoed the thoughts of Otto Clarke, a Treasury official and author of the 'Economic Survey for 1947'. Clarke recorded in his diary that Dalton was not trying, and that Shinwell was 'in a state of hopeless fog'. Attlee, he wrote, had 'not an ounce of will to govern or ability to control the situation.' Not one of them had 'the shadowiest concept of what they meant by planning'.[24]

In May, Attlee created a Cabinet committee (GEN/179; Attlee, Morrison, Bevin, Dalton and Cripps) to handle the worsening economic situation. At its first meeting the ministers considered a Treasury memorandum pointing out that prices in the USA had risen by enough to justify an additional loan of £1,000 million, and recommending cutting imports by £200 million in 1947–48.[25] A cut in imports would entail a cut in rations and the Minister for Food was concerned that 'the present diet of our people is generally considered inadequate'.[26] Not only physiologically but also psychologically inadequate, as it was monotonous and dull. 'There is a growing dissatisfaction', Strachey wrote, 'with a food situation which, two years after the war, deteriorates rather than improves.' At one point the banality of the Cabinet's concerns was characterised by the statement that there was 'no United States dried fruit at all … this would have the worst effects on all cake and bun making, as well as on the housewife.'[27]

Banality was compounded by shortages of beer in West Yorkshire, caused by inadequate stocks of coal.[28] While Attlee was planning grand initiatives – independence for India, consolidating the Atlantic alliance – the working man was denied beer and his wife had no currants for her buns – the subject of a Cabinet memorandum.

Within the Labour Party, too, concern was building concerning Attlee's leadership style. Morrison, always to be relied on to project himself as a leader, presented a paper to the Cabinet in which he emphasised the need to create new sources of supply.[29] 'We are in danger of making the worst of both planning and *laissez faire* worlds', he wrote, 'if we leave the expansion of overseas supplies too much to the self-interest of producers who have little incentive in present conditions and are up against heavy odds.' The message was clear: the government was barren of ideas; Morrison alone could think outside the box and produce inspiring leadership. Attlee allowed the initiative to wither and die.

As the date of convertibility approached the Cabinet considered a range of measures to solve the balance of payments crisis. Dalton warned that American credit would be exhausted by the end of the year[30] and every possible form of economy was considered. Even the banning of importation of American films was urged by Cripps[31] and, amazingly, the Cabinet discounted any negative effect on public morale.[32] At a time when the meat ration was to be cut to less than a shilling a week and cuts were increasingly resented, the public was to be denied even the pleasures of escapism. Two days later the Cabinet discussed how they might avoid making any public announcement at all.[33]

When the magic date of 15 July arrived, within a week the flight of currency from Britain was a cause for alarm. Durbin, PPS to Dalton,[34] wrote to Attlee to warn him of a severe balance of payments crisis. Of the American loan $1,000 million had been spent in eighteen months and at the present rate, he warned, Britain would rapidly run out of dollars. It would be folly to rely on more American aid. The government needed to reduce its dollar expenditure on the diplomatic and military accounts, implement cuts in the import programme, and re-allocate coal, steel and manpower to assist the export industries.[35]

In the same week nineteen left-leaning backbenchers[36] wrote to Attlee to express their concerns about cuts in imports, cuts in foreign commitments, positive measures for expanding production and trade, possible cuts to the housing programme, the need to expand overseas trade if

Marshall Aid[37] did not materialise, the need for a heavy tax on capital gains and the need for a profits tax that encouraged distribution of profits.[38] Ten days later Attlee received a document signed by 116 Labour MPs, asking him to scotch rumours that the government was weakening in its resolve to carry through the nationalisation of the steel industry.[39]

Attlee had foreseen difficulties within the party as conflicting claims built up and appropriated slender resources. During July, therefore, he canvassed opinions from MPs conversant with swings of opinion, who would report these honestly. In early August he received two responses from two very different Members.

Sir Hartley Shawcross felt that there was resentment of austerity, principally because the burdens of the current situation were not being evenly shared. There was no restriction on luxury foods, such as pineapples. Sporting events for the lower classes were being limited, whereas events such as Goodwood were going on as normal. Morale would be greatly restored if those who could afford restaurant meals were to sacrifice some of their points. Another source of resentment, he said, was felt by those living alone or without children. There was no immediate solution to this problem, but, if there were to be cuts in food, could such people be treated preferentially?[40]

Tom Driberg, Member for Maldon, sent similar advice that ranged over a number of issues. Certainly 'fair dos' and what he called 'symbolic socialist gestures' were important. For example, the royal wedding should be picturesque but not too lavish, and Princess Elizabeth's husband should live on his pay, not on the Civil List. There should also be attacks on luxury restaurants and 'Riviera idlers'. Above all, Attlee should be bold in his proposals. He should scorn any proposal for a coalition – an idea that was being discussed within the party – and should outline a bold and coherent socialist plan.[41]

Matters came to a head at a Cabinet meeting in late July.[42] Attlee stated the two objectives involved in resolving this crisis: to preserve the standard of life in Britain and to maintain Britain's position in the world. Morrison, again staking his claim for innovative leadership, accused the government of drift and argued for 'a coherent and realistic plan for dealing with the situation'. He stated that he would be disposed to 'inform the United States government that from a given date we should be compelled to stop all further dollar expenditure on Germany'. Bevan urged drastic action, such as withdrawal from Palestine or a complete ban of American films. He also insisted that any hardships imposed on civilians would be matched by 'severe measures to restrict our expenditure overseas and must be shared equally by the whole population'. From both left and right Attlee was under attack.

Attlee's concern, his desire to know all shades of opinion within the party, was prompted by the imminent debate on an Emergency Powers Bill, scheduled for 6 August. From the left of the party – Foot, Crossman, Mikardo, Wigg, Castle, Wyatt, Mallalieu and others – came urging that that in the forthcoming debate he should stress that the government would meet the crisis with more and not less socialism. Specifically, he should repudiate the Opposition's demands for cuts in the housing programme. There should be more rapid demobilisation to reduce the strength of the Armed Forces to 750,000 by March 1948, and a clear statement both of goals and of how they would be achieved. The public needed reassurance that there would not be a 'buyers' strike' and that the government would vigorously pursue alternative buying options in 'soft currency' areas.[43]

In preparation for the Emergency Powers debate Leslie Rowan sent Attlee a memorandum on 2 August. Its premise was that there should be as much co-operation with the Opposition as possible in a national crisis, but no coalition. 'I feel so strongly that it is essential to do everything which is possible and practicable to ensure the maximum support for a programme that is vital to the country's welfare', wrote Rowan. Plans for the nationalisation of iron and steel had been leaked and so Attlee should reveal the revised plan 'in the public interest but combining this with a practical approach designed to secure the full co-operation of the industry.'

Most importantly, there should be 'a month of brotherhood' (a variant on the Dunkirk spirit theme) and Rowan gave Attlee a document prepared by two naval officers, arguing that: 'the present state of the country ... is ignorance, apathy, bewilderment, hopelessness, despair and disillusionment – in varying degrees amongst individuals, classes and groups.' Politicians were not trusted, but this was a chance for Attlee 'to show his greatness. His choice is simply: the agony of collapse or the crusade of unity.'[44]

This was most laudable, but beyond the abstracts there were problems that defied simple moral rearmament solutions. The Conservative Party was not slow to point these out when the debate opened on 6 August. This evolved into a three-day affair, of which the first day and a half were devoted to the economic situation and the closing day and a half to the Supplies and Services (Transitional Powers) – or more simply, Emergency Powers – Bill.

Oliver Stanley, the Conservative Member for Bristol West, launched the attack. He first trained his fire at Dalton, broadening this to include 'whoever got us into this crisis'. His challenge to Attlee came at the end of his speech in a rousing, non-partisan coda. 'We on this side of the House are prepared to do nothing at all to save socialism, but we are prepared to do anything to save this country.'[45]

Responding, Attlee was bluntly logical, repeating points that he had made consistently during the previous two years: Britain had incurred gigantic liabilities during the war. It was vital to rebuild the economy which was, it emerged, more damaged than had been thought. Prices in the western hemisphere had risen by 40 per cent and the fuel and weather crises had been severe setbacks. Hard, long, sustained effort was now called for from everyone. This was a time for communal effort and the government welcomed the co-operation of the Opposition. When Labour joined the coalition government in 1940, he reminded the House, it didn't insist on nationalisation. Attlee trusted that the Opposition would now behave in similar fashion.[46]

The speech was a workmanlike and accurate description of events leading to the crisis; it was also uninspiring, a flat recital of events ending with a call for continued austerity. From both the Opposition benches and from Labour back-benches – in the shape of Ian Mikardo[47] – came criticism of the Prime Minister for lack of leadership, lack of fire and passion. The Cabinet was accused of poor co-ordination,[48] adding another charge to the many levelled at Attlee. Both Cabinet and Prime Minister emerged badly damaged.

Two days later, on a Sunday evening, Attlee broadcast to the country on the BBC. Trade has always been central to our economy, he said. But with our houses and factories bombed to ruins we had a heavy handi-cap. We needed time to recover and so we borrowed from the United

States and Canada, hoping to repay the loans by 1949. But the shortage of labour and materials, as well as the world shortage of food, caused problems, exacerbated by the lack of coal and power. Then came a very severe winter. Meanwhile American food prices rose by 40 per cent. Pending post-war settlements, forces were kept overseas. There was a shortage of dollars and a drain on resources. As a result, the American and Canadian loans would be exhausted by the end of the year. The crisis was as grave as any in the nation's history. Everyone must make sacrifices and be ready to serve wherever needed. He was certain of ultimate victory. The reward would be the survival of the British way of life.[49]

On the following morning the Parliamentary Party met amid mutual recrimination, as Gaitskell recorded in his diary:

> *Several angry and excited backbenchers made speeches critical of the government and the PM. I was depressed because much of what was said was unrealistic. The usual sort of stuff. 'People are ready to follow a lead for austerity if only you'll give it.' 'People are ready for a more left-wing policy.' ... The PM replied rather ineffectively ... His speech last week certainly was, as Evan [Durbin] said, catastrophic.[50]*

Never had the party required more decisive leadership, more charismatic than Attlee's bloodless style. Unprecedented criticism was levelled at the Prime Minister for hesitating over the nationalisation of iron and steel, for failure to reduce the size of the armed forces, and for lack of drive in promoting economic growth. A. J. Cummings reported in the *News Chronicle* that Attlee, 'exhausted and feeling deeply the humiliation of recent days', had offered to resign;[51] Frank Owen, editor of the *Daily Mail*, wrote that he was ready to go to the King and hand in the seals of office.[52]

The Opposition leaders stepped up their offensive, backed by the right-wing press. On 16 August a Churchill broadcast reignited the 'Gestapo' rhetoric of the election:

> *I warn you solemnly that if you submit yourselves to the totalitarian compulsion and regimentation of our national life and Labour there lies before you an almost*

measureless prospect of misery and tribulation, of which the lower standard of
living will be the first result, hunger the second, and the dispersal or death of a
large proportion of our population the third. You have not always listened to my
warnings. Please pay good attention to them now.[53]

The totalitarian theme was echoed by Macmillan, writing in the *Sunday Chronicle* ('We must either be slaves or starve. The trouble is that we look like doing both.'[54]), and by a *Daily Mail* editorial, 'When Britain becomes a concentration camp on October 1 the winter will be well on the way'.[55]

Throughout August the Cabinet discussed draconian cuts. Foreign travel allowances were reduced to £35 during any fourteen-month period; the individual petrol ration was abolished from 1 October; travel on foreign craft was forbidden; work on new houses was to cease.[56] There was growing concern that the measures would be so unpopular with the public that they would ultimately exacerbate the problems they were designed to solve. By September there was growing concern among the Labour 'Big Five' that Attlee was unequal to the task of providing the dynamic leadership required.

Cripps had for some time questioned Attlee's leadership style, particularly what he considered wastage of time in Cabinet committees.[57] His frustration with management by committee rather than by executive action grew as the government appeared direction-less during 1947, 'drifting in a state of semi-consciousness towards the rapids', as Dalton had described it. The only credible leader, he became convinced, was Bevin. As it happened, Dalton and Bevin had journeyed by road from Durham to London in late July and Dalton had hinted at such a move. Dalton and Cripps now decided to call on Bevin and sound him out. A suitable leak was arranged to the *Daily Mail*, who laid the groundwork with a headline, 'ATTLEE RESIGNING SOON. BEVIN TO BE PM.'[58] Bevin's refusal to consider the offer was splendidly expressed. 'Who do you think I am? Lloyd George?' he thundered.[59]

During August Cripps and Dalton continued to plot to supplant Attlee with Bevin.[60] Overtures to Morrison stalled for the simple reason that Morrison was busy promoting himself, rather than the Foreign Secretary, as the most suitable candidate. Bevin himself was unenthusiastic, asking rhetorically, 'Why should I do him out of a job? What's Clem ever done to me?'[61] Gaitskell recorded that there was a pervasive atmosphere of intrigue: 'You could not go in [to the Commons dining room] without several people looking at you hard and wondering whether you were involved in some intrigue or other, and also wondering what your position would be in the near future.'[62]

Determined to force his agenda, Cripps called on Attlee after dinner on 9 September. He urged him to resign in favour of Bevin and to take the Treasury himself. Unflustered, Attlee picked up the telephone, reached Bevin and said, 'Stafford's here; he says you want to change your job.' The attempted *putsch* collapsed when Bevin denied any such intention.

Bevin was central to any proposed toppling of Attlee. No other member of the 'Big Five' had the broad-based support or authority to be Prime Minister, either of a Labour government or of a coalition. Despite stalwart denials from both sides of the House that a coalition was being considered, Pierson Dixon of the Foreign Office confided to his diary rumours of a planned coalition under Bevin that would include both Attlee and Churchill. Bevin would, he wrongly believed, 'find it hard to resist the lure of the premiership'.[63]

Without Bevin Cripps found himself facing his leader with no support for the *putsch* he had proposed. In an inspired move, whether rehearsed or *ex tempore*, Attlee confided in Cripps that he planned changes in the Cabinet and its structure. There had been pressure from the left to appoint a Minister of Economic Affairs; would Cripps take on the new position? With this move Cripps would move up in the hierarchy, overtaking both Morrison and Dalton; at a stroke Attlee secured the loyalty of another lieutenant. As Dalton described the attempted coup, 'The movement begun by Cripps … to put Bevin in Attlee's place has turned into a movement to put Cripps in Morrison's place, or at least in the most important part of it.'[64] With a deft Cabinet reshuffle, Attlee could now consolidate his position.

In descriptions of the first Attlee Cabinet one hears the creak of age. The members were 'tired', 'exhausted by their work in the war', essentially old. The events of the summer of 1947 underscore that quality. There were men of stature – Bevin, Cripps, Dalton – whom Attlee needed on the bridge; there were others – Shinwell, Wilmot – who brought no stature to his Cabinet. This was the time to shed them, to bring into the government men who would lead the party in the 1960s. With attention to balance, he reconstructed his Cabinet.

Morrison left for a holiday in Guernsey and Attlee notified him of his attenuated powers on 15 September, commenting that the removal of economic responsibility would allow him more time for his work as Leader of the House and other non-economic work of the Lord President's Committee. Morrison replied four days later with comments on proposed changes and overall acceptance of the principles behind the Prime Minister's actions.[65] For Attlee the reorganisation was invaluable; it restored his authority, gave Cripps the ascendancy he sought, removed Greenwood from the Cabinet, and dealt deferred payment to Shinwell for the fuel crisis. Three future leaders of the party were promoted: Gaitskell (aged forty-one) to succeed Shinwell at Fuel and Power, Wilson (aged thirty-one) to succeed Cripps at the Board of Trade and Callaghan (aged thirty-five) to be Parliamentary Secretary to Alfred Barnes, Minister of Transport. Other younger men, later to achieve Cabinet rank, – George Brown, Patrick Gordon Walker, Michael Stewart – also moved up.

For George Brown the promotion was the opposite of what he expected when he learned that Attlee wished to see him. Brown had been deputed to speak to Bevin when the Cripps coup was attempted. To his surprise, Bevin's response was violent: '… now you are acting as office boy for that bastard Dalton! I don't want to see you again.' After a tongue-lashing from Bevin and a 'real clobbering' from the Chief Whip, Brown was summoned to see Attlee two days later. He reckoned that his future in the party was far from bright and was surprised when Attlee offered him the job of Under-Secretary of State at the Ministry of Agriculture! 'So there I was', he recalled, 'a full-blown junior minister, with barely two years in the House of Commons and one abortive revolt behind me.'[66]

One further event was to shape Attlee's Cabinet during 1947. In November, on his way to present the autumn budget, Dalton casually let slip to a reporter an element of his proposed tax changes. When this was printed in an early evening edition, Dalton was still speaking in the House; clearly he had been indiscreet. Dalton offered his resignation.

Attlee responded, saying, 'I have given the matter my earnest consideration and have come to the conclusion with great regret that it is my duty to accept it.'[67] Dalton's fall was greeted by widespread rejoicing.[68] It also enabled Attlee to put Cripps in the more constitutional position of Chancellor and face the end of what Dalton called Labour's *annus horrendus* from a position of greater strength.

The year eventually came to an end; Attlee broadcast to the nation that this had been 'a year of great strain'. He concluded with the familiar message that, although times were hard, if everyone carried the same spirit into 1948, all would eventually be well.[69]

For Attlee himself the year that had begun after a leisurely Christmas holiday at Chequers had thrust him into unprecedented crises. Leo Amery sent an ironic New Year's greeting. He had, he wrote, just been reading Trollope's *The Prime Minister*, in which Trollope 'depicts the poor Prime Minister of seventy years ago, bored to death with having nothing to do between August and February, no department of his own, no Cabinet meetings, nothing except the occasional appointment of a bishop or Lord Lieutenant, and trying to identify individuals among the crowd of guests that his wife insists on inviting.'[70] The very opposite of Attlee's life. The Prime Minister of 1947 must have read Amery's letter with a wry grin.

ENDNOTES

1   *The Times*, 1 September 1947.
2   Peter Clarke, *A Question of Leadership*, p. 197.
3   Bodleian: MS. Attlee. dep. 45, *passim*.
4   *Manchester Guardian*, 11 November 1946. Bodleian: MS. Attlee. dep. 45.
5   *Hansard*, HC Deb, 26 November 1946, cols. 1417–20. Bodleian: MS. Attlee. dep. 47 and dep. 48, *passim*.
6   TNA: PREM 8/440. Jay to CRA, 19 June 1946.
7   TNA: PREM 8/440. CRA to Dalton, 24 July 1946.
8   *The Diary of Hugh Gaitskell, 1945–1956*, entry for 12 August 1947, p. 29.
9   *Daily Herald*, 25 October 1946; referred to by Anthony Eden in House of Commons debate of 7 February 1947, *Hansard*, vol. 432; col. 2160.
10 Bodleian: MS. Attlee. dep. 49.
11 Letter to Tom Attlee, 30 August 1945.
12 Kenneth Morgan, *Labour in Power 1945–1951*, p. 285.
13 Letter to Tom Attlee, 29 December 1946.
14 Diary entry of 30 January 1947, J. W. Wheeler-Bennett, *King George VI, His Life and Reign*, p. 662.
15 Bodleian: MS. Attlee, dep. 49, 20 January 1947.
16 Dalton, *High Tide and After: Memoirs, 1945–1960*, pp. 187–192. The 'glad, confident morning' quotation is from 'The Lost Leader', a poem by Robert Browning.

17   Kenneth Morgan, *Labour in Power, 1945–1951*, pp. 330–331.
18   Bodleian: MS. Attlee, dep. 55, 21 June 1947.
19   Hennessy, *Never Again, Britain 1945–1951*, p. 275.
20   Bodleian: MS. Attlee, dep. 53. Memoranda, 31 May 1947 to 4 June 1947.
21   Bodleian: MS. Attlee, dep. 54, 16 June 1947.
22   Bodleian: MS. Attlee, dep. 55. 20 June 1947. Montgomery wrote to thank Attlee on the same day.
23   *News Chronicle*, 29 April 1947. Bodleian: MS. Attlee, dep. 52.
24   Clarke Diary, 20 April 1947. Cited at Hennessy, *Never Again Britain*, pp. 290–291.
25   TNA: PREM 8/489, GEN. 179/1st Meeting, 5 May 1947.
26   TNA: PREM 8/489, CP (47) 170, 31 May 1947.
27   Ibid.
28   *Hansard*, HC Deb, 28 April 1947, col. 174W.
29   TNA: PREM 8/489, 'Planning for Expansion', CP (47) 169, 2 June 1947.
30   TNA: PREM 8/489, CM (47) 52nd Conclusions, 5 June 1947.
31   TNA: PREM 8/479, CM (47) 54th Conclusions, 17 June 1947.
32   TNA: PREM 8/489, CM (47) 56th Conclusions, 24 June 1947.
33   TNA: PREM 8/489, CM (47) 57th Conclusions, 26 June 1947.
34   Durbin was close to Attlee, having worked as his personal assistant during the war.
35   Bodleian: MS. Attlee, dep. 57. Durbin to Attlee, 23 July 1947.
36   The signatories included Michael Foot, Dick Crossman, Ian Mikardo, Barbara Castle, Jim Callaghan, Fred Lee, Bill Mallalieu, Woodrow Wyatt and George Wigg.
37   See Chapter 15.
38   Bodleian: MS. Attlee, dep. 57. 23 July 1947.
39   Bodleian: MS. Attlee, dep. 57, 4 August 1947.
40   Bodleian: MS. Attlee, dep. 58, 1 August 1947, Shawcross to CRA.
41   Bodleian: MS. Attlee, dep. 58, 1 August 1947, Driberg to CRA. Tom Driberg retained an ambivalent view of the Attlee government, generally feeling that the PM's brand of 'Toynbee Hall socialism' was 'benign' and that its reforms were all inevitable anyway. (Driberg, *Swaff: The Life and Times of Hannen Swaffer*, p. 222.
42   TNA: CM (47) 65th Conclusions, 29 July 1947.
43   Bodleian: MS. Attlee, dep. 58, 1 August 1947.
44   Bodleian: MS. Attlee, dep. 59, Rowan to CRA, 2 August 1947.
45   *Hansard*, HC Deb, 6 August 1947, vol. 441, cc. 1473–86.
46   *Hansard*, HC Deb, 6 August 1947, vol. 441, cols. 1486–1511.
47   *Hansard*, HC Deb, 8 August 1947, vol. 441, cols.1856–62.
48   From Archer Baldwin, the Tory spokesman on Agriculture, who charged, 'What a team! Each of them is playing his own hand.' *Hansard*, HC Deb, 6 August 1947, cols 1511–12.
49   Bodleian: MS. Attlee, dep. 58, 10 August 1947.
50   *The Diary of Hugh Gaitskell, 1945–1956* (ed. Philip Williams), entry for Tuesday 12 August 1947, pp. 26–27.
51   *News Chronicle*, 12 August 1947.
52   Bodleian: MS. Attlee, dep. 61.
53   Bodleian: MS. Attlee, dep. 61, 16 August 1947.
54   *Sunday Chronicle*, 10 August 1947.
55   *Daily Mail*, 11 September 1947.
56   TNA: PREM 8/479, CM (47) 74th Conclusions, 25 August 1947.
57   TNA: CAB 21/1701, 'Organisation of Cabinet Committees, 1946–1947', Bridges to Brook, 5 July 1946.
58   *Daily Mail*, 20 August 1947; cited by Pimlott, *Dalton*, p. 514.
59   Bullock, *Ernest Bevin: Foreign Secretary*, p. 456.
60   Bullock, *Ernest Bevin, Foreign Secretary*, pp. 454–455.
61   Mayhew, Diary entry for 29 July 1947, *Time to Explain*, p. 104; Donoughue and Jones, *Herbert Morrison, Portrait of a Politician*, p. 414.
62   *The Diary of Hugh Gaitskell, 1945–1956*, Entry for 14 October 1947.
63   Dixon, *Double Diploma*, p. 246. Cited by Morgan, *Labour in Power 1945–1951*, p. 352.
64   For Dalton's account see Dalton, *High Tide and After*, pp. 240–246.
65   Bodleian: MS. Attlee, dep. 60.
66   George Brown, *In My Way*, pp. 50–51.
67   Bodleian: MS. Attlee, dep. 63, Dalton to CRA and CRA to Dalton, 13 November 1947.
68   Morgan, *Labour People*, p. 120.
69   Bodleian: MS. Attlee, dep. 66, 3 January 1948.
70   Bodleian: MS. Attlee, dep. 66, Amery to CRA 18 January 1948.

CHAPTER FIFTEEN

BUILDING THE ATLANTIC ALLIANCE, 1947-1951

After talks in London in May 1950 Bevin and Dean Acheson, the American Secretary of State, issued a joint memorandum. 'Both sides', they said, 'were in accord that, while agreement on ultimate economic objectives exists, most of the major difficulties between the two countries since the war appear to stem from financial or economic issues.' Their aims were the same: 'maximise world levels of trade and standards of living.'[1] That statement, *prima facie* unremarkable, represented a milestone in the development of the Atlantic alliance, a principal goal of the Attlee administration since 1947.

In less diplomatic language it might have been expressed as, 'For three years America was afraid that Britain would go bankrupt or go communist or both so we kept our distance. Now we're prepared to do business.'

By the end of 1946 Attlee recognised that American economic and military presence was crucial to the rebuilding and defence of Western Europe. Three problems, however, would affect his ability to link Britain as a force with the Western Superpower to deter encroachment from the Colossus in the East: acquiring Truman's agreement to play an active role in Europe; persuading the American Congress of the virtues of continuing involvement, of once more 'pulling Britain's chestnuts from the fire'; and, third, the maintenance of harmony within his own party.

During 1947 the government's programme for reform and Attlee's own position had been threatened. For Attlee, however, the year had important compensations. On 15 August India and Pakistan became independent, events that redounded enormously to his prestige. When he deftly turned the tables on Cripps, Attlee not only shored up his position as Prime Minister but also acquired an important ally in the form of the new Minister for Economic Affairs. When Dalton was compelled to resign, Attlee's position was stronger than it had·ever been. With rediscovered confidence he broadcast on 3 January 1948 that the coming year was to be devoted to Britain's foreign policy.

By both accident and design, events of 1947 fundamentally shaped foreign policy for the balance of Attlee's first government. The year opened with Attlee and Bevin on the defensive against attacks from Crossman and the Keep Left movement. Attlee was increasingly certain that controversies within the Cabinet were being leaked to the Keep Left activists, an accusation that Michael Foot categorically rejected.[2]

Attlee was caught in crossfire. The first majority socialist government was blamed for its hostility to Moscow, while the newly elected Republican US Congress was vigilant for signs that Britain was 'going communist'. Meanwhile, the immediate struggle was to afford the commitments that Attlee and Bevin planned to undertake. It was generally accepted that these would stretch Britain's resources, but no one believed that a crisis was imminent. Dalton, for example, recognised that Britain could not maintain 1,500,000 men in the Armed Forces and Supply at an annual cost of £1,000 million, but he believed that a gradual scaling down over two years was possible.[3]

In fact, Britain's financial position was perilous and *The Times* accurately divined that the government had been forced into 'a contest for priority between foreign and domestic policies'.[4] For some time Britain had struggled to maintain her position in Greece, where Soviet pressure was being applied by communist guerrillas from Albania, Bulgaria and Yugoslavia.[5] In January Bevin, convinced of the strategic importance of Greece and Turkey, proposed that three battalions remain in Greece until the USSR withdrew Soviet forces from Bulgaria.[6] The cost of maintaining financial and military support to Greece, estimated at between $250 million and $280 million in 1947[7], however, was daunting.

Ultimately the Cabinet reached the decision to request assistance from Washington, but Bevin hesitated, fearing that this would be interpreted as a shift in British policy.[8] On 21 February, however, he instructed Lord Inverchapel to deliver two Notes to General Marshall, the new

Secretary of State, informing Washington that Britain was no longer able to support Greece and Turkey alone.

Bevin need not have been concerned; Truman was already receiving discouraging reports from Ambassadors Lincoln MacVeigh in Athens and Bedell Smith in Moscow, urging immediate financial support for Greece.[9] In February 1946 George Kennan, deputy chief of the US Mission in Moscow, had sent to Washington the 'long telegram', his view that the Kremlin suffered from 'a neurotic view of world affairs' and urging that Russian expansionist pressure 'be contained by the adroit application of counterforce'.[10] The President requested his Counsel Clark Clifford to prepare a report on Soviet-American relations and was sobered by the report's conclusions.[11]

It did, however, come as a shock that Britain proposed to end support on 31 March, barely five weeks away. Marshall had just left Washington for Princeton; Inverchapel, at Acheson's suggestion, informally sent copies of the Notes so that State Department officials could study them before Marshall's return. 'They were shockers', Acheson recalled.[12] He immediately requested reports on the situation in Greece and its implications. Loy Henderson delivered these to Acheson's house the following evening and the two State Department officials 'drank a martini or two towards the confusion of our enemies'.[13]

Despite the immediacy of the crisis, the Notes were something of a relief, as Truman could now act, and when he made a decision he acted quickly. On 27 February he invited congressional leaders to the White House, where Acheson made a clear statement of the strategic position. The Soviet Union was pressuring the Straits and there was a risk of Soviet influence spreading to the Middle East, Africa and Europe if Greece fell into their orbit. The world was divided between irreconcilable ideologies; it was the worst situation since the era of Rome and Carthage.[14]

Senator Arthur Vandenberg told Truman that he would support the President if he made a statement to Congress and the nation along the same lines as Acheson. At a Cabinet meeting on 7 March Truman announced in typical fashion, 'It seems the United States is going into European politics'.[15] The State Department and Clifford worked together to prepare Truman's address to Congress, conscious that aid to Greece was merely the first step in an evolving policy.[16] Truman requested immediate military aid of $400 million for Greece and Turkey. Speaking calmly but firmly, he ended his address: 'Should we fail to aid Greece and Turkey in this fateful hour, the effect will be far-reaching to the West as well as to the East. We must take immediate and resolute action.'[17]

Thus was the Truman Doctrine born and, with it, a policy that guided Attlee's government until 1951.

In the same month the Council of Foreign Ministers held its fourth meeting in Moscow between 10 March and 24 April. Bevin stopped briefly en route to Moscow to sign the Treaty of Dunkirk, a mutual defence treaty with France. From the start the going in Moscow was difficult; the mood was expressed, albeit in diplomatic language, by Marshall's report. The development of a self-supporting Germany, he said, had been thwarted by resistance from the Soviet Union to establishing a balanced German economy, despite the Potsdam agreements. Now that the Bizone had been created by merging the British and American zones, the Soviet Union was bitter in denouncing the West – all propaganda to divert attention from their breaches of Potsdam agreements on economic unity.[18]

Marshall's conclusions provided the final evidence – if evidence were needed – that convinced the President of the importance of American presence to European stability. Aware that any involvement in post-war Europe would need to be 'sold' to Congress, Truman proposed that Acheson prepare the ground with a speech in Cleveland, Mississippi, a small riverside town between Memphis and Jackson, in May. Popular reaction would reflect the views of the American heartland.

Acheson's speech stressed the need for the United States to import goods to narrow the 'financial gap between what the world needs and what it can pay for'; there would be additional calls on the US for emergency financing of foreign purchases, and – a third imperative – the Truman administration would distribute aid 'where it will be most effective in building world political and economic stability, in promoting human freedom and democratic institutions, in fostering liberal trading policies, and in strengthening the authority of the United Nations.' Countries seeking to 'preserve their independence and democratic institutions and human freedoms against totalitarian pressure' would receive top priority, Acheson declared. It was, he urged in a ringing finale, 'our duty and our privilege as human beings'.[19]

Four weeks after this trial balloon, in a speech at Harvard University, Marshall announced outline principles of the European Recovery Plan.[20] In a little over three months the Notes delivered to the State Department concerning Greece and Turkey had set in motion a fundamental shift in American policy. Attlee's initiative had been more successful than he could have dared to hope. There were ugly precedents for a President moving ahead of public opinion with respect to Europe – Woodrow Wilson after the First World War, Franklin Roosevelt in his 'quarantine' speech of 1937 – but Truman responded positively and swiftly, using Acheson's speech as a thermometer of public opinion before allowing Marshall to take the definitive step that drew the battle lines of the Cold War in Europe.

The thrust of both speeches was to stress the moral responsibility that America bore to alleviate hunger and suffering in countries most affected by the war. Marshall was careful not to be specific, not to impose American solutions. Instead, he placed the onus on European countries collectively to formulate a statement of their needs and to communicate them to Washington. It was manifestly a statement of intent. The impetus, however, needed to come from Europe. America's role, he said, 'should consist of friendly aid in the drafting of a European program and of later support of such a program so far as it may be practical for us to do so. The program should be a joint one, agreed to by a number [of], if not all European nations.'[21] For Truman the European Recovery Program and the Truman Doctrine were 'two halves of the same walnut'.[22]

The clear message, immediately understood by Attlee and Bevin, was that European foreign ministers must seize the initiative. Characteristically, Bevin was not slow to set the wheels in motion. He promptly contacted Georges Bidault, the French Foreign Secretary, and after a meeting on 17 June they invited Molotov to join them in formulating a response to Marshall's *démarche*. Unsurprisingly, Molotov declined, denouncing the plan as an imperialist plot to subjugate Europe. The Soviet Union put pressure on Czechoslovakia and Poland not to participate, and this hint was taken by all Eastern European countries. Attlee's policy again came under criticism from Keep Left as slavishly pro-American.

Cautious of the negative connotations of socialism in the USA and faced with revolt from the left wing of his party, Attlee thought it vital to demonstrate to the United States Congress that Britain's leaders were moderates rather than fellow travellers. This resulted in the publication of the Labour Party pamphlet, *Cards on the Table*, an imaginative document written by Denis Healey, designed to bridge the gap between the government's left-wing and right-wing critics. Justifying the Atlantic alliance as likely to reinforce Britain's position as a third power, it was fiercely attacked at the party conference[23] and condemned by the Keep Left group as supine Conservatism – 'crypto-Fulton-Winston' in the memorable words of Zilliacus.[24]

The spring and summer of 1947 were difficult months for Attlee. The nationalisation programme of 1945–46 had succeeded beyond expectations, but had now slowed to a halt, and 'the rumour spread that the government's commitment to nationalise iron and steel was to be abandoned in deference to protests from the steel interests'.[25] Amid cries for more not less socialism and continuing criticism of foreign policy from Laski in the Scottish socialist journal *Forward*, amid swirling rumours that Attlee would be replaced, the Prime Minister used the Labour Party conference, held over Whitsun at Margate, to unleash Bevin on critics of *Cards on the Table*. Michael Foot described his broadside as devastating, sinking 'without trace all the disputes about demobilisation and defence expenditure'.[26]

Attlee reassured not only the British public but also the American press that Britain was a going concern. In September he made a rousing speech at a luncheon for American correspondents. Britain was going through acute economic difficulties, he admitted, but he expressed optimism on long-term projects. He mentioned coal and steel as important, and, understanding the sentimental mien of the American public, expatiated on the treatment and condition of British children. All in all, he concluded, there was much cause for optimism.[27]

Stalin condemned Marshall's approach and increased pressure on the Western Allies at the Foreign Ministers' Conference when it met in London in November. When the conference achieved nothing, Attlee and Bevin postponed the scheduled foreign affairs debate to buy time for policy decisions. They resolved on a more robust attitude towards Russia, as Attlee intimated in a broadcast to the nation.[28] He was wagering high stakes in advance of Congressional approval of Marshall funds.

It was left to Bevin, however, to launch a broadside assault when the foreign policy debate was held on 22 and 23 January. He denied that the Marshall Plan was 'directed against the Soviet Union or used for any ulterior purpose', commenting that 'the United States and the countries of Latin America are clearly as much a part of our common Western civilisation as are the nations of the British Commonwealth', and moving on to an impassioned defence of American motives. America was not the 'Shylock of Wall Street' that her opponents claimed; there was 'no political motive behind the Marshall offer other than the valuable human motive of helping Europe to help herself, and so restore the economic and political health of this world.' It was, he conceded, an American interest, but it was everybody's interest, not exclusively American.[29]

Bevin's calculated defence of the purity of American motive was mandatory diplomacy; its very presence makes the British stance explicit. The decisive move was being made; Britain was abandoning its attempts to maintain a position as a third force. Henceforth Attlee would work to strengthen the Atlantic alliance, as he made clear when he wound up the debate on the following day. Correctly reading that the House was prepared to support a more aggressive posture towards Moscow, he condemned the fanatical nature of communism, comparing its exclusive nature to that of early religion. There was no room for thought or other views, he said, although 'they are required to bless one day what they have cursed the day before'.[30]

Then, echoing Bevin, he returned to the Marshall Plan in a clear statement of policy. He could not understand how people could oppose the plan when they had nothing to put in its place. How else could peace be brought to millions threatened by Soviet imperialism? Britain was achieving a social revolution by peaceful and democratic means. 'We are showing how we can get an overall economy without sacrificing human rights and liberty. That is the work we have before us today.'[31]

The unsuccessful meetings of foreign ministers in March–April and November 1947 had now brought the USA and Britain together to the far side of the Rubicon. Truman had tested the water with Acheson's speech in Mississippi; Attlee had done the same with his January broadcast. Each subsequently advanced his position. The Soviet Union was not slow to respond.

First came the Soviet-engineered coup in Czechoslovakia between 12 and 25 February. President Beneš, fearful that his country would be thrust into civil war, yielded to communist demands for a new government. Democracy was replaced by a 'People's Democracy' in a one-party system. A month later the Russian representative on the Control Commission, Marshal Vasily Sokolovsky, accused the Western Allies of acting unilaterally to create a separate, 'western' federal republic of Germany. The war-mongering Western Allies were thus acting counter to the 1945 agreements, and the peace-loving Soviet Union had no option but to withdraw. So saying, he left the meeting and never returned.[32]

The Soviet Union had succeeded in finding an 'incident' that could be used as *casus belli* and on 24 June blockaded all traffic by road and rail to Berlin. Additional harassment, cuts in electricity supply and inter-zone transit in the divided city increased the insularity of the three western zones of Berlin. At the same time Stalin announced his intention to introduce a new currency, the Ostmark, to the Soviet zone.

Access to Berlin from the western zones of Germany was restricted to the three agreed air corridors to the city. Confident of the Red Army's massive numerical superiority in conventional forces, Stalin gambled that the two options open to the West were capitulation and evacuation of the capital or the use of nuclear force to pressure the Soviet Union to back down.[33] The supply of two million Berliners by air would, Stalin believed, be logistically impossible.

Attlee and Truman recognised that not only Western prestige but the future of all Germany was at stake and determined to answer pressure with pressure.[34] The only option was a massive airlift of food and essential supplies into West Berlin. Residents in the western zones of the city had adequate supplies for approximately six weeks. There was no time for delay; daily delivery of approximately 5,000 tons of supplies was needed, and the USA and Great Britain between them had, in the early days, enough aircraft to deliver barely 1,000 tons a day. Immediate action was required both to increase reserves in the city and to bring a vast fleet of transport aircraft to European airfields.

In the last week of June the airlift began and a supply line operated for eleven months in an unprecedented and brilliantly executed operation. The financial cost to Britain of the operation rose to over £1,000,000 each month.[35] Throughout the operation Attlee kept firm control of the British position as chairman of the Germany Committee (GEN/241); he and Bevin, working closely with Acheson, orchestrated a carefully executed strategy. The Soviet Union lost enormous face; the joint achievement of Britain and the United States, a conclusive step in consolidating the Western Alliance, hastened talks on the establishment of NATO. American commitment to rebuilding Western Europe, the goal towards which Attlee had inched since the end of 1946, was confirmed.

As late as the autumn of 1947 he could not have been certain that he would succeed; the Marshall Plan's passage through Congress was uncertain; Keep Left threatened further to undermine what Truman's political opponents denigrated as a socialist government. It would be overstating the case to assert that Attlee and Bevin orchestrated the reaction of Truman, Marshall and Acheson, but they certainly contributed to a dramatic shift in American policy, a shift towards an involvement in Europe that the most optimistic Atlanticist at Potsdam would have regarded as unlikely.

The unity of Attlee and Truman was tested from time to time – notably over the issue of Palestine – but both were team players and able to compartmentalise the issues that confronted them. As a result, they moved in step, if not always in lockstep, through the tumultuous last two years of Attlee's ministry.

Until 1950, the point at which Soviet and Western interests collided most sharply, Europe was at the centre of relations between the two leaders. The formal foundation of NATO on 4 April, the interdiction of movement of claimed reparations to the Soviet Union, and the first Soviet nuclear test on 29 August heightened tension between East and West.

As late as December 1950, when the public's attention was fixed on Korea, English political commentators continued to see the broader strategic position as ultimately Euro-centric. 'Grave as the crisis is in

Asia, it is in Europe that the danger lies', claimed *The Times*, a sentiment echoed by the *Manchester Guardian* who saw Asian events through
a European lens. 'If there should be a war with China', an editorial
opined, 'the danger of early war in Europe will become much greater. If
the atomic bomb should be used in Korea or China, it could hardly fail
to be used elsewhere in the world in the fairly near future.'[36]

In 1948 and 1949 however, there were significant developments in
Asia, most of which would assume importance after Attlee had left
Downing Street. On 18 June 1948 there was a Declaration of Emergency
in Malaya after three European plantation managers were murdered.
Although the state of crisis continued for twelve years and although the
administration of Malaya bore all the hallmarks of declining imperial
power accompanied by gross incompetence, the Labour government
was able to 'dodge the bullet'. The emergency played a part in the
increase of defence estimates[37] and one brigade was sent to Malaya;
over the following three years the insurgency was steadily pushed back.
When, on 6 October 1951, the High Commissioner Sir Henry Gurney
was ambushed and killed by guerrillas, the general election was just
nineteen days away and it fell to Oliver Lyttleton to deal with the crisis.

In Indo-China the Viet Minh were gaining influence and for the first
time the 'domino theory' became common parlance – if Indo-China
fell to the communists, then Siam and Burma would follow. When
Mao Zedong's communists defeated the Kuomintang and established
the People's Republic of China in October 1949, Hong Kong became
Attlee's Asian equivalent of Berlin – a matter of prestige as well as
considerable economic investment.[38] Gradually, China apart, the United
States began to assume French and British responsibilities in Asia.

When North Korea invaded South Korea on 25 June 1950 both Attlee
and Truman were uncertain about Soviet intentions. Both assumed that
the invasion was directed from Moscow but were unsure whether the
invasion was a test of American resolve or a diversion to draw attention
before a conventional attack in Europe. The State Department proposed
to issue a statement containing a reference to 'centrally directed communist imperialism', a reference that concerned Attlee, who argued for
allowing the Russians a line of retreat that would not embarrass them if
they wished to disassociate themselves from North Korea.[39]

For Attlee and Bevin, despite differences over the recognition of Mao's China, there was no hesitation over immediately joining the United Nations force in South Korea. It was a simple obligation in Attlee's view: America and Britain were playing on the same team in Europe; Britain was obliged to join the American team in Asia. Truman, an equally direct leader, would have seen the obligation in very much the same light.

Attlee had not met Truman since the tripartite conference in Washington in 1945. Now, he felt, it was important for the two leaders to clarify global policy. Bevin accordingly asked Sir Oliver Franks, the British Ambassador in Washington, for advice on the timing of a meeting. 'The international situation has become increasingly dangerous', he cabled, and 'the chance of further outbreaks on the Korean model must be taken into account.' The Prime Minister would not be coming to beg favours, Bevin stressed, but 'to make clear that what we want to do is to make the utmost contribution within reason for the common purpose.'[40]

Franks replied that the meeting should not be rushed as Attlee's presence would suggest that 'the world situation must have suddenly got worse.' Better, he urged, to delay the visit. A particularly cogent passage of Franks' cable draws a distinction between the American views of 'the Britain they have helped in the last five years and the Britain they knew in each of the two World Wars'. Once the Korean War broke out, 'American opinion swung back to the older view of a Britain from whom much should be expected and demanded.' The Prime Minister might experience a sense of disappointment if he made a visit in the current climate. The administration appeared to view the Anglo-American partnership as reviving but would probably not welcome a rejuvenated wartime partnership. Not yet, at least.[41]

A further problem was that, according to Acheson, the administration was finding it difficult to make up its mind on major matters of foreign policy.[42] This, of course, was precisely why Attlee proposed a visit. Concerned that there were differences over the strategic value of South Korea, he wanted to establish how far and at what cost the peninsula should be defended.

After the landings at Inchon on 25 September and the UN offensive north of the parallel, British and American strategy diverged. Once massed Chinese forces attacked UN forces on 25 October and drove

them headlong back into South Korea, General MacArthur mooted
the possibility of a tactical nuclear strike. During the following month
setbacks continued and on 28 November Truman told his staff meeting,
'We've got a terrific situation on our hands ... MacArthur said that there
were 260,000 Chinese troops against him out there.'[43]

Two days later Truman gave a press conference at which, under
persistent questioning about the bomb by reporters, he blundered badly.
Merriman Smith of United Press asked him if 'the use of the bomb is
under active consideration'. Truman replied simply, 'Always has been.
It is one of our weapons.' Pressed by Frank Bourghholtzer of NBC on
whether use of the bomb was dependent on authorisation from the UN,
the President responded, 'The action against communist China depends
on the action of the United Nations. The military commander in the
field will have charge of the weapons, as he always has.'[44]

This was dynamite. United Press released a bulletin stating that 'the
United States has under consideration use of the atomic bomb in connection with the war in Korea', an announcement elaborated by Associated
Press, who added that the use of the bomb lay within the authority of
the American commander in the field, Douglas MacArthur. The reports
caused consternation verging on panic in London. The White House
issued a clarifying statement, stressing that only the President's order
would authorise use of the bomb, but the damage had been done. This
was precisely the situation that anti-nuclear groups had most feared.
They were concerned that Russian – or in this case, Chinese – conventional forces would simply overwhelm Americans. The precedent had
horrifying implications for Europe. Attlee told the House in the course
of a foreign policy debate that he had sent a message to the White
House, requesting talks.[45] The announcement of Truman's positive
response was greeted with cheers.

From within the Labour Party reaction to Truman's comments was
violent and immediate. Seventy-seven Labour MPs signed a letter to the
Prime Minister, deploring Truman's statement and demanding that the
government withdraw British forces from Korea if the war were carried
beyond the Manchurian frontier.[46]

Before Attlee's arrival Truman held a series of crisis meetings in
Washington on 3 December. They failed to resolve the issues at stake,

infused as they were with a sense of unreality. The US Army's youngest major-general at forty-five, Chief of Staff five years later, MacArthur enjoyed the reputation of a military genius; accordingly the obvious – that he be relieved – was unspoken. There was talk of a ceasefire, which Acheson resisted.[47] Finally General Ridgway succeeded in persuading Truman and his despondent advisers to regain the initiative.[48]

By the time Attlee arrived in Washington Truman was resolved not to be talked into withdrawal. At their first meeting he stressed that Europe was America's principal strategic concern, but that Asia had large claims. Attlee pressed his view that by reinforcing the troops in Korea the West would play into Russia's hands by leaving Europe exposed.[49]

There was a fundamental difference between American and British policy regarding China. Whereas in 1950 and for the decade thereafter the State Department spoke of 'a Sino-Soviet bloc', Britain from the outset recognised 'Red' China and sought to detach her from the Soviet Union. This, Attlee argued, entailed recognising Chinese ambitions and attempting to reach agreement. When he pressed this view on Truman he made little headway.[50] Attlee would have been content to see Asia abandoned if that would save Europe from Soviet incursions, a view that Truman emphatically did not share. After a meeting aboard the presidential yacht, *Williamsburg*, Truman noted in his diary that it was 'a very satisfactory gathering' but that 'the position of the British on Asia is, to say the least, fantastic. We cannot agree to their suggestions. Yet they say they will support us whatever we do!' Attlee's stance, described by Truman, was 'that all should be given up in the Far East to save Europe', to which Truman replied with a firm 'No'.[51]

Acheson was concerned that Attlee's persistence, coupled with Truman's tendency to answer questions as they came up, would commit the President to accepting a ceasefire if, as Attlee argued, the position of the UN forces was untenable and the price of a ceasefire was reasonable. He saw Attlee as 'a skilled negotiator' who 'soon led the President well onto the flypaper'.[52] Truman and Acheson adamantly refused to abandon the South Koreans and 'gave Mr Attlee a lesson in political consistency'. At the end of their meetings, Attlee 'went home pledging full support to [Truman's] determination to stay in Korea – something he had come to Washington without the slightest desire to do.'[53]

One may reasonably ask just what Attlee's priorities were in Washington. The talks were presented to the world as intervention by the Prime Minister to stay the hand of a bomb-toting President, but discussions of the bomb occupied just one meeting between the leaders and a mere two sentences in the joint communiqué.[54] His visit served to reaffirm the solidarity of the Atlantic alliance, to reassure the American public that, although the two countries differed in some ways, they were both democratic countries and 'where the Stars and Stripes fly in Korea, the British flag will fly beside them'.[55]

When on the final day the two leaders privately discussed the use of the bomb, Attlee pressed for an assurance that no decision to use it would be taken without prior discussion and, preferably, a formal agreement with Britain. In characteristic style, Truman assured him that such a decision would not be taken unilaterally, but he declined to sign such an agreement. If a man's word was no good, he assured the Prime Minister, it was not improved by putting it on paper.[56] Eventually a brief statement was included that the President hoped that world conditions would never justify the use of the atomic bomb and he would at all times keep the Prime Minister 'informed of developments which might bring about a change in the situation'.[57]

On one subject, at least, Attlee was able to be satisfied. Both Truman and Marshall reaffirmed their commitment to European defence, although they regretted that, in light of the Korean crisis, they would not be able to move to Germany two divisions from Asia and one from the United States as they had planned.[58] Congress, however, would need to be convinced that there was a real possibility of defending Europe. How, they asked, did Britain view their plan to have 3,000,000 men at arms in Europe by 1952?

Field Marshal Slim, the CIGS, confirmed Britain's commitment to use the proposed defence budget of £3,600 million to raise twenty divisions over three years. The morale of European troops would be greatly boosted, he added, by the appointment of a NATO Supreme Commander and by the transfer even of a National Guard division to Europe.[59] Attlee pressed this point in a note that he handed to Truman, emphasising Britain's need for raw materials in order to contribute significantly to European defence.[60] Acheson had listed in May the seven cardinal points of Western strategy[61] but, since the outbreak of the Korean War, Attlee had been concerned that American commitment to NATO would wane. Instead, the linkage that Truman and Marshall saw between Chinese aggression and Russian ambitions in Europe actually reinforced their resolve to strengthen the Western Alliance.

Since the signing of the Treaty of Brussels in March 1948 and the North Atlantic Treaty a year later, NATO had existed more in concept than in substance. With the eruption of fighting in Korea, the American Chiefs of Staff had prevailed on Truman to appoint a Supreme Commander of a European army that would include German troops. In September the President announced his intention to increase the strength of American forces in Europe and to double the defence budget to $30 billion.[62] Then on 28 October he summoned to the White House the only American officer eligible for the job, General Eisenhower.[63] As a direct result of the Washington meetings Eisenhower visited the twelve NATO capitals in January 1951 and by February had installed his headquarters at the Hôtel Astoria in Paris.[64] Largely thanks to Attlee's and Bevin's efforts, congressional isolationism had been overcome and American prestige was firmly vested in collective European security. This was a remarkable culmination of policy that Attlee had brought to fruition.

Attlee returned to London and a hostile reception from the Opposition in the Commons. Churchill maintained that there was no guarantee of even consultation before a putative American use of the bomb. Only the vast superiority of the United States gave Britain a chance of survival.

> *The argument is now put forward that we must never use the atomic bomb until, or unless, it has been used against us first. In other words, you must never fire until you have been shot dead. That seems to me undoubtedly a silly thing to say and a still more imprudent position to adopt.*[65]

Attlee's position, however, was more in tune with the mood of the House than Churchill's. Most references to the bomb during the debate were to express gratitude for the West's nuclear superiority. The nice distinction between the right of veto and consultation was blurred and the issue conveniently faded away.[66]

Attlee broadcast to the nation on 16 December and in the New Year announced the measures that he and Slim had promised Truman and Marshall. The government had decided to 'increase and accelerate their defence preparations still further'. He stressed that the government did not believe war to be inevitable but was striving to prevent it. He revealed a plan to call up 235,000 reservists in the summer for fifteen days of training. The Navy and the RAF would also be recalling men from the reserve lists. As to the cost, in 1951–52 preparations for defence would total about £1,300 million. Over three years he expected it to rise to 'as much as £4,700 millions'.[67]

It was an ominous announcement. Increased defence expenditure set in train an irreparable rift within the Labour Party and imposed further hardship on an exhausted population. The added implication that, six years after the defeat of Germany, it was necessary to spend £4,700,000,000 to avoid another war was far from welcome.

Attlee had been loyal to his word. He had consolidated the Atlantic alliance and, in so doing, had sowed the seeds of the fall of his own government.

ENDNOTES

1   TNA: PREM 8/1202, 3 May 1950.
2   Michael Foot, *Aneurin Bevan*, vol. 2, *1945–1960*, p. 89.
3   Dalton, *High Tide and After*, p. 197.
4   *The Times*, 12 February 1947.
5   Gaddis, *The United States and the Origins of the Cold War*, p. 348.
6   TNA: CAB 128/9/14, CM (47) 14, 31 January 1947.
7   Additionally, the cost of support to Turkey was estimated at $150 million in 1947. Wheeler-Bennett and Nicholls, *The Semblance of Peace*, p. 563.
8   Bullock, *Ernest Bevin, Foreign Secretary*, p. 370.
9   McCullough, *Truman*, p. 540.
10 Kennan, *Memoirs 1925–1950*, pp. 547–559. 22 February 1946.
11 Clifford, *Counsel to the President*, pp. 123–129.
12 Acheson, *Present at the Creation*, p. 217.
13 Ibid., p. 218.
14 Gaddis, *The United States and the Origins of the Cold War*, p. 349.
15 McCullough, *Truman*, p. 545.
16 Ibid., p. 541.
17 *The Public Papers of the Presidents, Harry S. Truman, 1947*, pp. 178–179. Acheson, op. cit. pp. 222–3.
18 *Fourth Meeting of the Council of Foreign Ministers, Moscow, March 10 to April 24, 1947;* Report by General Marshall, 28 April 1947.
19 The Requirements of Reconstruction', US State Department, *The Record of the Week*, 18 May 1947, pp. 991–4. Speech of 5 May 1947.
20 *Foreign Relations of the US, 1947*, 5:60–62.
21 General G. C. Marshall, Commencement Address at Harvard University, Cambridge Massachusetts, 5 June 1947.

22   Seth Johnston, *How NATO Endures*, p. 66.
23   Healey, *The Time of My Life*, pp. 105–106.
24   At the 1947 Labour Party conference in Margate.
25   Michael Foot, *Aneurin Bevan*, vol. 2, *1945–1960*, p. 69.
26   Ibid., loc. cit.
27   Bodleian: MS. Attlee, dep. 60, 10 September 1947.
28   Bodleian: MS. Attlee, dep. 66, 3 January 1948.
29   *Hansard*, HC Deb, 22 January 1948, vol. 446, col. 402.
30   *Hansard*, HC Deb, 23 January 1948, vol. 446, col. 617–618.
31   *Hansard*, HC Deb, 23 January 1948, vol. 446, col. 622.
32   Roger Miller, *To Save a City: The Berlin Airlift, 1948–1949*, p. 19.
33   The American Chiefs of Staff considered General Clay's proposal to send an armed convoy to end the blockade but Attlee and Bevin, as well as the French, violently opposed this. Acheson, *Present at the Creation*, p. 262.
34   See TNA: PREM 8/989, fols 46–51, an exchange of telegrams between Attlee in London and Bevin in Washington, for a clear exposition of the issues at stake from the Western perspective in early April 1949.
35   TNA: PREM 8/989, fol. 64. GEN 241/9th Meeting.
36   *The Times* and *Manchester Guardian*, both of 4 December 1950.
37   Bullock, *Ernest Bevin, Foreign Secretary*, p. 612.
38   Ritchie Overdale, 'Britain and the Cold War in Asia', in *The Foreign Policy of the British Labour Governments 1945–1951* (R. Overdale ed.), pp. 128–129.
39   Overdale, *op. cit.* p. 131.
40   TNA: PREM 8/1156, T3663, FO to Washington, 11 August 1950.
41   TNA: PREM 8/1156, T2233, Washington to FO, 16 August 1950.
42   TNA: PREM 8/1156, T2320, Washington to FO, 26 August 1950.
43   Ken Hechler, *Working with Truman*, p. 167.
44   *The Public Papers of the Presidents, Harry S. Truman 1950*, No. 295, pp. 724–728.
45   *Hansard*, HC Deb, 30 November 1950, col. 1440.
46   Bodleian: MS Attlee, dep. 114, 30 November 1950.
47   Acheson, *Present at the Creation*, p. 475.
48   Ridgway, *The Korean War*, p. 62.
49   TNA: PREM 8/1200, 1st Meeting, 4 December 1950.
50   TNA: PREM 8/1200, 2nd Meeting, 5 December 1950.
51   Ferrell, *Off the Record: The Private Papers of Harry S. Truman*, pp. 202–203.
52   Acheson, *Present at the Creation*, p. 481.
53   Margaret Truman, *Harry S. Truman*, pp. 503–504.
54   TNA: PREM 8/1200, Joint communiqué, 8 December 1950.
55   TNA: PREM 8/1200, Speech to National Press Club, 6 December 1950.
56   McCullough, *Truman*, p. 826.
57   TNA: PREM 8/1200, Joint communiqué, 8 December 1950.
58   TNA: PREM 8/1200, 4th Meeting, 6 December 1950.
59   Ibid.
60   TNA: PREM 8/1200, Memorandum CRA to HST, 6 December 1950.
61   TNA: PREM 8/1202, Report on Tripartite Ministerial Meeting, 11 May 1950. The seven points were (i) we must appreciate the danger confronting us; (ii) we must be prepared in the military field; (iii) we must try to build the economic underpinning for this military preparedness together with the maintenance of a high standard of living; (iv) we must make use of Germany's productivity; (v) we should endeavour not to lose the East while we are trying to win the West; (vi) we must bear in mind the importance of the presentation to the world of our actions; (vii) we must have an effective organisation through which to act.
62   Bodleian: MS Attlee, dep. 108, 10 September 1950.
63   Ferrell, *The Eisenhower Diaries*, pp. 178–179.
64   Ferrell, *The Eisenhower Diaries*, p. 187.
65   *Hansard*, HC Deb, 14 December 1950, col. 1368.
66   Eden's biographer wrote that 'It was not easy to counter the Labour myth that Attlee, single-handedly, had prevented Truman from using atomic weapons over Korea. Eden suspected – rightly – that this was indeed a total myth, but he could not be sure, and the portrayal of Attlee in this heroic role, although carried to absurdity, formed an important part of the Labour counter-attack.' Rhodes James, *Anthony Eden*, p. 339.
67   *Hansard*, HC Deb, 29 January 1951, cols. 579–584. Bodleian: MS Attlee, dep. 118.

CHAPTER SIXTEEN

FROM LORD HAW-HAW TO BURGESS AND MACLEAN, 1945–1951

The British Security Service (MI5) was riding high at the end of the Second World War. The success of DOUBLE CROSS, a campaign of disinformation that deceived the German High Command until after D-Day, had been sensational. German espionage in Britain had been totally defused and there was no perceived threat from the Soviet Union, Britain's ally since 1941. According to one MI5 officer, there were only two or three officers in the Russian section at the end of the war.[1] Maxwell Knight, head of B5(b), the counter-subversion section, cried for more attention to communist espionage, but both Jasper Harker, the Deputy Director General, and Guy Liddell, Head of B Division, had lost confidence in Knight's judgement.[2]

From its foundation in 1909 until 1940 MI5 had been run by one Director, Major-General Sir Vernon Kell. Under Kell's regime officers were chosen according to criteria that had as much to do with sporting ability as skill in inductive reasoning. Recruitment was not a scientific process, as Sir David Petrie, Kell's successor, reported.[3] Emphasis was placed on a candidate's being 'the right sort of chap', and the MI5 establishment was conservative in outlook and demeanour. The shadow of Kell affected a wartime group whom Sir John Masterman described as 'a team of congenial people who worked together harmoniously and unselfishly, and among whom rank counted for little and character for much'.[4]

The instinctive suspicion of Labour ministers towards such a department was sharpened by their conviction that the Security Service had organised the affair of the Zinoviev letter that derailed Ramsay

MacDonald's campaign in 1924.[5] During the second MacDonald government, moreover, Dalton had complained that the secret service personnel was 'excessive', and urged economy.[6]

To MI5 officers the Labour Cabinet was an unknown quantity. Liddell recorded his first meeting with Attlee to discuss internment of aliens soon after the fall of France in 1940. Liddell spoke his mind to Attlee and Greenwood on the need to set aside 'the liberty of the subject, freedom of speech etc.' in the fight with Hitler and, rather to his surprise, Attlee and Greenwood agreed.[7] In 1942 Morrison, incensed by a cartoon in the *Daily Mirror*, had shocked Liddell by demanding an investigation of the newspaper to identify subversives.

As the post-war election approached, Liddell and Findlater Stewart discussed what attitude a Labour government would have towards MI5. Stewart believed that 'Dalton or someone even more to the left might insist on examining [MI5's] records and that, if they were not confined strictly to people advocating the overthrow of the constitution by violence, the whole department might be in serious trouble.' Liddell, probably recalling his surprise at his wartime encounters with Attlee, Greenwood and Morrison, replied that 'the general form was that the Labour Party were far more interested to make use of our services than the Conservatives'.[8]

Sir David Petrie, Director General of MI5 since 1941, was due to retire and, having heard that all was not well at MI5[9], Attlee appointed a committee to select his successor. When it became known in December that the committee had chosen Sir Percy Sillitoe, the Chief Constable of Kent, senior officers in the Service felt that the choice of a policeman reflected the personal preference of the socialist Prime Minister, heralding a downgrading of MI5's importance. In fact, Attlee distanced himself from the selection process and Sillitoe was selected ahead of highly qualified applicants such as General Ismay, William Penney and General Kenneth Strong. Sir Alexander Cadogan recorded that Sillitoe was unanimously selected as the best candidate.[10]

This was decidedly not the view of senior officers in MI5 who disliked 'having a rozzer at the top' and regarded Sillitoe as an ill-educated showman. To demonstrate their contempt for the outsider they went out of their way 'constantly to make lengthy Latin quotations to one another in his presence.'[11] Liddell in particular, as he had hoped to succeed Petrie, was critical of the appointment for a number of reasons. He initially blamed Attlee for the choice and refers to the Prime Minister as 'Little Clem', a nickname used with affection by Bevin, with contempt by Attlee's critics.[12] In fact, it was Morrison who doubted Liddell's suitability. He had learned from Ellen Wilkinson that Liddell might have been involved in the betrayal of Willi Muenzenberg, an ex-communist assassinated by NKVD agents in 1940, and reported this to Attlee.[13] An additional question mark was raised by Liddell's many friendships with homosexuals and left-leaning intellectuals with whom he spent several Friday evenings at the Chelsea Palais.[14]

Had Liddell been able to be more objective he would have seen the inevitability of an appointment from outside MI5. In 1943, when the successor to Petrie was discussed, Liddell had been the initial choice. There were, however, doubts about his administrative ability.[15] When Duff Cooper, head of the Security Executive, asked him who might succeed Petrie, Liddell replied that 'although [he] did not wish to appear conceited [he] was certain that if [he] did not do the job there was nobody else.'[16]

While the new appointment was being made Sir Findlater Stewart completed his report on the Service's future. Pointing out that during the war MI5 had had responsibilities to different departments, he recommended that it was time to regularise the position. 'The minister responsible for it as a Service (though not for action taken by other ministers on its advice) should be the Minister of Defence, or, if there is no Minister of Defence, the Prime Minister as chairman of the Committee of Imperial Defence.'[17]

Attlee, who had appointed himself Minister of Defence pending reorganisation of the three Service Ministries, took personal control of the Service and approved its new charter. It was a symbolic decision that, to Liddell's surprise, heightened MI5's importance, as the Director General would have unprecedented direct access to Downing Street.[18] When Liddell and Sillitoe met in February 1946 to discuss collaboration, Sillitoe said that he would be seeing the Prime Minister once a fortnight 'on the latter's special instructions'.[19] Attlee and Sillitoe met sometimes more, sometimes less frequently, not quite every two weeks, but considerably more frequently than any subsequent Director General 'for the remainder of the twentieth century'.[20]

Attlee gained considerable traction from Churchill's claim during the election that, if socialism were to be effective in Britain, the Labour Party would have to fall back on some kind of Gestapo. In private, however, he was scrupulous to avoid using MI5 in a way that could incur such accusations. As a result, there developed a close and efficient working relationship between Downing Street and MI5's Curzon Street headquarters, as both the Labour Cabinet and the ostensibly apolitical senior officers of MI5 collaborated in an unprecedented fashion in matters of security.

The Prime Minister acted to dispel the atmosphere of excessive secrecy surrounding the Service. One the one hand, MI5 'wanted at all cost to avoid the stigma of being called the British version of the Soviet secret police'. 'On the other', one officer wrote, 'there was so much secrecy within secrecy ... [that] ... I felt like a small boy unwillingly let into a prefects' pow-wow.'[21] Sillitoe also felt that MI5's 'popular reputation for excessive secrecy was in no way exaggerated'.[22] When he broke the Service's unwritten rules by booking airline seats in his own name and writing his memoirs, MI5 officers were outraged.

Attlee endorsed Sillitoe's openness by writing a forward to his memoirs. 'A Director General of MI5 needs very special qualities', he wrote. 'He has to have the technical qualities required for Intelligence work. He must be able to control a team of individualists engaged on important secret work. At the same time he has to have a very lively appreciation of the rights of the citizen in a free country ... In a world where so many millions groan under the tyranny of the police state, it is good to read the life of a man who exhibits the qualities which have made the British policeman the protector not the oppressor of society.'[23]

Every word in Attlee's foreword is carefully chosen. Conscious of the political capital that Churchill had hoped to make with his 'Gestapo' accusation, Attlee was scrupulous to ensure that the accusation could not be justly repeated. Hence the adherence to the Security Service's new Charter, as proposed by Stewart, that the Service's *raison d'être* was the defence of the realm and that all its activities must contribute to or be relevant to that goal.[24]

Sillitoe took up his appointment on 1 May 1946 and was almost immediately involved in a contentious issue. Attlee instructed him to clear up
MI5's comprehensive files and to dispose of personal files not strictly necessary for the defence of the realm. A few days later Liddell recorded that
Cabinet discussions were being leaked and that Attlee had instructed Sillitoe
to investigate. While MI5 was the only body equipped to handle such an
investigation, Liddell was concerned that, according to the new charter, it
would be acting beyond its powers. He requested a letter from the Cabinet
Office, instructing MI5 to investigate the leaks before proceeding.[25]

The issue of superfluous files was not one that Attlee allowed to drop.
He returned to it at a meeting with Sillitoe towards the end of June, as
Liddell's diary records. 'I asked the DG what the PM had in the back
of his mind', Liddell recalled. 'He said that he was quite sure he was
still afraid that the Opposition might accuse him of running a Gestapo.
This of course is quite ridiculous as far as MI5 is concerned, since I am
certain that Winston was merely referring to the socialisation of industry
and controls which caused the appointment of a staff of a Gestapo kind
to see that the regulations were carried out.'[26]

Liddell is disingenuous in this assertion. Attlee needed the Security
Service to maintain a close watch on the Communist Party of Great
Britain ('CPGB') while not appearing to use totalitarian methods to do
so. It was a curious conundrum: Churchill had appealed to the electorate's fears that socialism entailed a degree of control by the state and
had fanned those fears by referring to a 'Gestapo'. Although Attlee had
skilfully defused the charge, the underlying truth remained.[27]

The policy of appearing scrupulously open in relations with MI5 led,
on occasion, to difficulties. During the summer of 1946, as the issue of
Palestine increasingly showed Britain in imperialist colours, the government needed to justify the arrest of members of the Jewish Agency
who, they were certain, had connived with Haganah to commit acts
of sabotage. Attlee had publicly committed himself to produce any
documents found in Palestine that linked the Agency with Haganah's
activities, but he had been 'less definite about the production of documents that led him to decide on the arrest of members of the Agency'.
This led to friction between Attlee and the Security Service: Attlee and
the government felt that it was a matter of worldwide importance that

Britain demonstrate that the arrests were justified, a step that would involve revealing the sources if it were to be credible. MI5, naturally, was reluctant to reveal sources as this would put at risk a highly placed source in Palestine. Convinced that their Intelligence was accurate, they were placed in a difficult position when they wished to withhold their source. The issue came to a head in early July, when MI5 prepared a brief for the Colonial Office and Prime Minister on the activities of Haganah, Palmach and Irgun.[28]

On the following day Attlee called a meeting attended by George Hall, the Secretary of State for the Colonies, 'C', the Director of MI6, Sillitoe and Liddell from MI5, and General Ismay. He felt that he had been wrong-footed by the Colonial Office in being told that he could use information in a telegram from the High Commissioner in Palestine and subsequently embarrassed when he learned that the release of that information would compromise the Security Service.[29] The incident clearly illustrates Attlee's attitude towards the use of MI5: he recognised the need for Intelligence services and their secrecy but he wanted to be as open as possible in his dealings with them. He had erred on the side of being overly candid.

Aside from counter-insurgency in Palestine, Attlee depended on MI5 for two functions: counter-subversion (the role of F Division) and counter-espionage (B Division). In the first years of his government counter-subversion assumed primacy.[30] From 1948 on, the two functions were largely fused. No one can have been in doubt in 1945 as to where Attlee believed the source of subversion would be found.

He had long been a relentless critic of the CPGB, consistently resist-ing their attempts to associate themselves with the Labour Party.[31] In a speech at Blackburn in 1940, starting from the assumption that 'things will be different when the old order is supplanted', he condemned Nazism, the evil that Britain was fighting, and attacked communism, preferable to Nazism because it embraced the noble ideal of workers' freedom, but worthless as the CPGB were 'dummies of the ventriloquist Stalin'.[32] He regarded them as 'irresponsible and unstable' and impla-cably hostile to democratic socialism. An early effort to destabilise the government in 1946 can have come as no surprise.

During the summer the government encountered a delicate problem caused by the housing crisis. Four million homes had been damaged during the war and the rebuilding programme was badly hampered by lack of materials and labour. As a result, large groups of homeless squatters occupied empty military camps, a problem that the Cabinet addressed in August. There were considerable public relations problems involved in ejecting the homeless, particularly if the camps were to be used for resettlement of Poles or for German prisoners of war – as was frequently the case. Attlee observed that the important point was that camps vacated by the Army should not remain empty for long and that, in some instances, it was better to allow squatters to remain there if the camps were not earmarked for any other purpose.[33]

The press seized on the story and it quickly became a *cause célèbre*. Whether or not the initial occupation of camps was instigated by the Communist Party, once squatters occupied buildings in London, thus gaining greatly more visibility, the CPGB saw this as a rare opportunity to embarrass the government. In early September there were five invasions of empty premises in Kensington and Holland Park. In the largest of these, 800 people occupied Duchess of Bedford House in Kensington High Street[34] in a move both instigated by the Communist Party and used by them as a recruiting tool.[35]

The building had been requisitioned by the Ministry of Works and had been empty for about twelve days. On the following day *The Times* reported that 1,500 squatters had entered and after the first wave others joined the group. Home Office reports state categorically that the movement of the squatters was planned by the London District Committee of the CPGB; neither MI5 nor the Metropolitan Police had any advance warning.[36] Apparently planning had been in progress for some weeks but the decision to occupy was not made until two days before. On 14 September Ted Bramley, secretary of the London District Communist Party, and four other communist leaders were arrested for 'conspiring together with other persons to incite persons to trespass on property, and aid and abet and direct such trespasses against the peace'. Bevan, as Minister of Health, spoke for the government: 'The government are confident that local authorities will take firm and prompt action on these lines in defence of organised government and the principles of social justice on which the system of allocation of available housing is based.'[33]

As a tactic to place the government in a difficult position the move was inspired. There was enormous sympathy for homeless squatters and when the Cabinet discussed their options it was clear that force would be used to evict them. This would certainly increase public sympathy. By forming committees at Duchess of Bedford House and ensuring that only committee members spoke to the press, the CPGB orchestrated the operation to gain maximum public sympathy. After taking the decision to evict the squatters and to take a hard line in the High Court,[37] the government was able to find alternative accommodation and persuade squatters to vacate the flats without violence. For Attlee and his colleagues it was a lesson in CPGB tactics.

In Attlee's early dealings with MI5 there is a sense of uncertainty on both sides. Indeed, it is slightly comical to imagine the taciturn Prime Minister being briefed by officers for whom secrecy and need to know were paramount. Liddell mentions occasions when he awaited a response from Attlee and, receiving none, proceeded uncertainly to the next item on his list. 'I found the PM an extremely difficult man to talk to', he recorded. There were pauses after Liddell dealt with each item on the agenda, and after his briefing came another long pause until Liddell rose to leave. 'He then bundled out of his chair in a somewhat confused state.'[38]

Attlee's taciturnity is well documented. Douglas Jay commented that 'he would never use one syllable where none would do,'[39] and it is easy to imagine him receiving Intelligence from Liddell or Sillitoe in silence. There is, however, more to his silence. In taking personal responsibility for MI5 he was assuming a function that was new to him. In political, even military, matters he was accustomed to hearing two or more sides of an argument and guiding a meeting to accept what he perceived as the consensus. Here he was confronted by a different consideration to which he needed to adapt. In conditions of strict secrecy the Director General of the Security Service briefed him on inevitably complex subjects which, like icebergs, had their bulk hidden below the surface – as he learned during the row over sources in Palestine. At the end of the briefing there followed no Attleean summary, no consensus. Instead, in characteristic style, he uncoiled himself from his chair and ended the meeting. He learned how to handle the Service as he went along. By the time he understood its complexity and was comfortable with its powers, he knew what he wanted from it. He saw no need to comment or to discuss the Intelligence that Sillitoe or Liddell brought. Despite his discomfort, Liddell found Attlee 'uncommunicative and unresponsive, but quite pleasant'.[40] The Security Service, which flourished by listening to indiscreet talk, was disquieted by a man across the desk who said nothing.

The government's needs from MI5 were largely defined by its shifting foreign policy in 1946 and 1947. The wartime alliance with the United States was consolidated in ABCA, a four-power military pact between Britain, the USA, Canada and Australia; an agreement was signed providing for exchange of information between London and Washington in 'collection of traffic, acquisition of documents and equipment, traffic analysis, cryptanalysis, decryption and translation and acquisition of information regarding communication, organisations, practices, procedures and equipment'.[41] This wholesale sharing of information did not, however, involve sharing of atomic secrets. Once Attlee decided to proceed with Britain's independent nuclear deterrent, the need for counter-espionage became more acute.

Soviet espionage first came to Attlee's notice in September 1945 when Igor Gouzenko, a cypher clerk with Soviet military Intelligence ('GRU') in Ottawa walked out of the Soviet Embassy with over one hundred classified documents. Among these were GRU telegrams referring to an agent codenamed ALEK, the British atomic scientist Alan Nunn May. The discovery that the Soviet Union had a network in place to spy on their recent allies so soon after the war came as a shock. Attlee had not yet abandoned hope of maintaining cordial relations with Moscow and Washington – the charade of the Council of Foreign Ministers lay a few months in the future. At a time when he was beginning to doubt Truman's sincerity over sharing atomic research, the Gouzenko affair rankled. It offended his sense of loyalty to the wartime alliance and confirmed his growing feeling that Britain was on her own. As events turned out, it was a 'bookend' to his policy towards the USSR and the CPGB.

As late as May 1947 Attlee and Bevin attempted to maintain Britain's position as one of the 'Big Three'; Bevin stated baldly in the House that 'His Majesty's government do not accept the view submitted ... that we have ceased to be a great power'.[42] By the end of the year, however, that ambition was shelved and, after the rape of Czechoslovakia and the blockade of Berlin, both Attlee and Bevin accepted Britain's diminished status. That acceptance ushered in greater dependence on the Security Service.

In May 1947 Attlee formed GEN 183, the Cabinet committee on Subversive Activities, and because there 'was no way of separating the sheep from the goats', it was resolved that no members of the Communist Party were to be employed in sensitive jobs.[43] This laid the foundations for the first step in vetting and over the following six months Attlee considered the steps that he should take and in December resolved on the introduction of what became known as the 'Purge Procedure'.[44] Cautiously, and in step with MI5, he moved to introduce the procedure early in 1948.[45]

By 1948 anti-communist rhetoric in the United States was increasingly shrill and a Congress that had viewed Britain askance since the end of the war needed to be convinced that the country was not 'soft on communism' for much-needed Marshall Aid to flow. From this followed Attlee's decision that, if the special relationship were to be developed, the government must be seen to step up its anti-communist posture. London's relations with Moscow could no longer be viewed as the policy of an autonomous state. Britain's trade relations with the Soviet Union, her Intelligence apparatus, the make-up of her government – all became susceptible to inspection from Washington.

Between the end of 1947 and the fall of the Attlee government in 1951 the special relationship with the USA was carefully built. Among Attlee's team were several junior ministers and prominent members with links to the Intelligence services: Christopher Mayhew, an old Haileyburian and wartime Major in the Intelligence Corps; Hugh Gaitskell and Richard Crossman, who had worked for Dalton in SOE; Kenneth Younger, Director of E Division in MI5; Rex Fletcher, later Lord Winster, had worked in Naval Intelligence. On the back benches was Tom Driberg, who continued to report to Max Knight on the CGPB.

It was Mayhew who proposed to Bevin in 1947 a propaganda offensive against the Soviet Union,[46] a proposal that led to the founding of the Information Research Department to disseminate anti-Soviet 'grey' propaganda, heavily slanted factual material.[47] Highly secret, it was soon betrayed to Moscow as Soviet spy Guy Burgess worked for Mayhew at

IRD before Mayhew sacked him for being 'dirty, drunk and idle'.[48] The Secret Intelligence Service (MI6) took control of IRD, one of its many expansionist moves as the secret war against Russia flourished with the approval of Langley.

Attlee now operated with Rooseveltian dexterity. While championing openness, he enhanced the range of covert activities of the Security Service. Ostensibly, the government's interest was in identifying members of any extremist organisation; in fact, it was members of the CPGB who were targeted.[49] After the election of 1945 there were about a dozen MPs who were 'either secret CP members or were close to the CP, sharing its beliefs and enjoying the company of its leaders',[50] and in November 1946 Attlee asked Liddell for any 'positive information' that suggested a member of the Labour Party's position 'might constitute a danger to the state'.[51] At some point he also obtained from MI5 a list of crypto-communists; in 1949 Morrison told Liddell that he would like a list of fellow-travellers as he 'intended to smoke them out of the Labour Party'. Liddell recorded that 'I dodged this one, but if pressed I should have to tell him that such a list was in the hands of the PM'.[52]

However real the threat of communist penetration of Britain may have been, there was a tendency to see the evil influence of Moscow in every kind of dispute. One such situation arose in November 1947 on the eve of the wedding of Princess Elizabeth and Lieutenant Philip Mountbatten. Three days before the wedding Attlee summoned Sillitoe and expressed his concern that the Soviet Union was inciting strikes in an attempt to wreck the occasion. A waiter, Frank Piazza, had been dismissed by the Savoy Group in a demarcation dispute over carrying dirty plates to the kitchen, an action that provoked a strike of about 700 of the group's catering staff. Sillitoe believed that it was a simple industrial dispute rather than a Moscow-sponsored conspiracy. In that case, demanded Attlee, why was Piazza not deported as an undesirable alien? Liddell notes that he reminded the Director General 'that so far from deporting people of this kind, it was the Home Office policy not to regard membership of the Communist Party as a bar against naturalisation'.[53]

That statement might be true of employees of the Savoy Group but in more sensitive employment where national security was concerned, Attlee was determined that all members of extreme groups should be barred from employment. His solution, the 'Purge Procedure', was first raised with MI5 in December 1947 and discussed at the highest levels over the next two months. In early March Liddell commented that the statement Attlee proposed to make in the House of Commons was 'extremely good.'[54] Liddell and his colleagues did, however, have concerns that the procedure was clearly aimed solely at the Communist Party and that it would be difficult for Attlee to appear even-handed in his treatment of communists and fascists.[55]

When Attlee announced the introduction of the Purge Procedure in March 1948 the mood of the House was expressed by Charles Mott-Radclyffe, who agreed that 'few would deny the right of this or any other government to take adequate steps to ensure the security of the state. Indeed, the government would be failing in their duty if they did not do so.' If an individual with access to confidential documents held political beliefs that transcended loyalty to the state, then 'clearly action must be taken and, what is more, it must be taken while there is still time.'[56]

Opposition, predictably, came from the communist Willie Gallacher, MP for Fife-West, who correctly saw the tactic as a move to dispel American doubts of British security. He contrasted communism, which 'fights for the complete independence and economic prosperity of this country', with the unholy alliance of 'Tories and Labour leaders [who] are selling this country to the big dollar boys of America'.[57]

Liddell, with the cynical view of politicians common to Intelligence officers, observed that as he had expected, MI5 had been represented as 'whipping boys' who had bungled in the past and now the Labour Party was going to get everything under control.[58]

Initially the procedure applied only to government and Civil Service employees but, as Sir Norman Brook pointed out to Attlee, many private firms held government contracts for secret work and it would be prudent to extend the procedure's scope.[59] After some uncertainty as to how this should best be handled, it was agreed in Cabinet that the Minister of Supply was entitled to instruct a firm to remove a suspected extremist from secret work. Aware of the public reception that it would receive, the government never announced this extension of screening.[60]

The Purge Procedure in Britain has been criticised as a form of 'British McCarthyism'. The comparison is grotesque. The wild claim of

Senator Joe McCarthy that he had the names of 205 communists in the State Department[61] far outstrips the activities of the Purge Procedure in Britain. Ten months after the measure was introduced Attlee responded to a question in the House from Sir Waldron Smithers, revealing that a mere seventeen cases had gone before a tribunal. Of these eleven had resulted in the dismissal of an employee.[62] Attlee denied that the procedure was 'a purge' in the sense that Sir Waldron had used the word, but was cautioned by Cyril Osborne, MP for Louth, to 'bear in mind what has happened in America, and see that the committee's duties are carried out properly'.[63]

The Purge Procedure, whether or not it was successful in keeping communists out of sensitive posts, certainly succeeded in putting the CPGB on the defensive. There was, Liddell informed Attlee, 'a general atmosphere of depression in the Communist Party in view of recent happenings. They felt that they had lost the initiative.'[64] The procedure involved a massive amount of work, vetting 300,000 individuals with an additional annual intake of 50,000. There is no evidence that Security Service officers resented this work or disagreed with the Prime Minister as to its desirability.

Indeed, relations between Attlee and the Service remained cordial and in 1949 Sillitoe achieved a notable 'first' when he invited Attlee to come around to the Service's head office for a drink. A cocktail party was arranged for 16 March and Liddell saw a very different Prime Minister from the taciturn auditor of his Intelligence reports, commenting that Attlee 'was in extremely good form, firing questions at everybody and telling stories'.[65]

In Africa, too, the government was challenged by communist subversion. By late 1949 it was clear that the Groundnuts Scheme in Tanganyika had run into severe problems. This was an ill-conceived project that never had any realistic prospect of success and, after three years of setbacks, John Strachey, the Minister of Food, was blaming the failure of the scheme on communist sabotage.[66] At a meeting in January 1950 Attlee asked Liddell if he had heard anything about trouble with the scheme's staff. Liddell replied that MI5 was waiting for details of an alleged plot involving Professor A. H. Bunting, who, Liddell said, had a history of communism. Attlee added that Bunting had been reported as saying that he intended to 'wreck this Imperialist scheme'.[67] Liddell had the impression that Strachey had convinced Attlee that this was more than an airing of petty grievances and was 'seeking a cloak to cover up deficiencies of the Groundnuts Corporation by drawing the communist red herring across it'.[68] Attlee, ever susceptible to such a red herring, at first supported Strachey's request that all Europeans involved in the Groundnuts scheme should be investigated, but Sillitoe and Liddell successfully persuaded him that this would be an appalling waste of MI5 resources.[69]

Groundnuts provided light relief from a succession of events that provoked alarm in Britain and the United States in late 1949. On 16 September, 'under a melodramatic bond of secrecy', it was announced at a Joint Intelligence Committee meeting that the Soviet Union had exploded an atomic bomb.[70] When Liddell reviewed the events of 1949 he selected that as 'the event of the year', commenting that it had 'thrown everyone's calculations out of date'. By 1957, he reckoned, 'the Russians should have sufficient atomic bombs to blot out this country entirely'.[71]

Within days of the detonation, Mao Zedong announced the establishment of the People's Republic of China. Truman and his advisers, however, continued to see the USSR as the controller of 'Red' China, assessing the Chinese as 'complete satellites', a view that they held throughout the Korean War. As Acheson patiently explained to Attlee after the Chinese intervention, 'The central enemy is not the Chinese but the Soviet Union. All the inspiration for the present action comes from there.'[72]

In the same month decrypts from VENONA indicated that there was a British spy at the heart of the American atomic programme. The FBI deduced that the spy was Klaus Fuchs, who had worked at Los Alamos and had returned to Britain to work at the Atomic Energy Research Establishment in Harwell.[73] After intensive but inconclusive surveillance MI5's Jim Skardon succeeded in extracting a confession, and Fuchs was sentenced to fourteen years imprisonment in March 1950. Edgar Hoover immediately demanded that an FBI agent be allowed to interrogate Fuchs, a demand that the Home Office initially refused. Later that month, however, on a visit from Washington, Kim Philby told Dick

White, Roger Hollis and Liddell that if the FBI were not permitted to interview Fuchs, 'Hoover was quite capable of reducing [British] liaison to a mere formality',[74] an outcome that would undermine the special relationship. Consent was accordingly given by the Home Office.

Attlee's response to the Fuchs revelations was to raise the level of vetting for sensitive work. In April 1950 GEN 183 established the Committee for Positive Vetting, chaired by John Winnifrith. Sillitoe, however, objected that MI5 would be unable to handle the volume of enquiries that positive vetting would generate.[75] In October the committee proposed a compromise between screening methods in force in Britain, which were judged inadequate, and American methods, which were described as 'repugnant to British thinking'.[76]

While Winnifrith's committee prepared its report two events combined to heighten Attlee's concerns concerning communism. A Joint Intelligence Committee study[77] concluded that it would be simple for the Soviet Union to deliver component parts of a nuclear bomb that could be assembled in Britain and remotely detonated.[78] Two weeks later the North Korean Army crossed the 38th Parallel – 'as big an Intelligence surprise as Pearl Harbor'.[79] The apocalyptic vision that Liddell had recorded on 1 January seemed suddenly less remote.

In the general election in February the government's massive 1945 majority dwindled to just five seats. Attlee chose not to announce measures for positive vetting despite American pressure. The government whose openness Attlee had championed in 1945 was in a state of ethical siege, encircled by political enemies and Atlantic allies.

Nor was the siege lifted when Guy Burgess and Donald Maclean disappeared over the weekend of 25–27 May 1951. Maclean had been identified as HOMER, a Soviet spy mentioned in VENONA transcripts, and was to have been interrogated by MI5 in June. His disappearance (correctly) suggested the existence of a 'Third Man' who had assisted the pair to leave Britain. American concerns over British security surged once more.

In this climate of mistrust the domestic political sands ran out under the Attlee government. The United States called a conference in London to discuss atomic energy and its surrounding security. Heightened criteria called for 11,000 individuals to be subjected to positive vetting, a

mammoth task.[80] Before the government could yield to these requirements – as it certainly would have felt obliged to do – a general election
was held on 25 October and the Tories were returned to power.

ENDNOTES

1   Derek Tangye, *The Way to Minack*, p. 141.
2   Masters, *The Man Who Was M: The Life of Maxwell Knight*, p. 162.
3   'When the war broke out, each officer "tore around" to rope in likely people; when they knew of none
    themselves, they asked their acquaintances.' TNA: KV4/88; Andrew, *Defend the Realm*, p. 219.
4   Sir John Masterman, *On the Chariot Wheel*, p. 212.
5   For an analysis of the effects of the Zinoviev letter, see Andrew Williams, *Labour and Russia*, p. 18.
6   Andrew, *Secret Service*, p. 342.
7   TNA: *Liddell Diary*, entry for 25 May 1940. KV4/186.
8   TNA: *Liddell Diary*, Entry for 29 May 1946, KV 4/196.
9   Deacon, *The Greatest Treason*, p. 139.
10 Andrew, *Defend the Realm*, p. 321. Cadogan's diary entry of 14 November 1945, CAC, ACAD 1/14,
    cited by Daniel W. B. Lomas (2013): 'Labour Ministers, Intelligence and domestic anti-communism,
    1945–1951', *Journal of Intelligence History*, 12:2, p. 116.
11 Conversation with Anthony Sillitoe, reported in Richard Deacon, *The Greatest Treason*, p. 142.
12 TNA: *Liddell Diary*, entry for 9 September 1947. KV4/469.
13 Deacon, *The Greatest Treason*, p. 140.
14 West, *A Matter of Trust: MI5 1945–1972*, p. 24.
15 TNA: *Liddell Diary*, Entry for 1 July 1943, KV 4/192.
16 TNA: *Liddell Diary*, Entry for 8 July 1943, KV 4/192
17 TNA: CAB 301/31. See also Andrew, *Defend the Realm*, p. 323.
18 TNA: *Liddell Diary*, Entry for 25 April 1946, KV 4/467.
19 TNA: *Liddell Diary*, entry for 26 February 1946. KV4/467.
20 Andrew, *Defend the Realm*, p. 323.
21 Tangye, *The Way to Minack*, pp. 142–143.
22 *Sunday Times*, 22 November 1953.
23 Sillitoe, *Cloak Without Dagger*, Foreword by Clement Attlee, p. v.
24 TNA: Report of Enquiry into the Security Service by Sir Findlater Stewart, PREM 8/1520.
25 TNA: *Liddell Diary* entry for 10 May 1946. KV4/467.
26 TNA: *Liddell Diary*, entry for 28 June 1946. KV4/467.
27 Tangye, *The Road to Minack*, pp. 142–143.
28 TNA: *Liddell Diary*, entry for 8 July 1946. KV4/467.
29 TNA: *Liddell Diary*, entry for 9 July 1946. KV4/467.
30 Chapman Pincher, *Their Trade is Treachery*, p. 44.
31 Bodleian: MS. Attlee, dep. 3, 31 July 1941; dep. 33, 27 February 1946; dep. 69, 1 May 1948.
32 Bodleian: MS Attlee, dep. 1, 20 January 1940.
33 TNA: PREM 8/227, CM (46) 78th Conclusions, 14 August 1946.
34 TNA: PREM 8/227, 8 September 1946.
35 See http://www.bbc.co.uk/history/ww2peopleswar/stories/01/a2053801.shtml
36 TNA: PREM 8/227, Home Office Report, 11 September 1946.
37 TNA: PREM 8/227, CM (46) 80th Conclusions, 9 September 1946.
38 TNA: *Liddell Diary*, Entry for 19 November 1946, KV 4/467.
39 Douglas Jay, Attlee Foundation Lecture, 1983.
40 TNA: *Liddell Diary*, Entry for 14 April 1948, KV 4/470.
41 TNA: HW/80/4, 5 March 1946. This comprehensive shopping list led to an unprecedented
    co-operation and a supplementary power for MI5. With the establishment of the American base at
    Menwith Hill in Yorkshire in 1954 came the ability of the Security Service to use American personnel
    to monitor British phone traffic, an activity beyond the charter of MI5. 'US spy base taps UK phones
    for MI5', *The Independent*, 22 September 1986.
42 *Hansard*, HC Deb, 16 May 1947, col. 1965.

43   TNA: GEN 183/1, 29 May 1947, CAB 130/20.
44   TNA: GEN 183/1, 21 December 1947, CAB 130/20.
45   TNA: *Liddell Diary*, Entry for 5 December 1947, KV 4/469.
46   Mayhew, *Time to Explain*, pp. 107–8.
47   David Leigh, 'Death of the Department that Never Was', *The Guardian*, 27 January 1978.
48   Mayhew, *Time to Explain*, p. 110.
49   Liddell informed Attlee that there was little to fear from Fascists at the time of the introduction of the Purge Procedure. TNA: *Liddell Diary*, Entry for 24 March 1948, KV 4/470.
50   Beckett, *Enemy Within*, p. 104.
51   TNA: *Liddell Diary*, Entry for 19 November 1946, KV 4/467.
52   TNA: *Liddell Diary*, Entry for 21 February 1949, KV 4/471.
53   TNA: *Liddell Diary*, entry for 17 November 1947. KV4/469. For an account of the incident, *Daily Telegraph*, 1 June 2006.
54   TNA: *Liddell Diary*, entry for 4 March 1948. KV4/470.
55   TNA: *Liddell Diary*, entry for 4 February 1948. KV4/470.
56   *Hansard*, HC Deb, 25 March 1948, cols. 3394–95.
57   *Hansard*, HC Deb, 25 March 1948, col. 3399.
58   TNA: *Liddell Diary*, entry for 25 March 1948. KV4/470.
59   Brook to Attlee, 7 December 1949, TNA: PREM 8/946. Cited by Lomas, *op. cit.*, p. 124.
60   Andrew, *Defend the Realm*, p. 385.
61   In a speech at Wheeling, West Virginia on 9 February 1950.
62   *Hansard*, HC Deb, 24 January 1949, cols 556–557.
63   *Hansard*, HC Deb, 24 January 1949, col. 557.
64   TNA: *Liddell Diary*, entry for 14 April 1948. KV4/470.
65   TNA: *Liddell Diary*, entry for 16 March 1949. KV4/471.
66   The Groundnuts scheme, which caused an almost total write-off of £49 million, was an attempt to cultivate 150,000 acres of land in Tanganyika (modern Tanzania) to produce a source of oil, at the time strictly rationed. In two years only 2,000 tons of nuts were harvested and the project was cancelled in January 1951. 'Groundnuts' became shorthand for government incompetence.
67   TNA: *Liddell Diary*, entry for 2 January 1950. KV4/472.
68   TNA: *Liddell Diary*, entry for 28 January 1950. KV4/472.
69   TNA: *Liddell Diary*, entry for 31 January 1950. KV4/472.
70   TNA: *Liddell Diary*, entry for 24 September 1949. KV4/471.
71   TNA: *Liddell Diary*, entry for 1 January 1950. KV 4/472.
72   *Foreign Relations of the United States (FRUS), 1950*, vol. 3, pp. 1711–14, Cited by Andrew, *For the President's Eyes Only*, p. 190.
73   TNA: *Liddell Diary*, entries for 12 and 20 September 1949. KV 4/471.
74   TNA: *Liddell Diary*, entry for 27 March 1950. KV 4/472.
75   TNA: CAB 130/20, GEN 183/5th Meeting, 5 April 1950.
76   TNA: CAB 130/20, P. V. (50) 11, 27 October 1950.
77   TNA: CAB 158/9, JIC (50) 21, 12 June 1950.
78   A fictional scenario for such an operation is vividly portrayed by Frederick Forsyth, *The Fourth Protocol*.
79   Andrews, *For the President's Eyes Only*, p. 184.
80   TNA: CAB 130/20, GEN 183/7th Meeting, 17 August 1951.

CHAPTER SEVENTEEN

LOSING MOMENTUM, 1948–1951

No government can live on crisis peak forever. It must either fall or find itself in the plain beyond. The British government has reached the plain beyond. A few months ago, this present government, the most strongly backed in British history, was so hedged about by economic pressures that utter failure and a general election seemed inevitable, unless staved off by coalition or complete dictatorship.[1]

So wrote Honor Balfour for her American audience as she surveyed the political landscape early in 1948. The government could boast of substantial achievements but it had dipped 9 per cent in the opinion polls. Even Attlee's popularity had fallen by 6 per cent.[2] Although Marshall Aid promised to relieve the sharper edges of austerity, two and a half years after the end of the war, Britain appeared no closer to reaching 'the plain beyond'.

In retrospect, the Attlee era was at its halfway point. The first thirty months had seen breathtaking changes, then nine months of reverses until, at the end of the year, the government could reasonably hope for steady improvement. The next thirty months were to be a mirror image of the preceding period. After the triumphant introduction of the National Health Service in July, a series of hammer blows struck Attlee's administration until its fall in October 1951.

'We are far from being out of our troubles', Attlee broadcast, 'but we have made a fine start and I am certain that we shall in the same spirit carry on through 1948 and achieve ultimate success.'[3] The 'same spirit' that Attlee demanded was one of self-sacrifice, a quality personified by his Chancellor of the Exchequer, Stafford Cripps. Until ill health forced his resignation in October 1950 Cripps seemed to personify asceticism and the very morality of the government. Six years younger than Attlee, he was ambitious. Gaitskell, attending a Cripps dinner to discuss policy with Bevan, Wilson, Jay and others, recorded that he felt 'that Stafford was surveying his future Cabinet'.[4]

Cripps's daily routine was legendary. Rising at 4.00 a.m., he worked for three hours, then took a light breakfast and a cold bath before working punishing hours at the Treasury.[5] As the New Year began, there was rising confidence that the 'austerity and self-flagellation that he exhorted'[6] might provide the definitive solution to Britain's problems. Somehow, despite crippling economic difficulties, the government had pushed ahead with its policy of nationalisation. With Cripps at the controls and a period of grace provided by Marshall Aid, one last bout of self-sacrifice might be enough for Attlee's government to finish the job.

During the first half of 1948 the launching of the National Health Service – and, therefore, Aneurin Bevan, Minister of Health – assumed centre stage. Bevan, a brilliant and mercurial Welshman who could 'charm the birds off the bough', was fourteen years younger than Attlee, the son of a coalminer, an autodidact and passionate champion of the poor. He took a proprietary view of the NHS and a dim view of the middle-class medical profession resolved to impede it. Elected Member of Parliament for Ebbw Vale at the age of thirty-one, he soon established himself as a brilliant debater[7] and equally soon became an object of bitter controversy within the party. Attlee respected his brilliance, his socialist credentials and popular appeal and, ever hopeful that his talents would overcome his flamboyance, for some time viewed him as his probable successor.[8]

Bevan presented to the Cabinet radical and comprehensive plans for the NHS in October and December 1945.[9] By January 1948 he had made huge progress, but reached impasse with the medical profession over the role of general practitioners within the proposed system. Fearful that doctors would be remunerated as mere employees of the NHS, unable to sell their practices, the British Medical Association fought hard to block Bevan's proposals. Morrison, aware of the kudos that would accrue to Bevan with the introduction of the Health Service, suggested to Attlee that 'in view of the difficulties that have arisen in the discussions between the Minister of Health and the BMA', the matter might be brought before Cabinet.[10] Bevan had, in fact, sent the Cabinet a memorandum, laying out his plans for overcoming the BMA's objections.[11] The paper was both analytical and polemic. Bevan assumed total responsibility for the project and, without being resentful or vengeful, demonstrated determination to succeed. In his dealings with the BMA he was able to compromise without compromising principles.

These were precisely the qualities that many members of Attlee's Cabinet lacked and it is easy to understand how, for Attlee, the NHS project became a critical yardstick of Bevan's right to lead the party. When Bevan presented his paper to Cabinet, he argued his case strongly[12] and, a week later, displayed an ability to conduct a planned and effective offensive over the whole battlefield.[13] Only Ernie Bevin among Attlee's ministers displayed the same vision. That vision was translated into a short and simple motion for the Commons, approved by Cabinet four days later.[14]

This was the way Attlee liked to do business. In an interview with *The Lancet*[15] Bevan gave forthright answers to questions; to Attlee, Bevan sent concise suggestions of how he might answer questions in the House.[16] In a matter of two weeks Bevan had overcome Morrison's challenge, gained public support, and armed his leader against Tory opposition. No wonder Attlee was impressed.

Before Bevan addressed the House on the lingering concerns of doctors about their status, he and Attlee met in Downing Street to discuss tactics. His draft statement was cleverly calculated, answering each of the BMA's objections in turn, allowing doctors to choose between a basic salary of £300 and a capitation fee. The statement ended with a ringing declaration: 'I look forward now to a future of active and friendly co-operation with the profession in putting into operation next July a great social measure, which can be made a turning point in the social history of this country and an example to the world.'[17]

In May the party held its conference in Scarborough. Attlee's position as leader was now secure, a fact noted in the press.[18] Both in the party and across the country his personal standing was immense. He added to this in June when he defused the London Dock Strike with a speech that was 'human and full of common sense'.[19] Far from projecting himself as a figure of authority, Attlee spoke of his experience in Dockland, as someone who understood the cause of the dockers but was able to measure how much their lot had improved.

A warning note was sounded in conference by Morrison. Since 1946 he had opposed the nationalisation of steel[20] and now he called on the party to 'consolidate', to put a brake on what appeared to the public a relentless drive for public ownership. Over the next months he developed that theme, driving a wedge between left and right and, more ominously, between himself and Bevan.

On the eve of the introduction of the NHS Attlee broadcast a speech, sending an advance draft to Bevan. Typically, he proposed to give credit to all who had contributed over the years to the creation of the service. Bevan, equally typically, reacted angrily, insisting that credit should go to the Labour Party alone. Why, he demanded, should the Tories receive a mention? Attlee compromised, equitably retaining a reference to Churchill.[21] This was more than courtesy; the groundwork, including the Beveridge Report of 1943, had been handled before Labour came to power. It was as characteristic of Attlee to recognise that as it was for Bevan, whom Churchill described as 'just as great a curse to this country in peace as he was a squalid nuisance in time of war', to object.

On the same day Bevan spoke in Manchester, claiming that Britain now held the 'moral leadership of the world' and undertaking to press ahead with the full programme of nationalisation. So far, so controversial, but when he referred to the Tory Party as 'lower than vermin', his hyperbole achieved three things: it gave the press a stick with which to beat the party; it issued a direct challenge to Attlee, whose tone had been deliberately conciliatory. It also scandalised the floating voter. Attlee wrote him a surprisingly moderate letter, pointing out the unfortunate timing and urging more restraint 'in your own interest'.

Meanwhile, a split in the party was developing, the dominant issue being the nationalisation of iron and steel. In the debate on the address Attlee confirmed that there would be no relaxation in the government's determination to press ahead.[22] On the day of the debate, Attlee received a letter from Ivor Thomas, MP for Wrekin, informing him that he was resigning from the Labour Party, principally over iron and steel. He added a broader criticism:

For a long time I have been uneasy over a wide range of the government's domestic policy. I have been particularly perturbed by the growing concentration of power in the hands of the state, the costliness of doctrinaire planning, and the surrender of the government to its more extreme members and supporters.[23]

Attlee replied, asking Thomas to speak to Cripps, believing that the Chancellor could explain the need to make gestures to the left. Thomas, who subsequently wrote a coruscating attack on British socialism, was not to be moved. 'Millions', he subsequently wrote, 'who voted Labour in 1945 have already said, "Thus far but no further."'[24] This had been Morrison's precise concern at Scarborough.

The nationalisation of iron and steel was thus elevated to even greater importance as a symbol of a fundamental rift in the Cabinet. Attlee spent much of the rest of the year papering over the cracks, making positive, exhortatory speeches pointing out that the dire things predicted in 1947 had not come to pass[25] and making sure to rein in Bevan. When the latter was invited to address the United Auto Workers Union in Milwaukee, Attlee instructed him to decline. Bevan accepted the decision with a poor grace.[26]

In mid-December it became known that Clement and Violet were looking for a small country house in Buckinghamshire. Their love of Chequers was common knowledge and they had, in fact, been looking sporadically for some months. Now, with the party split in the open, the press speculated that they were preparing to lose the election and buy a home near Chequers[27] and that perhaps Bevan had advised them to buy quickly as prices were at rock bottom.[28]

In late 1948 a decision was made to court the woman voter, and in his New Year's broadcast for 1949 Attlee spoke to 'The Labour Woman'. While he was cautiously optimistic for the future and celebrating achievements in 1948, the underlying note was 'it is not possible to promise an early end of austerity conditions.'[29] This theme returned to Labour's electoral strategy in February, when equal pay for women was proposed in a policy document prepared at a party conference in Shanklin.

Few events illustrate more clearly than this conference that the party had run out of steam by early 1949. Shrouded in secrecy, the weekend conference brought together the entire Labour leadership to thrash out a draft statement of policy in preparation for the election that had to take place before July 1950. A document prepared by Morrison for the party Executive in 1948 was dusted off and re-presented. The battle cry was basically the same as in 1945 – Labour looks forward and not backward to the 'dark, dreary period between the wars'. Socialisation had been broadly accepted, so a 'shopping list' of further industries was considered: ICI, sugar, water supply, shipbuilding, the meat trade, cement, industrial assurance and minerals. To inject some festive spirit into the document the plan to create communal holiday camps was introduced and these, in an atmosphere of austerity, proved to be remarkably successful. The fundamental message was broadly 'Give us five more years to tidy up what we've done'.[30]

As a call to action, the document, entitled *Labour Believes in Britain*, failed to reignite the country's imagination. Attitudes towards the implementation of Labour's programme had altered over four years. In a radio interview in July 2013 Shirley Williams recalled the sense of excitement of 1945. There was an extraordinary sense of possibility, she recalled. The Attlee government was 'full of stars and Attlee was a great cosmologist'. Above all, she said wistfully, she had been 'born into a world where dreams were possible'.[31]

That the atmosphere had changed by 1949 was made clear when Attlee spoke in Newark on 1 May. The party was on the defensive, reiterating that 'The question which will have to be answered at this election is whether the policy [we] inaugurated is to be carried on or whether the clock is to be put back.' The Labour Party, Attlee declared, was not the slave of abstract formulae but a party with a definite philosophy. It had principles to apply to the practical problems that it encountered. Boasting of the Health Service, he mentioned that 'this great social advance has aroused interest in America and that President Truman is seeking to inaugurate a comparable system in the United States.' Sixty-five years later the issue is still being fought over in Congress.

Later that month came another defection over iron and steel when Lord Milverton wrote to Addison regretting that he could not support the government.[32] Three weeks later, resisting efforts from Attlee to dissuade him, he resigned from the party. His resignation speech in the Lords, predicting that 'a great deal more than iron and steel [was] destined for this particular furnace', built up to an attack on Bevan as 'the new moral leader of the Labour Party' and of the Cabinet, whose moral stature, he charged, was not worthy of the principles it proclaimed.[33] For the first time, a prominent Labour peer charged the government with moral turpitude.

The government meanwhile was embroiled in an illegal stoppage by dockers, striking in sympathy with seamen on six Canadian ships in British ports. The stoppage soon spread from Avonmouth and Bristol to Liverpool and London. Attlee was furious that the government was on the defensive and forced to take counter-action.[34] The situation became acute when perishables aboard the ships began to deteriorate and a decision was taken to send in troops to unload the ships.[35] Lord Ammon, chairman of the National Dock Labour Board, demanded decisive action from Attlee and, as the strike in London dragged on, made public statements highly critical of the government. Once more the party seemed in disarray. The strike was settled but the antagonism of George Isaacs, Minister of Labour, and Ammon had been damaging.[36]

The dispute, which involved the T&GWU, had lasted a month before the footprint of Bevin was visible. As a former T&GWU leader, he wrote to Chuter Ede with suggestions of how the situation might be dealt with. 'I am not attempting to influence your committee', he wrote, 'but in his personal talk with me this morning the Prime Minister asked me to convey to you clearly what was in my mind.'[37]

This letter gives an interesting insight into Attlee's *modus operandi*. Bevin was his closest associate in the Cabinet, but it seems that Attlee had avoided asking him for his opinion until late in the day – indeed, when the government was on the verge of declaring a state of emergency. Bevin is careful not to tread on the Home Secretary's toes, but the implication is clear: that he had allowed the Home Secretary and the Minister of Labour to handle the matter until it became obvious, late in the day, that it had spiralled out of control. Only at this point, it seems, did he speak to Bevin. While the compartmentalisation of government policy is understandable, it is amazing that Bevin, with more trade union experience than any other Cabinet member, was not consulted earlier.

Through the summer of 1949 two issues dominated Cabinet meetings: devaluation of sterling and the date of the forthcoming election. They were intimately connected. Gaitskell argued strongly for immediate devaluation and for an election in November 1949, before the winter. If that were not desirable or practicable, he felt that it should be delayed until May or June 1950.[38] Morgan Phillips, the party Secretary, also urged Attlee to decide early on timing. On the one hand, he wrote, the continuing American recession and the economic problems affecting Britain suggested an early election. On the other hand, poll figures were improving and Labour did better in the spring or summer. Members had been told that time was needed for the Iron and Steel Bill and that, therefore, the election would not be held before 1950.[39]

Devaluation had been discussed intermittently since 1945 and with increasing urgency in the second quarter of 1949. A rapid decline in dollar reserves and speculation against the pound in anticipation of deval-uation threatened Britain's economic stability as seriously as the crisis of 1947. Opinions of experts at the Treasury differed sharply and, with Cripps initially resisting devaluation, there was no clear lead in Cabinet to provide a solution to the crisis. Attlee was ill equipped to offer leadership on economic matters, while Morrison and Bevin were undecided. For the moment, at least, it was Cripps' voice that was heeded. In July, however, Cripps left for a five-week stay in a Swiss sanatorium and Gaitskell, Jay and Wilson, all economics specialists, reached the conclusion that devalu-ation was unavoidable and won Bevan over to their view.[40] With Cabinet approval, Wilson took a message to Cripps in Zurich, giving him little option. Cripps did, however, stipulate that any announcement must wait until he and Bevin returned from an IMF meeting in Washington in September. During August the Cabinet decided to proceed; at the end of the month a decision was taken to devalue sterling from $4.03 to $2.80, a significant once-for-all step.[41] In great secrecy Cripps returned to London on 18 September, attended a Cabinet meeting, met business and union leaders, and broadcast the decision on the evening of 19 September.

Reaction was immediate and negative, although the press was not as damning as Attlee had feared.[42] His Parliamentary Private Secretary, however, warned him that there was 'a gathering belief in newspapers and elsewhere that the rise in the cost of living over the next few months [would] be very substantial, and much greater than the Chancellor implied'. As a result, he said, there was the feeling that 'the Chancellor was insufficiently candid about the internal effects of devaluation'.[43] Three weeks later Cripps circulated a report prepared by the Central Office of Information on the public reaction – one of 'bewilderment, often of disappointment and sometimes of despondency'. The government was criticised, not for devaluing but for failure to tell the facts to the public and to be frank about the effects on the cost of living. There was also the concern that businesses would profit while the 'wage-earner bore the whole brunt of a rising cost of living'.[44]

Curiously, the public tended to blame Washington for Britain's economic ills, but the government's credibility was damaged. An international economic crisis was avoided at the price of a national crisis of confidence. Attlee explained devaluation in a speech at Llandudno, but his message – that devaluation was no magic wand and that there would be price increases – failed to dispel the public's growing unease.[45]

Attlee instinctively wanted as much time as possible to pass between devaluation and the election, which had to be held before July 1950. For that reason he initially favoured an election in June 1950. Cripps, however, felt strongly that it would be unethical to produce a Budget before an election, without a renewed popular mandate.[46] February then became the more likely month, despite Morrison's objection that bad weather would reduce the Labour turnout. Weighing the two options, Attlee yielded to Cripps' ethical concern and February was chosen.

For the next three months both parties prepared for battle. During those months Britain's economic situation improved dramatically; the balance of payments and dollar reserves improved and the government was able to point to devaluation as a success, as 'plucking a kind of victory from the jaws of defeat'.[47] At the end of October Attlee broadcast an important speech, underlining the continuing need to reduce expenditure by £250 million and reduce production costs if the country was to benefit from the effects of devaluation.[48] The country had a welfare state, he said, and that obliged everyone to pull together. He spoke to the same theme in the House, indicating that the £250 million would come from school meals, transport, agriculture, from the Ministry of Food and – what might have been a controversial issue – from the National Health Service, which would charge a shilling for prescriptions.[49] Bevan had agreed to this four days before.[50]

The proposal to introduce charges for NHS services four months before an election is puzzling. Hilary Marquand drew attention to the difficulty of differentiating between those exempted and those not exempted when applying prescription charges.[51] Bevan's initial response was that the Ministry of Health could not become involved in sorting claims. It would make the charge and Ministries wishing to exempt certain classes would have to make their own arrangements.[52] The question of administering the charge was referred to Cripps,[53] who duly submitted a proposed machinery, pointing out that the £10 million that the Government originally hoped to save by this measure would, in fact, be nearer £6 million. Despite the relatively small saving, the decision to impose charges was endorsed.[54]

At this point Bevan made a U-turn. In a paper for the Cabinet he registered his 'great misgiving' at the decisions taken. It would, he argued, be 'tactically unfortunate' to introduce prescription charges with an election imminent. Moreover, the government 'should be lucky if the actual saving proved to be in the order of £5 million or so'.[55]

It beggars belief that between October and late January, during which time all parties knew that an election was scheduled for February, an explosive issue saving a relatively small amount of money was made public. Attlee and Bevan agreed to shelve it until after the election, but damage had already been done by the announcement in the House.

The election would be, Attlee predicted, 'undoubtedly the most keenly contested of all elections in the life of our party'.[56] He himself remained, Lord Calverley judged, 'Labour's match winner'. Bevan and Wilson might be more flashy but Attlee was the man who won solid votes.[57] There had been some signs of relief from austerity when the foundation stone for the LCC Concert Hall, later named 'Royal Festival Hall', was laid in October – a shrewd pre-election move – and the release of unemployment figures in January gave a boost to Labour's full-employment claims. In 1920–21 the number of unemployed had varied between 857,000 and 2,549,400. The average between 1921 and 1938 had been 1,720,000. Under Labour the figures between 1946 and 1949 had ranged from 303,600 to 468,300, an average of 361,000.[58]

These were figures that the government could be proud of. Nonetheless, the Conservative Party attacked the government as 'a bureaucracy brooding over a dispirited broken people'. Their manifesto treated the government as a promising but headstrong child that had stumbled into power and proceeded from incompetence to, frankly, being rather deceitful. It is a document larded with suggestions of dishonesty, such as:

> From the time they acquired power **they pretended** that their policy was bringing the prosperity they had promised. **They tried to make out** that before they got a majority the whole history of Great Britain, so long admired and envied throughout the world, was dark and dismal. **They spread the tale** that social welfare is something to be had from the state free, gratis and for nothing. They have put more money into circulation, but it has bought less and less. The value of every pound earned or saved or paid in pensions or social services has been cut by 3s. 8d. since they took office. It is not a £ but 16/4.
>
>   **There is no foundation for the socialist claim** to have brought us prosperity and security. Ministers themselves have declared that but for American Aid there would have been two million people unemployed.
>
>   During these bleak years Britain has lurched from crisis to crisis and from makeshift to makeshift. Whatever temporary expedients have been used to create **a false sense** of well being, none has effected a permanent cure. Devaluation is not the last crisis nor have we seen the worst of it yet.[59]

Interspersed with suggestions of dishonesty are the firm words of a tolerant parent whose patience is at an end. 'Britain's difficulties will not be resolved by some trick of organisation, nor will prosperity come as a gift from government … With a high spirit, through great endeavours, relying on our native skill, every man and woman must bend their energies to a new wave of national impulse.'

Nationalisation, naturally, drew intense fire. 'We shall bring Nationalisation to a full stop here and now', the manifesto promised. 'We shall repeal the Iron and Steel Act before it can come into force. Steel will remain under free enterprise … The nationalisation of omnibuses and tramways will be halted. Wherever possible those already nationalised will be offered to their former owners, whether private or municipal.'[60]

The Labour manifesto, by contrast, was doctrinaire, somewhat shrill, devoting much space to attacking the Conservatives for being conservative, culminating in two sentences that read more like a polemic Soviet tract than a manifesto for a British election:

> *Shall we continue along the road of ordered progress which the people deliberately chose in 1945, or shall reaction, the protectors of privilege and the apostles of scarcity economics be once more placed in the seats of power, to take us back to the bleak years of poverty and unemployment? Those years must never return.*[61]

Attlee's government comprised old men, as distant from John Kennedy's 'new generation of Americans, born in this century, tempered by war'[62] as could be imagined. Attlee had just celebrated his sixty-seventh birthday. Bevin (sixty-eight) and Cripps (sixty-two) were seriously unwell and both would be dead in two years. Morrison and Dalton were sixty-two; Bevan seemed positively youthful at fifty-two. Perversely, Churchill, 'The Happy Warrior', remained full of pep in his seventy-sixth year.

Attlee's own account of the election opens rather in the manner of a Tintin comic book. 'Accordingly, after opening the local campaign', he wrote, 'I set off from Downing Street with my wife at the wheel of our car, accompanied by our old companion of past contests, Philpott of the *Daily Herald*, and one detective.'[63]

As ever, he conducted an undemonstrative campaign.[64] The modest family Humber carried him and Violet over 1,300 miles, to meetings and rallies across the country, seven or eight a day, finishing close to midnight.[65] On election day in Walthamstow, his new constituency since Limehouse had been absorbed into Stepney, he polled 21,095 votes, a majority of 12,107 over the Conservative candidate, while the Liberal and Independent Labour candidates lost their deposits. For the Prime Minister it had been a satisfactory and successful campaign.

For the Labour Party as a whole the result suggested disappointment but not disillusion. Instead of the 11.7 per cent swing in Labour's favour that had driven the 1945 landslide, there was a 3.6 per cent swing against the government. With a massive turnout of 83.9 per cent the Labour Party won 13,226,176 votes, 46.1 per cent of the votes cast. Although the Conservatives received significantly fewer votes – 11,507,061 or 40 per cent of the popular vote – as a result of redistribution of seats, Labour finished with an overall majority of five, a slender margin that ruled out attempting any dramatic or controversial measures. It was a dispiriting result for all parties. Morrison joked that, 'The British people are wonderful. They didn't mean to chuck us out, only to give us a sharp kick in the pants. But I think they've overdone it a bit.'[66]

When the government conducted its *post mortem* several explanations were offered. Attlee felt that the most important factor had been the redistribution of seats as a result of the Representation of the People Act.[67] He had recognised the negative effect the Act would have on the Labour vote but felt that 'it was the responsible thing to do at the time'.[68] Morrison believed that the so-called 'shopping list' of industries to be nationalised, 'nationalisation for the sake of nationalisation', had been damaging – essentially the position that he himself had taken.[69] He also blamed Bevan, without naming him, for divisiveness.[70] The 'vermin' speech had undoubtedly aroused the undying hatred of the Tory voter, although its wider effect was questionable.

A balanced and probably accurate assessment of the result came from Gaitskell who admitted that he could not observe 'any great difference in the attitude of the audience from 1945'. The Labour Party, he felt, had demonstrated that they were capable of governing, but this positive factor was, in his view, offset by the 'collection of grievances' that inevitably accumulated against them. Rather to his surprise, Gaitskell was impressed by the Prime Minister's handling of the election, commenting that he 'displayed his remarkable political instinct and gifts at their very best.' He had countered Churchill with skill and made an outstanding broadcast. For a man 'normally thought of as a poor broadcaster and a man with no gift for leadership', Gaitskell found this 'rather extraordinary'.[71]

The first question to be settled was whether Labour could continue to govern without forming a coalition, and on 25 February, the Cabinet resolved to continue alone. This was constitutionally correct, but several newspapers were pessimistic as to the government's lasting more than a few weeks.[72] The King's Speech Committee recommended that the Address should contain a passage stating that, 'In view of the parliamentary situation resulting from the general election, my government do not propose to introduce legislation involving matters of acute party controversy unless such measures prove, in their view, to be immediately necessary to the maintenance of full employment and the national well-being.' There was no mention of the Iron and Steel Bill in the speech.[73]

The Labour Party had won the election but its wings were severely clipped. There was a sense of siege and recognition that the government would not be able to finish the job. The toll of ministers at the polls was, fortunately, not serious. Creech Jones failed to gain re-election, not a severe setback as Attlee had planned to replace him anyway. Sir Frank Soskice, the Solicitor-General, also lost his seat but remained in office until a safe seat in Sheffield fell vacant. Much more damaging to the government were the illnesses of Cripps and, later, of Bevin. The former he was able to help by appointing Gaitskell to support him as Minister of State for Economic Affairs.

When Attlee asked Gaitskell to make the move to the Treasury from Fuel and Power, he mentioned that it would involve a cut in salary, as a Minister of State received £3,000 rather than the £5,000 that Gaitskell had received as a minister. Gaitskell recorded that he was 'a bit taken aback' but accepted the move, despite his concern that it appeared to be a demotion. Attlee assured him that he would make it clear that it was not, and on the following day Gaitskell learned that his salary would continue at £5,000. He suspected that Attlee had deliberately misinformed him, applying a loyalty test, but he was never able to find out whether this was so or if, as Treasury officials told him, it was a genuine mistake.[74]

Within a week Attlee had formed his new Cabinet and wrote to Tom,

The distasteful business of reconstructing the Cabinet is now through. It always means relegating some friends to the back benches. Our folk are in very good heart. I find that the view is general that my broadcast had a very considerable effect as did the tour. We lost some good men particularly Soskice and Chris Mayhew.[75]

The make-up of the Cabinet had changed greatly since 1945. When Labour first came to power the acknowledged bosses were the men who had held high office in the wartime coalition: Attlee, Bevin, Morrison and Cripps. The 1945 election brought different and younger men into the House of Commons, some of whom, notably Gaitskell, Wilson, Jay, Gordon Walker, Crossman and Brown, were already marked for high office. Somewhere between these groups was Bevan, ten years younger than Attlee yet of a different generation from Gaitskell. The youngest member of the Cabinet in 1945, Bevan was now a legitimate and natural target for the younger men as a member of 'The Old Guard'.

In Gaitskell's view, Bevan and Bevin had been disappointing and had weakened their positions during the 1950 election. He records Cripps as commenting that 'Bevin and Bevan between them had lost the election'.[76] When the new Cabinet was appointed Gaitskell was horrified that Bevan was again given the Ministry of Health, an appointment that he described as 'the worst of all unquestionably'.[77] A brilliant debater, a passionate orator prone to overstep the etiquette of debate (as in the 'vermin' speech), Bevan managed to impress and alienate his colleagues in equal measure. His commitment and visceral adherence to socialism were enormous strengths. Yet he was capable of immense errors of judgement and, ultimately, was not a team player, a cardinal shortcoming in the Prime Minister's eyes.

Bevan returned to the Ministry of Health. According to Gaitskell, this was at the urging of Bevin; according to Dalton it was Morrison who suggested it. Both sources quote the same reason: that Bevan should be made to clear up the mess he had allegedly created.[78] If this is the true explanation, it illustrates Attlee at his most myopic. Bevan's authority was circumscribed by the establishment of a committee chaired by the Prime Minister to control expenditure on the Health Service, which had the effect of treating Bevan as a wayward child. In adopting the disciplinary mien of a headmaster he widened the gap between Bevan and himself, and between Bevan and the Morrison-Gaitskell faction, creating the climate that was to prove toxic a year later.

That climate was foreshadowed in April when Cripps wrote to Attlee fixing the annual NHS budget at £350 million. In the first year costs would be as high as £392 million and, therefore, the government needed to decide on possible charges to impose in case the NHS costs exceeded £350 million.[79] Three weeks later he wrote again, saying that he would step down by July at the latest. He needed a year for 'a complete rest and renewal of mental energy and vigour'. He apologised for the inconvenience caused.[80]

Attention shifted from domestic politics in June with the outbreak of the Korean War.[81] Cripps remained at the Treasury until July, when he wrote to Attlee that, instead of resigning at the beginning of August, as originally planned, he would take three months' leave and then see whether he was sufficiently recovered to return.[82] In the event, he stayed until October.

To replace him Attlee chose Gaitskell. He was the most qualified, had been groomed by Dalton, and most recently had effectively handled Cripps' job during his absence. Appointing Gaitskell, however, meant not appointing Bevan, and therein lay the significance of the appointment.

Overtaking Bevan in one bound to become the fourth man in the hierarchy, Gaitskell gained prominence and visibility that Bevan had previously enjoyed as the youthful heir apparent. Not unnaturally, that sudden elevation caused resentment and envy in various quarters, as Gaitskell himself recorded. 'Of course it is impossible not to create jealousies, but I am not too worried. I suspect that Nye is not so much jealous as humiliated at my being put over him.' Wilson, on the other hand, he described as 'inordinately jealous, though in view of his age there is really no reason for it.' Jealousy, he commented, is not always rational.[83]

Michael Foot, in something of a whitewash, attributes Bevan's objection to nobler motives. Political leaders in a democracy, Bevan believed, particularly Labour leaders, 'should *represent* something and somebody; they must speak for the major sections of the movement'.[84] The new Chancellor did not do that. Instead, he swelled the number of middle-class socialists − of whom the Prime Minister was one − who were displacing the working class as leaders of the party.

In the autumn of 1950, with Dalton and Cripps gone, Bevin seriously ill, and the Labour Party no longer, in his view, representative of its core membership, Bevan blamed Attlee for allowing the party to deviate from its philosophical base and become a bloodless entity concerned only with re-election. Bevan had proclaimed on the eve of the 1950 election, 'I am not interested in the election of another Labour government. I am interested in the election of a government that will make Britain a socialist country.'[85] Now, on the heels of the party conference in Margate, Bevan expressed to Attlee his 'consternation and astonishment at the appointment of Gaitskell'.[86] Attlee responded immediately with a dismissive note, ending with the comment, 'I do not think that your views are shared by many people'.[87]

In January a further source of contention between Bevan and Gaitskell appeared. American Republicans demanded that China be branded an aggressor by the United Nations, pressuring other countries to support the initiative. The Cabinet initially agreed that Britain should not support it, but Gaitskell warned Attlee that he would resign unless Britain supported the American position. The Cabinet decision was reversed and Britain supported a modified American proposal.

Bevan, moved two weeks before to the Ministry of Labour, was forced to recognise that he had less bargaining power than Gaitskell. This bitter truth now fashioned his tactics. A surprising interlude followed when he brilliantly argued the government's position in the Defence debate on 15 February.[88]

Three weeks later Attlee, having waited for Bevin to step down from the Foreign Office, and becoming increasingly anxious as Bevin's illness and absences were providing ammunition for the Tories in the House, told his closest political ally that it was time to move on. 'I knew he wouldn't go until I pushed him', Attlee said later. 'He knew it too.'[89] Attlee wanted to keep him in the Cabinet and appointed him Lord Privy Seal. This action, taken on Bevin's seventieth birthday, 'broke his spirit', damaging the friendship between the longstanding allies.[90]

Bevin's resignation on 9 March was a milestone. One by one, Dalton, Cripps and Bevin had left the stage. Now the talent pool to provide Bevin's replacement was curiously shallow. Neither Younger nor Hector McNeil, ministers of state under Bevin, were ready for the job, nor was there a Foreign Office equivalent of Gaitskell, who had earned his spurs as Bevin's understudy. Attlee had delayed facing the future for too long.

When he appointed Morrison to succeed Bevin he laid bare the government's dilemma. A group of ageing, possibly superannuated, men were still dividing the same offices among the same, numerically diminished, favoured few as six years before.[91] Morrison's accession set the wheels in motion for Bevan's resignation. Whether or not Bevan hoped for the job, that resignation was as certain as the outcome of a Greek tragedy. Principles would be bandied about. Power was, ultimately, the sole issue.

Between late March and late April the most divisive drama of Attlee's government was played out. Ostensibly a conflict between

Gaitskell and Bevan, it arose from the appointments to replace Cripps and Bevin. Possibly Nye Bevan believed that he should have become either Chancellor or Foreign Minister; certainly he was incensed that neither was offered to a progressive left-winger. The rupture was a row over the direction – and the future leadership – of the Labour Party. Bevan, encouraged by his wife Jennie Lee and by Wilson, believed that he must act swiftly to establish his leadership of the left of the party. All he needed was an issue.

On 20 March Gaitskell and Attlee met and agreed that the cost of the NHS should be capped at £393 million annually, that there would be a reduction of £10 million in hospital costs, and that £20 million would be raised by charges for spectacles, dentures and prescriptions. Attlee wrote the same day, emphasising that presentation of the issue was important. He foresaw that this might become the issue over which Bevan would fight.

Soon after Attlee went into St Mary's Hospital for treatment of a duodenal ulcer, Bevan, at a meeting in Bermondsey, replied to a heckler with the statement of principle, 'I will never be a member of a government which makes charges on the National Health Service for the patient.' This out-of-context declaration became philosophical bedrock; even though, a few weeks before, it was Bevan who had piloted the government's defence programme, now a clear threat to the NHS. Six days later, Gaitskell announced in Cabinet his proposal to reduce NHS expenditure for the following year by £23 million, including £10 million from charges for dentures and spectacles. Bevan objected furiously, charging that in a budget of over £4,000 million it should be possible to find £13 million for defence without abandoning the principle of a free NHS. If the Cabinet agreed to the charges he would resign.[92]

Bevan and Wilson headed immediately to see Attlee in St Mary's Hospital, confident that a compromise could be agreed. According to Wilson, Attlee promised to speak to Gaitskell and urge him to 'be more reasonable'.[93] With the possibility of an election ever-present, Attlee urged them not to split the party.

When Gaitskell arrived at the hospital later that evening, he indicated to Attlee that no compromise was possible as he was committed to announcing the Budget on the following day. If necessary, he would resign to avoid an open rupture. Attlee, pipe clenched between his teeth, muttered 'Have to go. Have to go.' Gaitskell assured him that he would have his resignation in the morning. Attlee shook his head furiously and repeated more distinctly, 'No. *He* [Bevan] will have to go.'[94]

On the following afternoon Gaitskell presented his Budget.[95] Bevan held his cards close, receiving notes from Callaghan,[96] Addison, Greenwood, Stokes, Freeman and others, urging him not to precipitate a crisis. By the time that the Parliamentary Party next met, Truman had fired MacArthur, partially defusing criticism from the left that the government was the lackey of imperialist America. Bevan stated that he would not resign, tempering his statement with a clear hint to Gaitskell that he too might moderate his position. In Cabinet Morrison pressed the point and demanded his support for the government.[97]

Two days later Bevin died, a huge blow for Attlee. Writing to Violet Bonham Carter, he captured Bevin's massive prominence, describing him as 'the shadow of a great rock in a weary land'.[98] By the following week Attlee recovered enough to write to Bevan. Ever the master of compromise, he believed that the split could be repaired and wrote on 18 April,

> *My dear Nye,*
>
> *I gather all went off well at the party meeting and I am grateful to you for the line you took.*
>
> *The death of Ernie has rather overshadowed these differences, and I hope that everyone will forget them.*
>
> *I think that it is particularly essential that we should present a united front to the enemy. The next few weeks will be very tricky with the USA going haywire over MacArthur.[99] Hope to be back at work by the end of next week.*
>
> *All the best, Yours ever, Clem*[100]

By 19 April it was clear that the gulf between Bevan and Gaitskell would not be bridged when Gaitskell rejected the compromise solution of telling the public that the charges were temporary.[101] A deputation of Morrison, Ede, Gaitskell and Chief Whip Whiteley visited Attlee in hospital, after which Attlee sent a brusque ultimatum to Bevan. The decision had been taken that Cabinet ministers must toe the line, as Attlee made clear:

Cabinet ministers must accept collective responsibility for government measures.
Decisions of the Cabinet taken after full consideration must be supported by all.

I must, therefore, ask you to let me know how you stand in this matter. I have
discussed the issues with you very fully.

I shall be glad to know today that you are prepared to carry out loyally the deci-
sions of the government.[102]

Over the weekend of 20–22 April, Bevan corralled Wilson and Freeman
to his cause. On Saturday afternoon he wrote to Attlee a damning indictment of the Budget, 'wrongly conceived', 'based upon a scale of military
expenditure ... which is physically unattainable', 'wrong because it is the
beginning of the destruction of those social services in which Labour
has taken a special pride and which were giving Britain the moral leadership of the world.' He continued, 'it would be dishonourable of me
to allow my name to be associated in the carrying out of policies which
are repugnant to my conscience and contrary to my expressed opinion.'

Noting that Bevan had 'extended the area of disagreement with ...
colleagues a long way beyond the specific matter to which as I understood you had taken objection', Attlee accepted Bevan's resignation and,
over the next two days, those of Wilson and Freeman. In the six months
since Cripps's resignation the voice of the left had been muted.[103]

Attlee later speculated that, had he not been in hospital, he might
have prevented Bevan's resignation. Had Morrison and Gaitskell not
adopted entrenched positions, Attlee argued, a compromise could have
been reached.[104] This is unlikely – or, if it could have been achieved,
it would have been at the cost of Gaitskell's resignation. However the
matter was dressed up, it was an issue whose resolution would affect the
evolution of the Labour Party. Both Bevan and Gaitskell were acutely
aware of that; it was too important to allow a compromise, however
attractively supposed concessions were packaged.

The second issue concerns Attlee himself. Ernest Bevin's accusation
that he 'never had a constructive idea' is not as insulting as it seems *prima
facie*. His strength lay in channelling the ideas of others, fashioning them
into acceptable and workable initiatives. Without the practical trade
union negotiating experience of Bevin and the rigid but creative influence of Cripps, Attlee, now flanked by Morrison and Gaitskell, looked

less like the pioneer of 1945 than the middle-class leader of a middle-of-the-road team. Eden saw the government's weakness as a result of sheer exhaustion. Most had served during the war years and that had taken a toll on their health, he noted. More importantly, perhaps, their message too was tired. After extensive nationalisation, the public 'was sure that it had had enough and suspected that it had had a surfeit'.[105]

The slowing down of the leadership was further emphasised by less than adept handling of foreign affairs. Morrison had shied away from taking over from Bevin, as the Foreign Office would be unlikely to improve his position as Attlee's putative successor. He was correct: in his short tenure two crises greatly diminished not only Morrison's but also Attlee's standing, undoubtedly contributing to public doubts as to Labour's ability to govern. Each crisis was rooted in Britain's declining power and required a modern, nuanced approach, but in each case Morrison's diplomatic imagination was found wanting.

In Iran his response to the nationalisation of the Anglo-Iranian Oil Company was gunboat diplomacy in which Morrison was 'foolish to rattle a sabre one knows one cannot use'.[106] Acheson saw Morrison's response as 'Russian roulette' and warned Franks that a serious cleavage was opening up between London and Washington.[107] Attlee stepped in while Morrison was in Washington, overruled his Foreign Secretary over the use of troops, adamant that the affair be referred to the United Nations.

By that time it was known that an election would be held, as Attlee had announced on the radio (a technological first) the date of 25 October. His reasons were noble but not shrewdly calculated: the King was to take a six-month tour of Australia and New Zealand and it would be irresponsible not to have in place a government with more authority before he departed. When it emerged that, for reasons of health, the King would be unable to undertake the tour, Attlee resisted the temptation to postpone the election until 1952 when the economy should have improved.[108]

The King's advisers, presumably believing that the Tories would win the election, were concerned that His Majesty should cover himself against any allegation that he had intervened on their behalf by influencing Attlee's timing. Accordingly 'Tommy' Lascelles, the King's

Private Secretary, wrote to Attlee to ensure that 'there may be no misinterpretation of recent events by historians in the future'. He wanted it to be recorded 'in our secret archives' that, when he urged an election before departing on his tour the King had no idea that he might have to cancel the trip. Even then, Lascelles wrote, on the eve of his serious operation, he had not abandoned his plans.[109] It is ironic that Attlee, a socialist Prime Minister with a deep belief in the value of the monarchy, had acted out of respect for George VI and called an election at a highly unpropitious time.

Less than three weeks before the election, the Egyptian Prime Minister revoked the 1936 treaty with Britain and the agreement over Sudan. This *démarche*, the first thrust in a campaign to drive Britain from Egypt, greatly alarmed London and Washington but met with less than firm resistance from Morrison. Labour's foreign policy was no longer an election asset. The word 'foreign' does not appear in the 1951 manifesto; 'abroad' appears but twice in the final paragraph.

The election of 1951 was vitally important, as the Conservative manifesto made clear in its opening sentences:

> *We are confronted with a critical election which may well be the turning point in the fortunes and even the life of Britain. We cannot go on with this evenly balanced party strife and hold our own in the world, or even earn our living. The prime need is for a stable government with several years before it, during which time national interests must be faithfully held far above party feuds or tactics.*

Yet neither party produced a manifesto that stirred the blood. The Labour Party, reasonably, ran on its record of full employment; the Tories claimed that the government had destroyed the national unity of 1945 in an 'attempt to impose a doctrinaire socialism upon an island which has grown great and famous by free enterprise'.[110] Repetitive formulaic claims were bandied to and fro. The Labour Party had slipped to an approval rating of under 40 per cent;[111] with few Liberal candidates standing, the outcome, as Attlee wrote to Tom, was 'anyone's guess, depending largely on which way the Liberal cat jumps'.[112]

The Liberal cat jumped decisively to the right. Although the Labour Party increased its vote, finishing with nearly 49 per cent of the popular vote to the Tories' 48 per cent, there was an overall Conservative majority of seventeen. Attlee was out of office for the first time in eleven years, but he emerged from the election with undiminished prestige in the public eye. As he approached his sixty-ninth birthday he was awarded the Order of Merit and he set about marshalling his forces for a period of opposition.

It turned out to be a longer period than he could have imagined.

ENDNOTES

1   *TIME*, 9 April 1948.
2   Figures cited by Balfour in her article for *TIME*.
3   Bodleian: MS Attlee, dep. 66, CRA, New Year's broadcast, 3 January 1948.
4   Williams (ed.) *The Diary of Hugh Gaitskell, 1945–1956*, Entry for 23 April 1948.
5   Morgan, *Labour in Power 1945–1951*, p. 363.
6   Ibid.
7   'Rab' Butler described him as 'the greatest parliamentary orator since Charles James Fox'.
8   See Francis Beckett, 'Clem Attlee's Secret Lady Friend', *New Statesman*, 28 February 2000 and Patricia Beck's comments that 'He terribly wanted Bevan to succeed him as leader. He was very disappointed about that.' Gaitskell recorded that Attlee had lamented to him that, apart from Bevan, there was 'no one else' to succeed him. That resolved Gaitskell to keep Bevan down. (*The Diary of Hugh Gaitskell 1945–1956*, 10 August 1951). See also *The Backbench Diaries of Richard Crossman*, Entry for 8 March 1955, pp. 396–397 and p. 406.
9   TNA: CAB 129/5, CP (45) 205, 5 October 1945 and CAB/129/5, CP (45) 339.
10   TNA: PREM 8/844, Morrison to CRA, 15 January 1948.
11   TNA: PREM 8/844, CP (48) 23.
12   TNA: PREM 8/844, CM (48) 6th Conclusions, 22 January 1948.
13   TNA: PREM 8/844, CM (48) 8th Conclusions, 29 January 1948.
14   TNA: PREM 8/844, CM (48) 9th Conclusions, 2 February 1948.
15   *The Lancet*, 27 January 1948.
16   In preparation for the debate on 9 February. In the event, Attlee did not speak.
17   TNA: PREM 8/884, 6 April 1948. *Hansard*, 7 April 1948, cols. 165–166.
18   For example, *News of the World* and *Daily Express*, both of 23 May 1948. Bodleian: MS Attlee, dep. 70.
19   A description by David Graham, a party worker who heard him speak. The thrust of the speech was collective responsibility. Dockworkers who refused to unload cargoes were ignoring collective obligations and depriving people of their rations. Broadcast, 28 June 1948. Bodleian: MS. Attlee, dep. 71.
20   TNA: CAB 128/5, Cabinet Conclusions, 4 April 1946.
21   Bodleian: MS Attlee, dep. 71 and dep. 72, 4 July 1948.
22   *Hansard*, HC Deb, 26 October 1948, cols. 31–32.
23   Bodleian: MS Attlee, dep. 74.
24   Thomas, *The Socialist Tragedy*, p. 41.
25   For example, at the Lord Mayor's Banquet and on 15 December at an American press luncheon. Bodleian: MS Attlee, dep. 76.
26   Bodleian: MS Attlee, dep. 76.
27   *Daily Telegraph*, 15 December 1948.
28   *Manchester Guardian*, 15 December 1948.
29   Bodleian: MS Attlee, dep. 77.
30   Bodleian: MS Attlee, dep. 79.
31   Interview with Baroness Williams of Crosby, BBC Radio Four, 11 July 2013. She was fifteen years old when Labour won the 1945 election.
32   Bodleian: MS Attlee, dep. 83.
33   *Hansard*, HC Deb, 23 June 1949, cols. 156–158.
34   TNA: PREM 8/1081, CM (49) 38th Conclusion, 26 May 1949.
35   TNA: PREM 8/1081, GEN 291/2nd Meeting, 10 June 1949.

36   Immediately the strike was settled, Attlee dismissed Ammon, who had committed the cardinal sin of not being a team player. Attlee reminded him that, in addition to chairing the National Dock Labour Board, he was also a member of the government and that, therefore, to his great regret, he must ask for his resignation from the office of Captain of the Gentlemen at Arms (government Chief Whip in the Lords). 'I need not tell you how painful it is for me to have to take this action in the case of an old friend and loyal colleague. Bodleian: MS Attlee, dep. 86, 21 July 1949.

37   TNA: PREM 8/1081, Bevin to Ede, 11 July 1949.

38   Bodleian: MS Attlee, dep. 87, Gaitskell to CRA, 19 August 1949.

39   Bodleian: MS Attlee, dep. 86, Phillips to CRA, 19 July 1949.

40   *The Diary of Hugh Gaitskell*, Entry for 3 August 1949.

41   TNA: CAB 128/16, Cabinet Conclusions, 29 August 1949.

42   TNA: PREM 8/973, CRA to Cripps, 21 September 1949.

43   Bodleian: MS Attlee, dep. 88, Pumfrey to CRA, 22 September 1949.

44   TNA: PREM 8/973, E. P. C. (49) 114, 15 October 1949.

45   Bodleian, MS Attlee, dep. 88, 22 September 1949.

46   TNA: PREM 8/1027, Cripps to CRA, 16 July 1949.

47   Morgan, *Labour in Power 1945–1951*, p. 386. There is an analysis of devaluation in the context of economic recovery at pp. 386–8.

48   Bodleian: MS Attlee, dep. 90, 24 October 1949.

49   *Hansard*, HC Deb, 24 October 1949, cols. 1016–23.

50   Bodleian: MS Attlee, dep. 91, 20 October 1949.

51   TNA: PREM 8/1239, LP (49) 76, 25 October 1949.

52   TNA: PREM 8/1239, LP (49) 77, 1 November 1949.

53   TNA: PREM 8/1239, LP (49) 19th Meeting, 4 November 1949.

54   TNA: PREM 8/1239, LP (50) 1st Meeting, 20 January 1950.

55   TNA: PREM 8/1239, CP (50) 14, 26 January 1950.

56   Bodleian: MS Attlee, dep. 92, 15 November 1949.

57   Bodleian: MS Attlee, dep. 89, 11 October 1949.

58   Bodleian: MS Attlee, dep. 94, January 1950.

59   *This is the Road*, Conservative and Unionist Party's 1950 manifesto, paras 6–9.

60   *This is the Road*, Conservative and Unionist Party's 1950 manifesto, paras 35–37.

61   *Let Us Win Through Together*, A Declaration of Labour Policy for the Consideration of the Nation, party manifesto 1950, p. 9.

62   John F. Kennedy, 'Inaugural Address', 20 January 1961.

63   *As It Happened*, p. 274.

64   'An Appeal to the Heart: Mr Attlee's Tour', *Manchester Guardian*, 15 February 1950.

65   Bodleian: MS Attlee, dep. 94. The itinerary proposed on 13 January 1950 illustrates a typical day.

66   *News of the World*, 7 March 1965, cited by Donoughue and Jones, *Herbert Morrison, Portrait of a Politician*, pp. 453–454.

67   *As It Happened*, p. 272.

68   Harris, *Attlee*, p. 446.

69   Donoughue and Jones, *Herbert Morrison*, p. 456.

70   *Daily Telegraph*, 28 February 1950.

71   *The Diary of Hugh Gaitskell, 1945–1956*, Entry for 21 March 1950, p. 166.

72   'How Can Government be Carried On?', *Manchester Guardian*, 25 February 1950.

73   Bodleian: MS Attlee, dep. 98, 28 February 1950.

74   *The Diary of Hugh Gaitskell, 1945–1956*, Entry for 21 March 1950, p. 173.

75   Letter to Tom Attlee, 2 March 1950. Mayhew was elected to the safe seat of Woolwich East after Bevin died on 14 April 1951.

76   *The Diary of Hugh Gaitskell, 1945–1956*, Entry for 21 March 1950, p. 167.

77   *The Diary of Hugh Gaitskell, 1945–1956*, Entry for 21 March 1950, p. 174.

78   *The Diary of Hugh Gaitskell, 1945–1956*, Entry for 21 March 1950, p. 174 and note.

79   Bodleian: MS Attlee, dep. 100, Cripps to CRA, 2 April 1950.

80   Bodleian: MS Attlee, dep. 100, Cripps to CRA, 26 April 1950.

81   See Chapter 15 for an account of the war and its effects on Anglo-American relations and the defence budget.

82   Bodleian: MS Attlee, dep. 103, Cripps to CRA, 11 July 1950.

83   *The Diary of Hugh Gaitskell, 1945–1956*, Entry for 3 November 1950, p. 216.

84   Michael Foot, *Aneurin Bevan*, vol. 2, *1945–1960*, pp. 296–297.

85   Hunter, *op. cit.* p. 22.

86   Foot, *op. cit.* p. 297.

87   Attlee to Bevan, 21 October 1950, cited by Foot, *op. cit.* pp. 297–298.
88   *Hansard,* HC Deb, 15 February 1951, cols 729–740.
89   Conversation with Kenneth Harris, *Attlee,* pp. 471–472. 90 Bullock, *Ernest Bevin, Foreign Secretary*, p. 833.
91   When Bevin resigned Dalton told Attlee that he (Dalton) should not be considered for the post as that time had been and gone. Of Morrison's at the FO. Dalton wrote, 'Morrison's appointment was most unfortunate. He had great talent in some other directions, but he had no aptitude for managing foreign affairs. Nor did I ever think that he really understood them … Someone who worked with both Bevin and Morrison said: "Ernie can't pronounce the names either. But he does know where the places are."' (Dalton, *High Tide and After*, pp. 360–361)
92   TNA: PREM 8/1480, CM (51) 25th Conclusions, 9 April 1951.
93   Foot, *op. cit.* p. 321.
94   *The Diary of Hugh Gaitskell, 1945–1956*, Entry for 30 April 1951, p. 246 reports Attlee as saying '*they* [Bevan and Wilson] will have to go' while Foot *op. cit.* p. 321 reports Attlee's words as '*He'll* have to go.'
95   *Hansard*, HC Deb, 10 April 1951, cols. 826–868.
96   Jim Callaghan was particularly assiduous in urging circumspection. He wrote a second note on 10 April urging solidarity, together with Robens, Michael Stewart, Arthur Blenkinsop and Fred Lee.
97   TNA: PREM 8/1480, CM (51) 27th Conclusions, 12 April 1951.
98   Bodleian: MS. Bonham Carter, dep. 156, folio 89, 24 April 1951.
99   Truman had dismissed MacArthur on 10 April and provoked a firestorm among Republicans in Congress.
100 Foot, *op. cit.* p. 327, Harris, *Attlee*, p. 476.
101 TNA: PREM 8/1480, CM (51) 29th Conclusions, 19 April 1951.
102 Harris, *Attlee*, p. 477. 20 April 1951.
103 Bodleian: MS Attlee, dep. 119, 22–23 April 1951.
104 Based on a conversation between Attlee and Kenneth Harris, *Attlee*, p. 479.
105 Eden, *Full Circle*, p. 8.
106 *The Observer,* 7 October 1951.
107 Acheson, *Present at the Creation*, pp. 506–509.
108 It did, in fact, improve and the public-relations gains were garnered by the Conservatives.
109 Bodleian: MS Attlee, dep. 125, Lascelles to CRA, 21 September 1951.
110 Conservative Party general election manifesto, para. 5.
111 Attlee, by contrast, had retained an approval of 57 per cent in polls.
112 Letter to Tom Attlee, 21 October 1951.

CHAPTER EIGHTEEN

PASSING THE TORCH, 1951–1955

The 'War of Attlee's Succession'[1] began as soon as the election was over and lasted until December 1955. It was a troublesome period for the party and, for Attlee, profoundly distressing. At the time – and consistently thereafter – he was criticised for lack of leadership, for allowing polarisation to divide the party and to destroy its chances of returning to office. That judgement is not entirely fair.

Attlee could have retired with honour after the 1951 election. He was not a man who would cling to office with no clear purpose.[2] The traditional explanation is that he was motivated by a desire to block Morrison's accession, but, while that certainly formed part of his reasoning, it is an inadequate explanation. It was not in character for him to allow possibly terminal stasis for personal motives; there must have been a plan. If we work within the facts – first that he did not retire in October 1951, second that he did retire in December 1955 – we must conclude that within those termini certain events persuaded him that he could step down. Things were in place by December 1955.

What was it that he wanted in place? That Morrison should become superannuated? That Bevan should be marginalised? That Gaitskell should have broad support? That there should be an adequate semblance of party unity? Whatever the relative proportion of those elements, the absence of the right mix drove him to stay on as leader for an election that he knew Labour would not win, to dismiss as irrelevant a long history of working with Morrison, and to abandon his long-held hope that Bevan could succeed him. For four years he was not supine, but patient. He refused to advance until the terrain was favourable.

When Hugh Dalton looked back at the election of 1950 he saw it as a watershed. On the far side lay the triumphs of the post-war government. 'The five shining years of majority Labour rule were finished now', he wrote. 'At the election in February our high tide had ebbed quickly, quicker than we knew. There were signals flickering already on the political horizon, but we did not see them. And there was a political time bomb deep in the rapidly changing social pattern of British society.' The effects of that were yet to be felt, but 'in the '50s the Labour Party was to suffer, first defeat, then deadlock, then worse defeat, then the beginnings of a perhaps fatal illness.'[3]

For Attlee the release from responsibility of government after eleven years was a blessed novelty, as he wrote to Tom 'it seemed odd to look forward to a whole day with nothing particular to do'.[4]

Younger members were less philosophical. Crossman recorded that 'there were the very first quiet signs of impatience with the determination of the old gang to keep all control in their hands [and] clear signs that the old gang are determined to do so.'[5] Attlee came under criticism from both left and right. Gaitskell had clearly taken Bevan on over NHS charges and the party was split between Bevanites and the right wing, who, believing that Bevan had lost the election for Labour, united in a desire to see him humbled.

Denis Healey applauded Bevan's 'proletarian virility' that had 'hypnotised many middle-class intellectuals' but commented that the trade unions saw merely 'the familiar figure of the self-serving agitator'.[6] He believed that Bevan had destroyed his chance of winning the leadership. The division between right and left was 'tribal'.[7] The right had no candidate with Bevan's charisma and the only viable candidate in 1951 was Morrison. The argument, therefore, became about Bevanism, a split that Healey describes as 'a theological disputation'.[8] Yet it was Bevanites more than Bevan who incurred the greatest odium.

Gaitskell believed that Morrison's stock had fallen greatly, possibly fatally, since he became Foreign Secretary. It was a period of transition with younger Members closing the gap between themselves and the older leaders. Griffiths, Gaitskell believed, was the obvious successor, a view shared by Dalton, who discussed it with Crossman.[9] The issue that concerned Gaitskell was whether Griffiths was strong enough to overcome Bevan. 'Anyway', he added, 'this is all hopelessly premature.'[10]

Aside from the disingenuousness of Gaitskell's last sentence, the comment is a sad indictment of the leadership. Of the talent that took command in 1945 the survivors were growing stale. Bevan appealed to Crossman, to the public, to Attlee himself, as a broad thinker. 'Nye may sometimes be pretentious and superficial', Crossman recorded, 'but it's a relief to talk to a politician who really gets excited by ideas.'[11] He described Attlee as 'a prissy little schoolmaster'.[12]

Very quickly the dispute boiled down to Bevan. The left had a 'hypnotising' candidate; the right offered more of the same in the shape of Morrison. To Healey the 'Great Debate in British socialism ... consisted in one side talking nonsense and the other side keeping mum.'[13]

George Brown felt that Bevan could very well have become the leader, were it not for his friends around him.[14] The issue, however, was that those 'friends' were heady wine to the party at large, if not to the PLP. At the 1951 party conference four of the top six elected to the NEC were Bevanites – Bevan, Castle and Driberg taking the first three slots and Mikardo coming sixth. 'A band of cheeky, irreverent outlaws merrily challenged a humourless party establishment'.[15]

Attlee was determined to lead the party in Opposition as well as in government. As aware as any of his critics of his shortcomings, he strove to keep in touch with changing shifts of opinion and somehow contrived to stay in the centre of the party, whichever direction it took.[16]

A brief truce was called when George VI died on 6 February 1952. Attlee was devastated and for once spoke at greater length than Churchill. He had become close to the King – or as close as a commoner comes to royalty – as he expressed to Tom:

> The last ten days have been very busy with all the various events following the
> King's death ... It was curious that I should speak on the resolutions in the House
> just as I had done with George 5th ... I was very much attached to the King and
> knew him very well, seeing him week after week.[17]

Gaitskell believed that indecision and faction over the defence debate in March damaged the party. In spite of a three-line whip, Bevanites and other rebels, a total of fifty-seven Members, had abstained on an amendment, causing violent rage against the 'Fifty-Seven Varieties'. Instead of expelling the rebels, 20 per cent of the Parliamentary Party, Attlee attempted to expel only hard-core Bevanites, agreeing with Kenneth Younger that this was a deliberate move to provoke a split.[18] 'They're not all bad', said Whiteley, the Chief Whip. 'In fact the vast majority are perfectly good chaps ... But there's five or six, like Bevan, who are out to wreck the party and, unless we deal with them now, the party's done for.'[19]

To Attlee and his contemporaries the greatest sin was MacDonaldism. Ceaseless vigilance was required to keep the front bench on the straight and narrow. A resolution to withdraw the whip from Bevan was carried at a PLP meeting but, rather than expel him, the NEC voted in favour of Attlee's proposal that Bevan give assurances regarding future conduct and remain in the party.

Attlee's hope was that he could separate Bevan from his supporters for, as Crossman and Wilson recognised, the 'Group' would not be taken seriously without Bevan.[20] Wilson cautiously threw his lot in with the Bevanites. Having resigned alongside Bevan in 1951, he appreciated the need to show solidarity. Although he brought some reality, the Bevanites resented him, questioning his socialist commitment and believing that he was using them as a stepping stone.[21]

German rearmament provided Bevanites with a solid issue over which to challenge the leadership; they consolidated their position, becoming a structured entity. Morrison reproved Crossman, warning him that 'we shan't be able to tolerate much longer the sort of organised opposition you are running. It simply won't do.'[22] To refer to Bevan and his supporters as 'a party within a party' was hyperbole; the organisation amounted to no more than Ian Mikardo's secretary, a typewriter, and a self-important coding system that classified quite ordinary documents 'Confidential' or 'Secret'.[23]

The party conference at Morecambe in September was to be the battleground. If the Bevanites could establish one of their number – Wilson or Crossman – on the NEC, that would add greatly to their credibility. In the event, they did more than that, capturing six of the seven top places in the voting. To add piquancy to the result, Morrison and Dalton lost their seats. Wilson and Crossman joined Bevan, Mikardo, Driberg and Castle. Jim Griffiths was the only representative of the old

guard elected to the Council. For Morrison this was crushing evidence
of his decline; for the leadership it was a clear signal that to the party at
large the old guard was out of touch. The point will not have been lost
on Attlee, but his possible solutions were circumscribed.

The Morecambe conference embodied the party's tendency to doctrinal self-immolation that Attlee had struggled since 1935 to eliminate.
Michael Foot described Morecambe as 'rowdy, convulsive, vulgar, sple-
netic',[24] while for Douglas Jay it was simply 'one of the most unpleasant
experiences I ever suffered in the Labour Party'.[25]

Throughout the conference Attlee kept his head below the battle-
ments. Opening the debate on domestic affairs, he made, in Crossman's
opinion, 'what must have been the flattest speech ever delivered by a
leader.[26] After reading the Obituary Notice, which included Cripps
and George Tomlinson, the chairman asked Attlee if he had anything
to add. To Crossman's astonishment he doodled and shook his head.
To say nothing at that point, Crossman believed, was reprehensible. 'A
warm speech about them both could have been used to pull the conference together.'[27] To the electorate Attlee remained the party's most
valuable asset and the battle raged, not to remove him but to position
his successor.

When Morrison was defeated in the NEC election, 'not by word or
gesture, in public or in private, did Attlee express the smallest regret'.
When Arthur Deakin upbraided the Bevanites for splitting the party, he
'looked at [Attlee] and … almost said … it should not be my job to raise
this question. It should be the responsibility of the leader of the party to
challenge the antics of these people'.[28]

The issue continued to be 'these people' as much as Bevan himself;
he too was attacked at Morecambe. Healey criticised his 'knee-jerk
anti-Americanism' and detected a swing against Bevan.[29] The TUC,
solidly behind Morrison, believed that Bevan could be separated from
his group and suggested an approach to him to discuss removing Attlee
and replacing him with Morrison as leader and Bevan as his deputy.[30]

Morecambe was a rallying call for the Bevanites. Attlee, silent at
the conference, left the counter-attack to Gaitskell. At Stalybridge on
5 October, the latter made a provocative speech described by the
Manchester Guardian as 'a call to battle'. He attacked the Bevanites, whom

he characterised as 'frustrated journalists', describing the conference as 'mob rule'.[31] He upbraided them for releasing 'a stream of grossly misleading propaganda with poisonous innuendoes and malicious attacks on Attlee, Morrison and the rest of the leadership'. The defeat of Morrison, he said, was 'not only an act of gross political ingratitude but a piece of blind stupidity'. It was time to restore the authority of the 'solid, sound, sensible majority of the movement'.[32]

Until Stalybridge the alignment of forces was unclear. Bevan was the symbol of change, opposed by the forces of reaction – old men who had ruled the party since 1935. Had Attlee spoken out against the Bevanites at Morecambe he would have emphasised that generational gap. Instead, Gaitskell, eight years younger than Bevan, took up the cudgel. Whatever the damage to Attlee's status as leader, a champion of orthodoxy had emerged. No longer was the dispute a spat between Bevan and Attlee; a leadership struggle was now in the open. Deakin, impressed by Gaitskell's bluntness after Attlee's restraint at Morecambe, believed that he had identified the next party leader.[33]

When Gaitskell looked back at that period of 1952 he listed the contenders for the Opposition front bench. Discounting Bevan, he saw Jay, Soskice, Robens and Brown as the coming men.[34] Perhaps, as he had once observed of Cripps, he was forming his own Cabinet. He felt that his Stalybridge speech had impressed Morrison, but commented that Attlee was 'as inscrutable as ever'. Interestingly, he distinguished between Attlee in Opposition and Attlee in government, noting that he was 'concerned with party unity' and perhaps 'not as honest as he should be in Opposition'.

Party unity continued to be a recurring motif for both Attlee and Morrison. Both had lived through the MacDonald era – ancient history for Bevan and Gaitskell – and both openly attacked the Bevanites, censuring those who operated a 'party within a party'. Bevan was sufficiently encouraged by the outcome of the conference to say that he no longer needed the group – an astute exploitation of necessity.[35]

At an October PLP meeting Morrison underlined Attlee's position that only official groups should discuss party policy to avoid any repetition of the ILP schism of 1931. 'Chuck it, Nye,' he urged 'and when we get away from here let's think very seriously about the situation and how to right it.'[36]

But under the *bonhomie* and the chaff lay serious division. In October Attlee was re-elected unopposed as leader. Bevan challenged Morrison for the deputy leadership and won 82 votes against Morrison's 194, sending a message that he was far from marginalised. Dalton noted in his diary that 'the hatreds in this Labour Party are … so harmful that one would almost prefer not to be here.'[37] Crossman commented sourly that the adhesive uniting the party was not socialism but Tory-bashing.[38]

Remarkably, despite ever-widening divisions, 1953 was a relatively peaceful year. Bevan returned to the front bench; his group no longer threatened ideological schism. The conference at Margate saw Morrison back on the NEC when a TUC-sponsored amendment gave the deputy leader a seat *ex officio*. Nonetheless, Morrison confirmed Deakin's conviction that he had feet of clay when he backed out of running for Treasurer of the party. 'Morrison is finished', said Harry Douglass of the Steelworkers' Union. 'When trade union allies choose an ally to go into battle, they don't expect him to pull out at ten to twelve. We'll never trust him again.'[39] 'Jesus Christ!' added Deakin, 'that's the bloody last time.'[40] In October Bevan again challenged Morrison for the deputy leadership and was again defeated. Much the same result, but in 1953 nineteen more members abstained, finding themselves unable to vote for either of them. As the year came to an end Crossman reflected that 'there has never been a government which by its incompetence has given an Opposition so many opportunities and that there has never been an Opposition which by its incompetence and division has muffed so many opportunities.'[41]

Still Attlee remained inscrutable, dubbed by Morrison's biographers as 'disastrously vacillating'.[42] In fact, rather than vacillate, he had made solid progress. In separating Bevan from his group he gave him the opportunity to show the 'steadiness under fire' that he sought in his successor. Gaitskell had demonstrated that quality at Stalybridge but, believing that the party should be led from left of centre, Attlee still clung to the notion that a reformed Bevan might, in time, fit his specifications. Meanwhile, he kept his counsel.

The truce survived the first week of 1954 until Dulles, the American Secretary of State, unilaterally declared a *jihad* against communism. On 12 January he announced the American intention 'to depend primarily upon a great capacity to retaliate instantly, by means and at places of our choosing'.[43] Thus was born the doctrine of 'massive retaliation', designed in the evangelist halls of the Republican Party and scarcely tailored to meet Bevanite approval.

Early in February, at a conference in Berlin, Soviet and Western delegates failed to agree on the future of Germany. Bevan, writing in *Tribune*, rhetorically demanded why the Soviet Union should cave in and allow 'the creation of the twelve German military divisions upon which Dulles and Eden have set their hearts'. In a speech in the East End he challenged party policy and declared, 'If a third world war breaks out and our cities are laid in ruins and someone asks me why I did nothing to stop it, I cannot say: "Because it was against Standing Orders".'[44]

With exquisite timing in the following month a story broke of an American H-bomb test in the Pacific. The *Daily Herald* published a front-page story, 'Call Off That Bomb!';[45] this was followed up by articles in the *Manchester Guardian*. Quite suddenly it was a national issue. Attlee spoke at the Parliamentary Committee on 31 March and on the following day made what Crossman called 'the best speech of his life', an impassioned attack on atomic weapons and the need for high-level talks.[46]

Opening a debate on the issue on 5 April, Attlee spoke with studied calm, moving a Motion 'in no party spirit'. There was a need for a 'calm and realistic appreciation of the position of the world'. Civilisation was in grave danger. Not only was the hydrogen bomb greatly more destructive than its predecessor, it could be made greatly more so. Urgent action was necessary.[47]

Responding, Churchill attacked Attlee for abandoning the Quebec agreement. It was an unreasonable, inaccurate harangue that did no damage. Attlee benefited from the exchange, clearly putting country before party.

One week later, when Eden reported to the House on meetings held in London with Dulles on the subject of collective security in south-east Asia, Attlee appeared to 'feed' him questions. Bevan, seeing the exchange as a charade reflecting a cosy arrangement between two friends, attacked Eden for proposing a 'a NATO in south-east Asia for the purpose of imposing European colonial rule'. It was a brief exchange, but it highlighted differences on the Opposition front bench.[48]

At a PLP meeting the next day Bevan announced his intention to resign from the shadow Cabinet. Attlee urged him not to walk out of the meeting, advice that Bevan ignored.[49] At the following day's meeting Attlee, instead of remaining largely silent as on the previous day, launched an attack on Bevan, who, repeating his intention to resign, stormed from the platform.[50]

From 1951, when Bevan resigned from the Cabinet, to 1955 when his expulsion from the party seemed certain, Attlee agonised, fumed, ultimately despaired of Bevan's suitability as party leader. At some point in that downward path he was able to see the younger man with cool objectivity and admit that he was too unpredictable to succeed him. This culmination of events in the early months of 1954 confirmed that admission. He decided to marginalise Bevan and, knowing his tendency to make gestures in anger, provoked him to commit himself to resignation. Bevan reacted spontaneously – probably without having consulted his group.[51]

His shadow Cabinet slot passed to Wilson, the first runner-up from the previous October. Not unnaturally, despite his loyalty to Bevan, Wilson, not wishing to resign from the shadow Cabinet before even joining it,[52] asked Crossman to speak to Bevan to obtain his approval. Bevan refused. Crossman asked Bevan if he regarded Wilson as expendable, to which Bevan replied. 'Yes, and you too.'[53] Wilson, believing that Bevan had isolated himself, decided to shed the tag of 'Nye's Little Dog' and chart his own course.[54] Freeman saw this as the next move in Wilson's long game to rejoin the party mainstream after taking the correct course by resigning in 1951.[55] For 'the unity and strength of the party', Wilson searched his soul and found himself able to take a seat on the front bench.

Crossman warned Bevan that Wilson was more likely than Bevan to become Prime Minister, that he was just the right man to succeed Attlee. Bevan replied, 'If he's that kind of man, I don't want anything to do with him.' Bevan's aim was to destroy Attlee's reputation ('We have to expose the futility and weakness of the little man'). Crossman believed that it was Attlee's success in the hydrogen bomb debate that aroused this latest antipathy.[56]

Morrison now attempted to administer the *coup de grace* to Bevan in an article in *Socialist Commentary*, allegedly read by Attlee. This charged that

Bevan had alienated voters with his 'vermin' speech, that his resignation in 1951 had cost Labour the election, and that he was playing into
the Tories' hands with his position over Indo-China. Such an attack
defied the resolution of the Parliamentary Party forbidding attacks on
colleagues. If Attlee had approved the article, this was a neat gambit to
discredit Morrison while damaging Bevan.[57]

The right wing of the party, convinced that Labour would never win
a general election while Bevan was prominent, aimed at his political
extinction. In September at the annual conference in Scarborough
Gaitskell decisively defeated Bevan for the treasurership of the party.
The Bevanites were also defeated on the issue of German rearmament,
but by a much narrower margin.

For Bevan himself the Scarborough conference was notable for his
final alienation of the trade unions; he made a strident speech, claiming
that in three years he would break the leaders' hold over their members.
He protested that 'the right kind of leader is a desiccated calculating machine who must not allow himself in any way to be swayed by
emotion.' Although he strenuously denied that this insult was designed
for Gaitskell, he had once more crossed a line.[58] As with the 'vermin'
speech, with his defiance of Attlee in the House, with this personal
attack on a shadow Cabinet colleague, he once more assisted Attlee in
moving him to the sidelines.

Even for a politician as mercurial and flamboyant as Bevan,
Scarborough was a signal triumph of systematic alienation. He followed
this with arrogant treatment of Morgan Phillips, the Labour Party's
General Secretary, on a trip to China, where he treated Phillips as a mere
paid employee of the party. Phillips recounted the story to Gaitskell, and
it is clear that he too was now measuring Bevan for the drop.[59]

Attlee had succeeded in isolating Bevan while striving to maintain
semblance of party unity among the centrist majority. Fortunately, since
the atomic weapons debate in April he was riding high in the polls.
Crossman, however, was less than impressed by the reality, recording
that 'the right wing are frozen into a rigid attitude of suspicious fear and
hatred of their left-wing colleagues … Meanwhile little Attlee manipu-
lates and twitters to and fro in the centre.' By Christmas, he wrote, 'Nye
has virtually gone into retirement and the official leadership might have

been expected to feel easier and more self-confident, it has actually been more ineffective than ever, with the underlying ill will between the right and left in the party just as strong.'[60]

During March Attlee, in uncharacteristically open fashion, attempted to explain his position to Wilson and Crossman. To Wilson he admitted that he had regarded Bevan as his successor but over the past four years he had eliminated himself. 'I can't see a successor,' Attlee added. 'That's the trouble.'[61] To Crossman he was even blunter. 'Nye had the leadership on a plate,' he admitted. 'I always wanted him to have it. But, you know, he wants to be two things simultaneously, a rebel and an official leader and you can't be both.'[62] To Tom he had commented four years before simply that Bevan had 'too much ego in his cosmos'.[63]

Gaitskell could not understand why Attlee, Leader of the Opposition, behaved less decisively than Attlee, the Prime Minister.[64] The orthodox Labour Party's attempts to distance itself from Bevan led inexorably to a movement to expel him from the party. The episode reflected poorly on Attlee as leader but illustrates the lingering affection that he felt for Bevan, even when his actions put him in an untenable position. The background to the question, which came to a head at a special party meeting on 16 March, involved three issues, three occasions on which Bevan had been at odds with the party's Standing Orders: on 13 April 1954 concerning Eden's statement concerning south-east Asian defence and atomic energy, in January and February 1955 concerning the three-power talks, and, most recently, in a confrontational challenge during a House of Commons debate in which Bevan had unreasonably demanded Attlee's and Morrison's presence and, along with sixty-one other Labour Members, had abstained rather than support a Labour amendment.[65]

For anti-Bevanites, even middle-of-the-road Members, this was a heaven-sent opportunity to destroy the colourful rebel. The Parliamentary Committee favoured the strongest disciplinary action, backed by a threat that the committee members would resign *en bloc* if the whip were not withdrawn. Party unity demanded a show of reconciliation and Attlee interceded. On 29 March Bevan offered a comprehensive apology, regretting any pain he might have caused Attlee.[66]

Attlee's reluctance to expel Bevan sandwiched him between two possible outcomes, neither of which he wanted. He disappointed the anti-Bevanites, failed to put adequate restraints on Bevan (or any other rebel), and hardened the conviction of Gaitskell and his contemporaries that younger blood was needed to lead an effective Opposition back to government. To their consternation, however, Morrison had become rejuvenated by his second marriage in January and was tackling parliamentary business with renewed zest and vigour.[67]

In April Churchill finally stepped down and Eden, his successor, called a general election for 26 May. It was not a thrilling campaign. Labour produced a brief manifesto of fewer than 3,000 words, awash with nebulous abstracts, uninspiringly entitled *Forward with Labour*. It spoke of the brotherhood of man, the opportunity of building a world of peace, freedom and justice and looked back to 1945 while urging 'Now is the time to go forward with Labour.' It was far from being a blueprint for action.

To no one's surprise, Labour lost eighteen seats, the Conservatives gaining an overall majority of fifty-nine. More significantly, the loss by Labour of 1,500,000 votes prompted the press to ask whether Bevan was worth a million and a half votes. Nor was Attlee spared blame. His reluctance to distance the party from the Bevanites ignited demands for him to step down. At the first party meeting after the election he offered to do so, but, with no acceptable successor, the offer languished.

If Attlee did not want Morrison to succeed him he was surely relieved by Labour's loss of the 1955 election. Had Labour won, then Morrison would have been the only choice for Prime Minister once Attlee stepped down. As it emerged, his successor would have time to establish himself before an election five years down the line.

Pressure for change in the party's leadership now came from an unexpected quarter. Hugh Dalton, he of iconoclastic temper and a booming voice,[68] symbol of the older generation and gently mocked by his younger protégés, launched 'Operation Avalanche'. Its aim was to displace shadow Cabinet members aged over sixty-five to reduce the average age of the shadow Cabinet. As a parallel, but unexpressed, goal it aimed to reduce Morrison's chances of succeeding Attlee – in Dalton's eyes, an equally important facet of rejuvenating the party. To anchor the operation he urged Attlee to remain 'until HM is no longer an inevitable successor'.[69] 'My first job is to break the log-jam of ancients on the Parliamentary

Committee,' he told Gaitskell. 'I am writing a letter to CRA ... I want to see at least six vacancies on the Parliamentary Committee.'[70]

Directly after the election Dalton wrote to Attlee, urging a vigorous and effective parliamentary Opposition. 'It is high time', he wrote 'that a number of us should now stand down to make room in the shadow Cabinet for good younger men. There is no lack of these.' He did, however, concede that Attlee should continue as leader.

'There is an engaging naïveté about it; and at the same time a mischievous shrewdness', commented the *Manchester Guardian*.[71] In addition to Dalton, Ede, Shinwell and Whiteley stood down from shadow Cabinet elections. 'Seldom has it been so much fun to do one's duty', Dalton joyfully noted in his diary.[72] Morrison remained but he was one of the oldest on the committee and his chances of election were damaged. When Attlee set no firm date for his retirement, Dalton noted, 'This almost certainly the end of HM as a possible future leader. He'll be 68 next Jan, 69 in Jan 1957. Too old to succeed Attlee now.'[73]

Following a mild stroke in August, Attlee spoke openly of retirement, testing the water with the left.[74] Bevan declared that the only possible salvation for the party was for him to be deputy leader under Morrison. He feared that, if Morrison and Gaitskell led the party, it would disintegrate and never recover.[75] The Bevanites, therefore, were happy that Attlee should remain, keeping Morrison out. Attlee, not motivated by any passionate antipathy towards Morrison, foresaw the same outcome, doubting the depth of Gaitskell's commitment to socialism. In September, however, he gave an interview in which he spoke of the need for 'men brought up in the present age'.[76] The timing of the interview, just before the party conference in Margate, was a clear boost for Gaitskell.

At Margate, Gaitskell took the hint and, in the middle of a speech on nationalisation, inserted a passage that described his conversion to socialism, his inability to 'tolerate the indefensible differences ... which disfigure our society'. The speech received the largest ovation of the conference.[77] Brown commented that Gaitskell never aimed to water down socialism; he just wanted to bring it up to date.[78]

When it became clear that there would be a long session of Parliament Attlee announced that he would not retire in October but would continue as leader until the end of the session. Crossman commented that this was no bad thing while the party rebuilt itself. In the meantime, he wrote, it was a party without policy and without leadership, conceding that this was better than 'a party without policy but rent by personal rivalry for the leadership'.[79]

Over the next few months Gaitskell's name was heard more often. His stock had risen since Margate and, in line with Operation Avalanche, he was just forty-nine years old. Speculation became rife. At a dinner during the Tory Party conference Crossman and Brown discussed the succession. Brown greatly favoured Morrison as the new leader and when Crossman asked why 'gaga Morrison was better than gaga Attlee', he replied that with Morrison as leader the trade unions could re-establish their position and smash the intellectuals.[80] Brown was stating why the TUC would welcome Morrison rather than Gaitskell as leader.

In October Dalton told Oxford University Labour Club that if Attlee were forced to retire through ill health, the PLP should choose somebody able to carry on for some years. 'You do not want to have a caretaker who is approaching seventy.'[81] By the end of October he was able to write in his diary, 'HG [Gaitskell] has the leadership in the bag if it comes loose in the next four months.' One threat to this was Gaitskell's conservative economic policy. When Butler produced the Budget in October Gaitskell was at first mild in his criticisms. Urged to be more condemnatory, he inserted more virulent criticism of Butler to avoid the label of 'Butskell'[82].

Bevan was increasingly spending time on his farm in the Chilterns. Crossman, observing his withdrawal, commented to Dalton in November, 'A leader or deputy leader of the Labour Party is always pretty contemptible. Why shouldn't Nye convince himself that he is too big a man for these jobs?' To which Dalton roared in reply, 'You're quite right. That's the kind of job for which I've never felt any jealousy of the man who occupies it. Ernie Bevin, I and others weren't going to be little Attlees. Why can't Nye feel the same?'[83]

Attlee could have used his authority to patch up differences between left and right. He did not for two reasons: first, he realised that an externally applied bandage could only be temporary; second, he wanted to see a leader emerge who could win on the first ballot and lead with authority. As Morrison's support in the Parliamentary Party ebbed and as Gaitskell and Wilson worked together on the Finance Bill, producing 'the first effective fighting Opposition we've known for a long time',[84] Attlee believed that those conditions were in place. On 6 December he wrote to Tom in a fine example of Attleean modesty and understatement:

> I am tomorrow giving up the leadership of the party. As you know, I meant to go after the last election but stayed on to oblige. There is, however, so much speculation as to the next leader going on that I think it best to retire now ... There is a general wish that I should go to the Lords. Jowitt has given up the leadership and they rather want putting together.[85]

The contestants for the leadership were finally under starters' orders. Bevan issued a statement that, if other candidates also withdrew, he would allow Morrison to be elected unopposed. Gaitskell countered that he owed it to his supporters to stand. He had the 'highest regard for Mr Morrison, but ... the party should have the opportunity of choosing.'[86]

Bevan's tactic was a desperate attempt to secure a lien on the leadership. 'This last-minute manoeuvre is widely held to have made more certain the election of Mr Gaitskell,' said the *Daily Telegraph*. The *Daily Express* spoke of 'a last desperate bid to put the party crown into cold storage for himself'.

Few were surprised when Gaitskell won a landslide on the first ballot. For Morrison it was a humiliating defeat and he promptly resigned as deputy leader. Gaitskell appealed to him to reconsider but Morrison replied that the numbers spoke for themselves. Gaitskell was undoubtedly relieved, but went through the motions once more. The War of Attlee's Succession had reached its end. In more ways than one Gaitskell had succeeded. He had gained adequate momentum after the Stalybridge speech to leap-frog Attlee's concerns about him and manoeuvre him into admitting that the time was ripe for retirement. At a New Year's Eve party at the Gaitskells, when Attlee proposed a toast to the new leader, Gaitskell 'rushed into the room and stammered, "Oh Clem, thank you. I never expected this." "And you'd no right to," muttered Clem under his breath, just loud enough for Edna [Healey] to hear.'[87]

Meanwhile, as Attlee had predicted to Tom, in line with established custom, he became an Earl and left elective politics after thirty-four years at the age of almost seventy-three. As Tony Benn recalls, his faith in socialism was undiminished. About to enter the House of Lords, he spoke of the future. 'I don't want us, when we come in again to be swept in by some temporary discontent,' he vowed. 'I want to come in because a larger number of people have accepted the socialist creed.'[88]

ENDNOTES

1   This is the title of Part IV of Philip Williams' biography, *Hugh Gaitskell*.
2   Macmillan commented that he was 'never conscious at any time from the moment [Attlee] became Prime Minister until the day that he retired from the leadership of the party that Attlee was not in full command of the situation.' *Tides of Fortune*, p. 53.
3   Dalton, *High Tide and After*, pp. 352–353.
4   Letter to Tom Attlee, 14 November 1951.
5   Richard Crossman, *The Backbench Diaries*, entry for 20 November 1951, p. 38.
6   Healey, *The Time of My Life*, p. 150.
7   Pimlott, *Harold Wilson*, p. 173.
8   Healey, *The Time of My Life*, pp. 150–151. He speaks of the Bevanites as motivated by '*odium theologicum*'.
9   *The Backbench Diaries*, entry for 3 December 1951, p. 43.
10 *The Diary of Hugh Gaitskell*, entry for 23 November 1951, p. 308.
11 *The Backbench Diaries*, 6 December 1951, p. 49.
12 *The Backbench Diaries*, 26 November 1951, p. 42.
13 Healey, *The Time of My Life*, p. 150.
14 Brown, *In My Way*, p. 79.
15 Pimlott, *Harold Wilson*, p. 174.
16 *The Backbench Diaries*, 31 January 1952, p. 59.
17 Letter to Tom Attlee, 15 February 1952. Queen Mary, the King's mother told Attlee that his eulogy of George VI in *The Observer* was 'just what a mother would like to have written about her son'. Letter to Tom Attlee, 18 February 1952.
18 Kenneth Younger, Diary for 9 March 1952, cited by Williams, *Diary of Hugh Gaitskell*, p. 312.
19 Hunter, *The Road to Brighton Pier*, p. 47.
20 Pimlott, *Harold Wilson*, p. 175.
21 Pimlott, *Harold Wilson*, pp. 175–176. Of course, he was.
22 *The Backbench Diaries*, 23 July 1952, p. 125.
23 Hunter, *The Road to Brighton Pier*, pp. 51–2.
24 Michael Foot, *Aneurin Bevan*, Volume 2, *1945–1960*, p. 379.
25 Douglas Jay, *Change and Fortune*, p. 223.
26 *The Backbench Diaries*, 29 September 1952, p. 149.
27 *The Backbench Diaries*, 29 September 1952, p. 148.
28 Hunter, *The Road to Brighton Pier*, pp. 58–59.
29 Healey, *The Time of My Life*, p. 152.
30 Donoughue and Jones, *Herbert Morrison*, p. 521.
31 *The Backbench Diaries*, 6 October 1952, p. 154.
32 *The Times*, 6 October 1952.
33 Hunter, *The Road to Brighton Pier*, pp. 63–64.
34 Gaitskell, *Diary*, pp. 332–334.
35 *The Backbench Diaries*, 13 October 1952, p. 156 for Bevan's decision to disband the Group. Also entry for 18 April 1953, p. 217.
36 *The Backbench Diaries*, 23 October 1952, p. 167.
37 Dalton Diary, Entry for 11 November 1952. Cited at Ben Pimlott, *Hugh Dalton*, p. 615.
38 *The Backbench Diaries*, 3 December 1952, p, 187.
39 Foot, *Aneurin Bevan*, vol. 2, p. 405.
40 Donoughue and Jones, *Herbert Morrison*, p. 524.
41 *The Backbench Diaries*, Entry for 18 December 1953, pp. 282–283.
42 Donoughue and Jones, *Herbert Morrison*, p. 525.
43 Townsend Hoopes, *The Devil and John Foster Dulles*, p. 198.

44   *Daily Express*, 5 March 1954. Cited by Foot, *op. cit.*, p. 424.

45   *Daily Herald*, 25 March 1954.

46   *The Backbench Diaries*, entry for 6 April 1954, p. 305.

47   *Hansard*, HC Deb, 5 April 1954, col. 36.

48   *Hansard*, HC Deb, 13 April 1954, cols. 969–972.

49   Gaitskell, *Diary*, pp. 328–329. Gaitskell records that 'Clem said in his most Haileybury military accent, "Why can't you be a man and face the music?"'

50   Throughout Attlee's attempts to restrain Bevan, I am reminded of the comment of Aristophanes in *The Frogs*: ου cτη leontoσ skumnov εv poleι trefeiv / ην δ ektrafη tiσ, toiσ tropoiσ uphreteiv. (It's best not to raise a lion in the city, but if someone does, you have to humour it.) The words were written in 405 BC and refer to the brilliant, charismatic and unconventional Athenian general Alcibiades who, not unlike Bevan in Britain, was the cause of much divisive controversy in Athens. (lines 1431–32).

51   Gaitskell's view is that it was spontaneous, although he believes that Bevan was prodded into action by Jennie Lee – see *Diary*, pp. 328–329.

52   Mikardo, *Back-Bencher*, p. 153.

53   This moment of egotistical rage is well reported. See Dalton, *High Tide and After*, pp. 408–409, Gaitskell, *Diary*, *loc. cit.*, Hunter, *The Road to Brighton Pier*, pp. 78–79.

54   Donoughue and Jones, *Herbert Morrison*, p. 530.

55   Pimlott, *Harold Wilson*, p. 183.

56   *The Backbench Diaries*, 21 April 1954, pp. 314–317.

57   *The Backbench Diaries*, 6 May 1954, p. 325.

58   Bevan at the *Tribune* rally 1954. He denied that he was referring to Gaitskell, commenting that 'you could hardly call him a calculating machine – because he was three million out on the defence estimates.' This supports Francis Beckett's view that the slur was aimed at Attlee.

59   Gaitskell, *Diary*, Entry for 14 October 1954, p. 340.

60   *The Backbench Diaries*, Entries for 3 and 26 December 1954, pp. 374–376.

61   *The Backbench Diaries*, 8 March 1955, pp. 394–395.

62   *The Backbench Diaries*, 16 March 1955, p. 406. But as early as 1945 Attlee had had a constant concern that 'a silly speech by someone like Aneurin Bevan might easily be used to stampede the electors away from Labour'. (CAC: ATLE 1/24).

63   Letter to Tom Attlee, 24 July 1951.

64   *The Backbench Diaries*, 24 March 1955, p. 410.

65   For the comprehensive brief of the case against Bevan prepared by Gaitskell and sent to Attlee before the PLP meeting see Gaitskell, *Diary*, pp. 375–382.

66   *The Backbench Diaries*, 31 March 1955, p. 413.

67   Donoughue and Jones, *Herbert Morrison*, p. 533.

68   The booming voice was well known. Francis Beckett quotes a story that during the war Churchill heard a booming voice from an ante-room and, told by an aide that 'It's Mr Dalton speaking to Glasgow', growled, 'Why doesn't he use the telephone?' Beckett, *Clem Attlee*, p. 203.

69   Pimlott, *Hugh Dalton*, p. 621.

70   H. D. to Gaitskell, 30 May 1955, Gaitskell Papers, cited at Pimlott, *Hugh Dalton*, p. 622.

71   *Manchester Guardian*, 1 June 1955.

72   Dalton, *High Tide and After*, p. 417.

73   Dalton, *Diary*, 9 June 1955.

74   Henry Fairlie complimented Attlee on his skill at 'flying a kite' in *The Spectator*, 15 September 1955.

75   *The Backbench Diaries*, 7 June 1955, p. 426.

76   *The Observer*, 18 September 1955. Hunter, *The Road to Brighton Pier*, pp. 133–136.

77   Hunter, *The Road to Brighton Pier*, pp. 142–143; Donoughue and Jones, *Herbert Morrison*, p. 537.

78   Brown, *In My Way*, p. 81.

79   *The Backbench Diaries*, 13 June 1955, p. 431.

80   *The Backbench Diaries*, 7 October 1955, p. 446.

81   *Daily Herald*, 12 October 1955, cited at Pimlott, *Hugh Dalton*, p. 623.

82   'Butskellism', a conflation of 'Butler' and 'Gaitskell', was a term coined by *The Economist* in February 1954 to describe centrist economic theory.

83   *The Backbench Diaries*, 16 November 1955, p. 453. The printed text shows the sentence as '… aren't going to be little Attlees', an unlikely comment as Bevin had been dead for four years.

84   *The Backbench Diaries*, 2 December 1955, p. 453.

85   Letter to Tom Attlee, 6 December 1955.

86   Donoughue and Jones, *Herbert Morrison*, pp. 539–540.

87   Healey, *The Time of My Life*, p. 153.

88   Tony Benn, Attlee Lecture 1998, Royal Overseas League, 9 February 1998.

CHAPTER NINETEEN

ELDER STATESMAN, 1955–1967

A n earldom was a traditional reward for a former Prime Minister and Attlee was in many ways a traditionalist. In early December 1955 he told Eden, now Prime Minister on Churchill's retirement, of his intention to step down. Eden kept the confidence, telling only the Queen, and making the formal submission for an earldom.[1] When he accepted the honour ('the most ostentatious act he has ever committed'[2]) he was asked how it would feel to be addressed as 'Lord Attlee' rather than as 'Mr Attlee'. He replied simply, 'Practically everybody calls me "Clem".'[3]

Such modesty was typical of a man who was 'difficult to know and easy to underrate'.[4] Examples of his modesty are legion. In October 1968 Lord Longford told a story of how, after a debate in the House of Lords, he had invited Clement and Violet to dinner at a restaurant in Sloane Square. The Attlees conferred, said that they insisted on being the hosts as it was their turn, but since Clement had no cash on him, he asked to borrow the money from Longford and pay him back later. He was concerned that the restaurant would not accept his cheque. Longford assured him that the restaurant would certainly accept a cheque from a former Prime Minister, Earl Attlee, Viscount Prestwood of Walthamstow in the County of Essex.[5]

Other examples abound. In 1950, while still Prime Minister, he and Violet took a trip to the Loire Valley. He was amazed that he was treated differently from members of the general public at Blois and Chenonceaux, writing to Tom with childlike wonder that they had been admitted to rooms normally not shown.[6]

In 1951 Sir Arthur Goodhart was appointed Master of Univ. Attlee had kept up their friendship and, after his retirement, wrote to Goodhart, complaining that there was no room in 'Westcott', the bungalow that Violet commissioned, for the papers he had accumulated. Perhaps Univ might do something with them; otherwise he would 'consign them to the flames'. 'I don't know whether they contain anything of value for some future historian', he wrote, 'for I have never had the time to go through them.'[7] Goodhart understandably jumped at the offer and offered to 'drive down to Cherry Cottage at any time during the next few days' to collect them.[8] The notion of a former Prime Minister burning his papers because his bungalow was too small horrified the Master.

On a more practical level, he accepted an earldom to take him away from the Commons, insistent that he should be out of the way of his successor. He was amply aware of the need to rebuild the party, a task most easily performed with the fewest number of relics of 1945 in the House. The party faced a crisis greater than that posed by the Bevanites. Reporting the 1955 election on BBC television, Honor Balfour of *TIME-LIFE* magazines stated Labour's problems starkly, concluding that 'for some time the Labour Party has been in danger of losing its fundamental vitality … and the results show it'.[9]

Despite the infighting of the early 1950s, Attlee had stepped down at a moment when the party was reasonably united, with nothing on its mind other than the election of a new leader. Eden, an admirer of Morrison, believed that he delayed retirement only to ensure that Morrison would be too old to succeed him.[10] For all the talk of his relative youth, Gaitskell was only three years younger than Attlee had been in 1935, and he had held higher office than Attlee had held when he became leader. Gaitskell's task was to rebuild the party's structure, its image, the very soul of British socialism in a very changed climate. Lord Hailsham, the chairman of the Tory Party, echoing a widespread feeling, doubted 'that socialism in this country can survive a third electoral defeat'.[11] Naturally enough, Attlee soon established a routine. Violet drove him to Great Missenden Station for the 45-minute rail journey to Baker Street and onward by Underground to the House of Lords. A slight man sat in a corner seat of a third-class carriage, armed with a briefcase containing his needs for the day: 'a few copies of *Hansard*, two spare pipes, a two-ounce tin of cut Golden Bar … and a couple of detective paperbacks. Sometimes he would do *The Times* crossword. Occasionally he was recognised but very rarely.'[12]

Quite suddenly, he was a Grand Old Man of British politics, widely respected, a popular icon, a venerable relic of another age. It was a role to which he adapted easily. One biographer comments that 'there is no evidence that Hugh Gaitskell or, from 1963, Harold Wilson consulted him on matters of political strategy or party management.'[13] Although he was an active campaigner for Wilson in 1964, he would never have intervened uninvited; one can easily imagine how he as party leader would have reacted to such an intervention. Instead, he was content to observe politics with a quizzical eye, speak on the grand themes to which he had dedicated his life, and adopt a gently self-mocking air. In April 1956 he wrote to Tom with important news which, typically, he made light of. 'I gather that I have to take part in a ceremony on June 18th at Windsor,' he wrote. 'Rosebery has kindly offered me the loan of his father's robes for the occasion.' He offered Tom 'a little verse':

Few thought he was even a starter
There were many who thought themselves smarter
But he ended PM
CH and OM
An earl and a knight of the garter.[14]

If he looked at himself with a mildly satirical eye, he viewed his colleagues no less mischievously. When Dalton published the second volume of his memoirs, *The Fateful Years*, he commented that 'I wrote the Acts, Dalton wrote Revelations'.[15] When Leslie Hunter's *The Road to Brighton Pier* was published, he speculated that Morrison might have urged Hunter to write the book out of a pathological dislike of Attlee.[16] (Hunter's wife and Morrison were close friends.) Morrison's own autobiography he carefully placed in the 'Fiction' shelf of his library. As for Churchill, whose florid literary style was the very antithesis of his own taciturnity, he wrote to Tom that he had received the third volume of his history, 'rather better than its predecessors.' Despite Attlee's 'somewhat astringent reviews, the old boy sends me copies'.[17]

His reviews were certainly astringent. He referred to volume two of Churchill's *Second World War* as 'rather thin'. Of the second volume of *A History of the English Speaking Peoples* he concluded a longish, balanced review with a crisp, damning sentence, 'It might indeed be better called "Things in history which have interested me".'[18]

The objectivity of retirement gave him the necessary distance to polish and sharpen his barbs. On one occasion students canvassing for the Labour Party in Great Missenden called at his house. He dutifully listened to them; without declaring who he was, he said simply, 'Already a member' and closed the door.[19] His dry, dark sense of humour was given more exercise. He commented once that the West enjoyed an advantage over the Russians in negotiations over atomic weapons. Asked why, he said simply, 'Because we believe in the after-life.'

On his retirement he received tributes from people of all shades of political opinion. This greatly amused him and he wrote to Tom that only in Britain could that happen. One colleague in the House of Lords paid him a frivolous tribute, claiming, 'If Churchill had not been Prime Minister during the war, Attlee would have ended his days in a concentration camp. If Attlee had not been Prime Minister from 1945 to 1951, Churchill would have ended his days strung up from a lamppost in Whitehall.'[20]

In late July 1956 Colonel Nasser nationalised the Suez Canal. Through the summer and early autumn the crisis simmered, erupted and swiftly subsided; Attlee watched the process in disbelief. In July he spoke in the House of Lords, a measured, rational speech that balanced British interests with the policy of decolonisation, of building a post-imperial Commonwealth. He warned against any form of aggression and, equally importantly, against any collaboration with the French, tagged with an imperialist label after their unsuccessful struggle in Indo-China.[21] When, three months later, Eden yielded to pressure from Washington Attlee felt that Eden had handled the matter as ineptly as was possible.

In 1954 Attlee published his memoirs. They were not a success. The notes on his life preserved in the archive at Churchill College, Cambridge are understated, and the published version *As It Happened* is a truncated version of those notes. In truth, Clement Attlee is the least likely autobiographer imaginable; the very act of writing about himself, particularly of revealing motivation or justifying actions, would have seemed to him ostentatious and vulgar – the kind of thing that he left to Morrison and

Churchill. Many of the notes preserved in Cambridge were clearly written for his children and were never intended for publication. By the time he did write for publication there was a massive gulf between what he remembered – an enormous amount – and what he was prepared to reveal for public scrutiny. If he was economical with the spoken word, he was positively miserly with the written account.

Nonetheless, publishers approached him to suggest a second book but he was reluctant, writing to Tom that 'I've had two publishers after me to write a book but I doubt if I've much to say.'[22] Later that year, after three successful interviews with Francis Williams for the BBC, he worked with Williams to record his selected memoirs. The novel technology appealed to him and he wrote again to Tom, 'I have been working on a book which is to be the joint product of myself and Francis Williams, a kind of conversation piece. We talk together before a recording machine'.[23]

Rather than write about himself he undertook a form of writing for which his talents equipped him ideally. The book review, objective and concise, demanding an ability to summarise several hundred pages in a few well-chosen words, was perfectly suited to his style.[24] A selection of his reviews, illustrating the values by which Attlee lived and which he sought in others, was published in 2009. As the book's cover claims, 'they epitomise the intellect and humanity of … a man with profound qualities that are so poorly represented in today's politics'.[25] During the late 1950s there was a glut of war memoirs and Attlee was in demand as a reviewer. In common with many readers, he was shocked by some of the revelations and frank criticisms of Churchill in the diaries of Viscount Alanbrooke.[26] That was the very kind of material that he had eliminated from his own memoirs. In his review of *Triumph in the West* for *The Observer* he wrote tersely: 'If a diary is to enable tense minds to let off steam in private, it cannot be regarded as a safe historical source; and if it is written for use as a future historical document, it is suspect for the opposite reason. One cannot have it both ways.'[27]

Another talent came to the surface in Attlee's retirement from active politics. Never a great orator in the manner of Churchill or an acute debater like Bevan, he had always possessed an ability to summarise and clarify. This skill equipped him well for the role of elder statesman, looking back over his experience and translating myriad experiences into a comprehensive coherent summary. The lecture tour was the perfect vehicle for such addresses and he made two highly successful tours of the United States in 1957 and 1958. Two subjects emerged, naturally enough, as his preferred themes: the transition from Empire to Commonwealth and the Role of the United Nations in the preservation of peace.

In May 1960 he delivered the Chichele Lectures at Oxford. These were four lectures entitled *Empire Into Commonwealth*, on 'changes in the conception and structure of the British Empire during the last half-century'. As he modestly explained, the process of transforming Empire into Commonwealth had taken place in a period that covered his adult life. 'I have seen it happen, and have taken some share in bringing it about.'[28]

The lectures, spanning the wide arc of Britain's relations with colonies in Asia and Africa, as well as the independence of India, Pakistan, Ceylon and Burma, were a model of clarity containing insights and predictions that later events would prove accurate. As ever, the addresses bore the Attlee hallmark of brevity; they were the shortest Chichele Lectures ever delivered.[29]

During the summer he wrote to Tom from Italy, recalling his trip almost forty years before. 'Cadenabbia reminds me of my courting of Vi there in 1921', he wrote, 'with the strong scent of flowering shrubs.'[30] Back in England he planned a dinner in the House of Lords for Tom's eightieth birthday. Uncharacteristically, he had left the planning rather late and found that it was already booked for the actual birthday; he made arrangements for 20 October instead.[31] The dinner never came to pass, as Tom died on 11 October.

Britain changed dramatically in the five years after Attlee stepped down. The Suez affair led to Eden's resignation and Harold Macmillan's succession. The Labour Party lost a third consecutive general election in October 1959. The economic upturn, begun under Labour but now appropriated by the reassuring Macmillan claiming, 'You've never had it so good', supported the Tory claim, 'Life is better with the Conservatives, don't let Labour ruin it'. In truth there was little difference between the Labour and Conservative manifestos. The Tories, however, achieved the remarkable shift of being able to say, credibly, that 'the socialists have learnt nothing in their period of Opposition save new ways to gloss over their true intentions. Their policies are old-fashioned and have no relevance to the problems of the modern world.'[32] The Labour Party found itself facing the same criticism that it had used in 1945.

Attlee watched with amazement as Britain embraced materialism, and the Labour Party moved to the right to stay in step. As for the Conservative Party and Macmillan, he said simply, 'I always thought him rather a light-weight and recent happenings have confirmed that view.'[33]

That opinion of Macmillan was confided to a 39-year-old journalist with whom Attlee had developed a friendship since she came to Britain to cover the 1950 election for *TIME* magazine. Their initially inter-mittent correspondence became more frequent in the early 1960s, and Attlee clearly enjoyed their friendship.

'She was a maiden lady in her thirties,' recalls Anne, Lady Attlee, his daughter-in-law. 'Clem didn't make friends easily, but once he had chosen to be friends with someone, that was that.'[34] With Patricia Beck there developed a frank correspondence that is more revealing about the man than anything he wrote about himself.

The 1959 election was the first that Gaitskell had fought and he emerged from it well. Honor Balfour, observing the coherence of the rejuvenated party, described Gaitskell as 'a man who may prove to have done more for the British Labour Party in four years than Attlee did in twenty.'[35] Principally, he brought Bevan into line instead of destroy-ing him, which would have irrevocably divided the party. At every level Gaitskell asserted his leadership and a policy of moderation, broaden-ing Labour's appeal to the professional classes.

There was, nonetheless, a premature rush to write the obituary of the Labour Party – and, with it, to report the demise of Attlee's style of socialism. As clearly as 1945 had demonstrated that the Tories were out of date, so did 1959 demonstrate that the policies of the 1945–51 government were out of step with Britain of the Macmillan era. All three major parties fought the 1959 election under a new leader. The Labour years belonged to an age of austerity and rationing that Britain was happy to forget.

On his eightieth birthday Attlee gave a revealing interview before leav-ing for dinner in the House of Lords – the birthday treat he had planned for Tom. He looked back on taking Labour into the 1940 coalition and emerging without losing any members; on India, the nuclear deterrent, the Commonwealth, the Atlantic alliance. Asked how he would now spend his time he spoke of writing – 'not very much, I suspect' – and to pursuing his commitment to world government.[36] By any standards, this was an impressive panoply of achievements.

To the union of Europe, he remained adamantly opposed. Even before the subject became a fashionable talking point, he considered such a union 'out of date'.[37] This curious view reflects his certainty that in an atomic age power blocs and spheres of influence were irrelevant. World government was the only guarantee of world peace. It might be thought impractical, he conceded, but 'not as impractical as trying to run a world of sovereign states equipped with hydrogen bombs'.[38]

In the Chichele Lectures he commended the flexible structure of the Commonwealth, observing that 'foreigners find it difficult to understand how such loose methods can be effective'.[39] It was precisely that looseness that he applauded and whose absence in a united Europe concerned him. The notion of Britain's being locked into any kind of union with a handful of European countries whose governments might be unstable in the post-war years was anathema to him. He accepted that, for his generation at least, the question of joining 'the Six' would not be pressing, but he saw that for Gaitskell and Wilson it would be a dominant issue – as, indeed, it became. To his surprise he found himself, for the first time, sharing opinions with Beaverbrook.[40] Attlee himself was content to make half-serious comments about Britain's European neighbours. With his famously 'black' humour he joked of the Common Market in a brief *vignette* to anti-EEC backbenchers, 'The so-called Common Market of six nations. Know them all well. Very recently this country spent a great deal of blood and treasure rescuing four of 'em from attacks by the other two.'[41]

As with many of Attlee's one-liners, the last sentence has more than a hint of the truth. Twice in thirty years he had seen Europe plunged into unnecessary war; forty years after the event he could list the officers of his regiment and where they fell. Europe was more rather than less fragmented in 1945 and, while the issue of Germany, at the heart of Europe, remained unresolved, the notion of political union was premature.

On the other hand, as he stressed continually after Hiroshima, military alliances were outdated relics of Metternich and Bismarck. Under those circumstances he remained sceptical about the very feasibility of European union. He was prescient enough to foresee that it would become a vital issue for his successors – one of whom, Harold Wilson, cannily chose a referendum to resolve the issue in 1975 – but in the early 1960s he saw little point in even discussing the union of countries that might or might not exist by the end of the decade.

In January 1963 Gaitskell died suddenly from an attack of *Lupus erythematosus*. A Soviet defector, Anatoliy Golitsyn, later claimed that Gaitskell had been assassinated by the KGB in order to clear the way for a more leftist Wilson government, a claim taken seriously by several MI5 officers.[42] Edric Millar, who had brought Clement and Violet together, died in March. The cruellest blow followed in June 1964 when Violet collapsed while preparing Sunday lunch. Taken to hospital, she died overnight. By the time that Felicity, Martin and Alison arrived at Westcott, Clement had burned all his letters to her. No one was to be allowed to trawl through their life together.[43]

They had not been inseparable, as Attlee perforce was kept from family life by his work, but for forty-two years each had provided the other with absolute love and support. His mother had impressed on her children the self-sufficient quality of family, which for Attlee remained permanent and inviolable. Simply being with Violet, reading to her, sitting quietly together – this had been their shared bliss. Thirteen years older, he had assumed that he would die before her and providing for her widowhood – with lecture tours, writing book reviews, economising on writing paper as he manually altered 'The Rt. Hon. C. R. Attlee OM CH MP' to 'The Rt. Hon. Earl Attlee KG CH OM' – had been an obsession.

On the surface, they were an unlikely couple: she demonstrative, he restrained. She had been content to remain in his shadow, regretting but not resenting his job that kept them apart. She remained incurious about his work, certain of his motives of decency, even maintaining that he was never really a socialist – at least not a rabid one.[44] She had few friends among his colleagues – Isobel Cripps and Clementine Churchill perhaps knew her best. She had a reputation for being 'difficult' and Attlee's letters to Tom report periodically that Vi was 'better'. Unsure of herself, particularly in her relations with her twin sister Olive, she suffered post-natal depression when Janet was born; her doctor advised against having other children, advice that she ignored without ill effect.

She tolerated her husband's absences until he became Prime Minister. At Downing Street, however, his very proximity was a frustration, hedged about, as he was, by civil service protocol. Just two floors separated the Cabinet Room from their top-floor flat, and her 'difficult' side emerged once more as she berated the men who organised her husband's life, apparently to keep them apart.[45] Attlee would join her for lunch and tea whenever possible, but she yearned to be out of Downing Street and alone with him again. When Cripps and Bevin died, aged sixty-two and seventy, that desire to have sole possession for at least a few years became passionate, and when they moved to Cherry Cottage she was happier than ever.

Her pride in her husband was absolute, as was her knowledge that it was reciprocated. Superficial differences were trivial, separate interests irrelevant. She loved dancing while he did not. She enjoyed music; he was tone deaf. She mocked him gently and openly for his inattention at the bridge table. She drove him on election tours, packing just one suitcase and carrying a travelling iron to put a crease in the Prime Minister's trousers each morning. She gained a reputation as an erratic and accident-prone driver (despite having passed the Advanced Motorists' Test). Such minor differences and trivialities mattered not at all. She believed her husband to be the most wonderful man alive and he responded with the same solicitous devotion. When she died she left him alone in a way that he simply had not imagined possible. His life since 1955 had been reconstructed to provide for her after his death; he was quite unprepared for the actual sequence.

He quickly found living alone in the bungalow intolerable and resolved to move to London. 'I shall look forward to seeing you in town', he wrote to Patricia Beck. 'I could not have stayed here. The house is so much a projection of Vi's personality and most of my friends are in town.'[46] His friendship with Patricia now assumed greater importance for him. His eldest daughter Janet had decided to emigrate to Missouri in 1960. His son Martin and his family were living in Brussels. Felicity and Alison had young children who kept them busy. When he stayed with Felicity's family he felt out of place; he and Violet had not owned a television set[47] and he wrote to Patricia that 'I don't see much of the children as they are at school all day and on return are ardent televisionaries.'[48] Patricia provided the stimulus and companionship he lost when Violet died. He continued to consume books and valued the exchanges that he had with her. They shared books and ideas; gradually Patricia realised the extent to which he depended on her. For his part, he wrote increasingly warmly to her. There was a lively intellectual intimacy between them.

Francis Beckett, writing a biography of Attlee in 1997, stumbled on his letters to her and traced Patricia to St Andrews. Her description of her friendship with Attlee revealed his desperate need for her company. On one occasion, she told Beckett, 'I went to lunch with him, and when I got back he was on the telephone to ask if I'd have dinner with him at the Athenaeum. I couldn't face it.'[49]

There is no suggestion of impropriety on Attlee's part. He was able to talk to Patricia of his interests – his ideas for world government, party politics, history, literature, poetry. It is as if he had once again become the 'wholly romantic' young man of Oxford days. Or, perhaps, he had always been romantic but had concealed it well. Whatever the truth, he felt able to display a side of himself that was otherwise carefully hidden. As friends and colleagues died, he spoke of his own death, writing to Patricia, 'I shall die with lots of poetry in my heart and perhaps on my lips. However, for you, my dear, remember the last line of the sonnet, "Cueillez dès aujourd'hui les roses de la vie."'[50]

He acquired a manservant, Alfred Laker, and moved into a flat in King's Bench Walk in the Temple. His greatest concern in moving was the fitting of his copious library into the four-roomed flat. The general election of 15 October provided a welcome distraction as Attlee campaigned vigorously for the party. A small majority ended 'thirteen years of Tory misrule' and he was able to bask a little in what Wilson called 'a feeling of 1945'.

In January 1965 Churchill suffered his last severe stroke and died nine days later. Attlee, his long-time admirer and antagonist, was determined to attend the funeral, despite his own poor health. Exhausted by the effort and emotion, he was forced to sit, looking dazed and remote, on the steps of Saint Paul's cathedral.

Later that year, Alice Bacon, Minister of State at the Home Office, offered Attlee a lift in her official car to Epsom for Chuter Ede's memorial service. Their route took them through Wandsworth, and Attlee, 'dressed in a superb, old-fashioned morning suit with silk hat and rolled umbrella', regaled her with stories of his childhood in Putney and Wandsworth, pointing out landmarks and chatting in a way that she could not have imagined.[51] For fifteen years she had sat with him on the NEC and never heard him discourse so. But death was on his mind. 'Alice', he said, 'I've been to a number of funerals of my old colleagues lately – do you think I'll be the next?'

In May Frank Soskice, Solicitor-General and Attorney General in the Attlee governments, proposed that Attlee take a trip to the Caribbean in the company of his son David.[52] Attlee was delighted to get away from London for a month or so, and wrote to Patricia from Guadaloupe and Trinidad.[53] During the year he became greatly less mobile, and in November he confessed that he had failed to attend a Garter ceremony at the Palace and that he doubted he would attend the House of Lords.[54]

By March 1966, when Wilson called a snap election, Attlee was too frail to campaign. Despite gradual decline and a slight stroke, however, he was able to spend a weekend at Chequers in June at Wilson's invitation. Chequers had been his most valued perquisite of high office and this was a thoughtful gesture on Wilson's part.[55]

A year later, on 8 September 1967, he was admitted to Westminster Hospital with a minor complaint. He developed pneumonia and, within a month, died in his sleep. For three years he had fought furiously against the onset of old age. When he submitted, his demise was swift.

On 11 October his funeral, which he had meticulously planned, was held in Temple Church. He had paid no less attention to the content of a burial service at Westminster Abbey on 7 November; the convictions of the young idealist he had once been resonated in his choice of hymns – 'I vow to thee my country' and 'To be a Pilgrim'. The life of a man who rejected the 'mumbo-jumbo' of religion, who embodied as vigorously as any bishop the humanity of Christian belief, was celebrated as John Bunyan's words and Vaughan Williams' music echoed about the Abbey:

> *I'll fear not what men say*
> *I'll labour night and day*
> *To be a pilgrim.*

ENDNOTES

1   Eden, *Full Circle*, p. 319.
2   Bodleian: MS. Balfour, dep. 51.
3   Bodleian: MS. Balfour, dep. 26.4.
4   *Attlee As I Knew Him*, James Callaghan, p. 21.
5   *Attlee As I Knew Him*, Lord Longford, p. 30.
6   Letter to Tom Attlee, 3 June 1950.
7   Bodleian: MS. Eng. c.2881, folio 185, 11 January 1961.
8   Bodleian: MS. Eng. c.2881, folio 186.
9   Bodleian: MS. Balfour, Dep. 2.
10   Eden, *Full Circle*, p. 320.
11   'Operation Hat Trick', Speech at Conservative Party conference, 11 October 1958.
12   This description is that of Kenneth Harris, *Attlee.*, p. 545.
13   Nicklaus Thomas-Symonds, *Attlee: A Life in Politics*, p. 261.
14   Letter to Tom Attlee, 8 April 1956.
15   Letter to Tom Attlee, 24 March 1957. To Violet Bonham Carter he wrote that 'Hugh Dalton was very unreliable, being a great gossip (Bodleian: MS Bonham Carter dep. 197, 16 December 1963) and in the *Sunday Express*, 'Dalton's books are full of inaccuracies. If I started to refute them it would take me the rest of my life'. 19 January 1964).
16   Kenneth Harris, *Attlee*, p. 552.
17   Letter to Tom Attlee, 18 August 1957.
18   *The Observer*, 25 November 1958.
19   Bodleian: MS. Balfour, dep. 51.
20   Bodleian: MS. Balfour, dep. 51.
21   *Hansard*, House of Lords Debates, 2 August 1956, cols. 616–618.
22   Letter to Tom Attlee, 21 January 1959.
23   Letter to Tom Attlee, 19 July 1959. The resultant transcript was published as *A Prime Minister Remembers* in 1960. The historian Hugh Trevor-Roper, frequently critical of Attlee, commented that it might better have been called *What a Prime Minister Forgot*.
24   On one occasion, asked to submit a 500-word review, he sent in his piece of 499 words with the comment, 'I'm afraid it's a bit short.'
25   From the cover notes to Frank Field's book, *Attlee's Great Contemporaries*.
26   General Sir Alan Brooke, the wartime Chief of the Imperial General Staff, had been created Viscount Alanbrooke. His diaries, edited by Sir Arthur Bryant, were published as *The Turn of the Tide* (1957) and *Triumph in the West* (1959).
27   Review of *Triumph in the West, 1943–1946*, included in Field, *Attlee's Great Contemporaries*, p. 102. Attlee was loyal to *The Observer*. When the *Sunday Times* offered him £1,200 to write twelve book reviews over a year, 'being wedded to *The Observer*, [he] declined'. Letter to Tom Attlee, 19 July 1959.
28   *Empire Into Commonwealth*, Lecture I, lines 9–11.
29   Harris, *Attlee*, p. 556.
30   Letter to Tom Attlee, 9 June 1960.
31   Letter to Tom Attlee, 3 July 1960.
32   Conservative Party general election manifesto 1959, section 9, 'The Alternative'.
33   Bodleian: MS. Eng. lett. c.571, CRA to Patricia Beck, 19 June 1962.
34   Conversation with Anne, Countess Attlee, 14 October 2013.
35   Bodleian: MS. Balfour, dep. 27.
36   Bodleian: MS. Balfour, dep. 51.
37   Bodleian: MS. Balfour, dep. 51, Interview, 3 January 1963.
38   Bodleian: MS. Eng. lett. c.571, CRA to Patricia Beck, 20 August 1958.
39   *Empire into Commonwealth*, The Chichele Lectures, II, May 1969, lines 378–379.
40   Bodleian: MS. Eng. lett. c.571, CRA to Patricia Beck, 19 October 1962. 'I … am driven to be a strange bedfellow with the Old Beaver.'
41   Peter Hennessy, *The Prime Minister: The Office and its Holders Since 1945*, p. 173.
42   Leigh, *The Wilson Plot*, pp. 80–81; Peter Wright, *Spycatcher*, pp. 362–363.
43   Beckett, *Clem Attlee*, p. 314.
44   Harris, *Attlee*, p. 56.
45   Sir David Hunt's memoir *On the Spot* (1975, London: Peter Davies) gives a civil servant's picture of Violet's 'difficult' side.

46 Bodleian: MS Eng. lett. c.571, CRA to Patricia Beck, 20 June 1964.

47 Violet wrote to Lady Waverley on 15 February 1959, lamenting that Clem had been on TV and she had missed it as 'we haven't got television'. (Bodleian: MS Eng. c. 3337, fols. 68–69.)

48 Bodleian: MS Eng. lett. c.571, CRA to Patricia Beck, 10 January 1967.

49 Francis Beckett, 'Clem Attlee's Secret Lady Friend', *New Statesman*, 28 February 2000.

50 Bodleian: MS Eng. lett. c.571, CRA to Patricia Beck, 25 October 1965. 'Start gathering today the roses of life.'

51 *The Attlee I Knew*, Baroness Bacon, pp. 57–58.

52 Bodleian: MS Eng. lett. c.571, CRA to Patricia Beck, 25 May 1965.

53 By coincidence, David Soskice became a don at Univ, Attlee's former college, in the late 1960s.

54 Bodleian: MS Eng. lett. c.571, CRA to Patricia Beck, 23 November and 28 November 1965.

55 Wilson recorded that communication was difficult as Attlee was slurring his speech after his stroke. Nonetheless Wilson was treated to 'two memorable Attlee-esque replies to questions'. Wilson, *A Personal Record*, p. 246.

CHAPTER TWENTY

THE INEVITABLE PRIME MINISTER

La disparition de ce grand homme d'état que fut Lord Attlee me cause une peine profonde.[1] – Charles de Gaulle, President of France

A terrible wrong in the history of human society was righted and in consequence honourable relations and understanding were established between the people of Israel and the people of Great Britain. – Yigal Allon, Deputy Prime Minister of Israel

His name is inseparably linked with the beginning of the reconciliation between the British and German peoples. – Willi Brandt and Helmut Schmidt

An exceptional democrat who demonstrated admirable loyalty to his country and every human ideal. – Aldo Moro, Prime Minister of Italy

Clement Attlee's obituary in *The Times* was perceptive and accurate, addressing cardinal characteristics of the man and his government. Conceding that 'the absence of superficial qualities' had 'contributed to the failure of his party to dispel the air of drabness that settled over post-war socialism', it focused on his confidence in his own judgement, his pertinacity, his 'sturdiness of character' and 'unwavering resolution'. 'His integrity', the writer concluded, 'was absolute.'[2] In a few telling phrases, while remaining objective about his shortcomings, the tribute captured Attlee's essential qualities: his humanity and his integrity. The last, perhaps, was his most compelling virtue. Lord Longford spoke of his 'moral authority'; his moral disapproval was 'frightening to behold'.[3]

Perhaps because he never was and was never perceived as a ruthless politician, there has been a tendency to see his rise to power as an accident, rooted more in the misfortune of others than in ambition or ability. Such a tendency is wide of the mark.

Certainly his rise was boosted by events. At every critical point in his political career he succeeded in harnessing both public opinion and ethical constancy to his chariot. This called for exceptional skill and an astonishing degree of that quality which Napoleon most valued in a general – good, old-fashioned luck. Attlee would certainly have been a *Maréchal* in *La Grande Armée* if luck alone decided promotion.

But the leap from the obvious fact that he was aided by luck to the proposition that he did not seek power is logically false. There was a shrewd political side to his character that enabled him to capitalise on good fortune and benefit significantly from it. When he returned from Washington in December 1950 the popular perception was that he had single-handedly restrained Truman and his bomb-toting generals from launching World War III. Despite the blatant untruth of that view, he was not above allowing it to be the public perception. In July 1945, when Morrison schemed to replace him as party leader, he had no qualms about adducing respect for the monarch as his guiding reason for proceeding quietly to Buckingham Palace and 'kissing hands'.

When we follow Attlee's career from 1914 onwards we can identify the points at which Fortune intervened to grant him opportunity. On each occasion he moved with speed and determination to build on that good fortune. To suggest that he was without ambition, a compliant conduit for collective decisions, is to ignore the steely resolution he showed when necessary – for example, his decision that Britain build an atomic bomb in total secrecy.

His daughter-in-law Anne has no doubts about that resolution. 'He certainly had ambition,' she recalls. 'But it wasn't the kind of ambition that makes you go around, telling lies about people.' Ambition and integrity co-existed, and his ethical consistency was more than a political cloak. He had no hesitation in joining up when the First War broke out, but, as she points out, 'he said to Tom that life in the army was only worthwhile if one was in command'.[4]

His good fortune started with his surviving the First World War. The good luck of being wounded and unable to participate in the assault that wiped out his company possibly preserved him for future office. During the war he learned to lead men in battle, conducting a remarkably successful evacuation at Gallipoli. Once the war was over and the Labour Party was actively seeking candidates more in keeping with 'the officer type', the blueprint of Victorian respectability rather than twentieth-century upheaval, he had no scruples about retaining the field rank that he had earned. The handle of 'Major Attlee' had the right ring in 1918, evoking qualities of leadership, patriotism, reliability. It should be no surprise that he was still referred to as 'Major Attlee' well into the 1930s. The Minutes of the Paris meeting before the fall of France refer to him by his military rank.[5]

When he was demobilised in 1919 he left the depot in the morning, arranged his employment at the LSE in the afternoon and went to see Oscar Tobin in Stepney the following day. In reply to Tobin's offer he said crisply, 'Think it over.' Tobin assured that he had thought it over, to which Attlee snapped brusquely, 'No. I'll think it over.' As Lady Attlee chuckled, 'No one pushed Clem around.'

When he was co-opted by Labour colleagues as Mayor of Stepney in 1919–20 he rapidly established himself as the man in charge. Not only did he gain vital experience but he impressed colleagues and constituents with his ability, efficiency and decency. They never forgot.

Moral rectitude, however admirable, is rarely the weapon of choice for aspiring politicians; Attlee was fortunate that this quality shone through at the right time in the right place. First elected to Parliament in 1922, at a time when established values were crumbling and cynicism about Lloyd George's government was rampant, he had by 1931 accumulated experience as PPS to MacDonald, as Under-Secretary of War, with the Simon Commission in India, as Postmaster General and as Chancellor of the Duchy of Lancaster. As Lord Bridges commented, 'If a benign and far-seeing providence had wished to give to a future Prime Minister, in his first years in Parliament, experience of a very wide range of government work, the matter could hardly have been arranged more satisfactorily.'[6] Such a list of appointments for a relative 'freshman' in Parliament, however, suggests something more than good fortune.

He also retained his seat. In 1931, the year in which the Labour Party 'sustained the most crushing defeat in its history',[7] Attlee was re-elected by a slender margin. Morrison, Dalton, Henderson and Greenwood were less fortunate.

The outcome of the 1931 election is a vital pillar in the construction of the argument that Attlee was more fortunate than deserving. Morrison had been Minister of Transport and Dalton Under-Secretary at the Foreign Office from 1929 to 1931. Greenwood had served as Minister of Health and Henderson had held several posts, culminating in a stint as Foreign Secretary since 1929. All four, clearly, had deeper experience of government than Attlee and, had any one of them been returned to Parliament, the argument goes, then Attlee would not have become deputy leader of the tiny contingent that made up the PLP.

There are many critical moments in history, many roads to Damascus, and the putative course of events from 1931 to 1935, had one or all of the four remained in Parliament, provokes interesting speculation. Only the facts, however, are certain. By 1935 Attlee had established a sufficient reputation with Labour MPs to defeat Morrison and Greenwood with comparative ease. In four years he had demonstrated untiring devotion to the party. Questions concerning Morrison's candour – specifically that he spoke with forked tongue, was ambiguous about leaving the London County Council and devoting all his time to leading the party – were to recur throughout his political career.

It is an assumption of considerable dimension that, had he been on the Opposition front bench between 1931 and 1935, Morrison would have been the automatic choice of Labour Members. Even if one accepts the assumption, it requires a significant logical leap to assert that Morrison would have been elected leader or deputy leader in 1935. Attlee would have been on the same front bench and would have had room for manoeuvre to establish himself as a claimant if, as happened, there was a leadership election. Four years would have intervened and, if, as Wilson said, 'a week is a long time in politics',[8] Morrison would have had ample time to lose support and Attlee ample time to gain it. To assert that Morrison – or Greenwood – would have simply supplanted Attlee and maintained that position is the wildest speculation. When those two rivals had the chance to displace Attlee, they were dispatched with relative ease in two rounds of balloting in which Attlee led from the start.

Is there some residual 'gifted amateur' squeamishness that prevents us from accepting that ambition and ethical consistency are compatible? Do we, like Marc Antony, see ambition as 'a grievous fault'? Does it detract from Attlee's legacy to say that he was ambitious, hungry for the top job, principally so that he could pilot through Parliament the most comprehensive social reforms of any British government?

That he was ambitious is demonstrated by his running for the leadership at all. Between 1935 and 1940 he consolidated his position. Morrison and Greenwood did not simply vanish from view. Greenwood served as Attlee's deputy, while Morrison remained highly visible with the LCC. When Churchill took over from Chamberlain in May 1940, all three were needed.

The five years as Opposition leader, more than any other period, tested Attlee's ability to straddle the party left and the electorate, while maintaining a credible Opposition. It is for his performance during those years that he is most criticised. Simply put, the argument is that a more dynamic leader could have succeeded in stimulating defection from the Tory ranks much sooner and that, therefore, he must bear some responsibility for the events that led to war in 1939. Churchill, who since 1932 had given 'formal warning of approaching war', charged government and opposition equally for 'refusal to face unpleasant facts, desire for popularity and electoral success irrespective of the vital interests of the state'.[9]

Churchill himself, a constant goad to Baldwin over air estimates, failed to change government policy. The Tory government was mired in complacency, failing to grasp Hitler's true intentions. Attlee was urged by colleagues to make overtures to Sinclair and Churchill to form a Popular Front but he refused to move without a mandate.[10] Moreover, it is doubtful that Attlee could have succeeded where Churchill failed to rouse enough Tories to bring Baldwin or Chamberlain down. When Eden resigned over Chamberlain's dealings with Mussolini, when Duff Cooper resigned after Munich, there was no movement to unseat the Prime Minister. When Churchill delivered a magnificent oration two days later ('All is over. Silent, mournful, abandoned, broken, Czechoslovakia recedes into the darkness') he was heckled from the government benches.[11] It is hard not to agree with Attlee that it required more than dynamic leadership to reverse government policy. We can point to occasions when he might have scored a few more parliamentary points – when Baldwin confessed his error over

German aircraft building, for example[12] – but it took the shambles in Norway to make the folly of government policy plain.

From October 1940 Morrison served as Home Secretary throughout the coalition's time in office. Churchill recognised his value as he recognised the towering presence of Bevin. It helped Morrison not at all, however, that by 1942 Churchill had also learned to respect Attlee's worth and appointed him Britain's first Deputy Prime Minister – nor that Bevin stood firmly in support of Attlee. By the end of the war few Britons doubted the dedication, patriotism or ability of Churchill's deputy. When we mix into that equation a distrust of the Tory Party and a belief that the Labour Party offered a genuinely better future, Attlee's entry into Downing Street was a foregone conclusion. He had not achieved it by stealth or by misrepresenting the situation. He made no secret of the imminent austerity.

The years of 1922, 1935 and 1945 were of fundamental importance in twentieth-century Britain and in each of them Clement Attlee ran for election. In all three he was selected by a constituency that was aware of the importance of its decision. The first was local, the second partisan, the third national. In the first he defeated a Liberal who had held the seat at Limehouse since 1906 and was running with Conservative support; in the second he was elected over the supposedly superior claims of Morrison and Greenwood. In the third his party ejected from Downing Street the immensely popular Winston Churchill, who was riotously cheered wherever he appeared on his election tour.

Three things, arguably, were inevitable: that Clement Attlee would be elected party leader by the Parliamentary Labour Party in 1935, that he would become Deputy Prime Minister after May 1940, and that Labour would win the 1945 general election. The concatenation of those inevitable events led to a fourth – that Attlee would succeed Churchill as Prime Minister in July 1945; all the indicators suggested that outcome; only the massive stature of Winston Churchill and the relatively new science of polling obscured measured judgement.

Without drama, Attlee took the Labour Party and shaped it into a stronger organism. In later life he chuckled to compare his election as leader with Roosevelt's nomination as Democratic candidate for the Presidency in 1932. 'It is interesting', he wrote to Patricia Beck, 'to contrast the working of democracy in UK and USA, the huge long jamboree that made Roosevelt the democratic leader and the hour in the committee room in the House of Commons which made me Labour Party leader.'[13]

That shaping required tact, vision, courage and hard-headed political leadership. A brilliant Cabinet organiser, once he achieved power he was uniquely adept at using it, not for any personal agenda – except in rare instances like India and Abadan – but to establish and implement the will of the majority in Cabinet. Bevin had no illusions about the importance of this executive talent, reflected in the remarkable speed with which Bills were prepared and read. *The Times* singled out this ability: 'One of the most important functions of a Prime Minister is to dispatch business. Lord Attlee was a master of this. He could procrastinate when it suited him. Once he had made up his mind that a decision should be reached, he was unstoppable.'[14]

The clearest example of unstoppability was the granting of independence to India. The announcement of Mountbatten's appointment in February 1947 reads as though this were a culmination of benevolent policy, long designed to bring democracy to the subcontinent. Considering the speed with which events moved over the following six months, it is incomprehensible that they had limped for so long. It is hard not to see the appointment as the means by which national humiliation could be presented as a triumph. Whether or not the hasty withdrawal caused greater slaughter will never be known – particularly as the estimates of casualties are imprecise, varying from 100,000 to two million. Attlee believed that there was 'a very good chance' of avoiding bloodshed if Mountbatten could have remained as Governor-General of both India and Pakistan. This, he wrote, was 'foiled by the vanity of Jinnah'.[15] Attlee describes his decision to appoint Mountbatten as 'an inspiration' and this fits the facts. What he does not describe is the exact nature of the problem he was attempting to solve. At root this was a public relations problem, as his mind was already made up. Mountbatten, equipped with his own public relations officer – the first ever to accompany a Viceroy – provided the solution. At that point Attlee was, indeed, unstoppable.

That, in Bevin's view, he never had a creative idea is unimportant. Like a Hollywood producer, he had the 'Talent' around him for that. His continued presence at the top was as inevitable as his progress in reaching it. Equally, after twenty years as party leader and the loss of two elections, his departure was as inevitable as his accession. So great is the congruence between his career and its surrounding events that there is a risk of conflating party and leader.

One biographer asks the question, 'Would Attlee have succeeded as a leader in the modern day?' and answers firmly in the negative.[16] That conclusion is undeniable, for Attlee was considered an anachronism when he stepped down in 1955. He recognised that the issue of a united Europe, for example, was one that must concern his successors but one that he might avoid. Looking far beyond national boundaries and desperate to find a formula for peace in the atomic age, he referred to a united Europe as outdated. Who, one may ask, was old-fashioned?

To some extent he played the 'old duffer', much as Harold Macmillan affected Edwardian mannerisms while Britain hurtled into the moral maelstrom of the 1960s. He certainly played the role to effect. Sir William Hayter told a story of Attlee in Yugoslavia. A friend arrived at Brioni, where he was staying, and Attlee urgently asked him, 'Have you got the cricket scores? Nobody out here seems to know a thing about them.'[17] But behind the assumed façade of amiable grandfather there was a set of fixed Victorian values, an unambiguous moral code and more than a hint of respect for *l'ancien régime*. He could hold sincere socialist beliefs and at the same time accept, for example, a differentiated school system. Aged fifty-six when the Second World War broke out, he belonged firmly to the pre-war period. Curiously, it was the balance of being 'the Major' and a committed socialist that endeared him first to his own constituents, later to the nation.

Perhaps the most astonishing fact of chronology is that a mere eight years passed between Attlee's stepping down from the leadership and Harold Wilson's predicting the 'white heat of this (technological) revolution' at the 1963 party conference. By 1967 all three major parties were led by men born well into the twentieth century: Wilson and Edward Heath (both born in 1916) and Jeremy Thorpe (1929).

His kindness and decency were legendary. Punctilious in writing 'thank-you' notes, solicitous when colleagues were ill or when a family tragedy occurred, he received scores of appreciative letters. One delightful exchange occurred in June 1951. The government was hanging on to its tiny majority, daily besieged, when the Prime Minister received a letter from Ann Franklin, a fifteen-year-old schoolgirl, complaining that she had to wait a year before sitting the new GCE exam. The letter was written in six stanzas of verse, beginning:

> *Will you please explain, dear Clement,*
> *Just why it has to be*
> *That Certificates of Education*
> *Are barred to such as me.*

Instead of passing it to a secretary for a standard reply along the lines of 'The Prime Minister thanks you for your communication ...' Attlee replied, promising to speak to George Tomlinson, the Minister of Education. Writing by hand on 10 Downing Street writing paper in an envelope embossed 'PRIME MINISTER', he joined in the fun:

> *I received with real pleasure*
> *Your verses, my dear Ann.*
> *Although I've not much leisure*
> *I'll reply as best I can.*

> *I've not the least idea why*
> *They have this curious rule*
> *Condemning you to sit and sigh*
> *Another year at school.*

> *You'll understand that my excuse*
> *For lack of detailed knowledge*
> *Is that School Certs were not in use*
> *When I attended college.*

> *George Tomlinson is ill, but I*
> *Have asked him to explain,*
> *And when I get the reason why*
> *I'll write to you again.*

And he did. On 9 July he wrote again, explaining the reasons for the delay that Ann had to endure. It was a technical explanation that ended on a high note, pointing out that there were three levels at which she could sit the exam and wishing her every success when the time came. They stayed in touch; Ann wrote to tell her of her exam results in 1952 and Attlee replied with 'congratulations on your success'. In 1957, presumably when she graduated from university, her father wrote to thank him for his kindness. Attlee replied, saying, 'I am delighted to hear that any action of mine has been helpful. Please congratulate your daughter for me on her many successes and wish her all happiness.'[18]

Such concern was typical of the man. His manners, dress, courtesy to women, and habitual formality belong to the Victorian era, more conservative than progressive. That essential conservatism is illustrated by issues that his government left unresolved, issues central to a true socialist administration. Especially notable are reform of the House of Lords and of the education system.

Concern for the passage of the Iron and Steel Bill prompted the attenuation of the power of the Lords to delay Bills. That was practical politics but it did nothing to alter the make-up of the second chamber. Attlee worked closely with Addison on plans for reform and between February and April 1948 seven cross-party meetings were held. The government was represented by Attlee, Morrison, Addison, Jowitt and Whiteley; the Tories by Eden, Salisbury, Swinton and Maxwell Fyfe; the Liberals by Samuel and Clement Davies.

The goals were to establish a House in which heredity was no longer a qualification in itself, in which the composition was not such as to give a majority to any one party, and from which peers would be free to resign if they were not interested in governance. Hereditary peers who were Privy Counsellors or who held certain offices, or were in the male line of royal succession, would be members; so too would the 'Lords Spiritual' and Law Lords. Other members would be selected by the Crown from 'commoners of distinction' to be 'Lords of Parliament'.[19] At the end of the fifth meeting Attlee commented that 'there was a fundamental differ-ence between the government and the Conservative Party as to what the powers of the Second Chamber should be'. Salisbury agreed; the same comment was made after the sixth and seventh meetings, at which point discussion petered out and proposals for reform were shelved.[20]

As early as 1941 Attlee and 'Rab' Butler, the President of the Board of Education, met to discuss post-war education. To Tom he was quite clear that neither he nor the party wanted to abolish public schools, feeling that many essentially local schools could be absorbed into county secondary schools. Others, the 'national' ones, 'should be brought under control without killing their individuality'. That was about as far as the talks progressed beyond the vague goal that they should have 'a large proportion of scholars from the elementary schools'[21] and Attlee's view that 'variety and the maintenance of tradition was to be preferred to 'dull uniformity'.[22]

Butler, determined that 'educationally after the war Britain had to be one nation not two',[23] introduced the Education Act in 1944, creating the tripartite system of secondary education and the Eleven-Plus exam to determine a student's secondary path – whether to grammar school, technical school or secondary modern. When Labour came to power Ellen Wilkinson, the Minister of Education, was committed to the 1944 Act. The principal bipartisan aim was to raise school leaving age first to fifteen, later to sixteen,[24] even though this removed 160,000 people from the work force when they were badly needed.[25] Comprehensive education was loosely adopted as Labour policy, which focused on 'parity of esteem', the famous phrase of the Butler Act, yet in 1958 Gaitskell wrote to his old housemaster at Winchester that the abolition of public schools was an issue that had no value and 'that the ordinary man does not disapprove of the Public Schools and, on the whole, does not want much done about them'.[26] Nearly ten years later, Labour was still deliberately imprecise about plans for grammar schools.

On two questions, then, Attlee was far from a zealous socialist in pursuing reform. He avoided conflict with friends like the Marquess of Salisbury ('Bobbety' Cranborne) and Eden, with whom he would later serve in the Lords. As to education, he would hardly have abolished a source of supply for his government. In one of his many lists he records the public schools whose old boys had served on the Labour front bench. Eton leads the list with seven, followed by Haileybury (five), Winchester (four), Marlborough, Rugby and Saint Paul's (two) and by Harrow, Cheltenham, Tonbridge, Dulwich, Rugby and Oundle (one each).[27] John Colville, speaking with Attlee about Geoffrey de Freitas, an Old

Haileyburian, concluded that 'the old school tie counted even more in Labour than in Conservative circles'.[28]

Both questions were to become *causes célèbres* for later Labour administrations, but Attlee clearly had no difficulty in preserving the *status quo*. Along with a genuine and passionate wish to improve the living conditions of the less privileged co-existed a resolve to leave some symbols of privilege well alone.

One final issue needs addressing. In forging the Atlantic alliance, from 1947 a prime *desideratum*, Attlee made not one trip to Washington between 1945 and 1950. Unlike Churchill who, in addition to carrying on a voluminous correspondence with Roosevelt, crossed the Atlantic at the slightest opportunity, Attlee made just two visits to Washington. Those visits, together with the Potsdam conference, were the extent of the meetings between the two leaders.

Prime Minister and President were very different in style. Truman enjoyed an evening of poker and bourbon with male friends, while Attlee was shy to the point of being tongue-tied in company. Truman was famous for plain speaking; Attlee was curt, almost monosyllabic in conversation.[29] On the surface, at least, they had little in common. But when swift action was called for, as in the Berlin airlift, both moved quickly.

The issue that divided the two and in which both leaders appeared unable or unwilling to understand the other's position was Palestine. During the last days of the Mandate Attlee and Bevin were impotent without American support, while Truman's continued pressure was a vehement indictment of British policy. That the *entente* was allowed to slip is a criticism of both leaders, but, given the facts of the relative power of Britain and America, the onus to take the initiative was on Attlee.

Attlee typically described his government's achievements in six words during an interview with Honor Balfour in June 1967:

> *Honour Balfour: What was the greatest achievement of the Labour government?*
> *Clement Attlee: Indian independence.*
> *HB: What was the greatest problem you faced?*
> *CRA: Russia.*
> *HB: What was the West's most important operation in the face of that problem?*
> *CRA: The Berlin airlift.*

To an audience in Oxford he was more expansive. He was proud to have been involved in a unique phenomenon:

> *There is only one Empire where, without external pressure or weariness at the burden of ruling, the ruling people has voluntarily surrendered its hegemony over subject peoples and has given them their freedom, where also the majority of the people so liberated have continued in political association with their former rulers. This unique example is the British Empire.*[30]

All these achievements were in the credit column of his administration before 1951 when the Labour Party was returned to the Opposition benches. His presence after the Bevan–Gaitskell fracas of 1951 was vital. In 1953 he was distressed to note that 'the trouble in the party has broken out again just when I thought I had got things running smoothly. An article in *Tribune* upset the apple cart.'[31] By the 1955 election he was ready to leave and tried to do so but, he complained, 'at present they won't let me go'.[32] By December he was able to hand over the reins to Gaitskell reasonably smoothly and take his leave.

So ended twenty years of Attlee's leadership of the Labour Party. He had taken it over from a leader who could never have been elected Prime Minister, had won two general elections without losing a by-election, shepherded the party through viciously partisan squabbles, and ushered in a man with substantially the same background as himself. Haileybury and Oxford yielded to Winchester and Oxford; Gaitskell had not been his first choice to follow him, but Attlee was satisfied by the time he stepped down that he was the best, even the only possible, successor.

By then he accepted, in words he might have used, that he had enjoyed a long innings and put up his bat in the pavilion. He had stayed on as Labour leader and ensured that the next leader was truly of the next generation, an undeniably 'post-war' man. Once he had achieved that transfer of power he was able to withdraw, become an elder statesman, a man of his generation. The challenges after 1955 were very different from those of 1945 and he had no shame in admitting that he could play no useful part in them. Late in life, free of party responsibility, he returned to advocate the great themes of his life: the United Nations, world governance, world peace.

Lector, si monumentum requiris, circumspice.[33] So reads the inscription on a tablet close to Sir Christopher Wren's tomb in St Paul's Cathedral. Around the mortal remains of the architect stands the cathedral that best serves as his monument. Clement Attlee's legacy surrounds every British citizen in the fabric of society created by the reforms of the post-war Labour government. Attlee, to whose name the adjective 'modest' is indissolubly joined, would have shied in horror from any grand monument. 'Too much ego in his cosmos,' he might have muttered. His pride in his government's achievements was justifiably great, but it would never have occurred to him to claim personal credit for them. They were necessary reforms, long overdue, that his team brought to fruition in a staggeringly short time. He even infuriated Bevan by suggesting that part of the credit was due to the Tories and the wartime coalition.

It may be appropriate to end his biography with a short anecdote that illustrates his achievements, fame and modesty. After he stepped down from leadership of the Labour Party, he was travelling home – by the Underground, of course – and was accosted by a fellow traveller at Baker Street station.

'Good Lord!' said the traveller. 'Do people ever tell you that you are the spitting image of Clement Attlee?'

'Frequently,' replied the 1st Earl.

ENDNOTES

1   'The loss of the great statesman that was Clement Attlee causes me a deep pain.' President de Gaulle had a lingering fondness for Attlee, developed during his time in London as leader of the Free French during the war. In 1955 he wrote, 'I can still see Mr Attlee coming softly into my office, asking for the assurances needed to relieve his conscience as a democrat, and then, after he had heard me, withdrawing with a smile on his face.' (de Gaulle, *War Memoirs: The Call to Honour 1940–1942*).
2   *The Times*, 9 October 1967.
3   Lord Longford, *Reader's Digest*, October 1968.
4   Conversation with Anne, Countess Attlee, 14 October 2013.
5   Weygand, *Recalled to Service* (1952, New York: Doubleday), p. 415.
6   Lord Bridges, *Biographical Memoirs of Fellows of the Royal Society*, Vol. 14 (November 1968), pp. 15–36.
7   *As It Happened*, p. 108.
8   In 1964, the year he first became Prime Minister.
9   Churchill, *History of the Second World War*, vol. 1 'The Gathering Storm', p. 89.
10 CAC: ATLE 1/16.
11 *Hansard*, HC Deb, 5 October 1938, cols. 359–373.
12 *Hansard*, HC Deb, 22 May 1935, cols 367–368.
13 Bodleian: MS. Eng. lett. c.571, Letter to Patricia Beck, 20 August 1958.
14 *The Times*, 9 October 1967.
15 CAC: ATLE 1/13.
16 Nicklaus Thomas-Symonds, *Attlee*, p. 272.

17 Recounted by Crossman, *The Backbench Diaries*, p. 343.
18 The exchange of poems and subsequent correspondence is at Bodleian: MS. Eng. c.7100, fols 108–117.
19 Bodleian: MS. Addison, dep. c.189, fols 119–120.
20 Bodleian: MS. Addison, dep. c.189, *passim*.
21 Letter to Tom Attlee, 9 August 1941.
22 Bodleian: MS. Attlee, dep. 17, Speech in Leeds, 24 February 1945.
23 R. A. Butler, *The Art of the Possible*, p. 97.
24 Lord Redcliffe-Maud (formerly Sir John Maud), *Experiences of an Optimist*, pp. 51–59.
25 Carl Brand, *The British Labour Party*, p. 246.
26 Gaitskell to Cyril Robinson, 1 July 1958. Cited at Philip Williams, *Hugh Gaitskell*, p. 467.
27 CAC: ATLE 1/17.
28 Colville, *The Fringes of Power*, p. 613. Christopher Mayhew, another Old Haileyburian, recalls an occasion when his promotion was blocked by Attlee's concern that the press was commenting on his liking for the Old School Tie. *Time to Explain*, p. 95.
29 Attlee was staying at the White House in 1950 when Truman wrote an abusive letter to Paul Hume, music critic of the *Washington Post*, after Hume's savage review of a concert by Margaret Truman. According to Crossman, Attlee encouraged Truman to write the letter, saying 'That's the spirit'. Crossman speculated that 'Attlee was almost envying Truman for doing and being all the things he isn't'. *The Backbench Diaries*, p. 442.
30 *Empire into Commonwealth*, The Chichele Lectures, I, May 1960, lines 5–9.
31 Bodleian: MS. Eng. lett. c.571, Letter to Patricia Beck, 1 February 1953.
32 Bodleian: MS. Eng. lett. c.571, Letter to Patricia Beck, 31 July 1955.
33 'Reader, if you seek a monument, look about you.' The words are inscribed on a tablet in St Paul's, placed there by Christopher Wren's son.

BIBLIOGRAPHY

PRIMARY SOURCES
- The National Archives, CAB and PREM files; Dominion and War Office Files. (Cited in Notes with prefix 'TNA')
- The National Archives, Guy Liddell's Diaries (KV4 series). (Cited in Notes with prefix 'TNA')
- The India Office Records.
- *Hansard*, Parliamentary Debates (millbanksystems.com).
- Clement Attlee Papers: Collection of Anne, Countess Attlee.
- Bodleian Library, Oxford (MS. Attlee, dep. 1–146); Letters to Tom Attlee (MSS. Eng. c.4792–4); Honor Balfour Papers (MS. Balfour, dep. 1–9, 51); Christopher Addison's Papers (MS. Addison, dep. 183–94); Letters to Patricia Beck, MS. Eng. lett. c.571); Letters to Ann Franklin (MS. Eng. 7100, fols 108–119); Letters to Hartley Shawcross (MS. Eng. 2720, fols 20–26); Lord Simon's Papers, 1936–47 (MS. Simon, 83, 94, 96, 97). (Cited in Notes with prefix 'Bodleian')
- Churchill College, Cambridge (CAC, ATLE/1 and ATLE/2).
- Haileybury College Archive.
- University College, Oxford Archive and Corpus Christi College, Oxford Archive.
- British Library Newspaper Collection, Colindale.

SECONDARY SOURCES

- Acheson, Dean, *Present at the Creation: My Years in the State Department*. 1969, New York: Norton.
- Anderson, Perry, 'Gandhi Centre Stage' and 'Why Partition? *London Review of Books*, 5 July and 19 July 2012.
- Andrew, Christopher, *Defend the Realm: The Authorised History of MI5*. 2009, London: Allen Lane.
- Andrew, Christopher,, *For the President's Eyes Only: Secret Intelligence and the American Presidency from Washington to Bush*. 1995, New York: HarperCollins.
- Attlee, Clement, *As It Happened*. 1954, New York: The Viking Press.
- Attlee, Clement, *The Social Worker*. 1920, London: G. Bell.
- Attlee, Clement, *The Labour Party in Perspective*. 1937, London: Gollancz.
- Attlee, Clement, *Labour's Peace Aims*. 1940, London: Peace Book Company.
- Attlee, Peggy, *With a Quiet Conscience: A Biography of Thomas Symons Attlee*. 1995, London: Dove & Chough.
- Attlee, Thomas, *Man and His Buildings*, 1948, London: Swarthmore.
- Avon, Earl of, *Facing the Dictators*. 1962, London: Cassell.
- Avon, Earl of, *The Reckoning*. 1965, London: Cassell.
- Avon, Earl of, *Full Circle*. 1960, London: Cassell.
- Beckett, Francis. *Clem Attlee: A Biography*. 1997, London: Richard Cohen.
- Beckett, Francis, *Enemy Within: The Rise and Fall of the British Communist Party*. 1995, London: Murray.
- Bevan, Aneurin, *In Place of Fear*. 1952, London: Heinemann.
- Bevan, Aneurin, *Why Not Trust the Tories?* 1944, London: Gollancz.
- Bickerton, F., *Fred Of Oxford: Being the Memoirs of Fred Bickerton, Until Recently Head Porter of University College, Oxford*. 1953, London, Evans.
- Bohlen, Charles, *Witness to History 1929–1969*. 1973, New York: Norton.
- Bradley, Omar, *A General's Life*. 1983, New York: Simon and Schuster.

- Brookshire, Jerry, *Clement Attlee*. 1995, Manchester: Manchester UP.
- Brown, George, *In My Way*. 1971, London: Gollancz.
- Bryant, Arthur, *The Turn of the Tide*. 1957, Garden City: Doubleday.
- Bryant, Arthur,, *Triumph in the West*. 1959, Garden City: Doubleday.
- Bullock, Alan, *Ernest Bevin: Foreign Secretary*. 1983, New York: Norton.
- Bunyan, Tony, *The History and Practice of the Political Police in Britain*. 1976, London: Friedmann.
- Burridge, Trevor, *Clement Attlee: A Political Biography*. 1985, London: Jonathan Cape.
- Butler, J. R. M. (ed.) *Grand Strategy*, (6 vols.). 1956–76, London: HMSO.
- Byrnes, James, *Speaking Frankly*. 1947, New York: Harper.
- Cairncross, Alec, *Years of Recovery: British Economic Policy 1945–1951*. 1985, London: Methuen.
- Campbell-Johnson, Alan, *Mission With Mountbatten*. 1951, London: Robert Hale.
- Carter, Lionel (ed.), *Mountbatten's Report on the Last Viceroyalty*. 2003, New Delhi: Manohar.
- Churchill, Winston, *The Second World War* (6 vols.) 1948 1953, Boston: Houghton Mifflin.
- Clarke, Peter, *A Question of Leadership: Gladstone to Thatcher*. 1991, London: Hamish Hamilton.
- Clarke, Peter, *The Cripps Version: The Life of Sir Stafford Cripps*. 2002, London: Allen Lane.
- Clemens, Cyril, *The Man from Limehouse*. 1946, Webster, MO: Int'l Mark Twain Society.
- Clifford, Clark, *Counsel to the President*. 1991, New York: Random House.
- Colville, John, *The Fringes of Power: 10 Downing Street Diaries 1939–1955*. 1985, New York: Norton.
- Dalton, Hugh, *High Tide and After*. 1962, London: Muller.
- Dalton, Hugh, *The Fateful Years: Memoirs 1931–1945*. 1957, London: Muller.
- Danchev, Alex and Daniel Todman, *War Diaries of Field Marshal Lord Alanbrooke 1939–1945*. 2002, London: Phoenix.
- Darwall-Smith, Robin, *A History of University College, Oxford*. 2008, Oxford: OUP.
- Dellar, Geoffrey (ed.), *Attlee As I Knew Him*. 1983, London: London Borough of Tower Hamlets.
- Dilks, David. *The Diaries of Sir Alexander Cadogan 1938–1945*. 1972, New York: Putnam's.
- Dixon, Piers, *Double Diploma: The Life of Sir Pierson Dixon, Don and Diplomat*. 1968, London: Hutchinson.
- Donoghue, Bernard and G. W. Jones, *Herbert Morrison: Portrait of a Politician*. 1973, London: Phoenix.
- Durbin, Elizabeth, *New Jerusalems: Labour Party and the Economics of Democratic Socialism*. 1985, London: Routledge.
- Dutt, R. Palme, *Britain's Crisis of Empire*. 1950, New York: International Publishers.
- Epstein, Leon, *Britain: Uneasy Ally*. 1954, Chicago: Chicago University Press.
- Eubank, Keith, *Summit at Teheran*. 1985, New York: Morrow.
- Farnell, L. R., *An Oxonian Looks Back*. 1934, London: Hopkinson.
- Feiling, Keith, *The Life of Neville Chamberlain*. 1946, London: Macmillan.
- Ferrell, Robert, *Off the Record: The Private Papers of Harry S. Truman*. 1980, New York: Harper & Row.
- Ferrell, Robert, *The Eisenhower Diaries*. 1981, New York: Norton.
- Field, Frank, *Attlee's Great Contemporaries*. 2009, London: Continuum.
- Foot, Michael, *Aneurin Bevan* (2 vols.). 1975, London: Paladin.
- Fort, Adrian, *Archibald Wavell: The Life and Times of an Imperial Servant*. 2009, London: Cape.
- Frank, Gerold, *The Deed*. 1963, New York: Simon & Schuster.
- Gaddis, John Lewis, *The United States and the Origins of the Cold War 1941–1947*. 1972, New York: Columbia.
- Gardner, A. D. *Reminiscences*. Unpublished: University College, Oxford Library.
- Gilbert, Martin, *Churchill: A Life*. 1991, London: Heinemann.
- Golant, William. 'The Early Political Thought of C. R. Attlee', *Politics Quarterly* 40.3, July–September 1969.
- Golant, William, 'The Emergence of C. R. Attlee as Leader of the Parliamentary Labour Party', *The Historical Journal*, xiii, 2 (1970).
- Halberstam, David, *The Coldest Winter: America and the Korean War*. 2007, New York: Hyperion.
- Harriman, W. Averell, *America and Russia in a Changing World*. 1971, Garden City: Doubleday.
- Harris, Kenneth, *Attlee*. 1982, London: Weidenfeld & Nicolson.
- Harrod, Roy, *The Life of John Maynard Keynes*. 1951, London: Macmillan.
- Hayek, Friedrich, *The Road to Serfdom*. 2005. London: Institute of Economic Affairs.
- Healey, Denis, *The Time of My Life*. 1990, New York: Norton.
- Hechler, Ken, *Working With Truman*. 1982, New York: Putnam's.
- Hennessy, Peter, *The Prime Minister: The Office and Its Holders Since 1945*. 2000, London: Allen Lane.
- Hennessy, Peter,, *Never Again: Britain 1945–1951*. 1992, London: Jonathan Cape.
- Hickey, Michael, *The Korean War: The West Confronts Communism*. 2000, Woodstock: Overlook.
- Hollis, Christopher, *The Oxford Union*. 1965, London: Evans.
- Hough, Richard, *Edwina: Countess Mountbatten of Burma*. 1983, London: Weidenfeld & Nicolson.
- Howell, David, *Attlee*. 2006, London: Haus.

- Hunter, Leslie, *The Road to Brighton Pier*. 1959, London: Barker.
- Ismay, Lord, *The Memoirs of General Lord Ismay*. 1960, New York: Viking.
- Jenkins, Roy, *Truman*. 1986, New York: Harper & Row.
- Jenkins, Roy, *Mr Attlee: An Interim Biography*. 1948, London: Heinemann.
- Jenkins, Roy, *Purpose and Policy: Selected Speeches by the Prime Minister C. R. Attlee*. 1946, London: Hutchinson.
- Jenkins, Roy, *Churchill*, 2001, London: Macmillan.
- Johnston, Seth, *How NATO Endures: An Institutional Analysis*. 2012. D.Phil. Thesis: Oxford.
- Kennan, George, *Memoirs 1925–1950*. 1967, Boston: Little Brown.
- Khan, Yasmin, *The Great Partition: The Making of India and Pakistan*. 2007, New Haven: Yale UP.
- Kramer, Gudrun, *A History of Palestine: From the Ottoman Conquest to the Founding of the State of Israel*. 2008, Princeton: Princeton UP.
- Kynaston, David, *Austerity Britain*. 2007, London: Bloomsbury.
- Labour Party, *For Socialism and Peace*. 1934, London: The Labour Party.
- Labour Party, *Labour's Immediate Programme*, 1937, London: The Labour Party.
- Labour Party, *Leon Blum Before His Judges*, (Christian Howie trans.), 1943, London: The Labour Party.
- Lacey, Michael (ed.), *The Truman Presidency*. 1990, Cambridge: CUP.
- Leahy, William D., *I Was There*. 1950, New York: McGraw Hill.
- Leigh, David, *The Wilson Plot*. 1988, New York: Pantheon.
- Lomas, Daniel W. B., 'Labour Ministers, Intelligence and Domestic Anti-Communism 1945–1951', *Journal of Intelligence History*, 12:2, pp. 113–133.
- Macmillan, Harold, *The Blast of War 1939–1945*. 1967, London: Macmillan.
- Macmillan, Harold, *Tides of Fortune 1945–1955*. 1969, London: Macmillan.
- Mansergh, Nicholas (ed.), *Transfer of Power 1942–1947*. 1970–83, London: HMSO.
- Mathew, Theobald, *Forensic Fables*. 1961, London: Butterworths.
- McCallum, R. B. and Alison Readman, *The British General Election of 1945*. 1947, Oxford: OUP.
- McCullough, David, *Truman*. 1992, New York: Simon & Schuster.
- McKenzie, R. T., *British Political Parties*. 1955, London: William Heinemann.
- Milford, L. S., *Haileybury College Past and Present*. 1909, London: Fisher Unwin.
- Miller, Roger, *To Save a City: The Berlin Airlift 1948–1949*. 1998, Washington: US government.
- Milliband, Ralph, *Parliamentary Socialism: A Study in the Politics of Labour*. 1972, London: Merlin.
- Minney, R. J., *The Private Papers of Hore-Belisha*. 1960, London: Collins.
- Montgomery, Viscount of Alamein, *The Memoirs of Field-Marshal Montgomery*. 1958, London: Collins.
- Moon, Penderel, *The Viceroy's Journal*. 1973, London: Oxford UP.
- Moon, Penderel,, *Divide and Quit*. 1961, London: Chatto & Windus.
- Moore, A. M., *Recollections of University College 1896–1900*.
- Moran, Lord, *Churchill: Taken from the Diaries of Lord Moran*. 1966, Boston: Houghton Mifflin.
- Morgan, Janet (ed.), *The Backbench Diaries of Richard Crossman*. 1981, London: Hamish Hamilton.
- Morgan, Kenneth, *Labour in Power: 1945–1951*. 1984, Oxford: Clarendon.
- Morgan, Kenneth, *Labour People: Leaders and Lieutenants, Hardie to Kinnock*. 1987, Oxford: OUP.
- Morrison of Lambeth, Lord, *Herbert Morrison: An Autobiography*. 1960, London: Odhams.
- Mosley, Oswald, *My Life*. 1968, London: Nelson.
- Mountbatten, Pamela, *India Remembered: A Personal Account of the Mountbattens During the Transfer of Power*. 2007, London: Pavilion.
- Murphy, J. I., *Labour's Big Three*. 1948, London: Bodley Head.
- Nicolson, Harold, *Diaries and Letters* (3 vols.). 1968, New York: Atheneum.
- Observer, *Churchill by His Contemporaries*. 1965, London: *The Observer*.
- Overdale, Ritchie (ed.), *The Foreign Policy of the British Labour Governments 1945–1951*. 1984, Leicester: Leicester University Press.
- Paterson, Thomas, *On Every Front: The Making of the Cold War*. 1979, New York: Norton.
- Pearce, Robert, *Attlee's Labour Governments 1945–1951*. 1994, London: Routledge.
- Pelling, Henry, *A Short History of the Labour Party*. 1962, London: Macmillan.
- Pimlott, Ben, *Harold Wilson*. 1992, London: HarperCollins.
- Pimlott, Ben, *Hugh Dalton*. 1995, London: HarperCollins.
- Pimlott, Ben, *Labour and the Left in the 1930s*. 1977, Cambridge: Cambridge UP.
- Postgate, Raymond, *The Life Of George Lansbury*. 1951, London: Longman Green.
- Potter, Karen, 'British McCarthyism' in Rhodri Jeffreys-Jones and Andrew Lownie (eds.) *North American Spies: New Revisionist Essays*. 1991, Lawrence, KS: Kansas UP.
- Radice, Giles, *The Tortoise and the Hares*. 2008, London: Politico's.
- Redcliffe-Maud, John (Lord), *Experiences of an Optimist*. 1981, London: Hamish Hamilton.
- Rhodes James, Robert, *Anthony Eden*. 1986, London: Weidenfeld & Nicolson.

- Ridgway, Matthew, *The Korean War*. 1967, New York: Doubleday.
- Roberts, Andrew, *Eminent Churchillians*. 1994, London: Weidenfeld & Nicolson.
- Rowse, A. L., *Appeasement: A Study in Political Decline, 1933–1939*. 1961, New York: Norton.
- Sampson, Anthony, *Anatomy of Britain Today*. 1965, London: Hodder & Stoughton.
- Segev, Tom, *One Palestine Complete*. 2000, Boston: Little Brown.
- Sillitoe, Sir Percy, *Cloak Without Dagger*. 1955, London: Cassell.
- Spears, General Edward, *Assignment to Catastrophe*, 2 vols. 1954, London: Heinemann.
- Swift, John, *Labour in Crisis: Clement Attlee and the Labour Party in Opposition 1931–1940*. 2001, Basingstoke: Palgrave.
- Tangye, Derek, *The Way to Minack*. 1968, London: Michael Joseph.
- Taylor, A. J. P., *Beaverbrook*. 1972, New York: Simon & Schuster.
- Thomas, Hugh, *Armed Truce: The Beginnings of the Cold War 1945–1946*. 1987, New York: Atheneum.
- Thomas, Ivor, *The Socialist Tragedy*. 1949, London: Latimer House.
- Thomas-Symonds, Nicklaus, *Attlee: A Life in Politics*. 2012, London: I. B. Tauris.
- Truman, Margaret, *Harry S. Truman*. 1973, New York: William Morrow.
- US government, *The Public Papers of the Presidents, Harry S. Truman, 1945*. 1961, Washington: National Archives.
- US government, *The Public Papers of the Presidents, Harry S. Truman, 1950*. 1965, Washington: National Archives.
- Walter, David, *The Oxford Union: Playground of Power*. 1984, London: Macdonald.
- Weir, L. MacNeill, *The Tragedy of Ramsay MacDonald*. 1936, London: Secker & Warburg.
- West, Nigel, *A Matter of Trust: MI5 1945–1972*. 1982, London: Weidenfeld & Nicolson.
- West, Nigel, (ed.), *The Guy Liddell Diaries* (2 vols.). 2009, Abingdon: Routledge.
- Wheeler-Bennett, John, *King George VI: His Life and Reign*. 1958, London: Macmillan.
- Wheeler-Bennett, John, *Action This Day: Working With Churchill*. 1968, London: Macmillan.
- Wheeler-Bennett, John and Anthony Nicholls, *The Semblance of Peace: The Political Settlement After the Second World War*. 1972, New York: St Martin's Press.
- Wheen, Francis, *Tom Driberg: His Life and Indiscretions*. 1990, London: Chatto and Windus.
- Williams, Andrew, *Labour and Russia: The Attitude of the Labour Party to the USSR 1924–1934*. 1989, Manchester: Manchester UP.
- Williams, Francis, *A Prime Minister Remembers*. 1961, London: William Heinemann.
- Williams, Francis, *Nothing So Strange: An Autobiography*. 1970, London: Cassell.
- Wilson, A. N., *After the Victorians: The Decline of Britain in the World*. 2006, New York: Picador.
- Wilson, Harold, *A Prime Minister on Prime Ministers*. 1977, London: Weidenfeld and Nicolson.
- Wilson, Harold, *A Personal Record, The Labour Government 1964–1970*. 1971, Boston: Little Brown.
- Wolpert, Stanley, *Shameful Flight: The Last Years of the British Empire in India*. 2006, Oxford: OUP.
- Young. G. M., *Stanley Baldwin*. 1952, London: Hart Davis.
- Ziegler, Philip, *Mountbatten: The Official Biography*. 1985, London: Collins.

INDEX